Immaculate *DECEPTION*

and FURTHER RIBALDRIES

THE MIDDLE AGES SERIES

Ruth Mazo Karras, SERIES EDITOR

Edward Peters, FOUNDING EDITOR

A complete list of books in the series

is available from the publisher.

Immaculate *DECEPTION* and FURTHER RIBALDRIES

Yet Another Dozen Medieval French Farces in Modern English

Edited and translated by

JODY ENDERS

PENN

University of Pennsylvania Press

Philadelphia

Published by
University of Pennsylvania Press
Philadelphia, Pennsylvania 19104-4112

www.upenn.edu/pennpress

Printed in the United States of America on acid-free paper
10 9 8 7 6 5 4 3 2 1

A Cataloging-in-Publication record is available from the Library of Congress
ISBN 978-0-8122-5400-6 (hardback)
ISBN 978-0-8122-2529-7 (paperback)
ISBN 978-0-8122-9859-8 (eBook)

For my students. Yet again.

Contents

Abbreviations

Many medieval farces were untitled and "underdetermined." On their first or final pages, they largely read something like "*The Farce for [Two, Three, Four, or Five] Characters.*" On the opposite end of the spectrum, one finds chatty titles on the order of *The New Farce of the Chambermaids who Go to Mass at 5:00 A.M. to get their Holy Water* (our #7, *Bro Job*). I refer throughout to the present twelve plays—as to those of *Farce of the Fart* and *Holy Deadlock*—by the English titles that I've bestowed upon them. Inspired, moreover, by the occasional medieval "to wit" (*c'est assavoir*), I too venture alternate titles or subtitles when warranted.

For ease of reading, I favor parenthetical documentation when practical, which works in concert with the Bibliography. To facilitate consultation, I refer to frequently mentioned primary and secondary sources by the following abbreviations:

"ABT"	"About This Translation" from this book.
AF	*Against the Friars*. By Tim Rayborn.
AG	*Aspects of Genre*. By Alan Knight.
APF	*Art Poétique françoys (1548)*. By Thomas Sébillet.
ATF	*Ancien Théâtre françois*. 10 vols. Edited by M. Viollet le Duc.
CFSM	*Choix de farces, soties et moralités*. Edited by Émile Mabille.
CM	*La Comédie et les moeurs*. By L. Petit de Julleville.
CRCD	*Christian Rite and Christian Drama*. By O. B. Hardison Jr.
CWFR	*The Complete Works of François Rabelais*. Translated by Donald Frame.
DBD	*Death by Drama and Other Medieval Urban Legends*. By Jody Enders.
DLU	*Description et analyse d'un livre unique qui se trouve au Musée britannique*. By Octave Joseph Delepierre.
DNC	*Débat de la Nourrisse et de la Chamberière* (*RBM*, #49).

DSI	*Dictionnaire thématique et géographique des saints imaginaires, facétieux*. By Jacques Merceron.
"ETCF"	"Etudes sur le Théâtre comique français du moyen âge." By Pierre [Pietro] Toldo.
FCMF	*Five Comedies of Medieval France*. Translated into English by Oscar Mandel.
FF	*"The Farce of the Fart" and Other Ribaldries*. Edited and translated by Jody Enders.
FFMA	*Farces françaises de la fin du Moyen Âge*. 4 vols. Translated into modern French by André Tissier.
HD	*Holy Deadlock and Further Ribaldries*. Edited and translated by Jody Enders.
HDTW	*How to Do Things with Words*. By J. L. Austin.
HTF	*Histoire du théâtre françois depuis son origine jusqu'à présent*. By François Parfaict and Claude Parfaict.
LM	*Les Mystères*. 2 vols. By L. Petit de Julleville.
MBA	*Murder by Accident*. By Jody Enders.
MD	*Medieval Drama*. Edited by David Bevington.
MES	*The Medieval European Stage*. Edited by William Tydeman.
MFP	*Medieval French Plays*. Translated by Richard Axton and John Stevens.
MFST	*Music in the French Secular Theater*. By Howard Mayer Brown.
MTA	*Les Médecins au théâtre de l'antiquité au dix-septième siècle*. By Gustave Joseph Witkowski.
MTOC	*The Medieval Theater of Cruelty*. By Jody Enders.
PF	*Pure Filth*. By Noah Guynn.
PP	*Philosophical Papers*. By J. L. Austin.
RBM	*Recueil du British Museum*. Facsimile edition by Halina Lewicka.
RC	*Recueil de farces françaises inédites du XVe siècle*. Edited by Gustave Cohen.
Répertoire	*Répertoire des farces françaises*. By Bernard Faivre.
RF	*Recueil de farces (1450–1550)*. 13 vols. Edited by André Tissier.
RFlorence	*Recueil de Florence*. Edited by Jelle Koopmans.
RFMSJ	*Recueil de farces, moralités et sermons joyeux*. 4 vols. Edited by Antoine Le Roux de Lincy and Francisque Michel.

RGCF	*Recueil général et complet des fabliaux des XIIIe et XIVe siècles.* 6 vols. Edited by Anatole de Montaiglon and Gaston Raynaud.
RGS	*Recueil Général des Sotties.* 3 vols. Edited by Emile Picot.
RLV	*Recueil La Vallière.* Reprint entitled *Manuscrit La Vallière.*
ROMD	*Rhetoric and the Origins of Medieval Drama.* By Jody Enders.
RPF	*Recueil de poésies françoises des XVe et XVIe siècles.* Edited by Anatole de Montaiglon.
RSJ	*Recueil de sermons joyeux.* Edited by Jelle Koopmans.
RT	*Recueil Trepperel.*
RTC	*Répertoire du théâtre comique en France au moyen-age.* By L. Petit de Julleville.
RTLF	*Le Recueil Trepperel: Les Farces.* Edited by Eugénie Droz and Halina Lewicka.
RTLS	*Le Recueil Trepperel: Les Sotties.* Edited by Eugénie Droz.
SEF	*La Sottie en France.* By Emile Picot.
SFQS	*Sotties et Farces du XVe et du XVIe siècle.* By "Maître Antitus" [Thierry Martin].
SMFF	*Six Medieval French Farces.* Translated into English by Thierry Boucquey.
TB	*The Theatre of the Basoche.* By Howard Graham Harvey.
TFFMA	*Le Théâtre des farces en France au Moyen Âge.* 5 vols. Edited by Michel Rousse.
TFR	*Le Théâtre français avant la Renaissance.* Edited by Édouard Fournier.

Introduction

Nothing Sacred

Did you hear the one about the Mother Superior who was so busy casting the first stone that she got caught in flagrante delicto with her lover? What about the drunk with a Savior complex who was fool enough to believe himself to be the Second Coming? And that's nothing compared to what happened once farce got its grubby paws on the confessional. Welcome to the world of what one might call the "long Middle Ages." It's a fifteenth- and sixteenth-century French comedic world that is as much a medieval as a Renaissance and Reformation phenomenon. It's a world that stands to tell us a lot about where a Shakespeare or a Molière might have come from. It's an obscene, over-the-top, sacrilegious, satirical world that targets religious hypocrisy in that in-your-face way that only true slapstick can muster. It's the world of *Immaculate Deception*, where there was nothing sacred, especially the sacred.

Time and time again, the rowdy medium of farce gravitated toward a favorite target that proved one of the most formidable adversaries ever: the Catholic Church and, as the Reformation took hold throughout Europe, the Protestant *churches*.[1] As a descendant of sorts of the fabliau and a longtime companion to Chaucer, Boccaccio, and Marguerite de Navarre, farce asked: What *will* all those domineering, sexually rapacious priests, monks, friars, and the occasional nun do next? Can a titular Con-Man bluff his way through confession (#1)? Is that a sausage in those clerical hands or is the priest just happy to see Margot in *Blue Confessions* (#2)? Is the holiest of sacraments but a pretext for committing *Highway Robbery* (#3)? Are the *Confessions of a Medieval Drama Queen* merely one more way to keep a good—or a bad—woman down (#4)? Should a criminally erotic and socially subversive folie à deux be confessed in the first place (#5, *Confession Follies*)? Farce wants to know; and Brother Fillerup is only too happy to oblige with a handy demonstration (#6) or, like some of his colleagues, with a *Bro Job* (#7). Is that holy water spritzing out of the good Father's aspergillum? Or is it just the *farceur* casting aspersions again? And just wait till farce takes on the Resurrection. Make that *two* Resurrections. Two random drunks, Johnny Glad-Hand Palmer (#8) and Johnny Slack-Jaw (#9), are anything but Christ-like when they rise from the dead. They are followed here by two indulgence salesmen hawking quite the bill of goods in *The Pardoners' Tales* (#10); while Slick Brother Willy (#11) prefers to indulge other passions with the ballsiest sermon ever. And don't forget to get thee to the nunnery of our title cut, where most of the sisters avoid getting pregnant by engaging in sodomy (#12). Once you pierce through the outward appearances of faith, the dark underbelly of ecstasy suggests one hell of an immaculate deception. So, if you're wondering WWJD (*What would Jesus do?*), probably not what's about to transpire in this book.

In his *Art Poétique françoys* of 1548, Thomas Sébillet wrote that farce and its buddy, the sotie, were "designed to solicit pleasure and laughter" with all manner of phallic licentiousness, dissolution, nonsense, ridiculousness, and foolishness (*badineries, nigauderies, et toutes sotties esmouvantes à ris et Plaisir* [*APF*, 164–65; *AG*, 10]). But, this was more than just funny business. Comedy penetrates deep into matters of life, death, and the afterlife. The stakes were huge, as in the moral of our final story (#12): "it's illogical that one man would accuse another of the very same sin with which he himself is stained, sullied, and besmirched. Now wipe that smirch off your face because both are to blame" (*RFMSJ*, 2: 30). Nobody was fooling around, least of all the Church. And who better to speak up, act up, and act out than that lawyerly band of thespian brothers known as the Basochiens?

As documented in previous volumes of this series, the lion's share of medieval French farces were authored by members of the Basoche, a professional society of attorneys and legal apprentices founded in 1303 and that flourished between 1450 and 1550. At one time, it boasted as many as ten thousand members who, as theatrical practitioners of rhetorical delivery (*hypokrisis* or *actio*), litigated both real and fictional court cases (*FF*, 4–13).[2] And there was plenty to litigate too when speaking truth to ecclesiastical power. Performing a play could be dangerous. Early actors risked censorship, imprisonment, banishment, and even death, lest their humor fail to land. Already in 1398, a Parisian edict proscribed the production of any farces or saints' lives that had not been preauthorized (*LM*, 1: 414–15). In 1476, another edict barred the Basochiens, "under pain of banishment from the kingdom and confiscation of all their goods," from mounting farces, *sotties*, or morality plays not only at the Châtelet (their home court) but in any other public place (*MES*, 333).

Francis I threw a few outspoken Basochiens, *sots*, and *farceurs* in jail in 1516 (*MES*, 336n); and, by 1542, a formal legal complaint was filed in an effort to prevent parishioners from forsaking the sacred offices for the theater. The procurator general of Paris bemoaned the situation as follows: "the common people, as early as eight or nine o'clock in the morning—on holy days—would leave off the parish mass, sermons, and vespers to go off to these plays in order to save their places and to be there until five o'clock in the evening. Preaching stopped, because there would only have been preachers to listen to them." Worse yet, the shepherds themselves were abandoning their flocks, rushing through prayers, or moving up the recitation of Vespers so that they too could get to the show on time.[3] The Town Council of Amiens took action against similar lapses on 19 March and 23 October 1550, when its *échevins* permitted performances of the *Passion* and the *Acts of the Apostles* on the condition that there were "no farces nor impediments to sermons or vespers."[4] In 1559, their colleagues in Mons were maligning audiences who, "instead of going to vespers or to a sermon, spent their time watching plays, comedies, and farces."[5] And let's not omit an incident of 1562 that befell the Conards of Rouen, one of over a thousand *sociétés joyeuses* playing farces and soties all over France (*RTC*, 140).[6] The irreverent troupe allegedly pushed the boundaries so far that they were stoned by the "little people" (*TFFMA*, 5: 86).

Such was the cultural landscape in which an embattled Church decidedly viewed theater as a force for social (or antisocial) change at the expense of spirituality. And such was the universe of the unholy Trinity of farce: seeing, believing, and laughing, which makes for as good a description as any of the comic theater.

True-*ish* Confessions

Now joining the ranks of *Confession Lessons* (*FF*, #3) and *At Cross Purposes* (*FF*, #7), our first five plays invite us into the confessional. A con-man talks his way out of penance (#1); a sinful woman commits so many sexual good works that she doesn't merit an act of contrition (#2); a highwayman finds the sacrament a welcome means of getting his hands on a priest's money bag (#3); a female theologian vaunts her newly acquired authority to absolve her sisters (#4); and an abusive husband may or may not be trying to get right with the Lord on what may or may not be his deathbed (#5). The motif was so prevalent that Alan Knight speculated that "confession" might have functioned as a veritable synonym for "dialogue" (*AG*, 95); Aron Gurevich devoted an entire chapter to "Popular Culture in the Mirror of the Penitentials" (*Medieval Popular Culture*, 78–103); and, in the tour de force that is *Pure Filth*, Noah Guynn argued that "just as penitential theologians use problematic cases to test the limits of rules and norms, so, too, do farceurs ridicule, disrupt, and distort penitential practices in order to ask audiences to think carefully—if also playfully and perversely—about the nature, function, and efficacy of rituals of forgiveness" (113).[7]

For his own part, André Tissier was intrigued enough by the farces wholly or partly consecrated to confession that he differentiated between true vs. false vs. pseudoconfessions as heard by true vs. false priests (*RF*, 6: 378–83). Some confessions, he found, were true, as in our *Con-Man's Confession* (#1) and *Highway Robbery* (#3). Others were patently *false*, owing to the illegitimacy of both parties (#5, *Confession Follies*). And, then, there were the *pseudoconfessions* in which, say, a pretend priest hears a true confession (*Confession Lessons, FF*, #3). But what is farce to confession and confession to farce? Does a true confession to a false priest count? What about when it's a Mother Confessor brandishing a papal dispensation that empowers her to do so (#4)? What if the confession is neither full nor sincere or if the ritual doesn't proceed by the book? What if there is no remorse, no contrition, no absolution, no penance?[8]

My focus in this Introduction is less on the daunting theology than on the daunting theater phenomenology; but, mostly, it's this: when the Fourth Lateran Council made confession obligatory in 1215, it publicly mandated that the private be made "public," at least to the extent that a penitent would now give voice to normally unspoken truths. *Mais quelle coincidence!* The very act of making the private public is the business of theater and the funny business of farce. The question is *how public*? And, for that matter, *how theological*? As we shall see, the answers tend to be ambiguous; but they unfold uproariously in a medium that cannot abide secrecy. Farce will out. There are no "covert operations" (à la Karma Lochrie) and no "secret places" (à la Marie-Christine Pouchelle): not even for such intimate bodily functions as sex and excretion.[9] This is, after all, the genre that relies on "scatological foolishness to conjure eschatological truths": "more than demons and devils, . . . it is feces and defecation that are endowed with theologically destabilizing power" (*PF*, 5, 118). The *farceur* lets it all hang out: no "closet drama" allowed. Everything—and everyone—is out in the open, which, conveniently, was one of the historical settings for confession itself. Starting in the sixteenth century or so—a moment that coincides with the heyday of farcical performance—penitents could unburden themselves in the now familiar wooden booth (Lea, *History*, 395); but they could also confess in the open air, with about as much expectation of privacy as in the public square. Consider this fascinating piece of advice from Archbishop Walter Reynolds from across the Channel: "Let the priest choose for himself a common place for hearing confessions, where he may be seen generally by all in the church; and do not let him hear any one, and especially any woman, in a private place, except in great necessity."[10]

#ThemToo? Talk about an open secret, all of it fodder for farce's indecent exposure of clerical promiscuity, criminality, and abuse. (*Confesser*: *con* + *fesser* = "spank that cunt" or "bust that ass.") And what could be more biting than a theatrical performance of the "performativity" of the sacraments (in the sense understood by the ordinary-language philosopher J. L. Austin)? That is to say that, under the proper ritual circumstances, a duly ordained priest could alter a repentant sinner's reality when pronouncing absolution with *absolvo te*, thereby (per Austin's title), *doing things with words*. His utterance was as "performative" as when the bride and groom say "I do" and are, thereafter, legally married, having met the requisite conditions (marriage license in due form, sanctioned officiator, etc.) (*HDTW*, 12–24). Typically, a stage play is not a venue in which true performatives occur insofar as it is bracketed by what Erving Goffman famously dubbed "the theatrical frame" (*Frame Analysis,* chap. 5). By that, I mean that theater customarily hosts imitations of performatives—*pseudoperformatives*—not the real thing.[11] But the Basochiens were on intimate terms with real performative verdicts in real courtrooms. Particularly when playing their mock trials in the juridical spaces of the Châtelet, they were notorious for blurring the lines between reality and representation. The same held true in Passion plays, where men of the cloth might be cast as men of the cloth. Could a real priest in a theatrical role redeem another actor onstage? And how in heaven's name was one to distinguish between performative reality and theatrical representation (Enders, "Performing Miracles"; *DBD*, chap. 12)?

On the eve of the Reformation, those were the selfsame questions that saw Catholics and Protestants at each other's throats about Transubstantiation, the ultimate bone of contention between more literal-minded Catholics and more symbolically minded Protestants. When the celebrant of Mass pronounced the sacred words, "this is my body, this is my blood," there was intense disagreement as to what *really*—or *allegorically*—happened. Did the Eucharist and the sacramental wine metamorphose into the literal body and blood of Christ? Or was it, rather, a metaphorical reprise of what had transpired at the Last Supper? The need to come to grips with this theological and theatrical distinction between reality, reenactment, and representation informs, in different but effective ways, such scholarly works as Huston Diehl's *Staging Reform*, Andrew Sofer's *Stage Life of Props*, Michal Kobialka's *This Is My Body*, Glenn Ehrstine's *Theater, Culture, and Community*, John Romano's "Priests and the Eucharist," and Sarah Beckwith's work with "sacramental theater" in *Christ's Body* and *Signifying God* (90–91). And that very distinction, of course, had once given rise to O. B. Hardison's paradigm-shifting theory about the so-called origins of the medieval theater in the liturgy.[12] In this anthology, it is farce that ponders true and false, literal and allegorical, both or neither, or, as the contemporaneous Humanist philosopher Nicolas of Cusa would have had it, both *and* neither.[13] As it riffs on the theory and practice of what Stanislavski once dubbed "faith and a sense of truth" (*An Actor Prepares*, chap. 8), farce does what it does not just with words but with action.

Euphemism and "Comedification"

Centuries before *Les Mots et les choses* was a twinkle in Michel Foucault's eye, the relationship between words and things was taken up in one of the most widely circulated texts of the European Middle Ages, the *Roman de la Rose*. Surviving in over two hundred manuscripts and later translated by none other than Chaucer, the *Rose*'s quest for love was to endure as the joint effort of Guillaume de Lorris and Jean de Meun. Guillaume penned the first flowery, allegorical part in the 1230s; and, between 1276 and 1280, Jean picked up the thread in a markedly scholastic tone. It is the latter that interests us in that it explores a problem that has dogged language-users from the *Rose*'s Lover-Narrator to Lenny Bruce to George Carlin to Kathy Griffin. When debating Lady Reason, Jean de Meun's protagonist blanches at her lexicon for the myth of Jupiter's castration of Saturn. She has scandalously forsaken, he objects, the more polite "relics" (*relicques*) in favor of the unforgivably direct "testicles" (*couilles*): "Jupiter cut off his testicles as though they were sausages" (*les coilles cum se fussent andoilles*).[14] Instead of resorting to "crazy, bawdy talk," quoth the Lover, she ought to have euphemized (*parler par glose*). Indeed, these are the *coilles*, *andoilles*, and *glose* that will appear verbatim in *Blue Confessions* (#2).[15] So, would a rose—or a *roman de la rose*—by any other name smell as sweet?

If Lady Reason is crazy, she's crazy like a farce. Text and gloss, the practice of reading between the lines for hidden meaning, is very much the birthplace of literary criticism as we know it. In this book, it directs us toward farce's own contribution to the history of thought by inquiring: Which is more obscene? The God-created body part responsible for insemination? Or the euphemism that sanitizes its true meaning? Which is worse? Lenny Bruce's "getting your cock sucked" or "getting your *blah blah-ed*"? Which is more blatant? A censor's blurring (fogging) or bleeping? Or the sights and sounds they so glaringly spotlight by covering them up? And which is more rife with meaning? Transcribing the word *couilles*? Or eliding it as "*c. . . . . .*" in the nineteenth-century edition of *Blue Confessions* (*ATF*, 1: 375)?[16] As Koopmans and Verhuyck cleverly query in "Les Mots et la chose," do we opt for the *words*? Or do we go for *la chose*, as in "the *thing*:" "the penis" or *le petit chose*? I couldn't agree more with Ned Dubin's declaration that, in the fabliaux, euphemisms "usually serve to *underscore* obscenity, not attenuate it" ("Creative Choice," 189; my emphasis). So too for farce. By Lady Reason's logic, the euphemism is infinitely more obscene, transmuting a natural part of procreation into a prurient object of fornication. By farce's logic, that key linguistic question can lead to a bona fide dramaturgical crisis.

Given the importance of body language to the comic medium, the question of *to say or not to say* becomes one of *to stage or not to stage*. It's more than a matter of which word should denote which thing; it's which gesture should stage which thingy. In farce's grand meta-game of hide the sausage, the unsayable becomes sayable and the unstageable becomes stageable: all as it dares us to believe what we're seeing (and not seeing) right in front of us.

Throughout premodern French literature, there has always been something jarring about the commodification of the body, especially the female body. From fabliau to the genre of the *blason* that flourished between 1530 and 1540, poets were wont to emblematize body parts. With "a nose, a belly, a nail or a cheek," avers Bérénice Le Marchand, "the *blasonneurs* present a fragmented body, and a collage of all the pieces described would reconstitute a body in its entirety" ("Specular Dissection," 23–24). Farce fits right in with its own proffer of the corporeal part for the animate whole. Take the theaters of anatomy of *Shit for Brains* (*FF*, #8) or *Bitches and Pussycats* (*HD*, #8). In the former, wife Harpee is essentialized as a giant head and husband Harpo, as a giant ass (*FF*, 260–61). In the latter, the whole of womankind is reduced to either a loose asshole to be kept wide open or a gaping maw of a pie-hole to kept wide shut (*HD*, 242–45). It's all part and parcel of a distinctive dramatic technique to which I alluded briefly in *Holy Deadlock*: the quintessential melding of symbolic literalism with literal symbolism (*HD*, 11–12).[17] While Le Marchand doesn't hesitate to call the *blason* dehumanizing and fetishistic, she nonetheless adheres implicitly to its masculinist aesthetics when concluding that, "paradoxically, through fragmentation, poets are in search of unity and supreme beauty" ("Specular Dissection," 26). Farce's aesthetics lean more toward the toilet—nowhere more than in *The Resurrection of Johnny Palmer* (#8, sc. 3)—as it fixates on a clergy that is a literal pain in the ass. And—oh, holey holy!—a personified Church was to feel that pain in that very spot.

Sharing space with the forty-eight farces of the *Recueil La Vallière* is the mid-sixteenth-century *Moralité a sys personnages* (*RLV*, #57), a propaganda piece that "concretizes" the Church as the victim of anal rape. "Through one door or another," her allegorical enemies want in;[18] and, while wrong-way "furtive entry" might well be an abomination (*laron et interdict*), it is the same abomination that served, in *The Farce of the Fart*, as another literal butt of the joke about "accidental" honeymoon sodomy (*FF*, 82). Add a real case of accidental pregnancy by sodomy, and that sheds a nasty new light on the events of #12, *Immaculate Deception*.[19] Meanwhile, editor Beck issues these cautionary if contradictory remarks about the *Moralité*. On one hand, the "violently and grotesquely anti-Protestant play" is a "morality play, not a farce [which] could not have been performed by the same troupe or for the same public." On the other hand, there was "nothing obscene in and of itself about the [frequent] theme of the rape of the Church" (183–84). Seriously? Even the tamer assertion about genre is awkward when we recall that the *moralité* was often indicted in the same breath as farce.[20] Either way, the seminal message could definitely be that of the nuns of #12: "Take your theology and shove it up your ass!"

And yet, there's a big difference between a poeticized body part and a flesh-and-blood person who takes to the stage as a steaming heap of filthy, leaky, explosive sexuality. Farce reframes literal, spiritual, and satirical incarnations of *bodies of theological knowledge* as *knowledge of theological bodies*. It's a prickly, embodied literalism in which the gestural or corporeal (w)hole is quite a bit more than the sum of its yucky parts. This lands us squarely in the realm of synecdoche: the part for the whole or, as farce likes it, the part *in the* hole. Thierry Martin is even gracious enough to remind us in his edition of *Blue Confessions* that the infamous *coille* signifies both one testicle and the entire penis (*SFQS*, note 21). Feel free to groan audibly when I ask: Isn't that just ducky? *Synec-ducky.*

In light, therefore, of the farcical obsession with the literally symbolic and the symbolically literal, I make this modest proposal about theological embodiment in the form of a neologism. For farce's trademark sleight of hand and slight of bodies, for its fetishizing of a *blason*-like body, for its comical commodification: what do you say we call it *comedification*? If the *Roman de la Rose* tendered a philosophical investigation of euphemistic language, farce sticks us with a dramaturgical investigation of bodily practice. It wants to demonstrate that, in the hands of the medieval Church, sex is an act of violence and an abuse of power; whereas, in the hands of the powerless, sex is an act of pleasure (even if never fully devoid of violence). The real obscenity lies in how the Church—you should pardon the expression—fucks everybody over, which is the essence of the farcical show-and-tell. But how to show what you cannot tell and how to tell what you cannot show? Euphemize too much in farce, and you lose the comedic thrust; euphemize not at all and we're talking about pornography.

Pornography by Accident?

With superb guidance from such scholars as Kimberly Benston ("Being There") and Jonathan Walker ("Rhetorics of the *Obscaene*"), we are accustomed to thinking about obscenity and sacrilege. But, among the thornier questions posed by farce is whether there can be such a thing as a *bodily euphemism*. We needed one in *Extreme Husband Makeover* (*HD*, #11), where, in a post-Holocaust world, it seemed almost impossible to dramatize two husbands being forced into an oven (*HD*, 356–57). In this volume, various gestural euphemisms for the sex act are de rigueur. In *Highway Robbery* (#3), a thief's pat-down is a masterpiece of homoerotic stimulation; in *Slick Brother Willy* (#11), a brother's effort to shield his testicles moves Tissier to insert these two stunning stage directions: "*he makes a sketchy sign of the cross that degenerates into a caress of his groin-area*" and "*he hides his organ with his hand*" (*FFMA*, 2: 241, 249, 252). Oh, *really*? What do you suppose *that* looked like? At the very least, it's at variance with his comment elsewhere that sexual activity could be insinuated offstage only (*RF*, 11: 248–49, 240n).

Indeed, when preparing these translations, I frequently found myself hearing the voice of the title character of *Educating Rita*. When prompted to resolve the staging difficulties of Ibsen's *Peer Gynt*, she offered "Do it on t'radio." By and large, it's unimaginable that the fifteenth- and sixteenth-century theater could have been "pornographic" in today's sense of depicting real sex acts in real time. But that doesn't rule out the possibility of "protopornography" *by accident*.

More than in *The Farce of the Fart* or *Holy Deadlock*, the plays of *Immaculate Deception* gesture repeatedly toward graphic sex acts, real or virtual, public or private. The term *pornographie*, attested as early as the sixteenth century, derives from the late Greek *pornographos*, meaning to write (*graphein*) about prostitutes (*pornē*). But, in contemporary usage, the practice lies in that fifty-shades-of-gray area between eroticism, obscenity, and exploitation. In the *American Heritage Dictionary*, for example, pornography is "sexually explicit writing, images, video, or other material whose primary purpose is *to cause* sexual arousal." In *Webster's*, it's "the depiction of erotic behavior (as in pictures or writing) *intended* to cause sexual excitement." In *Oxford*, it's "printed or visual material containing the explicit description or display of sexual organs or activity, *intended to stimulate* erotic rather than aesthetic or emotional feelings." I've italicized what all three definitions have in common, namely, intentionality and causation, both notoriously difficult to access: even for the Supreme Court when, in *Jacobellis v. Ohio* (1964), they relegated the perception thereof to a community standard. Porn is in the eye of the beholder. The Justices knew it when they saw it. Ditto for medieval spectators. *If* they saw it, that is. So, did they?

Drawing on the theater phenomenology that I developed in *Murder by Accident*, I submit that there is a very good reason why intentionality perpetually comes up in definitions of pornography. From the standpoint of the initiator, there is no such thing as *unintentional sex*. What I'm about to hypothesize, however, and which this set of farces intimates, is that there is, in point of fact, such a thing as *unintentional pornography*.

This is neither the time nor the place to rerehearse the full taxonomy of *Murder by Accident* (chap. 5); but, drawing on such theorists as Jean Baudrillard, Steven Knapp, Walter Benn Michaels, Umberto Eco, Bernard Williams, Michael Kirby, Erving Goffman, and Steven Sverdlik, I crafted there a taxonomy of theatrical intentionality and argued for the existence of a highly sociable if largely implicit theatrical contract between all the parties who make and attend theater (esp. 91–102, 123–41). That contract is dependent on the spectators' ability to discern correctly the *actual intentions* of the multiple people mounting a play, regardless of how successfully or unsuccessfully those intentions are executed or bungled, attributed or misattributed, perceived or misperceived by audiences. Inspired by Austin's brilliant "Plea for Excuses," I contended that the theatrical contract would be breached by an intentional act like first-degree murder, but that not all breaches of social contracts are intentional. In Austin's scenario, he has conceived an overwhelming dislike for his donkey, ergo: ready, aim, fire! He shoots to kill, but he fells his *neighbor's* donkey instead. When wrestling with how to approach the neighbor, the shooter is unsure as to how to apologize: "'I say, old sport, I'm awfully sorry . . . I've shot your donkey *by accident*'? Or '*by mistake*'? Then again, I go to shoot my donkey as before, draw a bead on it, fire—but as I do so, the beasts move, and to my horror yours falls. Again the scene on the doorstep—what do I say? 'By mistake'? Or 'by accident'?" (*PP*, 133n; his emphasis). And that is what farce asks as it plumbs the depths of performing sexuality: *by mistake* or *by accident*?

On the face of it, it seems appalling even to ask; and in no way is the subsequent discussion meant to be lighthearted. If anything, it underscores the seriousness with which a comic medium can engage. Can sex occur *by accident*? *By mistake*? The issue was much in the news as I was preparing this book. Outrage upon outrage rightly accompanied the lack of legal repercussions for men like Brock Turner or Bill Cosby who had raped women who were unconscious, otherwise impaired, or legally and morally unable to consent to sex. For the theater, we do well to extrapolate a similar breach of the theatrical contract for certain "representations" of sex acts onstage.

In the same way that there is no murder by accident, there can be no sex by accident. Sex is and must be an intentional act; but that has never stopped theater or popular culture from dabbling in permutations. What if a man were to engage in *consensual* sex with his partner's identical twin unbeknownst to him? Even sex *by mistake* would *not* be "mistaken" by the improperly identified other party. Or, infinitely more dark and disturbing, what if a man premeditates the rape of one woman and assaults a different woman "by mistake"? The identity of the victim or, for that matter, of the participant does not negate the sexual assault. It is fair to posit that there can be *no sex by accident*; but the troubling *sex by mistake*? What I'm suggesting is that farce actually makes the case for *pornography by accident*.

Mea culpa—and keep this in mind when you read *Blue Confessions*—but what if, contrary to any preordained plan, a male actor were to become physically aroused during a given performance? Just because no record of it survives, thank God, that does not preclude the possibility. The spirit is willing; the flesh is weak. Farce enjoys all its slips of the tongue, to be sure; it has thoroughly mastered what we now call a Freudian slip or a *lapsus linguae*. I propose that, when assessing the extent to which medieval or modern farce is "pornographic" or "obscene," it is helpful to make room not only for a linguistic slip but for a *gestural slip*. A *lapsus gesti*? The dirtier the play—and *Blue Confessions*, *Bro Job*, and *Slick Brother Willy* certainly qualify—the easier that is to imagine, especially if medieval props masters went to town, as they usually did, with the special effects. Recall, for instance, the technical wizardry of filling animal bladders with red liquid to simulate the blood of the Passion plays (Gatton, "'There must be blood'"; *MTOC*, 192–202). As we shall see, those bladders could just as easily have been filled with milk for matters of not-so-religious ecstasy. Ladies and gentlemen, I give you the ultimate Baudrillardian robbery scenario in which simulation is indistinguishable from reality but, this time, it's a sexual scenario.[21] And, lest you find my hypothesis far-fetched, I regret to relate that I myself have borne witness to such a thing at a vexed experimental performance piece.

As mounted by a graduate student in one of my theater seminars at UCSB, the work was presumably intended as dramatic metacommentary on arousal and catharsis in S-and-M sex. Quite unexpectedly, what some of us saw was a piece of pornography. As one of the actors was being whipped, he became visibly aroused. Farce would have invited us to laugh; but this was no farce and nobody did. In my own case, I did not laugh because, from my particular seat, my view of the events was obscured. Others, however, saw quite plainly a spectacle that, for them, constituted a violation of the theatrical contract. We had signed up for representation, not reality. Per the definitions cited above, the agents or actants of pornography must have the intent to arouse; and, while a play cannot *be aroused*, a performer very much can be. It makes little difference to an offended spectator whether the actor's arousal was intended or not. Sometimes, of course, it's a matter of degree. A "wardrobe malfunction" is of another order of magnitude than an unplanned erection. But one thing is clear: while the graphic UCSB performance was not meant to be funny, the graphic sexuality of some farces most definitely was. The corollary question is thus: accidental pornography notwithstanding, can farcical obscenity be funny? The present anthology tenders an unambiguous reply: *yes*. And its *yes* is relentlessly problematic.

Farce always overplays its hand and, consequently, it can become what Austin dubbed an "infelicitous" or an unhappy "misfire."[22] As the medium fires away, moreover, it justifiably rubs the feminist community the wrong way and causes deep unhappiness. But, where a Catherine MacKinnon emphasizes legal reality, others like Laura Kipnis, Wendy Steiner, and my colleague Constance Penley favor the metaphorical. For MacKinnon, pornography sounds a lot like medieval hagiography in its presentation of "the sexually explicit subordination of women through pictures or words that also includes women presented dehumanized as sexual objects who enjoy pain, humiliation, or rape; women bound, mutilated, dismembered, or tortured, women in postures of servility or submission or display; women being penetrated by objects or animals."[23] Nevertheless, for the controversial Kipnis, "the world of pornography is mythological and hyperbolic, peopled by characters. It doesn't and never will exist but it does—and this is part of its politics—insist on a sanctioned space for fantasy" ("How to Look at Pornography," 119). Her observation, as germane to farce as to the morality play, holds true for any artist audacious enough to satirize a medieval ecclesiastical politics whose rules were meant to be broken. Some of those rules apply to the limits of not just sex but humor.

When writing on the reception of *The Liquid Sky* (1982), Steiner attributes to pornography many of the same potentially redeeming characteristics of farce: "the collapse of binary oppositions, as with the identical male and female models; the equation of art with assault; the inclusion of the audience in the action and therefore in the ethical responsibility for what is represented; and the outrageous cost of ecstasy" (*The Scandal of Pleasure*, 3). Farce *is* outrageous; but must it always be made to pay a price? And there's something else. For Penley, pornography can be funny. That's right. Whether it be projected on the screen of a playhouse, a television, a personal computer, or a handheld device, it can be as silly as men and women doing things with zucchinis. (As a resident of California, I hasten to assure you that we take vegetable abuse very seriously.) Porn is even funny in ways surprisingly evocative of medieval farce. Turning to the popular ditty "The Monk of Great Renown," in which a clergyman engages in rape, anal intercourse, and necrophilia, Penley notes that "the somewhat tamer stag films that I have seen prefer to attack the hypocrisy of the clerical class by having the priests and the nuns get it on in all sorts of combinations."[24] And just wait till you get a load of the eerie relevance of her work on the stag film *Getting His Goat* (1923) to *Blue Confessions* (below, #2, § "Sets and Staging"). Welcome to the farcical house of God.

Political Impieties

Centuries before Bill Maher, Jim Jefferies, Sarah Silverman, Colin Quinn, or Ricky Gervais ever launched joking indictments of religion, Tartuffery, and pedophile priests, farce was shining its harsh spotlight on them all. Even the taboo Holocaust as a matter for levity is the subject of the Netflix documentary *The Last Laugh* (2017). Is farcical humor offensive, disgusting, misogynistic, classist, elitist, ethnocentric, and irreligious? Totally. From *Monk-ey Business* (*FF*, #9) to *Tartuffe* to Diderot's *The Nun* to such cinematic offerings as *The Magdalen Sisters* (2002), *Philomena* (2013), and *Spotlight* (2015), there is nothing remotely amusing about centuries of sexual abuse in ecclesiastical communities. Or anywhere else. But can farce be *terribly funny* anyway? In these humorless times? Or must it be dumped into the dustbin of history?

Obviously, with my ongoing commitment to making these texts available, I deem them resurrection-worthy. So does the classicist Shadi Bartsch in a 2021 op-ed for the *Washington Post*, "Don't Yield Ancient Literature and History to the Alt-Right," in which she urges that an unabashedly political translation reframe what is no longer tolerable. Reframing is precisely what theatrical performance always invites us to do. But that's where the terrible fun begins. And the drama. And the politics of political incorrectness.

Impious and unorthodox, farce loves nothing better than to take on piety and orthodoxy of any ilk as it wages an extreme comical crusade against religious extremism. Of necessity, then, twenty-first-century humor will come face-to-face with a new fundamentalism about humor that is nowadays amplified by social media outrage. There's a reason why we speak of political *pieties*. Indeed, when I lecture on these materials, audiences are routinely too uncomfortable to laugh, at which point, we retreat to the safer ground of the Reformation. Then as now, many might laugh at a farce *about* religion, but not at religion as farce. *C'est la vie. C'est la farce.* Maybe it's not farce's sexuality that is pornographic after all but its political humor, the ultimate sacrilege.

As Andrew Kay points out in "The Joke's Over," the current political climate has had dire consequences for the pleasures of satire at a cultural moment when we have never needed it more. Today's satirist, he polemicizes, must reckon with a "cluster of menaces" that tend to "repel efforts at humor," the sheer scale of which "can hector him into muteness." To which I add: *her too.* It turns out that the Dark Ages had a lighter side; and France's over two hundred rollicking, frolicking, singing, and dancing comedies—more extant than in any other vernacular—have waited long enough for their moment in the spotlight. Is their perilous work to become a latter-day casualty in the cultural battles about humor? Or might we call upon theater to allow us to laugh along with medieval people at religion and at ourselves? Might we join in the frivolity and release that can provoke new thinking? Or is the impolitic laughter itself beyond the pale? As we come face-to-face and *farce to farce* with the monitoring of humor, it behooves us to ponder the ways in which comedy pushes the envelope of the theological and pietistic alike. Medieval people had a sense of humor, and God only knows they needed one. Do we?

When deciding how to approach profanity and profanation, many scholars turn for insight to political theorists like Giorgio Agamben, and why not? Medieval theology is political, just as medieval politics is theological. Among the characters that you shall meet in the pages that follow: a fantastical female confessor who indicts French Cardinals in Rome as a bunch of asses (#4) and an ersatz resurrectee who tells tales of the Reformation Wars of Religion erupting in Heaven (#9). For myself, I prefer the rhetorical spin of a little-studied text by Kenneth Burke, one of the greatest political rhetoricians of all time. Burke was also a literary critic and a playwright of sorts when trying his hand at a forty-page morality play in his *Rhetoric of Religion* (1961), the nominal subject of which was *logology* or the linguistic politics of theology. His stated purpose was "simply to ask how theological principles can be shown to have *usable secular analogues*" (2; my emphasis); but there was nothing simple about it when he illustrated the phenomenon with an "Epilogue: Prologue in Heaven" (273–316). Burke's epilogue is an imaginary dialogue between God and the Devil, complete with an expositor and stage directions. While I cannot do it justice here, perhaps readers will take it on faith that it owes less to *Paradise Lost* and more to ancient Greek mock encomia and medieval *moralités.* The "Prologue in Heaven" is a mise-en-scène, a riff on the "symbol-using animals" known as "Earth People," who cannot do without their drama: "their words for morality, drama and action will all imply one another" (278). "You get drama," he continues, "since drama is based on action. . . . That will be particularly important because of the large part that the arts of comedy and tragedy will play in their outlook, extending even to their ideas of ultimate salvation" (281). At one point in the dialogue, Satan goes so far as to demonstrate the new theology by analogizing it to a beautiful woman: "[the Earth People] will mean a seductive surface which perversely and reconditely alludes to the possibilities of motherhood, while underneath there lies a dying assemblage of bones, ooze, drip, slime and potential stench" (306). It's hard to come closer to farce than that. A "usable secular analogue" on its own terms, farce might well appear to be inimical to religion; but, in turning everything inside out and outside in, it demands a closer look at the rhetorical and theatrical foundations of faith. For Burke, when you think through religion, you get drama. For the Middle Ages and the Renaissance, you also get farce, a medium that can nurture more nuanced thinking *about* theology, even if it does so in the most brazen manner. Rather than police or censor its vile language, we might choose instead to explore, reinterpret, reshape, subvert, and, in a word, translate a theatrical body of work for new bodies politic.

In challenging us to laugh at moral abuse, in its critique of flagrant antisocial behavior, farce is sociably funny enough to reclaim its place in literary history and serious enough to participate in the larger critical conversation about medieval and early modern culture. For better or for worse—for better *and* for worse—it has always intervened to expose and even to right the wrongs of the past. Each time readers and practitioners translate imaginatively or materially from the page to the stage, they take up theater's call. In my own work, I've been profoundly influenced by Elaine Scarry's paradigm-shifting *The Body in Pain*, where she theorized that "physical pain does not simply resist language but actively destroys it, bringing about an immediate reversion to a state anterior to language, to the sounds and cries a human being makes before language is learned" (4). What the farcical corpus helps us to discover is that, *if pain defies language*, maybe pleasure does too. We might, therefore, look at and listen to all those laughing bodies in pain, the better to access the sights and sounds of their pleasure. And ours.

About This Translation

It is no coincidence that one speaks of a translation that is *faithful* or *unfaithful*. Nowhere is that more true than in these farces devoted to theology, which I call, more emphatically than ever, *adapted translations* (*HD*, 20). Ever operating in good faith and committed to rendering each and every word of the Middle French, I've still sought to capture their overall mood through contemporary cultural touchstones while attending to many of the needs of the prickliest medievalist. This time, however, for plays that survive in more than one version, I've taken things a step further with two bona fide composite editions for *Blue Confessions* (#2) and *Bro Job* (#7) (below, § "Critical Apparatus"). Otherwise, the main advantage of a multivolume project like this one is that I've already shared the majority of my editorial theories and practices (*FF*, 33–54; *HD*, 20–33). I'll confine myself to a few supplemental methods to the translational madness.

Feminist Dramaturgy: An Encore Performance

Farce is notorious for its violence, sexism, classism, and misogyny. But theater itself is always translation, always adaptation. Performance changes everything, especially when so much of theater's beauty, magic, and verve lies in its virtuality and mutability. With or without an extant script, theater is a vision *of* and *for* action: a move from image to speech, idea to embodiment, piety to prayer, page to stage, thought to motion, sight to sound, vision to action. The unseen becomes seeable; the unimaginable, imaginable; the unstageable, stageable. In *Immaculate Deception*, moreover, if the move from idea to embodiment is the literal *incarnation* of a rhetorical and theological practice, it is also a translational practice. More intriguing still: in an act requiring imagination and fidelity, the translator must attend to all of that as she reimagines a given story for the living stage. She becomes a virtual director, producer, and dramaturge in a process that is less about an author's (or authors') meaning (or meanings) and more about multiple subjectivities multiplied exponentially.

Myriad individuals collaborate to make theater: authors, producers, directors, set- and costume designers, actors, and audiences, all of whom inflect interpretation(s) in different ways that vary from performance to performance, place to place, time to time, person to person, and within the same person. Theater has no voice per se: only *voices*. And that's before we face the music—including the literal musicality—of the still more daunting challenge of what is unseen on the page, namely: all the pantomime, the dance, the melodies, the intonation. In a repertoire dominated by irrecuperable physical, visual, and auditory comedy, that is often what matters the most. Readers are probably familiar with the translator's *le mot juste*: to wit, "just the right word" for terms and expressions that seem *untranslatable*. In this series, I must also locate *l'acte juste*: "just the right stage action" that will bring home the message at some five centuries' remove. Verbal language is not the only conduit to the past. As art historians know full well, so too is nonverbal language and, in my own case, so too is the complex scenic use of silence, gesture, staging, tears, and laughter.

In the Middle Ages, silence doesn't always mean what we think it does; quite to the contrary, it can be teeming with life and rebellion. Nor does it necessarily denote consent. In comedy, silence can speak volumes, such that a faithful, feminist translation of farce might readily speak to us today. Once we draw on the transformative power of performance to adapt, alter, interpret, and even subvert, theater invariably offers a way for new generations to raise their voices, to be heard, and to act. A deceptively silly farce can present to the modern world a strategic deployment of words and acts that do not divide but, rather, unite all those who dream of a common language.

An unabashedly political feminist translation can both reframe and reject the original sexism by doing the very thing that theater invites us to do: adapt and inflect (*HD*, 20–22). But one thing is clear: we are unlikely to find that out unless we listen to and hear the palpable silences of the comic theater and, with any luck, inaugurate a translational movement of #ThemToo.

High Art, Low Art

Three volumes and myriad conversations into this project, I've noticed something about artistic sensibility and, more and more, *sensitivity*. Independent of the delicate farcical balance that is perpetually struck between pleasure and pain, it is my distinct impression that there is an investment in and an expectation of comedy that is different from what we bring to other creative media. When I teach these materials, for instance, it is not uncommon to hear a student profess to feeling excluded from all the lawyerly in-jokes, the isolated phrases in Latin or Italian, the allusions to specific historical events, or the arcane and even not-so-arcane references. My usual response is to quote the immortal words of Jerry Seinfeld: *not that there's anything wrong with that.* Be that as it may, the resentment to which satire can give rise frequently yields something like this: if the humor's not for *me,* it's not for *us,* and, therefore, not for *anyone.* To that, I say: jokes have eternally been made at somebody else's expense, the jokers' included. If, for Aristotle, comedy "sets out to represent people as worse than they are today" (*Poetics,* 1448a), I would venture to say that farce admits us into a world in which people are *nastier* than we are. While we have happily moved away from the excessive cruelty that perpetuates cultural stereotypes, not everyone is meant to get every joke. But does that mean that this is a repertoire that only the most dispassionate intellectual could love? I think not; but the reasons *why not* might fruitfully relax some of the strictures placed all too easily on comedy.

Take the sexism and elitism of farce's notoriously frank vernacular. Its idiom, constantly evolving, is gleefully grounded in the learned and popular culture of the fifteenth and sixteenth centuries. Current today, gone tomorrow: for us as for them. In the pages that follow, you will encounter a "Jesus H. Christ" here, a "Jeez Louise" or a "Crikey" there. You might even wince at the occasional archaism or anachronism, many of which, by the way, farce delights in deploying deliberately. And yet, I don't recall too many scathing readerly indictments of a translator's recourse to "alas" or "hark" in Homer or Shakespeare, nor of a director's to period-piece music. Nor did archaisms seem to bother anybody in Nathaniel Dubin's groundbreaking verse translations of the filthy *fabliaux.* But, somehow, when poetry is rendered as poetry, even the lowly *fabliaux* can be received as high art. No such luck for their farcical *compère.* Farce is relentlessly low art, the black sheep of the literary family, even though the translational situation is palpably the same. Its language, humor, and music must sound contemporary, regardless of all the changes with the times, and, interestingly enough, when my students stage these plays, that's not a problem. They routinely update a given text in accordance with whatever is dictated verbally or nonverbally by their communities. No matter that their rescripted or improvisational moments affect the rhythm, rhyme, or reason of one moment or another. They've gotten it exactly right. They've done just what they're supposed to do for a site-specific theater: adapt and readapt, inflect and reinflect, fashion and refashion, interpret and reinterpret. If anything, they have mirrored the premodern circumstances better than my books could possibly do in that we have, all of us, become translators.

Comedy, theater, and the comic theater are always of the moment and that moment always changes. Likewise for the present offerings, which are not meant to be carved in stone. Indeed, if I've managed to translate one highly local, humorously contextualized moment into another—that of my own American popular culture—then I do believe that I've been faithful. To anyone who complains that he or she wants *a literal translation*, this much, I can assure you: it doesn't exist and, no, you don't. Not if this repertoire is to live on. Read each play as if it were prefaced by a Magritte-like statement that *ceci n'est pas un scénario*. This is not a script. It is and it isn't. It must, it will, and it should change. And who knows? Open Access might well turn out to be the best possible venue for the dynamism of a dynamic theater.

On Anonymity, Naming, and Renaming

As in the two previous volumes, I refer to the twelve plays here assembled by the titles that I have bestowed upon them and to their dramatis personae by the names with which I've baptized or rebaptized them. I also continue to assign textually justifiable names to the many unnamed female characters. As you've doubtless gleaned from the Table of Contents alone, this ensemble is not particularly friendly to religion. Lest you suspect that I've transmuted a "feminist appropriation" (*HD*, 20–22) into a secular one, I hasten to emphasize that any joyously irreverent hostility toward theology is that of the original *farceurs*.

Critical Apparatus, Stage Directions, Composite Editions

With a renewed effort to fashion a critical apparatus that is useful for the specialist but will not overwhelm others, I've endeavored to keep the endnotes in bounds. Future volumes will be streamlined more radically but, for the time being, only the most germane matters of philology, history, or transmission are explored in the endnotes (more extensively when there is a scant editorial tradition or, as for the *RC* plays, online availability is spotty). Their scope tends to be limited to an English-language source or two, the better to get new researchers started; but do be aware that the Bibliography doesn't begin to cover all the scholars who have long inspired me. I employ parenthetical documentation whenever practicable, especially for the frequently cited works in the list of abbreviations. I also beg your indulgence for mentioning a great deal of my own work: its extensive bibliographies are easy to access. All translations of primary and secondary sources are mine unless otherwise indicated, as, for instance, for Donald Frame's *Rabelais* (*CWFR*).

In accordance with my past practice, I italicize any original Middle French stage directions, which appear unbracketed, as opposed to my own bracketed interpolations that signal such situations as these: nonspeaking characters that I've added to the casts of characters; dramaturgical guidance for set design, action, or pantomime; scene breaks; my best guess at what might be missing for an orphaned rhyme; a clarification of an obscure historical reference; a translation of a Latin phrase unlikely to be understood; the setup for a joke, and so forth. Regarding the two composite editions of *Blue Confessions* and *Bro Job*, I've introduced new editorial conventions to accommodate three types of parenthetical: my habitual square brackets for marking my own interpolations or stage directions; curly brackets for stage directions within those textual interpolations; and, for the first time, angle brackets to flag my translations of a second (or third) base text.

The quick-takes of my "Brief Plot Summaries" again shepherd your choice of what to read; and each play's "Production Notes" lay out the five categories of § "Plot," § "Characters and Character Development," § "Language," § "Sets and Staging," and § "Costumes and Props." That said, those categories remain as fungible and arbitrary as ever. It regularly proves impossible to separate a play's story line (§ "Plot") from its overarching metaphors (§ "Language") from its dramaturgical mise-en-scène (§ "Sets and Staging") from a protagonist's persona or speech patterns (§ "Characters and Character Development"). Unfortunately, one rare subsection is wholly absent in *Immaculate Deception*: "Performance History." Although Petit de Julleville stressed that over a thousand *sociétés joyeuses* played farces and soties all over France (*RTC*, 140), no concrete information has come down to us about a single production of our twelve plays.[1] Instead, I give a shout-out, when appropriate, to any noteworthy modern one.

Editions and Printed Sources

Immaculate Deception features plays from all four of the key medieval-Renaissance collections: the *Recueil du British Museum* (*RBM*), the *Recueil La Vallière* (*RLV*), the *Recueil Cohen* (*RC*), or *Recueil de Florence* (*RFlorence*), and, making its debut in my series, the *Recueil Trepperel* (*RT*). There are six farces from the *RBM*: *Blue Confessions* (#2), *Confession Follies* (#5), *Bro Job* (#7), *The Resurrection of Johnny Slack-Jaw* (#9), *The Pardoners' Tales* (#10), and *Slick Brother Willy* (#11); three from the *RC*: *Highway Robbery* (#3), *Confessions of a Medieval Drama Queen* (*Drama Queens* for short [#4]), and *The Resurrection of Johnny Palmer* (#8); two from the *RLV*: *Brother Fillerup* (#6) and *Immaculate Deception* (#12); and one from the *RT*: *The Con-Man's Confession* (#1). All four *Recueils* preserve plays that are believed to predate considerably the sixteenth-century dates of their compilation; all four exist in accessible postmedieval editions and, for the *RBM* and *RLV*, in both digitized and facsimile editions. Rest assured that, if an edition could be located, I've consulted it, along with any translation thereof (the latter, only after completing my travails). To facilitate perusal of the Middle French, I've favored referring you to the convenient digitized editions. If there is a better edition—oftentimes, by the incomparable André Tissier, Jelle Koopmans, or Thierry Martin—I incorporate its teachings. Each set of "Production Notes" will remind you of a play's provenance, but here are the basics.[2]

The *Recueil du British Museum*, discovered in 1840, contains sixty-four plays believed to date from 1540–50, of which forty-seven are farces. For our six *RBM* farces, I cite from Viollet le Duc's *Ancien Théâtre françois* (*ATF*), a ten-volume series for which a young Anatole de Montaiglon prepared the actual editions (*RF*, 6: 252n). The first citation always specifies *ATF*, after which the designation is dropped, followed by volume and page number; there are no verse numbers in *ATF*. When an ancillary lesson is needed from the original *RBM*, I send you to Halina Lewicka's facsimile edition, the legible Gothic typeface of which is decipherable even for the amateur. While each play therein is clearly demarcated by the large Roman numeral on its title page, its continuously paginated folio numbers can be difficult to see.

Therefore, in lieu of directing you to something like fol. 367v, I cite a local folio number (i.e., fol. i or v for *Slick Brother Willy*).

In the *Recueil La Vallière*, dating from approximately 1535–45 and copied around 1575, we find seventy-four plays, forty-eight of them farces. It was copied in Rouen (Normandy) in the 1570s and sold in 1780 by its owner, the Duke of La Vallière, whence its name. For the *RLV*, I largely adopt the same procedure as for the *ATF*, citing by volume and local page number from the four-volume *Recueil de farces, moralités et sermons joyeux* edited by Antoine Le Roux de Lincy and Francisque Michel (*RFMSJ*). Pagination in that edition is complicated, however, in that it is not continuous within a given volume (let alone over the four volumes). For guidance from the original manuscript, I number the folios as I did for the *RBM*; and an excellent facsimile edition of the *RLV* was published by Slatkine in 1972. Additionally, the Bibliothèque Nationale has digitized the entire *RLV* (Ms. 24341) but, regrettably, the reproduction is of poor quality.[3] I am happy to report that, at the time of this writing, Mario Longtin was hard at work on reeditions of all seventy-four plays, but under the revised name of the *Recueil de Rouen*.

The *Recueil Cohen* (*RC*), so named for its first editor, Gustave Cohen (1949), houses fifty-three plays, all called "farces," for which I cite his verse numbers. The *RC* was discovered in Florence in 1928, only to be lost again for many years, precluding all scholarly comparison with Cohen's *Recueil de farces françaises inédites du XVe siècle*. That changed in 2011 when, in the denouement of an editorial cloak-and-dagger story (*FF*, 39–40), Jelle Koopmans managed to relocate, reedit, restore, and republish the compilation under a new name, the *Recueil de Florence*, to which I turn for important new clarifications and corrections. The plays, asserts Koopmans and in contrast to previous assumptions, were probably printed in two installments during the first quarter of the sixteenth century (ca. 1504–21 and 1512–21); and their overall cleanliness prompts him to wonder whether they were much used at all (*RFlorence*, 7, 15). Even so, the originals are as inaccessible as ever. To date, no one but Koopmans has seen them, such that signs of strain have emerged. In the "Préface" to his online edition of *Sotties et Farces du XVe et du XVIe siècle* (*SFQS*), we can hear Thierry Martin's frustration: "In a private collection, Koopmans has found the *Recueil* believed to have been lost, but we are still waiting for him to give the proof of this rediscovery by showing the photographic reproduction that he purports to possess."[4]

Finally, the *Recueil Trepperel*, comprised of thirty-five plays, of which five are farces, was edited in two volumes by another towering figure from medieval studies: Eugénie Droz, who published *Les Sotties* and, in collaboration with Lewicka, *Les Farces*. Also discovered in Florence in 1928, the *RT* was a major find, despite a number of incomprehensible passages, inverted speeches, omissions, inappropriate archaisms, errors, and inscrutable allusions to unidentifiable events (*RTLS*, xii–xiii). Printed in Paris, it likely dates from approximately 1504–25 and may have belonged to a Parisian theater troupe (Bouhaïk-Gironès, *Les Clercs*, 227, 322–23).

As far as modern editions and, more rarely, translations are concerned, it's a pleasure to acknowledge the tour-de-force erudition of Tissier's thirteen-volume *Recueil de farces (1450–1550)* (*RF*), as well as the modern French translations he provided for all sixty-five in the terrific four-volume *Farces françaises de la fin du Moyen Âge* (*FFMA*). Bernard Faivre crafted a bilingual edition of *Slick Brother Willy* (#11) in *Les Farces* (1: 199–268); and, more recently, a full 136 farces and soties have been posted online in the superb *Sotties et Farces du XVe et du XVIe siècle* (https://sottiesetfarces.wordpress.com/about/). *And counting.* These invaluable and heavily annotated editions come to us courtesy of the genius of Thierry Martin, whose verve is inflected by an ebullient queer theory and who publishes under the playful pseudonym of "Maître Antitus." Just one caveat: Martin is so prolific that it is impossible to keep up. Since he updates his site regularly, its content will almost certainly have changed by the time you read this book. When citing his oeuvre, I refer to Martin's brief prefatory notes to each play as "Introd.," and to his verse numbers and endnote numbers, but with the same caveat: any note might have been renumbered or eliminated. (When not otherwise indicated, all dates of access are 25 January 2021.)

To my knowledge, none of the dozen plays of *Immaculate Deception* have ever been translated into English; but five have indeed been translated into modern French (details to come in their corresponding Production Notes): *Blue Confessions*, *The Resurrection of Johnny Slack-Jaw*, *The Pardoners' Tales*, *Slick Brother Willy*, and *Immaculate Deception*. At one point, a number were published online in Portuguese too; but they were subsequently removed, including *Slick Brother Willy* (initially accessed on 21 December 2015). Consequently, the number of medieval French farces available in English remains quite low. Counting the present twelve—and in light of my previous calculations (*FF*, 37; *HD*, 25)—Anglophones can now enjoy forty-eight farces of the some two hundred extant. For plot summaries of all the rest, several French-language resources are at our disposal, notably Petit de Julleville's *Répertoire du théâtre comique* (*RTC*) and Faivre's deliciously tongue-in-cheek *Répertoire* (1993). Occasionally, one or the other excludes a farce from consideration, seemingly deeming it a morality play, a dialogue, or simply not funny enough. And do be advised that the *RC* plays were not within Petit de Julleville's purview: his *RTC* was published in 1886, over fifty years before Cohen's *RC* of 1949. Likewise for Faivre's inability to cite all of Tissier's *RF* editions (1986–2000): his *Répertoire* appeared in 1993. Every now and then, I also cite from the oft-scandalized Octave Joseph Delepierre, aka Tridace-Nafé-Théobrome (*FF*, 416n), who catalogued and recapped the *RBM* plays in his *Description et analyse d'un livre unique qui se trouve au Musée britannique* of 1849 (*DLU*).

As in the past, when I reproduce the Middle French, I resolve abbreviations, regularize the spelling of titles and characters' names, and modernize such archaisms as "j" for "i" and "v" for "u." When reader-friendly, I add the odd diacritical as well: the preposition *à* receives its *accent grave* or a naked *e*, its *accent aigu* (*é*) or *accent grave* (*è*). I also capitalize or italicize the generic names of the characters of the play, even if they are not capitalized consistently in the Middle French: "The Wife," for example, for *La femme* or *La Femme*.

Order of Presentation: Intertextuality, "Intersexuality," and Casting

The *Farce of the Fart* was an anthology of some of my favorites; *Holy Deadlock* was a comical chronology of marriage; *Immaculate Deception* now speaks to us of religion and—take it on faith—one volume doesn't begin to cut it. We begin our journey with four—almost five—confession farces that frame the quintessential theatrical and theological questions of public vs. private, authentic vs. inauthentic, repentant vs. unrepentant. *Confession Follies* (#5) then serves as a transition to the various physical and spiritual remedies to be administered to the flock, primarily to women. After Brother Fillerup's tawdry prescription (#6), *Bro Job* enacts a cure so graphic that it's licentious even for farce (#7). Next, follow the pointing aspergillum and watch the dead rise in two respective (if hardly respectful) resurrections of two drunken John-Boys (the Fool-*Badin*'s typical moniker): *Johnny Palmer* (#8) and *Johnny Slack-Jaw* (#9). After all, miracles make for good business, stage business, and funny business as they do in the delightful *Pardoners' Tales* (#10), which then sets the stage for the crème de la crème. The cream definitely rises to the top after

Slick Brother Willy delivers a filthy sermon that foretells a lot more exposure than his naked butt (#11). Last, it's a nun's butt on the line in *Immaculate Deception* (#12), and not necessarily just the pregnant one's. By the way, our final three plays—a potential triple bill—are united by underwear and headgear, enjoying what Andrew Sofer has shown to be the phenomenological richness of props (*Stage Life of Props*, 1–60).

In terms of casting and consistent with the genre's reputation for etymological "stuffing," these farces dialogue with one another intertextually and "intersexually" as one medium or genre penetrates another (miracle play, Passion play, *moralité*, song, fabliau, poetry, etc.). Most medieval plays were performed by men; so, by all means, cast men, if you so desire. But go big. Go camp. Go drag queen. And don't hesitate to cross-cast or to bend the rules and play it "bent," underscoring the prospects of latent or blatant homoeroticism. Premodern French theater history hosts plenty of male-male attraction. Remember when young Lyonard's Saint Barbara of 1485 looked so much like a woman that he inadvertently seduced a priest (*DBD*, 29–42)? But medieval women correspondingly took to the stage: as early, we surmise, as Hrotsvitha's tenth-century adaptations of Terence. Throughout a "long Middle Ages" that stretched well into the sixteenth century with, say, Antonia Pulci's Italian convent dramas, we find such actresses as the unnamed young lady playing Saint Catherine in 1468 or one Françoise Buatier in 1535, whose Virgin Mary brought down the house in Grenoble (*DBD*, 17–43). Significantly, the first extant contract for an actress was issued in 1545 to a Marie Ferré, and it included farce work, authorizing her to play "histories, moralities, farces, and acrobatics [*histoires, morales, farces et sobressaults*] in exchange for 12 *livres tournois* per year."[5] What is more, all that gender-bending revelry can be amplified today. Why not cast actors who are not so much the twelfth-century hermaphrodites analyzed by Nederman and True ("Third Sex") as they are trans, gender nonbinary, gender-ambiguous, or, for Bychowski, "intersex" ("Isle"). Especially in a play like *Blue Confessions*, replete with big reveals, the gender of the actors might prove the biggest shocker of all, conceivably during the supremely liminal moment of the curtain call (as theorized by Bert States in *Great Reckonings* [197–206]). Nowhere more so than with Birdie of *Johnny Palmer* (#8), where the pronouns *they*, *them*, *their* work best. It all depends on how secretly—or manifestly campily—an actor wishes to convey his, her, or their *own* gender throughout the performance. To my eye, the whole vibe is very much akin to that of a classic Dunkin Donuts ad in which a quite obviously mustachioed man plays a woman;[6] or, in the converse phenomenon, where Melissa McCarthy parodies Sean Spicer or Kate McKinnon does Rudy Giuliani on *Saturday Night Live*. Or, wait! Also from *SNL*, "It's Pat!" (gender unidentifiable). Or, from cinema, it's Victor! It's Victoria! No, it's farce!

Oh, Brother! Costuming the Medieval Monastic Orders

So much *monk*-ey business, so little time. This book is a far cry from a primer on monasticism, which is why I bring this up under translation methodology rather than theology. But, if we are to understand our dramatis personae, something of the fundamentals of medieval religious life is in order. Dotting the farcical landscape of western Europe, as well as the pages of Boccaccio's *Decameron* or Marguerite de Navarre's *Heptameron*, were the omnipresent monks, friars, hermits, and brothers, fixtures one and all of daily life. Notwithstanding the proverbial wisdom that you can't judge a book by its cover or a monk by his habit (*l'habit ne fait pas le moine*), it turns out that you can indeed judge a monk by his cover and by his umpteen cover stories. Faced with farce's bands of Brothers Minor (*Frères mineurs*) and Brothers Preachers (*Frères prescheurs*), we too must be able to judge them instantaneously by their vestimentary and behavioral habits.

As recognized by the Second Council of Lyon (1274), those represented here belonged to the four medieval mendicant or "begging" orders, which came to prominence in the thirteenth century. The Order of Preachers, the Friars Minor, the Carmelites, and the Hermits of Saint Augustine renounced all worldly goods and property and were vowed to poverty. As "begging friars," they traveled from town to town; and their communities sprung up around larger cities, where they cared for the sick and preached the word of God. There, they subsisted on the charitable kindness of strangers or, as farce would have it, did anything but subsist. (For myself, I keep hearing Errol Flynn's Robin Hood to the portly Friar Tuck: "If this is poverty, I'll gladly share it with you.") Members of all four orders, for example, are named as the sex partners of the hyperactive penitent of *Blue Confessions* (#2): the Dominicans (*Jacobins*), the Franciscans (*Cordeliers* or *frères de la Corde*), and the less influential Augustinians (*Augustins*) and Carmelites (*Carmes*) (*AF*, 4; Andrews, *The Other Friars*). Who *are* they exactly? Thanks to such superb scholarship as that of Frances Andrews, Bernard McGinn, Jill Raitt, Keith Egan, Guy Geltner, Wayne Hellmann,

Richard Kieckhefer, Tim Rayborn, Simon Tugwell, and Adolar Zumkeller, it is possible to find out.[7]

The challenge today—whence the thumbnail sketches below—is how best to make this tall order of monks legible to contemporary audiences who are, for the most part, unfamiliar with their ways. Problems of cultural literacy become problems of costuming; but their true colors can be revealed by just that: some color-coding. From medieval heraldry to Huizinga's *Homo Ludens* (77–78) to Susan Crane's *Performance of Self* (10–38), we are what we wear or, as Slick Brother Willy would have it (#11), what we don't. The Dominicans ("Blackfriars" in Britain) donned a black cloak or *cappa* over their white habits; for the Franciscans, it was fifty shades of "Greyfriar"; while the Augustinian "all blacks"—no, that's not a soccer team—sported two types of black woolen tunic. The outdoor version had "long, wide sleeves, a black leather girdle and a large shoulder cape to which is attached a long, pointed hood reaching to the girdle"; the indoor version featured a scapular or "short monastic cloak covering the shoulders over which the shoulder cape is worn" (Derwich, "Clothing"). And the chaste Carmelites were mostly dressed in white; but, in *Blue Confessions*, we'll have some fun with their original, Elijah-black- or brown-and-white striped mantles.

Dominicans or Jacobins. Founded by Saint Dominic and recognized by the papacy in 1216, the Dominican Order of Friars Preachers (*frères prescheurs* or *Prescheurs*) dominated the medieval French religious scene. Since its brothers were sworn to preach, they were to be found near major urban centers, where their houses were called "convents" or *couvents* (a small lexical item that can aid in pinpointing the religious sensibility of any given farce). The Dominicans went by the name of "Jacobins" as well, owing to the location of their Parisian house on the rue Saint-Jacques (*Jacques* > *Jacobins*). Not only was that street a stone's throw from the Sorbonne: their church was also one of the stages of the storied pilgrimage route of Saint Jacques de Compostelle or the *Camino de Santiago* (*RF*, 6: 395n). In contrast to their more or less unschooled Franciscan brethren, the highly educated Dominicans played an important role in medieval education. Thomas Aquinas was a Dominican; and so too were the "hounds of the Lord" (a pun in Latin on *domini canes*) associated with the atrocities of the Inquisition, the Albigensian Crusade against the Cathars (*AF*, 21), and the prosecution of Joan of Arc. Like the Augustinians, the Dominicans followed the *Rule of Saint Augustine*, observing corporate and individual poverty (*AF*, 19–27). Interestingly, they took one vow only—that of obedience—with the vows of poverty and chastity implicit (Tugwell, "Spirituality of the Dominicans," 20–23). And who better to look for a legal loophole than a Dominican or—what do you know!—a Basochien?

Franciscans or Cordeliers. With the Dominicans under our belts, we can proceed to the Brothers of the belt—*les frères de la Corde* or *Cordeliers*—better known as the Franciscans ("Greyfriars" across the Channel). They were not monks per se but "little brothers" of the order of Friars Minor (*frères mineurs* or *fratres minor[e]s*), which was established in 1209 by Saint Francis of Assisi (*AF*, 16). Notoriously corrupt and promiscuous, they could be found hanging around cities like Paris, their nickname deriving from something else that was hanging: their distinctive rope belt or cincture (*corde*) with its three knots that symbolized their three vows. Chief among those vows was that of "radical voluntary poverty," which, as Rayborn explains, required that they "sell all of their possessions and give the money to the poor before they would be admitted" to the order. "With no permanent homes," he continues, "no possessions, no wealth, and no food, they set out into the world, adopting a mendicant lifestyle and begging for their food, taking shelter where they could, and considering it a badge of honor if they were abused or turned away, living just as they believed the first apostles did." Walking barefoot and subject to pain and humiliation, they were aiming at a true, papally sanctioned *imitatio Christi* (*AF*, 16). Needless to say, farce was at pains to up the humiliation by highlighting the deterioration of their lofty impulses into a quest for the fulfillment of material and earthly needs.

The Augustinians or Augustins. Other "Brothers Minor" to claim farce's attention were the Augustinians, sometimes dubbed hermits of Saint Augustine, Augustinian hermits, Augustine Monks, or, in England, Austin Friars. And let's not forget that hermits are popping up all over the place in medieval romance, say, any time a knight-errant seeks to have his dream interpreted. The Augustinians were dedicated, as their name implies, to the *Rule of Saint Augustine* (ca. 400), which had enormous impact in Italy, Switzerland, and Germany too, where Martin Luther was one such friar (from 1505 until his excommunication in 1520). The eight brief chapters of their doctrine give the essence of their spiritual father's theology: the quest for God through prayer, the peace and harmony of communal monastic existence, and service to the Church. In farce, of course, ministry, spirituality, and fraternity readily morph into forerunners of *libertinage*, *animalité*, and a *fraternité* that could put any latter-day frat house to shame. In the place of Augustinian prayer, farce chose parody. For preaching, it substituted the *sermon joyeux*; for forgiveness, grudge fests; for chastity, promiscuity; for discipline, indulgence; for obedience, disobedience; and for pastoral care, a good pastoral poke.

Carmelites or Carmes. The so-called Brothers or Friars of Mount Carmel belonged to the "Order of the Brothers of the Blessed Virgin Mary of Mount Carmel" (*Ordo Fratrum Beatissimae Virginis Mariae de Monte Carmelo*). It was founded, we think, in the twelfth century and went on to flourish in Spain and England, with French houses springing up in Montpellier and Paris as early as the mid-thirteenth century. Its members, who resided in individual cells, took vows of obedience, chastity, and poverty, living solitary lives of prayer, penance, work, silence, fasting, abstinence from meat (except in cases of severe illness), and strict separation from the world.[8] Presumed to be under the protection of the Virgin Mary and, thus, associated with the Marianic cult, their ranks included friars and cloistered nuns, plus uncloistered laypeople who had the right to marry (Egan, "Spirituality of the Carmelites," 50–56). For now, let's just say that the Carmelite nuns mentioned in *Bro Job* might dispute their adherence to those vows (below, #7, note 25).

Curses and Exclamations

Not up to speed with your Bible? Your liturgy? Your Latin? No problem. To a large extent, neither was the average spectator or, for that matter, the average clergyman. This was clearly a source of tremendous amusement for the Basochiens, who must have chafed at seeing illiterate priests in more lofty social positions than their learned, lawyerly selves. Out of the mouths of babes—and of the unruly clerics hitting on them—there issues mangled yet comprehensible Latin. The French call it "kitchen Latin" (*latin de cuisine*), for which I earlier coined the term "Flatin" (by analogy to "Franglais" or "Fritalian").[9] And their garbled language perfectly befits their garbled prayers, confessions, blessings, and the granting of absolution. As in *Holy Deadlock* (*HD*, #7, 216–22), no holy utterance is immune from "obscenic" mutation. A sacred prayer becomes a scatological drinking song; the *Kyrie, Sanctus*, or *Agnus Dei* of Mass is fodder for profane puns. And yet, blasphemous times call for translational piety. The theological stakes being what they are in this group of farces (and hereafter), I've sought a greater degree of specificity and consistency than before because of the sheer volume of curses, expletives, and even plain old exclamations. Yes, our characters are still swearing by every real and imaginary saint in the book—like Saints Muffie, Poontang, Meatstick, and Boozler—for which Jacques Merceron's encyclopedic *DSI* remains a godsend. But so repeatedly do they take the name of the Lord in vain that I've formulated the handy glossary below, which I follow almost without exception. As one would expect, *bieu* mostly stands in for *Dieu*, as does "gosh" for "God": the medieval equivalent of posting *beotch* online so that the censor doesn't catch *bitch*. But that general tendency only makes the random *Dieu* or *Jésus Christ* all the more shocking. Unfortunately, this précis isn't backward-compatible with *Farce of the Fart* or *Holy Deadlock*; but I'll stick with it in future translations. Bottom line: when it's *Dieu*, not *bieu*, you'll always see an idiom with "God"; and, by all means, add some of your own when the spirit moves you, like "Christ on a bike," "Jumpin' Jesus," and the like.

chair bieu = Jesus fucking Christ (literally, "Gosh's flesh")
corps bieu or *corbieu* = Jesus H. Christ on a cracker (the body of Christ is a wafer, after all)
croix bieu = Jesus H. Christ on the Cross
Dea or *Ouy, dea* = Jeez *or* good heavens *or* Lord, have mercy *or* for Chrissakes
Dieu le mauldie = God damn him
Dieu me/te doint joye = God give me/you great joy *or* peace *or* good day
Dieu mercy = Thank God *or* Praise the Lord
Je vous prometz! = I do solemnly swear *or* mark my words
ma foy or *par ma foy* = I swear *or* my goodness *or* goodness me *or* my, my, my *or* hello!
maulgré bieu de = what the fudge
midieulx, se m'aïst Dieu[x], or *se mesdieux* = God help me *or* Lord, have mercy
morbieu, mor bieu, or *mort bieu* = Jesus flippin' Christ
par bieu = by golly *or* omigod *or* for goodness' sake *or* for gosh sakes
par Dieu = by God *or* Good God Almighty *or* I swear to God *or* oh, for God's sake
par la chair Dieu = Christ in the flesh
par la mort sans remission = damn it to hell
par le Dieu qui me fist = in the name of the God who gave me life
par les saints Dieu = saints alive
par mon ame = bless my soul

par Nostre Dame = Hail, Mary, full of grace *or* Mother Mary *or* Mary, Mother of God
pour Dieu/de par Dieu = for God's sake *or* Good God
sang bieu = Jesus H. Christ (literally, the archaic "God's blood" or "s'blood")
ta foy, par ta foy = gimme a break
ventre bieu = Holy flippin' Christ
vertu bieu = Jesus H. Christ Almighty
vertu Dieu = Jesus Christ Almighty
vierge Marie = Mary, Mother of God

That said, not all exclamations are blasphemous or obscene. You can swear by garlic and onions, for example, as in #1, *Con-Man's Confession* (*RTLF*, v. 64), when you don't give a fig. But I've sought relative consistency for those too, even as different expressions sound different on different lips. Thus, for *helas* or *las*, I usually go with "Lord have mercy!" rather than the old-hat "alas"; but "Jeez" works better in *Confession Follies* (#5) or *Johnny Palmer* (#8); while, in *Slick Brother Willy* (#11), *helas* runs the gamut from "alas," "bummer," "pity," and "oh, well" to "it's awful." Keep an eye out as well for *certes* (alternatively "certainly" or "to be sure") and the affirmative *enda!*, for which, depending on the *personnage*, you'll read something on the order of "bless my soul," "you betcha," "damn straight," "holy shit," "amen to that," "fuckin' A," or "what do *you* think?" Ditto for *nenny*, which might be "no way," "no, no," "nuh-uh," or "not at all." Even the seemingly simple *c'est bien dit* can resonate as "well said" vs. "you can say that again!" while *or sus* encompasses "hurry up," "quick," "step on it," "pray," or "please continue." Any noteworthy linguistic idiosyncrasies are addressed under either § "Characters and Character Development" or § "Language." And I've left onomatopoeia as is for laughter, snickering, and shouting: *hon, hon, hon, hy, hy, hy, hen! Hen! Hen!*

Money, Money, Money

As I've observed before, it is nearly impossible to find accurate contemporary monetary values for the diverse medieval currencies that are bound to farce's dual propensity for exaggeration on one hand and understatement on the other (*HD*, 28, 351–52). Compared to *Holy Deadlock*, our characters obsess less about the denominations of the legal tender; but I adhere to the same currency calculator established there for *écus*, *ducats*, *francs*, *livres*, *sous*, and *deniers* (*HD*, 28–29). I refer you anew to the handy tables in Peter Spufford's *Money and Its Use in Medieval Europe* (397–410) and Marie-Thérèse Boyer-Xambeu's *Private Money and Public Currencies* (114–15). Also helpful is Tissier's calculation that a *denier* was worth one-twelfth of a *sou*; a gold *ducat*, ten to twelve *francs*; an *écu ordinaire*, about three *francs*; and both the *franc* and the *livre* (or *livre tournois*), equal to twenty *sous* (*RF*, 6: 449, 150n). In *Immaculate Deception*, my historically proportional translation of farcical finance again amounts to this: a gold *ducat* will be worth about $200 USD, an *écu*, roughly $100, and a *franc* or a *livre*, about $20. For the coins of lesser value, a *sou* will equal about $1, and a *denier*, about a dime.[10] In our first farce, we even encounter a *poujoyse*, worth only one-quarter of a *denier* (*RTLF*, 62n): literally, a currency you wouldn't give two cents about.

Prose, Verse, Music, and Choreography

Encore! Encore! Farce adores giving the public a song and dance; so, I continue to spotlight anything that smacks of a musical intertext or a call-out for performance (and I've doubtless missed some of those original cues). Melodically, linguistically, nonlinguistically, and corporeally—with song, words, laughter, and farts—refrains are heard time and time again, almost as farcical *koinoi topoi* in a medium that is wont to repeat itself (*FF*, 48–49) and which redundancies I carefully preserve. Characters not only say the same things: they *sing* or bodily express the same things. That sent me back to my musical touchstones: French music hall à la Edith Piaf or the televised variety show *Champs-Elysées* (1982–90); rock 'n' roll, country, rap, hip-hop, Broadway musicals, and so on. When venturing a rough translational equivalent for a medieval lyric, I return to my earlier system of signaling it with the copyright symbol (©), a process complex enough to warrant another "Appendix: Scholarly References to Copyrighted Materials" (as it did in *FF*, 401–6; and *HD*, 30–33). You will *not* see that sign for lyrics mentioned in passing in the Production Notes, where they cannot be construed as call-outs for performance (unless, of course, you're singing my commentary aloud for a price). You will see it, however, anywhere you might wish to incorporate a lyric or melody into a production. All such references should be considered unscripted; but, out of an abundance of caution, I attend dutifully and legalistically to all matters related to the staging of copyrighted materials.

In terms of versification, rhyming octosyllabic couplets are still the *lingua franca* and, occasionally, I retain them in rhymed or free verse, all the while renewing my caveat that I render doggerel as doggerel. Case in point: the slapstick sensibility of the *rondeau triolet* associated with such moments as a character's entrance (*FF*, 48). Elsewhere, deviations from the octosyllabic standard deserve special care, especially when the three women of *Drama Queens* (#4) introduce themselves in three separate rhyme schemes. Sometimes, I offer both prose and verse translations—even for a magnum opus like Brother Willy's *sermon joyeux* (#11). Feel free to choose one or the other or to edit as run-time allows. But, for now, it's time to run—and romp—through the faithfully faithless farce as it takes on religion.

Brief Plot Summaries

1. *The Con-Man's Confession* [*La Confession Rifflart*]

   For four actors: Matilda (Mehault/Mahault); Connor (Rifflart); the Priest (Le Prestre); and Jolly Roger (Rogier)

   Who's running this confession anyway? The Priest or the Con-Man? Browbeaten by his wife, Matilda, into making a clean breast of things at Easter, Connor comes out ahead by leaving the bemused Priest behind. If this is penance, it's quite the farce.

2. *Blue Confessions*, or, *Sweet Margot Spills* [*La Confession de Margot*]

   For two or more actors: The Parish Priest (Le Curé); Margot (Margot); and possible extras: monks, penitents, a bishop, etc.

   When Margot spills, she really spills. In making her X-rated confession to an excitable Parish Priest, she gets off easy. Him too. The Priest can but endorse her good works with brothers everywhere.

3. *Highway Robbery*, or, *A Criminal Confession* [*La Confession du Brigant au Curé*]

   For two actors: the Highwayman (Le Brigant); and the Parish Priest (Le Curé)

   On a dark, isolated path in the woods, a starving robber accosts his priestly target. Confession is the ruse by which one man makes off with all manner of booty and, the other, with his life.

4. *Confessions of a Medieval Drama Queen*, or, *The Theologina Dialogues* [*La Farce de quatre femmes*]

   For four actors: Dolly, the Fashion Plate (La Bragarde); Jezebel, the Strumpet (La Gorrière); Tartuffie, the Hypocrite (La Bigotte); and Ms. Theologina, the Lady Theologian (La Théologienne)

Does a female theologian have the right to hear the confessions of her sinful female followers? Armed with a papal bull, Theologina says she does. But a Fashion Plate, a Strumpet, and a Hypocrite may not be getting all they've bargained for.

5. *Confession Follies: Folie à Deux?* [*Le Badin, la Femme, et la Chambrière*]

   For four actors: The Fool, Fouquet (Le Badin); Gwynnie, the Wife (La Femme); Mandy, the Chambermaid (La Chambrière/Mannette); and [Bozo, the Valet, also a fool]

   Everybody's up to no good in an unhappy household dominated by violence and trickery. Revenge comes in the form of two masquerades, one of them, a confession. But who gets the better of whom? The miserable wife? The sassy chambermaid? The brutish fool? Most critics confess that they have no idea.

6. *Brother Fillerup* [*Frère Fillebert*]

   For four actors: Brother Filbert (Frère Fillebert); Colette, the Neighbor Lady (La Voysine); Donna, the Mistress (La Mestresse); Perrette, the Chambermaid (La Povre Garce, Perrete Venés-tost)

   Doctor? Lawyer? Pharmacist in chief? You name it, Brother Fillerup's got it. In one of the most sexualized prescriptions ever, he'll cure whatever ails you with fornication: especially the serving class.

7. *Bro Job*, or, *Cum Hither* [*Les Chamberières qui vont à la messe de cinq heures*]

   For four or more actors: [The Narrator]; Saucy (Saupi[c]quet); Pricker-Upper (Troussetaqueue); Florence, the Nurse (La Nourrice); Father Johan (Domine Johannes)

   First come, first served. As early as the 5:00 A.M. Mass, two chambermaids and a nurse are hot to trot for some holy water. The good father will not be delivering it from the church-sanctioned vessel.

8. *The Resurrection of Johnny Palmer* [*La Resurrection Jenin à Paulme*]

   For five actors: Johnny Glad-Hand Palmer, a Monk (Jenyn à Paulme); Joanie, Johnny's Sister (La Seur Jenyn); Joachim, a Brother (Joachin); Toni, Johnny's Cousin (Thoynon); and Brother Birdie, a Drag Queen (Caillette)

   Hold onto your hats—and your tennis rackets—because, in this fools' play of a farce, *heeere's* Johnny, resurrected from the dead! Has he really been to hell and back? Or has the drunken player, a member of the newly founded Order of Baboons, been sprung from somewhere else?

9. *The Resurrection of Johnny Slack-Jaw*, or, *The Harrowing of Heaven* [*La Résurrection de Jenin Landore*]

   For four actors: Johnny Slack-Jaw (Jenin [Landore]); Alison, his Wife (Sa Femme); the Parish Priest (Le Curé); and Adso, Novice to the Parish Priest (Le Clerc)

   In the Gospel according to the resurrected Johnny Slack-Jaw, heaven is one helluva partisan political scene that bears a striking resemblance to the Wars of Religion. What did Johnny learn in his voyage to the other world? Get ready for the ultimate April Fool and his magic.

10. *The Pardoners' Tales*, or, *Panderers' Box* [*La Farce d'un Pardonneur, d'un Triacleur et d'une Tavernière*]

    For three actors: the Pardoner (Le Pardonneur); the Snake Oil Salesman (Le Triacleur); and Frenchy, the Alewife (La Tavernière)

    With hysterical hawking cries, dueling salesmen traffic in all manner of unholy relics, indulging their every sinful appetite until it's time for gluttony. Uniting in trickery to get the better of the Alewife, the Pardoner and the Snake-Oil Salesman tender a mala fide "Panderers' Box."

11. *Slick Brother Willy* [*Frère Guillebert*]

    For four actors: Brother Wilbur (Frère Guillebert); Marvin, the Old Man (L'Homme Vieil, Marin); Blanche, his Young Wife (Sa Femme Jeune, La Femme); Agnes, the Gossip (La Commère, Agnès)

    Obsessed with the willy, Brother Willy delivers a sermon about it, an ode to it, and a bona fide Last Will and Testicle when he's caught in flagrante with old Marvin's nubile wife. Enter BFF Agnes to convince the cuckolded fool that a purloined purse is really the drawers of Saint Francis.

12. *Immaculate Deception*, or, *Nuns Behaving Badly* [*Farce nouvelle à cinq parsonnages*] (*Soeur Fessue*)

    For five actors: Mother Superior, the Abbess (L'Abeesse); Sister Crybaby, the First Nun (Soeur Esplouree/La premiere Soeur); Sister Goody Two-Shoes, the Second Nun (Soeur de Bon Coeur/La deuxieme Soeur);

Sister Frisky, the Third Nun (Soeur Safrete/La troisieme Soeur); and Sister Bunny (Seur/Soeur Fes[s]ue)

Poor knocked-up Sister Bunny! She was too much of a dummy to avoid pregnancy by engaging in the convent's usual sodomy. But she can debate Scriptures with the best of them; and it turns out that Mother Superior is in no position to judge her or anybody else.

The PLAYS

Actors' Prologue

If medieval priests sold indulgences, medieval theater troupes begged for the indulgence of their audiences. *Please don't throw us in jail for heresy: we're just actors playing our roles. We're just lawyers insisting that we not be held liable for verbal offenses not technically uttered in our own voices* (*MBA*, 39–40). To that, contemporary actors might add: *Please don't cancel us on grounds of political correctness.* Whence, in my own voice, this humble offering, a new sonnet to serve as a Prologue. Maybe don't give 'em that old-time religion. The times, they were a-changin' and, heaven only knows, ours too.

ANNOUNCEMENT FROM THE COMPANY

Oh, brother, where art thou? And sister too?
Come out! Come out and play, and bring your friends!
You think religion's meant to make you blue?
You scared it's gonna get you in the end?

Come, feast your eyes, 'cause that's them in the corner,
Them in the spotlight losing their religion.[©1]
It's not the crazy ramblings of some foreigner:
Let farce adjust your viewpoint just a smidgen.

Were medieval folks all theologians?
They didn't always know what they were gettin'.
A bunch were only going through the motions,
While climbing up a hot stairway to Heaven.

Trot out those Bibles, only time will tell—
and luck—if we are going straight to Hell.

1.
The Con-Man's Confession
La Confession Rifflart

CAST OF CHARACTERS

MATILDA (Mehault/Mahault)
CONNOR (Rifflart)
The PRIEST (Le Prestre)
JOLLY ROGER (Rogier)

PRODUCTION NOTES

The anonymous *Confession Rifflart à quatre personnaiges, c'est assavoir Mehault, Rifflart, Le Prestre, et Rogier* had appeared only in the *Recueil Trepperel* (#27) and in the Droz/Lewicka facsimile edition (*RTLF*, 55–62) until, in 2020, enter Thierry Martin with a new online *SFQS* edition (https://sottiesetfarces.wordpress.com/tag/recueil-trepperel/; accessed 6 January 2021). I know of no modern French or English translation. Of late fifteenth- or early sixteenth-century Picard provenance, it may have been associated with one of the extra-Parisian urban centers for theater such as Saint-Omer, Bethune, Arras, or Cambrai (*RTLF*, 56) or, for Martin, from the 1480 repertoire of the Conards of Rouen (*SFQS*, "Introd."). Faivre summarized the play in his *Répertoire* (112–13) but not Petit de Julleville, the *RT* having been discovered only in 1928 ("ABT," § "Editions"). Our short farce of 278 verses plays out in rhyming octosyllabic couplets (albeit with a slight error in *RTLF*, where two separate lines bear the verse number 28). Nevertheless, for ease of consultation, I've retained the edition's slightly imperfect numbering as is.

Plot

Behold! Here begins an ensemble of four—almost five—plays that penetrate the secrecy of the confessional: two from the *Recueil du British Museum* (#2, *Blue Confessions* and #5, *Confession Follies*), two from the *Recueil Cohen* (#3, *Highway Robbery* and #4, *Confessions of a Medieval Drama Queen*), and, for the first time in my series, this one from the *Recueil Trepperel.* Per the Fourth Lateran Council of 1215, obligatory confession was serious business (above, Introd.); but, to Connor—the *Con*ster, the *Con*-man—the whole thing is madness (*folie*), a big joke (*desrision*), and—what else?—a farce (technically, a *sottie* [v. 267]). He hasn't been to confession in at least four years, if at all. (It's all very Alice-in-Wonderland when he suggests simultaneously that he has "never been in his life" *and* that he has "stopped going" [v. 110].) That doesn't sit well at all with his wife, Matilda. Easter is coming, for God's sake (as it will be in *Highway Robbery* [#3] and *Johnny Slack-Jaw* [#9])! Besides, after Holy Week (comprising Holy Wednesday, Maundy Thursday, Good Friday, Holy Saturday, Palm Sunday, and the last week of Lent), Mardi Gras is coming too, when everybody lets loose. Sorbonne students will take to the streets for their quodlibetal disputations (Enders, "The Theater"), and throngs of citizens will parade about during the carnivalesque *fête des fous* (Bakhtin, *Rabelais*, chap. 1; Harris, *Sacred Folly*). It's also close to the couple's wedding anniversary . . . although one does wonder why anyone would marry at Lent. Not much of a reception.

That is the setup for a momentous question posed against the special backdrop of Easter laughter (Jacobelli, *Risus Paschalis*): What counts as confession anyway? Put a trickster in the presence of a clergyman scarcely more knowledgeable than he, and theology is in for a world of comedic trouble.

Matilda orders Connor to go confess and, shockingly, he obliges, albeit with about as much enthusiasm as Cousin in *Everyman*, who doesn't want to go on pilgrimage because of "the cramp in my toe" (ed. Ward, 45). After seeking counsel from his good buddy, Roger, Connor hatches a plan: use Roger's trick of going to confession without ever confessing (vv. 74–100). Trickery is no stretch, after all, for a *Conard* of a con-man skilled at feigned ignorance and role-playing. In response to the Priest's review of the seven deadly sins (*sept pechez mortelz*; vv. 162–75), the pseudopenitent runs through a whole list of them, including anger. But, if he is insincere, then Tissier's allusion to a "real confession" is puzzling (*RF*, 6: 379–80; above, Introd., "True-*ish*"): all the more so in that the most crucial matter is left unresolved. With something resembling a proper liturgical performative in the Austinian sense (*HDTW*, 14–24), the Priest implies that Connor has been absolved. "I hereby absolve you," he proclaims, "I grant you absolution and remission for all your sins. I just absolved you . . ." (*Je t'en absoubz vrayement, / Absoluction et remission. / Tu es absoubz presentement* . . . [vv. 188–90]). Indeed, Connor's own recital of the words of absolution is more on point (vv. 247–50; below, note 15). But what about remorse and penance?

I guess the Priest is no lawyer because it is only after pronouncing absolution that he thinks to place a condition on it: "But, sweet friend, you must now perform penance" (*Mais mon doulx amy debonnaire, / Il te fault penitence faire* [vv. 191–92]). In this farcical riff on *how to do absolution with words*, Connor seems most unlikely to obey the Priest's directive that he undertake a pilgrimage to Boulogne near Paris, a popular penitential journey at the time (*RTLF*, 56). So, was Faivre right about the play being pale and anodyne (*Répertoire*, 112–13)? I think not. Suspended absolution was hardly pabulum: not even in a charming, PG-rated romp.

Characters and Character Development

In the first sixty lines, we hear Connor's name four times, plus six "Matildas." It's as if the actors were afraid that an unruly crowd would miss the protagonists' names. Either that or Connor and Tilly were such beloved character types that the mere mention of those names would set up expectations for a whole shtick. For Rifflart, it's all in his name, which we've seen before in *For the Birds* (*HD*, #4). With occasional connotations of gluttony, card-playing, and violence, the verb *riffler* or *rifler* is another form of *rafler*, signifying "to rifle through," "to swipe," "to steal," "to nick," or "to clean up," as in "do well financially" (*RTC*, 189n). Recall, too, that there is often a Riflart in the Passion plays scourging Christ as fun and games (*MTOC*, 170–85; *RTC*, 189n). But, philologically disposed though this Connor might be to make out like a bandit, he is neither violent nor even sarcastic toward his "sweetheart," his "darling," his little chickadee (*bel oyselon*). We know little else about him other than that the working stiff—a roofer, posits Martin (*SFQS*, note 73)—could use a break from his manual labor on the town's two bell towers (vv. 140–45). This brings his story into intertextual dialogue with *Extreme Husband Makeover* (*RBM*, #6; *HD*, #11), where a Bell-Maker incarnated what it meant to "melt the bell" (*il est temps de fondre la cloche*), to wit: to resolve an ongoing, persistent, festering affair (*HD*, 344–45, 349–51). Not going to confession—or not confessing while you're there—would certainly qualify as a festering affair. As we shall see, if anyone winds up "as surprised as a Bell-Maker" (*être étonné* [*penaud*] *comme un fondeur de cloches*), it's the hapless Priest.

Our female lead, "Matilda"—*Mahault* is a form of Margaret—is most unhappy with her irreligious slacker of a husband whom she nonetheless honors with the polite *vous*. Her unhappiness even earns her the atypical privilege of opening the farcical proceedings as the female expositor—a copyist's error, says Martin, who believes that it should be the Priest (*SFQS*, note 2). He also believes that she is hustling hubby out the door because she has an assignation with Roger (*SFQS*, notes 16 and 54).

Next up is Jolly Roger, whose limited role is nonetheless a featured one. In the course of only two speeches (about 36 lines altogether), it is he who reveals the ruse of confession *sans* confession. But, because his first big speech is where the original text is corrupt (vv. 74–100), some imagination is required to fill in the blanks. Have some fun with that, speaking of which:

The unnamed Priest isn't having any—fun, that is—which is most unusual for farce. There is some implication that he is the selfsame deaf cleric whom Roger has just cited as uncommonly useful, and at whom farce could easily yell and scream. Either way, penitential theologians were concerned about the fate of the sacrament if a priest were deaf (Tentler, *Sin and Confession*, 126). This one seems just plain dumb. He might well be able to refer to good works (*oeuvres de misericorde*), the Ten Commandments, the articles of faith (*articles de la foy*), "ensconcement" in heresy (*dont tu es empesché* [v. 166]), and the shunning of the excommunicated (*excommunié*). But he is ill-equipped to see that farce will turn the tables on him and on the sacrament when he flies sinfully off the handle, angered at having had truck with a fool.

Language

In this and the next four farces, I tend to translate the honorific designations for the Priest—*Sire* or *Monsieur*—as the more familiar "Father." As for addressing the penitent, I normally go with the logical "my son" (or, later, "my daughter"). Here, however, I take care to retain the Father's multiple (and multiply overdetermined) terms of endearment for the "sweet," "good," "dear," and even "great-looking" Connor, with whom he uses *tu*: *bel amy*, *beaux* or *beaulz amy*, *mon amy*, *mon bel amy*, *beau doulx amy*, *doulx amy debonnaire*, *mon amy doulx*, *compains*, *beau filz*. Not surprisingly, we encounter a vocabulary of religious awe and astonishment (*merveille* or *merveilleux* at vv. 141, 207, and 232) as well as of sin (*meffais* or *pechez* at vv. 138, and 184). But most deserving of our attention is the authenticity of liturgical-*ish* language for getting things off one's conscience (v. 19), one's chest, or, as Middle French has it, one's belly or tummy (*la pance*, v. 15). Connor also invokes *papelartz* (v. 56), an ancestor of sorts to Molière's Tartuffe: the ultimate hypocrite engaged in false piety, a *faux dévot* who sets the stage not only for "Tartuffie" of our #4 but for the large-scale humanistic obsession with inner reality vs. outward appearances. It's all part and parcel of tipping a farcical hat to *mocquerie* (vv. 231–32) and to *nous conars* (vv. 55 and 85), possibly a shout-out to the local Rouennais acting troupe.[1] Droz and Lewicka doubt that our play was composed in Rouen owing to its telltale Picard dialect (*RTLF*, 56); but the metacommentary works either way for the send-up of idiotic priests, the true *conards. Ils déconnent, quoi.*

Sets and Staging

A path joins two sets: the home of Connor and Matilda, and the interior of a rudimentary church. Given the reference to the pilgrimage to Boulogne (v. 243), we are probably in the Paris area but not necessarily: the assigned penance could be comic overreach or underreach. Obviously, the focal point is the confessional, which should be situated center stage. In all likelihood, it's the now familiar booth-like structure, as evidenced by the editors' advice that, from verse 109 onward, the action takes place "in front of the confessional" (*RTLF*, 62n). Alternatively, one could confess Connor in a huge empty church. The Priest does comment that there's nobody else around (v. 113), one of farce's favorite winks to its spectators. It's almost as good as the Priest wondering what kind of Fools' play brought him there today: *je ne scay / Quelle* sottie *m'y mena* (vv. 266–67).

Costumes and Props

In light of the Priest's various penance propositions, he might have on hand a hair shirt and a sackcloth, the latter technically known as a "cilice" (< Latin *cilicium*). According to the *Catholic Encyclopedia*, this was "a garment of rough cloth made from goats' hair and worn in the form of a shirt or as a girdle around the loins, by way of mortification and penance" (http://www.newadvent.org/cathen/07113b.htm; accessed 25 July 2018). The roughhewn sackcloth could be made even more prickly and uncomfortable, moreover, by adding twigs and the like. To bring out the comedy, it is helpful if Connor is clad in a pair of work overalls on top of his rustic shirt and underwear (the *chemise* and *cotte* at v. 226).

Scholarly References to Copyrighted Materials (in order of appearance and indicated by © within the text)

"Dang Me." By Roger Miller. BMI Work #275944.
"Now I Lay Me Down to Sleep." ["All Night, All Day, Angels Watching Over Me."] By Otis Leon McCoy. (19th c.)
"All My Trials." By Joan Baez. ASCAP Work ID: 310153330.
"Skip to My Lou." Traditional.
"Get Happy." By Harold Arlen and Ted Koehler. ASCAP Work ID: 360219907.

[Scene 1]

MATILDA

[*To the audience*] In the name of the Lord who suffered his grievous Passion for our Redemption, may He bless you and keep you from evil. Ladies and gentlemen! Our very own parish priest has told you that the Holy Days are at hand. Easter is coming; so, it's time to go unburden yourselves with a full and true confession. It's cathartic—I'm just sayin'—and I only bring it up because of one of our own, goes by the name of Connor: he never felt like going. Thinks the whole thing is one big joke.[2]

Enter Connor

CONNOR

Hey, Tilly! with the great big heart in that tiny little package! Over here! Why so upset, my little dove, *ma gentille alouette*? How come you're not singing, Matilda? Somebody got you down? What happened to those good spirits of yours?

MATILDA

Connor, darling, sweetheart: I'd never want to displease you, but I will tell you what I've got on my conscience.

CONNOR

Matilda, just tell me what's on your mind. I'd never get angry. Again.

MATILDA

Then, my dear Connor, I'll tell you. It'll be four years at Lent since our wedding day; and the reason I'm so distressed is that I just found out you haven't been to confession this whole time. Sweetie, you've got to go. What are you waiting for? It's usually not too crowded at this hour, and there's not a moment to lose. Please.[3]

CONNOR

Good God, Matilda, sweetheart, that displeases the hell out of me! You know the kind of life I live. What are you trying to do? Get me killed? Arrested? Hanged by the neck till I'm dead?

MATILDA

Connor, you misunderstand completely. We can't have word getting out that . . . Now hear this! If you don't go, I swear: no Easter dessert for you! [Connor, Connor], no pudding, no pie.

CONNOR

Okay, fine, Matilda, let's get it over with. Since you insist, I'll go; but you'll have to tell me what to do because, in all my born days, that's the craziest thing I've ever heard! Since when does a man have to go to confession? It's *religulous*!

MATILDA

You big dumb ox! You don't have the sense that God gave a flea. I'll have you know there's not a man or a woman alive who doesn't have to fast at Lent and go to confession. The really devout folks go maybe three or four times.[4]

[*Matilda shows him to the door.*]

CONNOR

Easy, Matilda, don't let it ruffle your feathers!

[*To the audience too*][5] Do you seriously believe that jokers like us got any business at Church? Or going to confession? Are you kidding? Shove it, clowns! We're actors, not Bible thumpers!
Oh, the hell with it! One of these days, I really oughta check out the fine print in that marriage contract of ours. It'll be depressing as all get-out if it turns out I've gotta go to confession.

[*Matilda succeeds in pushing Connor out the door, but not before he snags a bottle of wine. Lights down on their home, where Matilda remains.*]

[Scene 2]

[*On the way to church*]

[CONNOR]

I guess that's that. Off to confession I go. Bummer. [I mean: did you ever hear anything so ridiculous?] A jolly good fellow like me who doesn't give a fig? Now, a figgy pudding, that's another story. [People, people, please!] I need some advice. There must be somebody out there who can help me out. [What do you know! If it isn't Jolly Roger!]

[Scene 3]

[*Enter Roger*]

CONNOR

Hey, Roger! I'm off to confession. Matilda's making me go; so, why not just take a rope and hang me![©] I mean, you wanna make a deathbed confession, fine. Knock yourself out. But why the hell would a man ever make a confession as long as he can still eat and drink? Then again, my wife's a pretty smart cookie.

ROGER

Dude. Con-Man. [Con. The Con-ster.] It's pretty standard. If you want, I can show you exactly how I go about it. Check it out:

When *I've* got to go to confession, I wait till there's a whole mob scene, right? Sometimes, the priest can't even get to me and, then, I just say I'll come back some other time. Gotta keep up appearances and all. It's what we do. And that, my friend, is how you go four years without gettin' confessed![6] Even when I do get in, I've got a whole system: step right up and start mumbling, that's the ticket. No need to play dumb or play the fool because, get this: my priest is deaf. I just whisper maybe one out of every three words and, when I get to the end, he asks "Is that it?" And, then, I go "Yes"; and, then, he absolves the hell outta me![7] Who cares how it works? Seriously, dude: he's all over me. Come hell or high water, inquiring minds, they wanna know. Whatever it is, he's gotta try and drag it out of me. "Get it all off my chest" and stuff: it's like my whole damn life depends on what I been eating. But, in the name of Saint Mary, hallowed be her name, I swear: he ain't outsmarted me yet! Why, only just the other day, he wouldn't let up: goin' on and on about "Is there anything else? Steal anything?", like I was tryin' to pull a Barabbas or something and get away clean. So, I did! Just got the hell outta there.[8]

CONNOR

Wow. Dude. I get the picture. I can't wait to give it a try, I swear. I'll see what he's got to say for himself.

[*Connor rehearses gesturally for Roger as the two men head to church.*]

[Scene 4]

[*Outside the church, there is a long line of parishioners, all moving so quickly through their confessions that Roger's strategy won't work. Connor continues to rehearse, now with a loud groan that he hopes the Priest will overhear.*]

CONNOR

All night, all day,© is there no end to this pain and suffering? Alas! My wretched heart cries out in the wilderness! Is there no shelter from the storm of this life? Oh where, oh where is a man to turn? All my trials, Lord, soon be over.©

[*Connor enters the church while Roger waits outside.*]

[Scene 5]

CONNOR

[Alas! be still, my wretched heart!
Is there no place to ease this pain?
Lest all my trials be in vain?
No peace? Is there no final rest?
He really puts me to the test.][9]

Hey, Father! God give you great joy, sir! The wife sent me in to confess 'cause I kinda quit goin'.

THE PRIEST

Closer, my son—and louder. Speak up, that I might hear you. There's nobody else around.

CONNOR

Hey, Father, I'm right here! [*Sotto voce*] 'Bout as close as I'm gonna get. [*He inspects the paltry ecclesiastical accommodations.*] But *here*? I don't play no empty house. You'd think the Church would have better digs.

THE PRIEST

A place for everything, and everything in its place. Take all the time you need, my son, there's no hurry. But, for God's sake, speak up!

CONNOR

Beggin' your pardon, Father, but—Mother Mary!—after you. I'm not worthy! I'd never presume to speak first. Definitely not my place. So, please, Father, after you. Go ahead. You first. Spill.

THE PRIEST

Lord have mercy, sweet friend, I can't possibly speak before you do, my son, because I don't know what you wish to confess. Pray, get on with it, friend. Summarize.[10]

CONNOR

But Father, folks are supposed to show you the proper respect on accounta your bein' a priest and all. Besides, I'm no dumb ox. I'd never be

so crazy presumptuous. [Wasn't brought up in a barn, you know!] So, please: don't get mad. If you want, I can just leave because there's no way I'm speaking before you.
[*With a wink to the audience*] I've never done anything so crazy in my life!

THE PRIEST

If that's how it's going to be, very well, I'll tell you this much: you're supposed to speak first and give a full account of all your sins that you can remember.

CONNOR

[*Miming various emotions and activities*] Father, I get, you know, [mad.] A lot. Like when I work a week or so on those two bell towers over there—wicked high—and all I get is two bucks for the whole day. [And I barely even fall down!]
So, I repent—okay?—like crazy. In the name of Saint Renley, *mea culpa*! My bad! Whatever. It's all my fault. I'm sorry . . . that I didn't get at least two and a half![11]

THE PRIEST

That's not quite the accounting I had in mind. Now, please: [*He tries to coax the proper words from Connor.*] ["God give you great joy and, bless me, Father, for you have sinned . . ." *C'est ma faute, c'est ma très grande faute . . .*]

CONNOR

[Nuh-uh.] It's not my *faute* if I slipped up when all's I got is these old clodhoppers. God give *me* great joy already and bless my soles! Folks is just a bunch o' heels. What else is a guy in need supposed to wear to work when—?

THE PRIEST

Seriously?
God help me, I do believe you're out of your mind. Or crazy. Or drunk. Now, I pray you: unburden yourself already because you're giving me a splitting headache!

CONNOR

[Nuh-uh.] And they can hang me in the public square—on a holiday, no less!—if I ever done anybody wrong! [Call the cops, if you want:] it's the truth, the whole truth, and nothing but the truth. I'll even slip the judge a few. You know how he is: not exactly the forgiving kind.[12]

THE PRIEST

I feel sorry for you, my son, I really do. Now, come a little bit closer and, I pray you: first, you'll confess to the seven deadly sins that weigh so heavily upon your conscience. Next, I'll take into account any good works you might happen to have performed, and then, it's on to the Ten Commandments—I'm fairly confident you've violated a few of those. Then, it's on to the articles of faith and to whether you've had contact with anyone who has been excommunicated and such. You owe it to yourself to confess to all that.

CONNOR

Sweet Jesus, Father, Lord of Lords! Sure thing. I'm totally down with everything you just said and—please—if you know of anything else, just come right out and say so. It's not like anybody's gonna hear. It'll be our little secret. On the QT. Very, very hush-hush. Go on, go for it! I'll confess to the whole kit and caboodle, whatever you come up with.

THE PRIEST

My son, for all your sins that you have now confessed, do you seek absolution?

CONNOR

You betcha, Father, sure thing.

[*The Priest gestures a blessing, but Connor makes no move of contrition.*]

THE PRIEST

Then, I hereby absolve you. I grant you absolution and remission for all your sins.

[*Connor rises and makes a move to leave.*] I just absolved you, my good, sweet son, but you must now perform penance.

CONNOR

Seriously, Father? What penance? Haven't I had enough trouble already?

THE PRIEST

My son, you must fast.

CONNOR

No problem till lunchtime but, if I gotta fast the whole day, what am I supposed to eat?

THE PRIEST

Then you must don a cilice. [*Connor looks confused.*] A sackcloth.

CONNOR

Got nothin' up my sleeve, but that sounds like a bunch o' *ciliceness* to me.[13]

THE PRIEST

Then, what do you wish to do, sweet son? Would you perhaps prefer to leave things at putting on a hair shirt? You would simply slip it on over your chest. [And cover up that gut.]

CONNOR

Jeez, no way! What's wrong with this *here* shirt? Plus, that thing's gotta hurt. It'd be all prickly against my skin and stuff—scratch me all over—[and that ain't no rib tickler]! Holy moly and saints alive, I'm astonished! Where'd you ever come up with a thing like that? What did my shirt ever do to you?[14]

THE PRIEST

Then, I'm at a loss. In the name of Saint Paul, the Apostle, I don't know how I can possibly be of service. Just say three "Our Fathers" and get lost!

CONNOR

They can put a noose around my neck if you want, but I only know just the one ["Our Father"].

THE PRIEST

Oh, for God's sake, that's the one. Say *that* one: *one, two, three* times! [And enough with the comedy routine.] I do believe you're just playing the fool here. Now: if you'd be so kind as to . . . get [the flock] outta here!

CONNOR

Lord have mercy, Father, what the flock? [You're gonna turn a deaf ear?] This is no act! I'd be mortified—grief-stricken, utterly devastated—if I were to lose count on you.

THE PRIEST

Fine. Then don't keep track. I'll simply direct that, this evening, before you lay you down to sleep,[©] you say the one "Our Father" over and over again, continuously without stopping, while you're taking off your shirt and undergarments. Seems to me you ought to be able to manage *that*.

CONNOR

But, every night at bedtime, it all comes off in one piece, you know? Or I just sleep in my overalls. Saves time the next morning when I gotta get up. [You think I wanna be riflin' through all my stuff?]

THE PRIEST

Astonishing. Never seen anything like it.
What do you think this is? A farce? In the name of the blessed Virgin Mary, I'm done talking to you today.

CONNOR

Whatever you say, Father, I swear! [*Whispering*] You won't *hear* another word outta me! Not one peep. Command away! Anything you want. Thy will be done pronto.

THE PRIEST

Then, without further ado—there's no need to make a whole production, you know—for the sins that you've committed, you must go on pilgrimage to Boulogne. [*Connor looks confused.*] [It's just outside of Paris, for God's sake!] Within the next forty-eight hours at the very latest, and don't you be thinking this is some line.

CONNOR
You got it, Father.

[*Connor leaves the Priest and rejoins Roger outside the church.*]

[Scene 6]

[CONNOR]
[*To both Roger and the audience*] And there you have it! From the heavy burden of all those sins o' mine, I'm absolved! Good deal! Got me a full pardon and all that jazz off that priest, which calls for a little musical number, don'tcha think? [How's about a little Thelonious Monk? No?] Okey-dokey, then. Mother Mary-Lou, Lou, skip to my Lou, my darlin':© this one's for you! Forget your troubles, come on, get happy!©[15]

[*Connor goes back inside the church.*]

[Scene 7]

CONNOR *returns to the Priest*
Hey, Father! I'm *baaaack*! It just occurred to me that I forgot to ask you to spot me a couple o' bucks. Truth is, I'm broke. Don't have two cents to rub together.[16]

THE PRIEST
And you seriously believe I'm gonna be forkin' it over? Good God Almighty, not one red cent!

CONNOR
And you seriously believe I'll be goin' if you're not pickin' up the tab? I got expenses, you know.

THE PRIEST

Have mercy on me, oh God, I turn to you in sorrow and repentance for . . . having heard your confession here today.

[*Exit Connor to rejoin Roger.*]

[Scene 8]

CONNOR

What the—? Jesus H. Christ! Some Fools' play, right? But the wife sent me, [remember?] And there's no man ever listens to his wife who don't wind up in the [w]hole . . . shame and blame game!

ROGER

Jeez, neighbor! You're the one who believed your wife! If you woulda done like me, I do believe you wouldn't have gotten so mad. But, hey, go on home to your wife!

[*To the audience*] And, as for all you gentlemen out there: you too! Don't take our little play the wrong way and, for God's sake, don't sue us!

Now, let us pray . . . that Our Father who art in Heaven watch over you, me, and the whole lot of us. And get better confessions than He got off Con-man over there.

[What do you say, folks? One more time?]
[The wife's at home. It's time to go!
Don't take offense, it's just a show,
Milords; so, there's no need to sue.
To one and all we say God bless:
No con-jobs when you go confess!][17]

The END

2.

Blue Confessions, or, *Sweet Margot Spills*

La Confession de Margot

CAST OF CHARACTERS

The PARISH PRIEST (Le Curé)
MARGOT (Margot)
[At least five Mendicant Friars: two Dominicans (Jacobins), a Franciscan (Cordelier), an Augustinian, and a Carmelite]
[A number of extra penitents of any sex or gender]
[A Bishop]

PRODUCTION NOTES

La Confession Margot à deux personnaiges, c'est assavoir Le Curé et Margot appears as #21 in the *RBM*, the edition that, for the most part, I follow in *ATF*, 1: 372–79 (again, paginated but without verse numbers; above, "ABT," § "Editions"). There is also a close copy at the Biblioteca Capitular Colombina in Seville, Spain. In 167 rhyming octosyllabic couplets, the anonymous *Blue Confessions* has been edited by Tissier as #37 of *RF*, 6: 367–422; and by Martin in *SFQS* (https://sottiesetfarces.wordpress.com/category/confession-margot/); plus, Tissier translated it into modern French (*FFMA*, 2: 289–96). It was summarized by Faivre in *Répertoire* (111) but not by Petit de Julleville, who excluded it as a *fabliau dialogué* that was "not really dramatic" (*RTC*, 5).

Most interesting of all: there is an earlier version that Tissier reproduces side by side in *RF* and which attests to the play's popularity. At 141 verses, it was published undated in Lyon by the celebrated Barnabé Chaussard and, while it is highly similar to its *RBM* successor, the differences are fascinating (*RF*, 6: 370–76). For one thing, it has a distinctly Parisian vibe; for another, it is, paradoxically, both more marked for performance *and* more graphic (below, § "Sets and Staging"). Whence, my composite edition for which new diacriticals are required. Both versions of *Blue* are housed in the British Museum; so, to avoid confusion with our usual *RBM* plays edited by Montaiglon in *ATF*, I've gone with "*RBM*-a" for the earlier version (a variation on Tissier's "Bma"). My interpolations from *RBM*-a are indicated by angle brackets and, inside and outside those brackets, you will find the usual square brackets, curly brackets, and italics for my own interpolations of text or stage directions ("ABT," § "Critical Apparatus").

Plot

Imagine, if you will, the scene in *A League of Their Own* where a priest is hearing the confession of Madonna's "All-the-Way Mae." He keeps dropping his Bible and, when Mae is finally done, he emerges red-faced to ascertain the identity of the penitent. Now, make way for the promiscuous Margot.

The plot is straightforward enough: her sex-laden confession to an aroused *curé* leads to absolution and penance—to the extent, that is, that lending a literal hand to brothers in need is a tough assignment. It is well worth recalling, moreover, that many of the theological terms for sin, faults, forgiveness, redemption, and penance (*meschief, penitence, dommaige, quitte*) have legal ramifications of acquittal and exoneration (as befits a bunch of Basochiens). Margot requests absolution—*J'en requier absolution* (1: 372; later, 377)—and, in *RBM*-a, the Priest absolves her "truly" and "for all to see" (*pour voir*) with the proper, performative *je vous absoulbz* (*RF*, 6: 410, vv. 89–94). But, in the *ATF* version, he jumps straight to the *in secula seculorum* [*sic*], clinched by her *amen* (1: 379). Farce hardly says *amen* to that.

For Margot, you see, absolution can't come soon enough because, as my mother used to say, it's like Grand Central Station in there. She has been a very busy girl with brothers, monks, and hermits galore (*freres, moynes, ermites*). Indeed, representatives of the four great medieval mendicant orders are on hand: a steady stream of Dominicans (*Jacobins*), Franciscans (*Cordeliers*), Carmelites or Benedictines (*Carmes*), and Augustinians. Thanks to what I believe to be an apt pun, there's even a Capuchin friar (another order associated with the Franciscans; below, note 14). But how, oh how, to tell them apart? Was sweet Robin a *Jacobin, Cordelier, Augustin ou Carme* (1: 372–73)? Margot's not too sure and—guess what? From time to time, neither are we, especially when *RBM*-a drops the Augustinian to double down on the Dominican: "Jacobin, / *Frere mineur,* prescheur *ou Carme*" (*RF*, 6:

394, vv. 17–18; my emphasis). The thing is: Jacobins *are* Brothers Preachers (*frères Prescheurs*). Or maybe the missing Augustinian is covered by another reference to the Brothers Minor, or maybe a later hermit in the woods is an Augustinian. Or maybe it's nothing but issues of versification. In any event, silent though Tissier, Faivre, and Martin are on the subject of why a given brother might incline toward a given sex act, that's clearly part of the theological punch packed by *Blue*. Margot has left all those mendicants begging for mercy.

Blue Confessions is a stunningly self-reflexive play that moseys on into the great debate from the *Roman de la Rose* about the nature of euphemism (above, "Introd.," § "Euphemism and 'Comedification'"). Around midway through our play's journey through masturbation, coitus, and ejaculate, it's Jupiter's castration of Saturn all over again—*les coilles cum se fussent andoilles* (*Rose*, 5537–38)–when Margot comes upon a hermit who is fiddling about with his "sausage." No Lady Reason she, Margot opts for sausages and bells (*andoilles* and *cloches*) as the petulant Priest demands cock and balls (*une coille, des coilles*), uttering the play's single most important line (not present in *RBM*-a): *Il ne fault point parler par glose* (1: 375). No speaking with veiled references, no talking in riddles, and, as I've translated it with a homonymic pun: in this "cock 'n balls" story, "no euphemisms allowed/aloud." *Au contraire* in the *ATF* edition, where Montaiglon or Viollet-le-Duc elided the original *couille* as "*c. . . . . .*" (*RBM*, iii; *ATF*, 1: 375). Margot's literal-minded confessor would doubtless have called that some kind of editorial balls.

Then again, sometimes a sausage is just a sausage, all the more so when you put it in your mouth and eat it. Much as the *Rose* spawned a fifteenth-century epistolary donnybrook between Christine de Pisan, Jean Gerson, and Pierre Col, so now do we find dueling versions of *Blue* waging their own debate about *le mot ou la chose* (Koopmans and Verhuyck, "Les Mots ou la Chose"). Which word should denote which thing, it asks, and which gesture, *which thingy*? As we shall see, our play transmutes a theological and linguistic issue of representation into a bona fide dramaturgical crisis. And it's a damn good thing the play is so funny because, failing that, it would pass for either a sinister how-to manual for perverted priests or a piece of pornography.

Characters and Character Development

Consistent with the play's central question, we do well to ask of the titular female lead: "What's in a name?" A "Margot" is an easy woman who is sweet, docile, "easy to handle," and "blessed," as in *Margot la Bénigne*. A Betty? Plus, any medievalist thinks immediately of "Fat Margot" (*la grosse Margot*) of François Villon's *Testament* (*Poems*, 127–29), such that the actress—or actor in drag—could be hyperbolically well-endowed. (A *marguet* is also a dick.) But, since "Margot" is also a diminutive for "Marguerite," it seems more than coincidental that there was a storied Marguerite whose life and literary tastes ran to the farcical: one Marguerite de Navarre (1492–1549), the sister of Francis I, the author of the *Heptameron*, and France's answer to Boccaccio. Who, then, is our Margot? I prefer to leave the more salient details to her; but she is wont to invoke adjectives of distress, anxiety, horror, shock, and awe (*espoventee, troublee, esperdue, esbahy*). Nor do I regard her as Tissier's naive ingenue to whom perversity is unknown (*RF*, 6: 386). Otherwise, what would she be confessing *to*? Think of her instead as a consummate actress with a permanent, Monty-Pythonesque "wink, wink, nudge, nudge" to the audience. In the *ATF* version, she is *trying* to sound as innocent as possible; in *RBM*-a, she is trying *not to*. It's almost as if the later Margot is offering up sausages, bells, thingies, and thighs to correct her vulgar predecessor's predilection for the virile member (*membre*). But, in the end, *both* Margots use euphemisms for "penis" or "vagina." (Not so, by the way, for the Priest, who's all about dicks, pricks, cocks, and balls [*des couilles*].) I've therefore incorporated the tonal and lexical idiosyncrasies into a single, complex Margot, and if you're worried about the verisimilitude of a simultaneously proper and improper character, don't be. Farce gives us such bipolarity all the time, often to highlight women's subtle intelligence with a marked change of stylistic register (e.g., *FF*, 103, 117, 395; *HD*, 116, etc.). Or have a look at comedian Wendy Liebman's signature clarifying afterthoughts ("When I quit my job . . . and got fired").[1] That's how I hear the back-and-forth between the two *Margots*: in reverse chronological order here with the *RBM*-a obscenity correcting and clarifying the more euphemistic *RBM* (my base text). To my ear, this is no binary choice between a dumb broad putting an *andouille* between her legs and a crafty nymphomaniac comfortable with her sexuality. Margot is an actress heaven-bent on getting a literal and metaphorical rise out of the Priest.

The unnamed Parish Priest (*Le Curé*) is operating in his capacity as a Father Confessor; and I strongly suspect that *le bon père* (1: 372) is a Dominican for the following reasons: (1) he appears educated enough to be a *Rose* reader, thereby reinforcing the overall cognoscente vibe; (2) poverty-observing Dominicans were authorized to hear confessions and would praise charitable good works (1: 378); (3) the *RBM* woodcut (Figure 1) pictures a dog, who could be the *domini canis* or "hound of the lord" (above, "ABT, § "Oh, Brother"); and (4) he twice designates the Dominicans as especially deserving of Margot's ministrations: "*les frères de nostre ordre / Comme les frères de la Corde, /* Prescheurs, *Carmes et* Jacobins" (1: 378, my emphasis; above, § "Plot"). It's conceivable that he's another farcical Franciscan *frère de la Corde*; but, if Margot likes it doggy-style, there is a logic to reading him as a Dominican, particularly in the Parisian setting of *RBM*-a. Remember that the Dominicans owed their "Jacobin" nickname to their habitat on the rue Saint-Jacques (*Jacques* > *Jacobins*) right near the Sorbonne—and that that habitat was one of the stops on the pilgrimage route of Saint Jacques de

Figure 1. Frontispiece, *La Confession Margot. RBM*, #21.

Compostelle (*RF*, 6: 395n; above, "ABT," § "Oh, Brother"). No wonder Margot has access to so many pilgrims hanging around. And there's something else about the good father. However steadfastly he repudiates euphemism in favor of the proper anatomical term, he's slower on the uptake for the female anatomy. Yes, it's *coille* on his lips for both "penis" and "balls." But, when it comes to "sticking it in," he goes with *la mistes vous en vostre ventre*? (*ATF*, 1: 376). *Ventre*, the Middle French "tummy" and the Latinate "uterus," is both a euphemism and *not one*. The perfect gestational metaphor for the communion being advocated when sweet Margot spills.

But wait, there's more! There is a virtual cast of characters just begging to be staged: all those mendicants. I've thus made room for at least five extras: two Dominicans, one Franciscan, one Augustinian hermit, one Carmelite, and a Bishop. And, since it's quite the procession of wayward brothers, I've done so in a way wholly consonant with medieval musical, theological, and theatrical practice: a processional (below, § "Sets and Staging").[2] The costumed presence of these flesh-and-blood characters—okay, mostly flesh—will also enhance the satire of the four orders.

Finally, casting is huge and anything but transparent, as I learned when workshopping what amounted to four different plays (two men, two women, cross-cast, and "straight"). As you read, try to envision the homosocial, cisgender, latent, blatant, or unclassifiable gender trouble wrought by actors who might be, for instance, men, women, drag queens, trans, or gender nonbinary.

Language

As in *Con-Man* (#1), the Priest is mostly *sire*, which I tend to translate as "Father." The occasional *messire* or *monsignor* pops up too—"monsignor," "milord," or "sir," depending on the level of formality. And, for the Priest, Margot is *m'amye*: usually "my daughter" but, sometimes, "my dear" or even "baby." In *RBM*-a, he also favors *Dame* or *Donne* (sometimes a woman of ill repute [*RF*, 6: 415n]) to the *fille* of *ATF*. I won't flag these each time but, for simplicity's sake, if you see a *Madame*, it's from *RBM*-a.

Beyond that, two specific linguistic items deserve our attention: the verb *fatrouiller* and the use of the past tense, both related to daunting dramaturgical challenges. At the play's climax, Margot describes her activities with a masturbating hermit as *fatrouiller* (*ATF*, 1: 377; *RBM*, fol. iv), a Rabelaisian synonym for coitus that connoted "fucking with no chance of getting the clap" (*RF*, 6: 411n; *SFQS*, note 34). But we're just a tongue twister away—or, in Tissier, a *typo* away (*RF*, 6: 410)—from *fratrouiller*, which would make for some fabulous wordplay for a cheating trickster *brother* (*frater*) who is messing around, mistreating, whacking (off), and hitting below the [Franciscan] belt (*rouiller*, *roeillier*, *faire rouler*). No messing around when roundly mocking the *frātrēs* (*rouillés*) who are "played" (*roulés*) by Margot. Speaking of which:

Props to Tissier for having zeroed in on a subtle point of grammar that may well tell the whole story. Right after Margot cites chapter and verse of her encounter with a sausage-wielding hermit, the Priest's emission contains a Freudian slip (either *his* or the author's): *Vous avez grand devotion / D'eschauffer celle povre beste* (*ATF*, 1: 377). We expect him to mean: "You were most charitable to have warmed up that poor creature." But, instead of using the imperfect verb tense—*vous* aviez *grand devotion*—the Priest praises her in the present: "How charitable you *are* to be [in the act of] warming up that poor creature [right now as we speak.]" Impossible to tell whether it's an error; but Tissier hints that Margot has taken another thingy in hand—*her own*: "Doesn't the Priest think that she is in the process of warming up another 'animal'" (*RF*, 6: 413n). For myself, I find it equally plausible that he is thanking her for warming up *his* animal, his *beste*, "creature" or "manhood." So does Faivre, opining ever so elegantly that Margot might be masturbating the Priest as she reenacts the same "manipulations with which she had gratified the hermit's 'sausage'" (*Répertoire*, 111). Nor is that the only time such linguistic ambiguity obtains. When promising absolution in *RBM*-a, the Priest employs an infinitive to similar effect. Margot will have earned her pardon, not for *having* lodged a pilgrim but for *lodging him* (*de heberger le pelerin*) (*RF*, 6: 404, vv. 75–79). What can I say? The main thrust is that it all depends on what the meaning of *is* is.

Sets and Staging

Per *RBM*-a, we are explicitly in a Paris that is teeming with such local landmarks as the church at Saint Germain-des-Prés and the eight statues of its foyer-like entryway (*la porche*), which were destroyed in 1793 (*RF*, 6: 370–711, 421n). Margot's confession could be heard in the open air, of course, but I've set it center stage in a confessional booth in a church that is as elaborate or as pared down as one wishes. But, before anything happens, it is crucial to bring legibility to the disorderly procession of brothers she describes, here, with two or more Dominicans and one each from the Franciscans, the Carmelites, and the Augustinians, sporting their characteristic vestments (below, § "Costumes and Props"). Margot's tableaux vivants are likely too prurient to stage; but try installing a choir stall upstage, visible to the audience at all times and, perhaps, a second choir stall behind the last rows of the theater (so that the audience can be conscripted into a religious or antireligious community). As the theater morphs into a pseudosacred space, add a Bishop to the proceedings to exemplify the coercive power of the Church: in ninth-century France, for example, he was empowered to flog people into accepting Christ.[3] The brothers might enter from the back of the house, begging as they go until they reach the upstage choir stall. Later, during Margot's actual confession, each time a monastic affiliation comes up, the corresponding brother will rise with the mention of his name and then quickly be seated. That piece of staging can be played for further laughs with the overdetermined Dominicans: Will the real Jacobin please stand up? And, when the Augustinian isn't mentioned the second time around, he might look as confused as did presidential candidate Ben Carson when he didn't hear his name during one of the Republican debates (6 February 2016). For twenty-first-century attendees, a theme song for each order would help too. For the Jacobin, you could go with "Dominique" of "singing nun" fame: its refrain of "Dominique-nique, nique" yields *nique! nique!*, the grammatical imperative for "Fuck! Fuck!" For the snow-white Carmelite, why not "Who's that yonder dressed in white?"—unless he's wearing the earlier striped mantle that was discarded in 1287. In that, case, make it "Jailhouse Rock." And so on, and so on. Let those brethren come. This is foreplay. Plus, at the afterplay, it's the ideal opportunity to align their mendicancy with the actors' convention of asking for financial contributions.

The *ATF* version features a number of stage directions, including the text's first words: *MARGOT se met à genoux devant le curé et dit en plourant* (*Margot kneels before the priest and, in tears, begins to speak* [*ATF*, 1: 372]). But the graphic *RBM*-a practically dares to be mounted, with Petit de Julleville ruling out that very prospect. It was too licentious, he averred, and no closing *envoi* (*RTC*, 5). Not so for *RBM*-a, counters Tissier, where such an *envoi* "establishes to a near certainty that the dialogue was not read and recited but 'played' on stage" (*RF*, 6: 377; *SFQS*, note 44). But how to play it? Was an audience of one enough? As Margot paints picture after picture, the Priest is clearly aroused or *excité* (*FFMA*, 2: 295; *Répertoire*, 111). How clearly? And what about the corresponding actions? Does *Blue*'s preoccupation with naming vs. euphemism extend to *staging* vs. euphemism? Farce has long been hard at work breaking down any semblance of a fourth wall (or a comically anachronistic confessional partition) between priest and penitent. How far is it willing to go in its breach of the confessional wall of silence?

Now comes the hard part for an audience of peeping Toms; and do bear in mind that *not seeing* something concealed behind a door or a curtain can be even more obscene than *seeing it*. Did the dramaturgical imagination supply a material meatstick for the living sausage (*endoille toute vive*) (*ATF*, 1: 375)? Was the privacy lattice of *Blue*'s confessional easily removable, such that various items could be passed back and forth? Maybe the Priest is feeling around to ascertain whether the penitent is a man or a woman. Maybe he sticks a comestible sausage through the passageway—we *hope* it's just a sausage—only to draw back a chicken neck. And there's no reason why a props master couldn't have filled an animal bladder with milk, the crème de la crème, for a gestural euphemism. No reason, that is, other than to avoid out-and-out pornography or, at least, the utterly convincing appearance thereof: the ultimate Baudrillardian confusion between simulation and reality (above, "Introd.," § "Pornography"). So, that's right: I'm suggesting that the latticed opening of the confessional might function as a glory hole. Thy kingdom come, thy will be done. Glory hole-a-lujah. Whence, the unanticipated relevance of Penley's work on the 1920s stag film, *Getting His Goat*.

Anyone with twenty seconds to spare can watch its plot unfold on the Internet. A trio of beautiful women is skinny-dipping at the beach when a geeky voyeur steals their clothes. When he demands sex in exchange for their outfits, the women seemingly consent; but, in true farcical form, the nasty trickster is tricked. They playfully take their revenge by substituting a different sexual partner whom they back up against a hole in a fence, which satisfies the blackmailer to no end: "the best girl I ever had in all my life." His partner was—wait for it—*a goat*. No kidding. The butt of the joke is *the butt of the goat*. I'm no veterinarian, but the specter of sodomy is surely as comical as it was in the allegedly accidental honeymoon sodomy of *The Farce of the Fart* (*FF*, 82). In *Blue*, the whole makes for a spirited, not meanspirited, practical joke on foolish men.[4] Has the question of pornography by accident vs. by mistake thus morphed into one of bestiality by accident vs. by mistake?

(above, "Introd.," § "Pornography"). One thing is for sure: when you make your decisions about staging, you can't be on the fence.

Costumes and Props

Long ample robes are eminently serviceable for hiding a world of evil: everything from erections to . . . you'll see. Margot might enter in a cloak with a hood (*capuchin*); and the Priest shall be dressed in accordance with whatever brotherhood you assign. He should have his surplice and stole, as in the fabliau "Estula";[5] and, if wearing the now familiar collar, he's definitely hot under it. The extra Brothers of the processional are clad in their signature regalia as laid out in "Oh, Brother" (above, "ABT"): the Dominicans in their black cloaks over white habits; the Franciscan "Greyfriar" in gray with his telltale rope cincture, and the Augustinian in his outdoor black garb with its long, pointed hood. If that's still not enough, give him a copy of Augustine's *Confessions* in one hand and a Germanic sausage in the other. The Carmelite shall emerge last: barefoot in either a white or striped mantle. In honor of the expression *bander comme un Carme* ("to get as hard as a Carmelite" [*SFQS*, note 8]), you could give him a huge codpiece. Stiff competition for the Franciscan.

Scholarly References to Copyrighted Materials (in order of appearance and indicated by © within the text)

"Dominique." By Soeur Sourire, aka Jeannine Deckers. ASCAP Work ID: 340100063.

"Jailhouse Rock." By Jerry Leiber and Mike Stoller. BMI Work #757227.

"Poor Jerusalem." By Andrew Lloyd-Webber and Timothy Rice. ASCAP Work ID: 460132212.

"Someone to Lay Down Beside Me." By Karla Bonoff. BMI Work #1376250.

"Jacob's Ladder." Spiritual.

"Knockin' on Heaven's Door." By Bob Dylan. SESAC Work Number: 514919.

"Goin' Down." By Suketu Khandwala, Taylor Momsen, and Benjamin Phillips. BMI Work #11639290.

"Hodie Christus Natus Est." From *Ceremony of Carols*. By Benjamin Britten (1942).

"Trouble." By Lenka Kripac and Thomas Salter. ASCAP Work ID: 505224635.

"Let's Hear It for the Boy." By Dean Pitchford and Thomas Snow. BMI Work #858383.
"Papa Don't Preach." By Brian Elliot. ASCAP Work ID: 460257114.
"Amen." By Jerry Goldsmith. BMI Work #34271.

[*At first, only the dimly lit choir stalls are visible upstage. As music plays,*[6] *a processional begins from behind the spectators. Members of each mendicant order walk toward the choir stalls, begging for contributions along the way. Once the brothers are seated, the lights come up on a confessional center stage. The Parish Priest might hastily be dispensing with a long line of penitents.*]

MARGOT *kneels before the priest and, in tears, begins to speak.*

Bless me, Father, for I have sinned. Why, only just today, I came to the aid of a brother in need: great need.[7] I did so in joy and gladness because he was so backed up he didn't know what to do with himself. ⟨And, since he was kind of a looker,⟩ I succored him as best I could. Which is why, Father . . . I don't know: ⟨Is there anything standing between me and my salvation?⟩ If I've sinned, I [humbly beg forgiveness and] ask for absolution.

THE PARISH PRIEST

Tell me what's on your mind, my daughter, ⟨I'm all ears. Let it all hang out. I'll gladly tender absolution.⟩ Let's have the whole list of your sins.

MARGOT

⟨Whatever you say, Father:⟩ I want very much for you to know them, so, ⟨sure: I'll spill.⟩ I won't leave out a [blessed] thing. Three or four times, he did me, Sweet Robin, in one fell swoop. Didn't even dismount.

[*Each mendicant brother in the choir stalls will rise briefly upon the mention of his name.*]

I don't know if he was—[*with a thick French accent*]—how you say? A *Jacobin*, a *Cordelier*, an *Augustin*, a *Carmelite*? [A Dominican, a Franciscan, an Augustinian, a Carmelite? It's all French to me.] ⟨A Brother Minor, [a major brother,] a Brother Preacher,⟩ [a major preacher], a lay brother, [a brother laid . . .] But—boy, oh boy and, oh, brother!—that was one holy order! He did it with great gusto too, I swear, ⟨super eager to minister to my needs.⟩

THE PARISH PRIEST

You have committed no sin. Blessed is he who does a good turn to men of the cloth for, in sure and certain hope, Paradise is his: ⟨and the power and the glory, forever and ever and ever.© [Thy Kingdom come, thy will be done!]

MARGOT

But, Father, uh-oh! That's just what I'm so ashamed of because . . . our parish priest . . . knocked me up . . . with a daughter . . . that I gave to my husband.[8]

THE PARISH PRIEST

Madame, just keep up the good works for the parish priest, and ye shall receive salvation in the sweet hereafter. [Blessed is he who cometh in the name of the Lord.]⟩

MARGOT

A monk came to bed with me too in the best room in the house. It was just the other night, maybe seven times or more, he put his knees between my legs and—. I don't know: am I damned for all eternity? Anything to say about a case like that?

[*The Priest is silent but not inactive.*]

⟨I say, Father, oh no! In my bedroom! I'm pretty sure that was a monk layin' butt-naked with me. Spread my legs and stuck his dick right in! Seven minutes in heaven. Just last night. [Thy rod and thy staff comfort me!] I don't know whether I'm burnin' in hell for it or what. What's your take? Did I transgress or anything? My brother.⟩

THE PARISH PRIEST

⟨Of course not. That's not how I see it at all.⟩ Bless my soul! I hold you to be a very good girl—very good—to have made such a glorious offering unto him. In the name of all the cardinals of Rome—⟨and all the cardinals up the Rhône too, up the papal way by Avignon⟩—I shall grant you absolution. [Just like last time.][9]

MARGOT

⟨But wait, Father, there's more!⟩ I'm not finished. ⟨Lemme give you the whole scoop.⟩ I also come to the aid of my next-door neighbor in need. A lot. First chance I get to be of service, I hightail it over there when my husband is asleep. And that one's really pricking my conscience. I don't know. . . . Is that remorse I'm feeling? Do I repent or what?

THE PARISH PRIEST

Now, why would you want to go and do a thing like that, ⟨*Madame*⟩? It makes no sense at all to repent for doing good. [Love thy neighbor as thyself.] From fire and brimstone, from the torments of hell, from the pains of Purgatory, ⟨for lending a helping hand to a neighbor in need, I shall absolve you. You've got a full pardon coming your way, for sure: absolute absolution. *Absolution-ly.*⟩[10]

MARGOT

But, Father, wait till you hear about the pilgrim sallying forth the other day on his merry way. He needed a place to stay and, this I must tell you: I was deeply moved by his plight. So, long story short, in Christian charity, I had him lodge in my chambers. I gave him plenty to eat and drink—a real feast—and, after . . . well. . . . Naturally, I had the bed made up and the sheets turned down and I had him lay down beside me.[©] And then, let's just say we both went to a whole lot of trouble. We practically ran out of breath. Such a joyful noise we were making [unto the Lord], that that bed of ours fell over! The whole house was shaking. The earth moved. [The angels wept.] Whence I was much astonished.

Now, on that one, I'm not sure what I've got to say for myself or whether I ought to be repenting. But I must admit—and it's no lie—I felt really bad about the whole thing. I wasn't exactly at my best. And don't you be thinking I'm lying. I'm telling the truth, I swear. [*There is no verbal response.*]

⟨I say, Father: did you hear the one about the pilgrim? Spoke softly and carried a great big stick? Asks me in the name o' God: "Is there any room at the inn?" So, I take pity on him, right? and I'm a good sport about the whole thing. I take him in, lay out a whole spread—anything he wants—I have him come to bed with me, and—[Jesus! Joy of man's desiring!]—he takes me up on it. Again and again. And again. [I'm givin' it to you straight here, Father . . .] All of which leaves me in fear and trembling . . . and with a great load . . . on my conscience because . . . Three times, that holy roller climbed on top of my ass—[and the cock crowed!]—banging so hard we damn near broke the bed! Down go the covers, down we go onto the floor, smack on our asses and—wham, bam, thank you ma'am!—we fucked like there was no tomorrow!

And then, oh so sweetly, my lord lifts me up.

Now for that sin, I'm sure I've got a penance comin'. Can you help me out?

THE PARISH PRIEST

There's no sin in that; and you'll get no penance from me. You've earned yourself a full pardon—and paradise in the end—for lodging a wayward pilgrim.⟩[11] You've been a woman of great constancy, my dear, taking him in like that. You were most kind to squeeze Mr. Pilgrim in at your place.

MARGOT, *weeping.*

Father, there's another matter that I really need to get off my chest. But I don't know if I dare say.

THE PARISH PRIEST

Why not?

MARGOT

Woe is me! It's the worst sin I ever committed in my life!

THE PARISH PRIEST

All the more reason to speak up and name it or the confession doesn't count.

MARGOT

Father, then I shall tell you, that all my sins might be washed away and that I be purged. The other day, off the main road in the woods, I came upon a hermit who had his hands full of a thing of great beauty. His fingers were all wrapped around it and he seemed to be making a fist.[12]

THE PARISH PRIEST

No euphemisms allowed. What was it?

MARGOT

I do believe it was some kind of living sausage.

THE PARISH PRIEST

Or could it be . . . a cock?[13] Spit it out! Cock or balls? What was it?

MARGOT

[*She might stick a hand through the latticed opening.*] Bless my soul, Father, it was like a little tonsured mini-Monk. In front, it was all red and it had a bald head with, like, a crown and a hood to protect it from the wind.[14] It was—[*O magnum mysterium et admirable!*]—well fashioned: big, fat, bulging, and beautiful to behold, ready to take on all comers, hard as a rock, stiff as a board the whole time. And, at the base, two beautiful . . . *bells*: so beautiful, such pretty little things that, ding-dong-ding, those bells were ringing! As soon as I saw it, [I just sensed something was up.] I knew in my heart of hearts that I had to move in for a closer look.

THE PARISH PRIEST

[*Ever more excitedly*] And then?

MARGOT

To tell you the truth, something tells me this beautiful thing was really cold—that's what *he* said—which is why, I suppose, he was rubbing it in his hands.

THE PARISH PRIEST

And then? Come on baby, [you're getting warm]. Out with it! What next?

MARGOT

I took it by the head and, believing it to be some sort of creature of the fields, I put it between my both thighs to warm it up. [And yea, I saw the ram butting westward, northward, and southward, and he did as he pleased and magnified himself.][15]

THE PARISH PRIEST

[And Jesus wept!] These are grave errors. Did you take one in the gut? In your womb, for God's sake! [*Benedictus est fructus ventris?*] Did you stick it in?

MARGOT

It went in all by itself and, then, it kind of jumps up. And, then, it comes in so sweetly that—[in and out, and in and out, and hide the sausage]—it was awesome.

THE PARISH PRIEST

[Talk about your second coming!] There's no harm in that. I'm thinking it's all good.

MARGOT

And then, when he was all finished messing around down there and he wanted to take the thing back out, it was all . . . Friar-Tuck-ered out.[16] 'Twas but a piteous thing: so tiny, so soft, so tender. It was pathetic: barely half the size it was in the beginning and—*O lacrimoso!*—oh, so gently weeping, on account of which—alas! wretch that I am!—I was beside myself when I saw it shrink into nothing like that: flying at half-staff, spoiled rotten from my misdeeds because . . . after, when he wanted to play with it again like before, he just couldn't do it because . . . I swear, it was all droopy: bent in the middle, all petered out. And, for this, I humbly beg God's forgiveness and your absolution. [I am sorry for these and all my sins.]

THE PARISH PRIEST

[Oh God, oh, the devotion!] Warming up that poor creature![17] [Praise the Lord, sing glory *hole*-a-lujah!]

[But what did I just tell you about euphemisms? Keep your eye on the ball. {*He shouts.*} No euphemisms aloud!]

MARGOT

⟨Yeah, yeah, yeah, daddy, fine. Did you hear the one about the hermit who was fisting a big hard cock? He sticks it way the hell up my snatch and comes so hard, it looks like a goddamn Hollandaise. I'm thinkin' I musta been some kinda major slut 'cause, when that hermit pulls his cock back out, he's got nothin'. Soft as a baby's goddamn bottom. So, there you have it. I confess. I repent. Whatever.[18]

THE PARISH PRIEST

Again, *Madame*, [no harm, no foul.] You were most reasonable and sensible—the soul of patience, full of the milk of human kindness—to let that hermit have his way with you as he deemed fit. I'm absolving you of the whole thing, sure as shootin'.⟩

MARGOT

[I'm not outta the woods yet, Father.] I rubbed its head too hard. *There's* the harm. *There's* the root of all evil. *Ecce homo!*

THE PARISH PRIEST

You meant well. He was in high spirits when he left, yes? Anything else?

MARGOT

Father, I've told you all I've done: [in word and deed, known and unknown.] At least as far as I can recall. ⟨I don't know what else to tell you but, as God is my witness, that's the low-down—and the down-low—on my conduct.⟩

THE PARISH PRIEST

⟨Then, *Madame*, ma-*donna*, Madonna, here it is straight up:⟩ you're a "woman" of good conscience and you've lived like a saint. ⟨Absolution shall be yours and, *instead of* penance, here's what you're gonna do right away. Again and again. In perpetuity. Doctor's orders.⟩

[*A Bishop, probably a Dominican, suddenly stands, initially seen only by the Priest. So too do the various brothers when they hear their orders mentioned.*]

[What I mean to say is:] *for* your penance: I hereby decree that you shall . . . Get thee to my brethren, ⟨my brothers of the cloth everywhere!⟩: like the brothers of the belt, the Brothers Preachers, the

Carmelites, and the Jacobins. Go visit those places where you're sure to find them congregating. Help my buddies out: every morning, every evening, [at matins, at vespers], for as long as you shall be in the full flower of youth.

[*The brethren begin to congregate around the confessional.*]

[That's right! Come out, come out, wherever you are!] ⟨The Franciscans—oh yeah!—with those long, dangling ... cords. [*Cordeliers* are well hung, but watch out you don't wind up with a bloody sphincter! I mean *cincture*.]

And my Brothers Preachers, the Jacobins, [just a stone's throw away:] Go see about them too, every morning. Consecrate thy body to their service. Climb the hell up Jacob's ladder!©⟩[19]

As for your friendly neighborhood priest, should he have need of thy service, don't be a tease. He who does a good turn for the poor father shall have Heaven on earth as his ... *her* ... his-and-her reward. Plus, it'll do that poor little [mini-]monk a world o' good. ⟨So, be ye crazy merciful to your parish priest, the one who governs you, instructs you, confesses you, and gives you communion. Don't be a stranger. [Commune like hell with him.]

And, while we're at it, same goes for all the folks from these here parts. I'm talkin' be a good neighbor! Commune with them too. [Be neighborly as hell.] Bend ye to their will, attend to them, delight them. Offer your body as a living sacrifice, wholly pleasing unto God. [*He holds up the Eucharist.*] May all partake of the sacred body at will. And *that's* what we call doin' penance![20]

As for that wayward pilgrim, one good turn deserves another: you'll do plenty unto him too.⟩ In the weeks to come, should one pop up, knock, knock, knockin' on heaven's door,© take him into thy chamber, have him lay down beside you,© and [lodge the hell out of him.]

⟨And let's not forget good old Herman's hermit in the woods. [The more, the merrier!] Go to him three times a day, bringing tidings of comfort and joy. And a bottle of good wine.

Likewise for the poor monk who aims to please: he'll do anything for you, sun up or sun down, whether you go to him or he comes to you. [Your body as a living and holy sacrifice, I say!—the kind he will find acceptable.] Don't hold back—[*fingering his Bible and perhaps something else*]—and don't you be lookin' too closely at the fine print.⟩

[You hear what I said?] I'm ordering you to do your duty by that hermit. Visit him early and often. [The Lord is thy shepherd; thou shalt not want. He maketh thee lay down in green pastures.] So, into the woods with you! Under the trees! Be a good girl now and [Austin-fry 'im!] Bring a picnic. [Eat, drink, and, whatever you do, do it all for the glory of God! Thy cup runneth over. With the good stuff, oh yeah!] And don't forget the ham because everybody loves a good pork!

Ham it up, I say! Leave 'em beggin' for mercy! Have yourself a *ho*-down. Ladies and gentlemen, have yourselves a bro-down!

And God shall have mercy on your soul. As soon He gets a minute. Unless something comes up.

[*The Bishop makes his presence known to all, upon which the brothers rapidly disperse and resume their previous positions in the choir stalls.*]

He [the Priest] lays his hand upon her head and says

And verily you shall be forgiven and your sins shall be effaced. Forever and ever. [Give thanks to the Lord for He is good.] *In saecula saeculorum.*

⟨But—my, my, my!—Would you look at the time! I've just about had my fill o' you for now and it's time to be off.

[*To the audience*] No, not *you*, not *yet*!

[*He glares at the brethren in the choir stalls and, with a nod of the head, indicates that it's time for them to circulate among the spectators to solicit financial contributions. All rise and move toward the audience except one.*]

[*To Margot*] As for you, [my daughter:] Come the morrow, as fervently as hell, you shall get your zealous ass straight over to Saint Germain-des-Prés [and have yourself a real field day because there's plenty o' sermons to be preached on that mount.] You'll "prostate" yourself at that big ol' statue and, by way of salutation, you'll go: "Get thee behind me, Satan!" Stick your head through the portal, stick your ass in the air, and, verily, Paradise shall be thy reward. [Holy is as holy does!]

[*He might give a kick in the ass to the one mendicant brother remaining onstage.*] [But don't be an asshole! Keep the acting in bounds. Don't be a drag and don't be a drag queen, or you're *really* gonna get it in the end!]

Believe you me, that much I know: We hope that you enjoyed the show,⟩ because *that*, ladies and gentlemen—and all you lady-gentlemen—is how make your way into Heaven. Ass backwards! Now give thanks to your lord, for he is good. Real good. *In saecula saeculorum. In suck-you-là! suck-yooh-la-la!*[21]

MARGOT
Amen.

[*The Priest might whip the audience into a singing frenzy.*][22]

Here ends Margot's Confession ⟨recently published [and hot off the presses]⟩

The END

3.

Highway Robbery, or, *A Criminal Confession*

La Confession du Brigant au Curé

CAST OF CHARACTERS

The HIGHWAYMAN (Le Brigant)
The PARISH PRIEST (Le Curé)

PRODUCTION NOTES

First edited by Gustave Cohen, the *Farce nouvelle à deux personnaiges, c'est à savoir Le Brigant et le Curé* appears as #10 in the *Recueil Cohen* (*RC*, 79–82). It was later reedited with myriad annotations by both Koopmans (*RFlorence*, 173–79) and Martin in *SFQS* (https://sottiesetfarces.wordpress.com/category/confession-du-brigant-au-cure/#sdendnote9anc). Of Norman provenance (*SFQS*, "Introd.") and comprised of 188 octosyllabic verses in mostly rhyming couplets, the play was summarized by Faivre in *Répertoire* (109–10) and briefly by Tissier in the context of *Blue Confessions* (*RF*, 6: 379). It also bears some similarities to an itsy-bitsy farce interpolated into the *Life of Saint Fiacre* (*TFR*, 28–32). Koopmans is confident, based on a textual allusion to the devaluation of the *escuz vieulx*, that *Le Brigant et le Curé* dates from after 1514 (v. 6; *RFlorence*, 173n, 179). I know of no modern French or English translation.

Plot

The time: Holy Week (*la longue sepmaine*); the place: a deserted path in the woods. As in *The Con-Man's Confession* (#1), Easter is coming, but so too is trouble. A Parish Priest (*Le Curé*) sallies forth to confess the flock, only to be accosted by a starving Highwayman, and, in order to save his skin, he distracts the bandit with—what else?—the sacrament of confession. The pair will cover all the bases: keeping the Sabbath, attending Mass, many of the seven deadly sins, plus the Ten Commandments, especially "Thou shalt not covet thy neighbor's wife," "Thou Shalt not take the name of the Lord in vain," and—wink, wink, nudge, nudge—"Thou shalt not steal." After a series of clerical queries that can best be qualified as going through the motions as they target the spectators' own misconduct, absolution is seemingly granted. The question is: *what* motions? But, first, a confession of my own about my initial reading of this *farce nouvelle*:

I didn't get it. The premise was unverisimilar, even for farce. I mean: what were the odds that, in the middle of a hold-up, a bandit would be moved, in honor of Easter, to confess his sins? And what was so funny about highway robbery or of the imminent threat of death by dagger (v. 51)? If anything, the events were borderline tragic, as in a morality play. Make that a *mortality* play or, worse: a bad comedy. I guess I was in good company. With the exception of Faivre, Koopmans, and Martin, critical analysis was virtually nil, save a passing reference in Bowen ("Cliché," 39) and Kent ("Signe trompeur," 98–105). Alan Knight deemed our play a "dialogue" (*AG*, 95), as did Martin (*SFQS*, "Introd."); and Cohen dismissed it as "lackluster and uninteresting" (*RC*, xii). *Wrong!* ruled an exasperated Koopmans: Cohen had "understood nothing" (*RFlorence*, 179). It turns out that, materially, gesturally, and comedically, the right hand doesn't know what the left hand is doing. *Literally*. One man reaches into the dark recesses of a penitent's conscience; the other, into the dark recesses of a money bag hidden on the cleric's person. The sacrament is but a piece of sleight of hand during which the countdown of sins facilitates the counting *up* of the Priest's coins—that is, as soon as the thief can get his hands on that sizable purse.

One good shakedown deserves another and, by the end, "they take their leave of one another, one lightened of the weight of his sins, the other of the weight of his *écus*" (*Répertoire*, 109). In a way, the entire farce is one grand pantomime buttressed by a series of double entendres for what's really going on: namely, an unburdening of a more physical nature. And the big joke is on the Priest who gets had as the audience gets the last laugh about how "enriching" confession can be (*Répertoire*, 109–10). In a word, the Highwayman makes out like a bandit and the Priest gets off easy. In more ways than one.

Two roads diverged in a yellow wood and, long I stood and looked down both as far as I could. But I'm a rather different traveler than Cohen, Faivre, or Koopmans. To my eye, both protagonists were *bent* in the undergrowth. Where Koopmans and Faivre find all the equivocation financial, I find it sexual too, and so does Martin (*SFQS*, note 41). The two are hardly mutually exclusive. It's not only the Priest's coin purse on the line but that other purse (*la bourse* or *l'aumônière*): the lexical and scenic double for the scrotum and the upcoming star of *Slick Brother Willy* (#11). *Highway Robbery* is the story of the literal cut-and-run of a metaphorical castration when the thief uses his scissors (*les forces*) to snip the Priest's purse strings (*RFlorence*, 175n). The whole thingy reminded me of the twelfth-century fabliau *Estula*, in which two hungry, cabbage-stealing bandits rip off a priest's surplice and stole, snagging his "head and tail" (Bloch, *Scandal*, 35–36). Ouch. Careful, folks, lest trickery cut you off at the knees. Or higher. This is no *quem quaeritis* trope of Holy Week in which the three Marys seek Jesus in his empty tomb. This farce seeks empty pants: *Quem quaeritis*, not *in sepulchro* but *in pantalones*?

If *Highway Robbery* can be said to have a denouement, it's less an unknotting than a cutting off. But who has screwed over whom? Only dramaturgy will tell. When the Highwayman threatens violence, is it also sexual violence? Is that threat pleasing to his prey? Does the Highwayman enjoy flirting with the Priest? Just how far is the Priest willing to go to save his (fore)skin? Which is the better proffer or the more daunting demand? Money? Sex? Absolution? Is the bottom line that the Highwayman gets paid *for* having sex with the priest? And does the Priest get "cleaned out" in every way? All in all, if the Priest is the butt of the joke, we must determine how literally to take that. Either way, a queer reading is de rigueur. On one unholy road, the specter of sodomy hints at where sinful clergymen ought to stick it: the chocolate highway to heaven.

And what of absolution itself, misspoken as *ego asuote* (v. 176) and not *ego absolvo te* (*RC*, 82n)? What of contrition? For Tissier, this is a "real, albeit theatrical confession" (as opposed to a "false" or "pseudoconfession" [*RF*, 6: 379]). For Faivre, it's the fake contrition of "impenitent penitents" and an "auto-glorification of their guilty activities" (*Répertoire*, 109). But pseudopenance and pseudoabsolution will not do at all. They are "unhappy" performatives in the Austinian sense in that they fail to come to fruition (*HDTW*, 20–24). Like the overgrown roots that the Highwayman claims to "cut off at the knees" (v. 105), the garbled liturgical language seems likewise to cut off salvation. Greedy clergymen are the real highway robbers, forcing others into lives of penury and thievery but subject to punishment from the outlaw actors of theater.

Characters and Character Development

Thin, drawn, and out of work, the unnamed Highwayman (*Le Brigant*) opens with a soliloquy on the pains of poverty, a clever piece of metacommentary on the life of the starving actor (vv. 9–12). Upon spying the Priest, he is motivated by hunger, anger, and resentment to improvise quite the little metaperformance of confession. And he knows exactly how to distract his mark: with the pleasures of the flesh. What with all his assertions about men, women, roots, shafts, pins, prickles, and pricks, he appears to issue a cis-gender rejection of the very homoeroticism that dominates the proceedings (vv. 94–106; below, § "Language"). But how far is he willing to go, phallic dagger in hand? Again, only dramaturgy will tell what to make of a dual delivery that alternates rapidly between *sotto voces* and direct address. The Highwayman also alternates between *vous* and *tu*, at first marking the social superiority of the priest with *vous*, which changes once he ascertains that they're alone. Otherwise, his French is fairly good, notwithstanding my occasional "ain't" for effect. From what little we hear of it, his Latin is good too—better than the Priest's (v. 34; *SFQS*, note 11).

Our ecclesiastical everyman may or may not be called "Maurice" (as in #5, *Confession Follies*);[1] and his dominant character traits are gluttony, lust, and greed (*SFQS*, "Introd."). He transports food and wine on his person, he enjoys a nice stiff one, and, throughout the pat-down, he is infinitely more concerned for his lost money than for the thief's lost soul (*SFQS*, note 24). Oddly polite at first (*vous* instead of the pastoral *tu*), he is sore afraid, which could account for his Latinate mumbo-jumbo approximating the liturgy (*SFQS*, note 29). And who wouldn't be afraid with a thief fumbling around in your junk? Unless, of course, the pat-down is exactly what the Priest is after in the woods. Are these woods the equivalent of the Bois de Boulogne as red-light district? After all, he's loaded with five or six hundred dollars on him (vv. 67, 133): all set up for the confessional money shot.

A potential third personage is invoked so vividly that one might wish to stage her in flashback with: "I remember it as if it were yesterday." The female tripe-seller, a fixture in Rabelais and the subject *La Trippière* in the selfsame *Recueil Cohen* (#52), is a character type in her own right. Notorious for her vicious temper and her double-edged knife (*SFQS*, note 62), she's always ready for a good tongue-lashing. Here, she embodies the play's central castration metaphor (below, § "Language").

Language

Between the Norman dialect and the messy versification, Koopmans's poetic anarchy (*RFlorence*, 179) mirrors theological anarchy. Just wait till you hear what they do to the liturgical *Sursum corda* ("Lift up Your Hearts") and the *Gloria Patri* ("Glory Be") (below, notes 8 and 20). Under normal farcical circumstances, prayers in "kitchen Latin" are decipherable, as in *At Cross Purposes* (*FF*, 241–44) or *Holy Deadlock* (*HD*, 217–21). But in *Highway Robbery*, the Latin is so corrupt that even a frustrated Cohen confessed that he couldn't make heads or tails of it (*RC*, 82n). And, then, there's the taking of the name of the Lord in vain. Indeed, this was the play that inspired my glossary ("ABT," § "Curses and Exclamations"). If you're wont to keep score: the most common euphemism for the blasphemous *Dieu* is *bieu*, spoken no fewer than ten times in a large variety of expressions including *la croix bieu*, *maulgré bieu*, *mort bieu*, *vertu bieu*, *ventre bieu*, *chair bieu*, and *corps bieu*, along with a profusion of *sang bieu* (vv. 33, 63, 116, 148, 165). But, beyond that, in violation of the Third Commandment, there are multiple instances of the uneuphemized *Dieu*: *Dieu mercy*, *pour Dieu*, *par Dieu*, *par le Dieu qui me fist*, the wholly impious *par la chair Dieu* (literally "God in the flesh"), and—way over the top at v. 89 for the Easter moment of eternal life—*par la mort sans remission* ("death without remission").

This is a stickup; so, there's plenty of fumbling around with that purse as scrotum (*la bourse*), obscenely confused with *la conscience* on occasion when denoted by the direct object pronoun alone (*la*). And, thanks to the thief's special scissors, there's a fair amount of snipping and cutting related to more than the pins and pricks of sinful cavorting with women (vv. 93–106; below, note 11). Technically, an *espinette* is a spinet—tickling the ivories? fingering the strings?; and the *espingles* are the pins used to stitch women into—or out of—their dresses. But the meaning grows thornier when aligned with the play's roots and thistles that impede the Highwayman's smooth passage. In addition to being associated with Lenten jousting in the famous theatrical city of Lille, an *espine* signified a penis (*SFQS*, notes 35 and 36), and a small one at that. No matter how you cut it, this prickle-tickle is designed to have the audience in stitches as it cuts and runs. Like the tripe-seller's knife, everything cuts both ways. The question is whether anyone gets split wide open. And where.

Sets and Staging

The action takes place, possibly on Sunday, in the woods where the Highwayman lies in wait. In light of the Priest's contention that he overspent on special Easter lighting (vv. 61–62), the illuminated church might be depicted in the background . . . unless that was a lie. His humble—or not so humble—manse might be located on either side of the stage or envisaged liminally before the curtain goes up. For Martin, the Priest is already en route, picking up a dead tree branch as both a weapon and a walking stick for the long and dangerous trek to the parish. Cities were "normally located in forests," he recalls, which were teeming with "wild dogs, wolves, and robbers" (*SFQS*, note 10). But I've started the Priest off at home, where he might engage in a host of religious or irreligious activities before setting off. Take your pick of the seven deadly sins—I'd go with homosocial lust—but, by all means: account for how he came by such a large sum of money in the first place. Has he been pilfering from the collection plate? Picking the pockets of an assembly line of penitents?

That aside, the main thrust of the play's financial, sexual, and theological equivocation is physical comedy. Since there are no stage directions, the action must be intuited and resolved during the snatching of the purse. What can I say? It's all in the hands. To borrow an Alanis Morrissette lyric—she did play God in *Dogma*, you know—he's got "one hand in his pocket and the other one's" . . . wherever. It's a delicate scenographic balance between what the audience must see but which the Priest cannot. We also know that the Highwayman has considerable trouble getting at the Priest's booty because "the opening is too small" (*le pertuis est trop petit* [vv. 120–21; *SFQS*, note 47]). Needless to say, the canonical penitential genuflection comes in handy; but anyone daring to stage *Highway Robbery* must decide how far to take the climax.

Costumes and Props

The Highwayman's threadbare clothes are well described in his first speech; and also wields the trademark pair of scissors for snipping off his victims' purses. If the Priest is staged at home, there might be any number of implements on hand for protection: a rod, a staff, a baseball bat, and—to channel Saint Julian the Hospitaller (v. 124)—an oar.[2] He bears the key prop too: a bulging purse stuffed with coins of every shape and size (*grans et menuz*). These include *escuz vieulx* (v. 6) and a *rouelle*, so-called because it's round (v. 55), whence today's *je n'ai pas un rond* ("I don't have one red cent"). If updated, try an enormous wad of small bills. In terms of comestibles, the cleric's references to his empty cup (vv. 55–56), jug of wine (v. 65), and food or breadstuffs (*la crouste d'ung pasté* [v. 176]) intimate that he might have stashed a repast for his journey. Plus, to highlight the intertext with *The Chicken Pie and the Chocolate Cake* (*FCMF*, 151–58), I recommend those very items: a chicken pie and chocolate cake. And do have some fun with anything else he's hiding under his cassock. Most important: some stale breadcrust, piecrust, or crackers to pass for a makeshift Eucharist during the pseudosacramental moment of absolution. And don't forget that chocolate for dessert.

Scholarly References to Copyrighted Materials (in order of appearance and indicated by © within the text)

"Brother, Can You Spare a Dime?" By Yip Harburg and Jay Gorney. ASCAP Work ID: 320093878.
"The Big Muddy." By Pete Seeger. BMI Work #114413.
"Battle Hymn of the Republic." By Julia Ward Howe. (19th c.)
"More, More, More." By Gregg Diamond. ASCAP Work ID: 430240205.
"Carry That Weight." By John Lennon and Paul McCartney. BMI Work #187794.

[*Several cross-cut mimed scenes of the Priest enjoying his bounty while the starving Highwayman walks alone on a deserted road still wet from a recent rain.*]

[Scene 1]

The HIGHWAYMAN *begins*

My brothers, can you spare a dime?©
I'm broke: not one red cent on me.
Just hang me from the highest tree!
Hang any man who can't squeak by!
[Say, brothers, can you spare a dime?©]

Come on now, folks: can't be hangin' on to that spare change! I'm tapped out, I said, on my last legs. [Just look at me!] You name it, I ain't got it. I'm a bag o' bones. It's been so long since I worked, I can't even fill out this here coat. I'm almost out of everything at home: bread, ham, cheese. Pity the fool who crosses my path before this day is out.[3]

[*He finds a hiding place. Lights down.*]

[Scene 2]

[*Lights up on the Priest in his manse.*]

The PRIEST

Well, what do you know! Easter is coming. I'd best take my chances and stop by the parish to confess the flock because they've certainly been most remiss. One might even go so far as to say they know not what they do. So, I suppose the very least *I* can do is get *their* load off *my* conscience. Praise the Lord, I'm all set, and not a moment too soon! But I better hurry. Come to think of it, a man without a staff is at the mercy of the dogs. [*He fetches a staff and a picnic lunch.*]

Onward, ho! [From ghosties and ghoulies and long-leggedy beasties and things that go bump in the night. . . . And, yea, though I walk through the valley of the shadow of death,] I will fear no evil. The Lord be with me, and Mother Mary too.[4]

[*He hides his purse deep on his person and departs.*]

[Scene 3]

[*In the woods*]

The HIGHWAYMAN

Jesus H. Christ on the cross! I'm just wasting my time out here. There's not a single living soul.

But [wait]! God strike me dead if that ain't some sucker headed right this way. Whoa-ho-ho! Better make sure he ain't got company.

[*Sotto voce*] Jesus H. Christ! Prepare to meet thy Maker, *Domine Padre*, 'cause you're gonna die!

The PRIEST

Looks like I'm making pretty good time. I'm almost there.
[*While he reaches for a snack, the Highwayman pounces. The Priest attempts to flee but is restrained by his captor.*]
[Help! Murder!]

The HIGHWAYMAN

[*Imitating him*] "Help! Murder!" Not so fast, there preacher man. Where do you think you're going there, sir?[5]

The PRIEST

What's this? Lord have mercy, Lord have mercy! For God's sake don't hurt me!

The HIGHWAYMAN

Anybody else comin'? Seen anybody walkin' or ridin' by this way?

The PRIEST

I haven't seen a single living soul.

The HIGHWAYMAN

You seem nervous, my fine fellow.

The PRIEST

At first, I thought there might be a bad element out here but, no, that's certainly not the case, praise the Lord.

The HIGHWAYMAN

This is a stick-up. And I won't be leavin' here today till I've counted up every cent you got.

The PRIEST

[*Sotto voce*] This is worse than I thought.
Lord have mercy! Don't let this come to blows!

The HIGHWAYMAN

Is this a dagger you see [before you? the handle toward my hand]?
One more word outta you, pal, and—[you tryin' to get crucified here?]—Jesus fucking Christ! I'll split your ass wide open![6]

The PRIEST

Not one word. I'm no fool. Nobody will ever know.

The HIGHWAYMAN

So, pony up. Fork over the dough.

The PRIEST

[*He speaks very loudly, hoping to be overheard.*] In the name of the God who gave me life: [no cup of mine runneth over]. I don't have a penny to my name.[7]

The HIGHWAYMAN

Keep your damn voice down! Can't have nobody gettin' in our way.

The PRIEST

Quite right, [my son], I'd forgotten, I swear. But, truth be told, I disbursed all my funds on the special lighting for the holidays. [He is the Resurrection, you know; He is the Light.]

The HIGHWAYMAN

Of all the dirty, underhanded—. Jesus H. Christ! You'll soon be singin' a different tune, lousy, tightwad priest. On your knees!

The PRIEST

I could give you a jug of wine, my good sir. Let's be friends.

The HIGHWAYMAN

Just fork over the dough, I said. Five or six hundred and nobody gets hurt. And, then, you won't have to worry 'bout nobody gettin' it off you.

The PRIEST

In the name of the God who gave me—. My whole life, I've never had that kind of money in my purse.

The HIGHWAYMAN

Better not make me angry 'cause if I have to blow my top . . .

The PRIEST

For that, I'd be truly sorry.

The HIGHWAYMAN

Which reminds me: this whole Holy Week, I've been meaning to get to confession.

The PRIEST

Aha! Then, by God, let's drop everything and I'll hear your confession! Pray, make yourself comfortable. Have a seat. Or stand erect. Or get down on your knees and—say it with me now—*benedicite Dominus*! [Bless me Father, for . . .]

The HIGHWAYMAN

Say it the hell for me!

The PRIEST

Benedicite et Domin . . . Domin . . . ummm . . . Dominus vobiscum . . . cum . . . cum . . . O cum all ye *fidelis et* cardiac workout! In the name of the Father, the Son, and the holy spigot: *in spiritus sancti, amen.*[8]

Now you: "[Bless me, Father,] for I have sinned. *Je me confesse . . .*"

The HIGHWAYMAN

Say it the hell for me, bub!

The PRIEST

"I confess my sins to God. *Je me confesse à Dieu.*"

The HIGHWAYMAN

Adieu? You tryin' to beat it already? Damn, sleazy priest![9]

The PRIEST

It's what you say at confession. [For your salvation.]

The HIGHWAYMAN

[For your *salivation*, you mean, you damn pervert!] One more word outta your trap and I'm gonna kill you.

The PRIEST

Pray, continue, my son. Do go about your business. Have you stolen from anyone? Have you been . . . poking around in what isn't yours?[10]

[*The Highwayman removes his scissors and attempts to cut off the Priest's purse.*]

The HIGHWAYMAN

Jesus flippin' Christ, what do *you* think? *Strip*-pokin'—you bet your ass—with plenty o' pretty girls. Gettin' me some action off one and, then—next! Up you go! Sharin' that booty right on down the line. Snippin' the stitches right off them dresses and, then, it's cut and run!

The PRIEST

And for that, may God forgive you, sir.
And how's it going with the sin of anger? If you're hot-tempered, that's simply not going to cut it.

The HIGHWAYMAN

When I'm walking the roads and I see a root or a thistle or some prickle-bush gonna stick me between the legs, I get downright snippy. So, I pretty much take the name o' the Lord in vain right off the bat. And, then, I cut that low-down sucker off at the knees and not one more word about it. All on the down-low. All the way down to the stub.[11]

The PRIEST

May God forgive you for that too. But you mustn't resort to self-help, you know. [Don't be a bad actor.] And you really must refrain from taking other people's money. [You owe it to yourself.]

The HIGHWAYMAN

Damn straight! [*Struggling to access the contents of the purse*] What the hell else am I supposed to do when I can't . . . quite . . . manage to get my hands on some o' my own![12]

The PRIEST

Which is all very well and good, but it angers the Lord. Now: what else have you been up to? What about pretty *boys* and *their* purse strings? With all that playing around, ever forced thy way into thy neighbor's junk?[13]

[*The dialogue and action come harder and faster, some of it possibly concealed behind the aforementioned bushes.*]

The HIGHWAYMAN

Good God Almighty, no!
[*Sotto voce*] Not yet! [Talk about tightening the old purse strings!]

The PRIEST

Pray, go on, then, proceed. To each man, his cross to bear. But God helps those who help themselves.

The HIGHWAYMAN

[*During the pat-down, he hits a cross and some foodstuffs.*] Jesus H. Christ! I'm helping myself as we speak!
[*Sotto voce*] To each *my* own. And I'm just gettin' started.

The PRIEST

Consider your position, my son. You must get it all out.

The HIGHWAYMAN

[*Sotto voce*] I'm doin' the best I can here but the damn hole's too small.

The PRIEST

[For what shall it profit a man if he gain the whole world and suffer the loss of his soul?] Leave no stone unturned, my son. It's for your own good.

The HIGHWAYMAN

My own good is right. In the name of Saint Julian, that's what I'm hopin' for: a profit! [And some goddamn hospitality.]

The PRIEST

Lord have mercy! Have you no faith in God? There's no need to rush. Easy does it.

The HIGHWAYMAN

[*Sotto voce*] No, no. I'm easin' on in right now.

[The PRIEST

{*With a shiver*} What the fudge! Haste makes waste!

The HIGHWAYMAN

{*Sotto voce*} And go fudge yourself! It won't go to waste, believe me.] Don't tell me I'm getting on your nerves.

The PRIEST

Not at all, my good man, take your time. I take great pleasure in freeing you from the wages of sin.

The HIGHWAYMAN

[*He finally gets a good grip on the Priest's bulging purse.*] And—good God Almighty!—them's some wages. There's gotta be about six hundred in there.[14]

The PRIEST

Your confession, my son. Before we adjourn, you must finish up. Come clean.[15]

The HIGHWAYMAN

"Clean's" the word for it, pal, and—good God Almighty!—I'll be cleanin' you out if it's the last thing I do! [*At long last, he is in the purse.*]

The PRIEST

Good heavens! So much sin to account for. Be sure to get every last one. [It's a cold, hard world out there.]

The HIGHWAYMAN

And cold hard cash in *here*! I'm gettin' it all, count on it—big ones, little ones—I'm makin' out like a bandit!

The PRIEST

May God have mercy on your soul. But what about . . . Is there anything else you wish to make known?

The HIGHWAYMAN

There was this one day a while back, somebody had left out this great big greasy cock. Well, a capon, actually. And all the fixin's. All night long. So, I just made off with it.[16]

The PRIEST

[*Off-balance, he falls over into a puddle.*] Lord have mercy, I . . . you . . . [in the Big Muddy©?] . . . not the c-c-c- . . . [17]

The HIGHWAYMAN

[The cock? The big fool said to push on.©] Jesus H. Christ! Wolfed that sucker right down—the jelly too—for which, I confess, I'm truly sorry.

The PRIEST

Uh-huh. But, say, what about Sunday service? When they ring the bells, you go to hear Mass, don't you?

The HIGHWAYMAN

I hear just fine from wherever I am.

The PRIEST

You bear a heavy load, sir, but—good God Almighty!—what's the hold-up? Go on.[18]

The HIGHWAYMAN

Will do.

[*Sotto voce*] I'm loaded, all right, thanks to you, praise the Lord!

The PRIEST

Pray, go on, my son, what next? This is no time for banal tripe.

The HIGHWAYMAN

Speaking of which . . . Ate me some tripe the other day off some tripe-lady when she was sellin' in the neighborhood. [I stuck in my thumb, and pulled out some . . .] Come around fast, she did; so, I stuck my knife all the way in and, then, sucked me up her whole pot. Good till the very last drop. Juice was drippin' out all over the place. Shut her filthy trap but good. And then I stiffed her. Beat a hasty retreat before she could stick me back.

[*He makes the cut and snags his prize, possibly distracting the Priest with a corresponding "purse"-grab.*]
[And boy, oh boy, did I ever hit the jackpot!][19]

The PRIEST
Good heavens! Now we're really getting somewhere! Are we all fessed up?

The HIGHWAYMAN
In the name of—Jesus H. Christ!—all fessed up and ready to blow! Can't think of a single thing left deep within the deep, dark recesses of . . . my conscience. Nope. All cleaned out.
[*Sotto voce*] And so are you. Unless there's still somethin' wedged in there.

The PRIEST
It's all in your best interest, I assure you. And, if I've played my part in good faith, so much the better for you.

The HIGHWAYMAN
[*Sotto voce*] [Way better.] My best interest is the whole "principal." So, finish up already and get on with it. Let's get this show on the road.

The PRIEST
But, to be forgiven for your sins, you must express contrition, my son, and show remorse. And I must assign penance.

The HIGHWAYMAN
You just give it some thought, there, Father, because, if you load me up with one more thing, I don't know how I can possibly bear it.

[*The Priest motions for him to kneel. He then locates a makeshift Eucharist from his picnic and attempts to stick the "wafer" into the "penitent's" mouth. Meanwhile, the Highwayman locates other comestibles.*]

The PRIEST
[*In saecula saeculor . . . saeculor . . . ummm. . . .*] In the name of that great chicken pie in the sky, I *ab . . . ab . . . absolvimus te*! Absolution-ly! Mine eyes have seen the glory of the coming of the Lord!© *In Spiritu sancti amen.*[20]

The HIGHWAYMAN

How wise you are, my friend, and endowed, sir, with a great big . . . [*to the audience*] crock![21]

[*While the Highwayman eats, the Priest beats a hasty retreat.*]

[Scene 4]

[*Alone again on the road*]

The PRIEST

Jesus H. Christ Almighty! And I got off okay too, by the hair of my skinny-skin-skin! Barely made it out of there before he sliced my ass in two! But—Jesus flippin' Christ on a cracker! I best pick up where I left off and stop by the parish to confess the flock . . . before I get flocked again! So, folks: maybe we didn't exactly take the high road here but, heads up 'cause we're comin' your way! Exit . . . that-a-way.

[*The Highwayman returns and the two actors head into the crowd to collect donations.*]

[The HIGHWAYMAN

Moe, moe, moe! How did you like it? How did you like it?©]

The PRIEST

Moe, moe, moe! How did you like it? How did you like the show?©
We hope you enjoyed it—the good Lord pardons you if you did—but, for now:

[*Doubled version begins here.*]

The time has come to say adieu.
Forgive us, Lord, unholy roads.
You liked the show? Then pardon *you*![22]

[*Doubled version ends here, possibly giving way to closing music.*][23]

The END

4.

Confessions of a Medieval Drama Queen, or, *The Theologina Dialogues*

La Farce de quatre femmes

CAST OF CHARACTERS

DOLLY, the FASHION PLATE (La Bragarde)
JEZEBEL, the STRUMPET (La Gorrière)
TARTUFFIE, the HYPOCRITE (La Bigotte)
MS. THEOLOGINA, the LADY THEOLOGIAN (La Théologienne)

PRODUCTION NOTES

The *Farce nouvelle excellentement bonne de quatre femmes* is one of the longer farces at 632 verses (although that's nothing compared to the *Pathelin*'s approximately 1,500). In addition to the typical rhyming octosyllabic couplets, it boasts the complex musical versification of a rondeau or motet.[1] Edited by Cohen (*RC*, #46, 369–78) and by Koopmans (*RFlorence*, 647–62), it appears in the *Recueil Cohen* only. I'm aware of no translation into French, English, or any other vernacular, whence more endnotes than usual; and only Koopmans summarized it (*RFlorence*, 647). He also surmises that our farce was written sometime after 1496, basing that assertion on historical allusions to the plague in Naples (v. 499) and to the military campaigns in Italy under Francis I (*RFlorence*, 661). Be on the lookout too for a number of intertextual echoes with *Blind Man's Buff* (*RC*, #45; *FF*, #6), which immediately precedes *Drama Queens* (for short throughout) and which almost reads as if an audience has just seen it. Alternate titles: *Confession Transgressions* or *True Concessions.*

Plot

Confessions of a Medieval Drama Queen is what you might call an *immorality* play. The content of the plot is the content of its characters, women one and all, which is a farcical rarity shared by only two other farces that I know of: *Immaculate Deception* (#12) and *Les Malcontentes* (*RLV*, #61). Three married sinners are awaiting the arrival of Madame Theologina (*ma dame la Theologienne* [v. 117]) when, true to morality-play form, they introduce themselves at length. There's Dolly, the primping Fashion Plate (*La Bragarde*); Jezebel, the preening Strumpet (*La Gorrière*); and Tartuffie, the dissimulating Hypocrite (*La Bigotte*). Let's just say that, between the three of them, they've got those seven deadly sins covered: gluttony, lust, avarice, pride, envy, wrath, and sloth. "Ensconcement" in heresy comes up as well, which could be punishable by death during the Reformation. So, it's a very good thing—or is it?—when Theologina shows up with a load of papal bulls that empower her to hear women's confessions (*des busles un grant tas* [v. 171]). In a lopsided sequence that mirrors the women's self-presentations, Theologina does just that. Dolly's confession spans 160 lines of dialogue (vv. 268–428), Jezebel's 120 verses (vv. 429–549), and a rushed Tartuffie's barely 50 (vv. 550–601).

Among many things, we learn why women might want to avoid the confessional in the first place. Male confessors are described repeatedly as dirty, gossipy, lecherous, and illiterate (*qui ne sçavent ne a ne boys* [vv. 154–55, 445–47]), a reproach historically associated with attendees of Passion plays (Sainte-Beuve, *Tableau historique*, 193; above, "Introd."). There's even a special term for their particular brand of "ass-holiness": they are *ânes fagotés*. It sounds like a "fagot of asses," but it actually refers to powerful cardinals who had been elevated way above their station and who, like Theologina, have recently returned from Rome (*RFlorence*, 652n). And don't forget the comedic genre, the *ânerie*, or those other donkeys, the Conards of Rouen.[2] Plus, if you think the notion of a papal seat crawling with asses is sacrilegious, just wait till you hear Jezebel's shocking line about casting theological pearls before religious swine: "the Pope was wrong" (*Certes le pape a eu tort* at v. 204). That farcically fallible Pope might even be a send-up of the days of a shadow-Pope in Avignon (1309–77).

Bottom line: whatever the theological issue, *Drama Queens* brings things to a head. Or lower. "Wily women work in mysterious ways"—*Engins de femme sont moult rusez / Ilz besongnent d'art subtille* (vv. 88–89)—and the Devil is in the details of the bull. It is formally and ceremoniously read aloud

(vv. 220–35) as in *The Edict of Noée* (*FF*, #2), *The Washtub* (*FCMF*, 144–48), and the *Miracle of Théophile* (*MFP*, 191–92); but with what powers does it truly vest our Mother Confessor? As we shall see, Theologina turns out to be the original originalist, a subscriber to the plain-meaning rule. Nothing is a done deal in these "Theologina dialogues."

Characters and Character Development

When the triumvirate—*triumfeminate*?—takes to the stage, is it the usual men in drag? Or is *Drama Queens* genuinely for women only? Probably not, given the play's closing lines about its student performers (below, note 55). But that can be changed up today, especially since the earliest-known contract issued to a French comic actress dates back to 1545, the heyday of farce (Scott, *Women on the Stage*, 59–62; above, "ABT," note 5). Starting with what the three allegorical figures of Dolly, Jezebel, and Tartuffie have in common: all three are living caricatures of their most pronounced sins; all three exalt outward appearances that camouflage what lies beneath, the perfect metaphor for the letter and spirit of this farce's literary law. All three profess great admiration for book learning, even if their wisdom (*sapientia*) and experience (*scientia*) leave something to be desired (vv. 128–30).[3] And all three will do whatever it takes to get ahead, "as need be." Their favorite term is *besogner*, which implies "need," "sex," "work," and, for Jezzie, what we now call "sex work." That said, each everywoman has her own distinctive style which, for Dolly and Jezzie, is the literal *style* of fashion sense. Inasmuch as the play alternates between octosyllables, heptameter, pentameter, and the odd *douzain*, I've retained that flavor in their introductory speeches by assigning elegant pentameter to Dolly, quicker and dirtier octosyllables to Jezebel, and Molièresque alexandrines to odd woman out Tartuffie.

Dolly, *La Bragarde*, is all about the clothes; and she is constantly applying *braguer* ("to be all *dolled up*") to the haves, the have-nots, and the fashion wannabes. To *braguer* is to show off ostentatiously or, Madonna-like, to "vogue." Her excess is in the dress. I also hear punning on *braguette*, that is: the codpiece that could clarify what's really going on under those ensembles. Dolly might be cast as a stunning blue-eyed blonde who, rather like the first wife of the *Fifteen Joys of Marriage* (8–15), bats her eyes and plays it up for anyone liable to get her into the latest couture. In contrast to Jezebel's intermittent vulgarity, Dolly is high style and at pains to distinguish her *brague* from her frenemy's *gorre* (here, "taste").

Next, meet a *Gorrière* who is up for anything and whose moniker translates loosely—is there any other way?—as "hussy," "floozy," or "strumpet." I've gone with "Jezebel" for the lusty, gutsy character. With a taste for sex, Jezzie talks salt and spice and military nice (or, pugilistically, not so nice). Instead of voguing, she adopts combative poses to illustrate the multiple mottos and aphorisms she spouts. All made up and into glam, dissolution, and debauchery, she's a sweet painted lady, a voluptuous Miss Piggy with lipstick. (*Gorre* denoted both "makeup" and "sow.") And there's something toxic about her too, if not as toxic as the perilous kingdom of *Gorre* in Chretien's *Knight of the Cart*. *La grand' gorre* meant not only "high style" but "syphilis" (*RC*, 378n). To borrow the plague-inspired lyric from *Pippin*, Jezzie's veneration of all things venereal has led to other matters venereal as she "spreads a little sunshine" transnationally.[4] She needs globs and globs of concealer for a poor complexion marred by pocks and pimples. And yet, she is as happy and gay as a drag queen (*frisque*; *dehet* [vv. 19; 41]). Put her in a T-shirt, if you wish, visible under all her finery, that reads "Confession or Bust." Finally, while Jezzie intimates, Con-Man-like (#1), that she is ignorant, uneducated, and unfamiliar with what to do at confession (not having been in four years [vv. 440–41]), that's likely just an act. She's perfectly capable of rattling off legalese (vv. 218–19) when it comes to absolution.

For her own part, *La Bigotte*'s spectacle of false devotion moves me to christen her "Tartuffie" in honor of Molière's storied character, but with a hint of the flamboyant piety of Arsinoé from *The Misanthrope*. Look closely under the veneer of her *bigoterie* or *bigotage*, and you'll see that something else entirely is brewing. Sanctimonious, holier-than-thou Tartuffie is a *fausse dévote*, a hypocrite; and that's working for her because churchgoers eat her right up. In light of her reference to "the flower of her youth" (vv. 541–42), she might be somewhat older than the other ladies and not as well-dressed. As the song goes, "she'd change her sad rags into glad rags if she could."

Now, enter one of the most intriguing characters of the repertoire: "Madame la Théologienne," the "Lady Theologian" whom I've dubbed "Theologina" (rhymes with "vagina"). *La Théologienne* has hightailed it from Rome with a momentous papal dispensation; and her journey was arduous, albeit difficult to understand. The muddled language seems to imply that she mounted a pack mule; but it's hard to tell which pairs of legs have given out (esp. vv. 189–203; below, note 24). If anything, her description conjures Chrétien's Lancelot again, whose horses kept dropping dead beneath his thighs in his frenetic quest to rescue the kidnapped Queen Guinevere. During Theologina's trip, something has been left for dead, never to rise again, and it's probably the horse. Either that, or she is riding, à la *Monty Python and the Holy Grail,* no horse at all while a squire runs alongside making clopping noises. Once on the scene, Theologina doesn't hesitate to make her expertise known. She is well-read in civil and canon law (*legiste, decretiste* [v. 145]), endowed with a fine logical and theological mind, and she interprets with the best of them (*en tous livres elle glose* [v. 141]). Perhaps that's why she manifests a particular dislike for Tartuffie, which is reflected in an aggressive change of linguistic register. Then again, her polite *vous* occasionally obfuscates which penitent (or penitents) she is addressing.

One last thing, and it's a horse of a different color or, rather, an ass. Between the *ânes fagotés* and Theologina's pack mule, you could consider staging a *male* animal (with the donkey's notoriously pronounced manhood). There was another farcical donkey, after all, in *The Jackass Conjecture* (*HD*, 160), stalling at the "bridge of asses." It's not a bridge too far.

Language

Religion, medicine, toiletries, and Platonic cosmetics (as in *Gorgias*, secs. 464–65): all come together in the homonymy of saints (*saints*), breasts (*seins*), and belts (*sainture, ceint*). Other metaphorical registers include gaming (card playing and bowling), impersonation-related metacommentary, and assorted emphases on the sexual prefix *con*, which would permit hearing "cunt" or "asshole" before the other syllables of such terms as con*trepoint* ("musical counterpoint"), con*trefaire* ("to imitate"), con*trouver* ("to fabricate" or "to find the right hole?"), or con*trepeter*, which sounds like counter-farting but which means imitation, parody, or payment in kind (*RFlorence*, 649n). Especially noteworthy is the play's veritable reading list, which, while not as extensive as the syllabi of *Un Vendeur de livres* (*RLV*, #15, forthcoming as *Chick Lit*) and *Folconduit* (*TFR*, 284–87), features the Vulgate (v. 137), *Le Compost* (an analogue of the *Farmer's Almanack* [*RC*, 378n]), Guillaume de Machaut's fourteenth-century *Remède de Fortune*, and . . . is that Ovid's *Metamorphoses*? Not quite. Dolly cites the *Virgille methamofosé* (v. 139), which, for all we know, might be a reference to the seven-thousand-verse, fourteenth-century *Ovide moralisé*, a highly influential medieval adaptation and commentary. And speaking of Virgil, the women are up on their folklore too, recounting how Virgil was hung out to dry in a basket by a woman who chose to punish him spectacularly for his amorous advances (vv. 90–91) (Figure 2).

Furthermore, between Jezzie's militaristic register and the town of Bagnolet, I see a fashionable tip of the hat to the famous satirical monologue, the *Franc Archier de Bagnolet* (v. 334). Among its subjects: the telltale cowardice of the soldiers of Charles VI, linked here to the women's frequent denunciations of lily-livered, chicken-shit men.

Two more linguistic issues now claim our attention, the first a four-word aphorism whose embrace of free will, good works, and intentionality is challenging to capture: *Voulenté repute le fait* (v. 332). The expression was glossed by the near-contemporaneous legal rhetorician Antoine Loisel in his *Institutes coutumières* (1607); but it can be traced as far back as Saint Bernard. Basically, it means that good will is fine, but, if actions are to "speak louder

Figure 2. Virgil dangling in a basket, by Lucas van Leyden (*Virgilius in de mand*). Woodcut, Amsterdam, Rijksmuseum Amsterdam. Inventory number RP-P-OB-1811. https://commons.wikimedia.org/wiki/File:Lucas_van_Leyden_051.jpg.

than words," they must be performed voluntarily and not under duress. If uttered sarcastically, it could resonate as "Do as I say, not as *you* do." But the real kicker is one of Theologina's most crucial but ambiguous lines. When chastising Tartuffie, she says "Si *voz faitz ne sont amendables, / Tout droit yrés à damnation*" (vv. 582–83). As student readers of Ronsard's carpe diem sonnet "Quand vous serez bien vieille" have discovered, *si* does not necessarily translate as "if."[5] In fifteenth- and sixteenth-century philology, it could signal the very opposite of equivocation as the "si" of *ainsi*: the "thus" or "therefore" of indubitable logical consequence. In a way, the entire legalistic reading of Theologina's bull depends on the correct reading of this line, which I won't spoil here (below, note 53).

Sets and Staging

Specific Parisian locales abound as nearby Bagnolet and Saint-Maur-des-Fossés give way to the heart of the City of Lights, artsy Montmartre, and various districts of ill repute: the Bois de Boulogne (male prostitution), Brières (amorous assignations), Saint-Germain-des-Prés (debauchery), and the Church of Saint Merri, the notorious site of the anti-Semitic *Mistere de la Sainte Hostie* (15th c.), which features a Dolly-esque "Evil Woman."[6] And yet, for all that site specificity, there's something timeless and "placeless"—very *moralité*-like—about our farce. Unfortunately, since Koopmans did not reproduce its two woodcuts, it is impossible to assess them for iconographic guidance; but, per his description, one depicts two knights on their knees and, the other, a man sounding a horn as a woman and a king leave a chateau. In all likelihood, the three confessions take place in the open air, conceivably against the backdrop of a raucous pilgrimage junket, about which the trio tenders copious details. Per Dolly's request they also perform a motet (v. 39); so, I suggest a musical number. It won't be quite the girl band of Biddy and the Pilgrimettes from *Holy Deadlock* (*HD*, 221–25), but, by all means, have them sing and dance. And, as Bert States would have advised in *Great Reckonings* (197–206), don't neglect the curtain call where, à la *Victor/Victoria*, all can be revealed. Or not. Is one or more of the players a man in costume? A victor/victorious? While it would be a shame to invite a man into an all-female cast, some of Theologina's shortcomings might be addressed by her sex.

Costumes and Props

For wordplay, it's helpful to have an oboe, a trumpet (from the woodcut), and a picnic basket onstage; but, otherwise, it's all about costuming. For Dolly, try a huge gold belt à la Cleopatra; for Jezebel, make it overdone garb, hair, makeup, and jewelry, and, because she's partial to the hard stuff, give her a flask or a bottle of liquor. For Tartuffie, who is clad in an ample cape that looks like a nun's habit, have her hands full of religious paraphernalia: rosaries, Bibles, and so on. And for Theologina, who might sport an elegant man-tailored black suit and priestly white collar, I recommend a pair of glasses. Her look is expressly clerical as she wields the surplice and stole stipulated by an original stage direction: *prent ung surplis et l'estolle* (*RC*, after v. 242; *RFlorence*, 652). Theologina also needs some wine and a comestible that, while resembling a communion wafer (as it did in #3, *Highway Robbery*), is really a bite-sized cookie, cracker, or breadcrust. Her key prop, of course, is that papal bull, a huge scroll, weighted down by dozens of hanging seals.

Scholarly References to Copyrighted Materials (in order of appearance and indicated by © within the text)

"C'est Moi." By Alan Jay Lerner and Frederick Loewe. Music Theatre International. https://www.mtishows.com/camelot.
"I'll Get You." By John Lennon and Paul McCartney.[7]
"Gotta Dance." By Hugh Martin. ASCAP Work ID: 370048707.
"Sweet Painted Lady." By Elton John and Bernie Taupin. BMI Work #1440132.
"Love Is a Battlefield." By Mike Chapman, Randall Hargove, and Holly Knight. ASCAP Work ID: 882360621.
"Rag Doll." By Holly Knight, Joe Perry, Steven Tallarico, and James Vallance. ASCAP Work ID: 480200315.
"Spread a Little Sunshine." By Stephen Schwartz and Roger Hirson. Music Theatre International. https://www.mtishows.com/pippin.
"Just One Look." By Gregory Carroll and Doris Payne. BMI Work #788840.
"Vogue." By Madonna [Ciccone] and Shep Pettibone. ASCAP Work ID: 520105119.
"I'm Called Little Buttercup." By William Schwenk Gilbert, Nicholas Cameron Patrick, and Sir Arthur Seymour Sullivan. From *H.M.S. Pinafore* (1878). BMI Work #4257023.

"You Keep Me Hangin' On." By Lamont Dozier, Brian Holland, and Eddie Holland. BMI Work #1720690.

"Stop in the Name of Love." By Lamont Dozier, Brian Holland, and Eddie Holland. BMI Work #1413855.

"One, Two, Three." Len Barry [Leonard Borisoff], Lamont Dozier, Brian Holland, Eddie Holland, John Medara, and David White. BMI Work #1126577.

"If I Only Had a Brain." By Harold Arlen and E. Y. Harburg.[8]

"Black Magic Woman." By Peter Alan Green. BMI Work #121091.

"Spring Carol." From *Ceremony of Carols*. By Benjamin Britten (1942).

"You Got Me Wrapped [Around Your Little Finger]." By Beth Rowley and Benjamin Castle. BMI Work #9833096.

"On the Wings of a Nightingale." By Paul McCartney. ASCAP Work ID: 450177005.

"Hello Dolly." By Jerry Herman. ASCAP Work ID: 380106250.

"Jubilation T. Cornepone." By Gene de Paul and Johnny Mercer. ASCAP Work ID: 400022800.

"Oh Happy Day." By Philip Doddridge. (18th c.)[9]

"Suspended from Class." By Tracyanne Campbell. ASCAP Work ID: 493817573.

"God Bless America." By Irving Berlin. ASCAP Work ID: 370029559.

"America the Beautiful." Katherine Lee Bates and Samuel Ward. BMI Work #34771.

"Signed, Sealed, Delivered, I'm Yours." By Lee Garrett, Lula Mae Hardaway, Stevie Wonder, and Syreeta Wright. ASCAP Work ID: 490293528.

"Doctor, My Eyes." By Jackson Browne. ASCAP Work ID: 340138550.

"Gee, Officer Krupke." By Stephen Sondheim and Leonard Bernstein. Music Theatre International. https://www.mtishows.com/west-side-story.

"Good Old-Fashioned Lover Boy." By Freddie Mercury. BMI Work #495994.

"Sweet Gypsy Rose." By Irwin Levine and Russell Brown. BMI Work #1294630.

"Bohemian Rhapsody." By Freddie Mercury. ASCAP Work ID: 320199817.

"Put on a Happy Face." By Lee Adams and Charles Strouse. ASCAP Work ID: 890113209.

"Tits and Ass." By Marvin Hamlisch and Edward Kleban. ASCAP Work ID: 892861121.
"Like a Virgin." By Thomas Kelly and William Steinberg. ASCAP Work ID: 420307199.
"Knockin' on Heaven's Door." By Bob Dylan. SESAC Work Number: 514919.
"You Give Love a Bad Name." By Jon Bongiovi, Desmond Child, and Richard Sambora. ASCAP ID: 550147303.
"Crazy Love." By Russell Young. ASCAP Work ID: 330259797.
"Let's Get It On." By Marvin Gaye and Edward Townsend. BMI Work #857218.
"Everything's Coming Up Roses." By Stephen Sondheim and Jule Styne. ASCAP Work ID: 350034303.
"We Hasten with Eager Footsteps." (*Wir eilen mit Schwachen.*) By J. S. Bach.
"Seven Deadly Virtues." By Alan Jay Lerner and Frederick Loewe. Music Theatre International. https://www.mtishows.com/camelot.
"Rag Doll." By Bob Crewe and Bob Gaudio. BMI Work #1223896.

[Scene 1]

[*Somewhere near Paris, outdoors, music plays.*][10]

DOLLY *begins*

And now, it's time to sing a little song of days gone by, so pleasing to the ear, of which we never tire, tales of love: the deeds, the twists, the turns, as you shall hear, of Fortune's faces that we know so well: outrageous tricks, ruses, manipulations by which, all things considered, any gal can take her mark for everything he's worth. By hook, by crook, every trick in the book: I've got the ways, the means, the schemes, the style: I always get my man, I'll do him royal. My fashion sense is all dollars and *sense*. The end, miladies, justifies the means to get that gentleman under your thumb. Where there's a will, conniving is my way—in good conscience and even better clothes. I'll dress the part and pull out all the stops. A fashion plate, thank God, is dressed to kill and, King of Kings, *c'est moi*:© the queen of queens! I'm all dressed up with everywhere to go and plenty up my sleeve: I'm all the rage. The endgame is my game and, when I smile at one man while I'm winking at the other, there'll be a change of Fortune. Spin my wheel! *Rien ne va plus*, gents, so, place your bets on me. I'm gonna get you in the end.© That's why I'm rightly called all over Paris "Madame"—I'll be your baby doll—I'm Dolly.[11]

JEZEBEL

And *I've* got style. I pile it on. Got makeup, powder, pancake, rouge. I'm happy and I'm gay! Just watch me shake my little ass. From soup to nuts, they eat me up. Got taste. Whipped cream with cherry on the top. [Ain't no one beats my Sundae best!] So, *servez-vous*: I'm *à la mode*. Love is my shepherd: I won't want. You name that tune, boys, gotta dance.© Sweet painted lady.© Even this here dress is painted on. So, just gimme your needle, boys, to thread: have you in stitches in no time. *En garde!* The royal standard's mine. I plant my flag, and it shall wave! Love is a battlefield.© Watch out 'cause, what so proudly I do hail, I don't wave everybody in!

I win! You lose: there's nobody can beat my style. I got a name: be careful you don't wear it out. I'm what you call a Jezebel.[12]

TARTUFFIE

I won't be left behind. Nay! Victory is mine! 'Tis what a zealot says. Victorious I reign, for I have played it straight: all on the up and up. [*Aside*] Ladies and gentlemen, you might say "the down-low."

I move in most mysterious ways behind the scenes. That's where the action is, my case made sight unseen. I practice sleight of hand, so crucial to my role, plus tricks of sacred trade, where secrecy obtains, lest there be penetration by a steely glance that would reveal the truth and pretense of my act. You take me for a zealot? *Moi?* I'm faking it. It all comes down to this: I am a hypocrite.[13]

DOLLY

Say, girls! What do you say we three sing a little motet to pass the time? Where *is* there a tenor when you need one?

JEZEBEL

[{*Briefly performing some high-camp dance maneuvers*} What? I said happy and gay. Hilli-ho! Just count on Mistress Jezziwig!] And I'll be takin' my sweet time too because the queen of style, *c'est moi*!© My motto is: the only pleasure in this life is pleasure in this life. Pleasure is as pleasure does.[14]

TARTUFFIE

I'm all dolled up at Mass, from my head to my . . . *mass*, just going through the motions: I'm mouthing the words. Monk-ey see, monk-ey do. Think I'm saying my prayers? Underneath this great cape, it's all bell, shtick, and candle. I speak softly, but I carry a big stick. Eyes like saucers, wide open, and mouth open too for communion. Just watch as I move through the aisles. Here I come! Off'ring up a whole fistful of candles. There's just one thing missing and that's God Himself. Make hay while the sun shines. [And, sometimes, where it don't.]

DOLLY

Leave it to that one to drag out the introductions. Some dolly you are! You call that a fashion statement? You're so fine, they'll never see ya leavin' by the back door, ma'am.© Fashion is a public face: you don't get all dolled up just to please yourself. Plus, everybody sees right through you. Not exactly what a real dolly would call intelligent design. And, by the way, nobody puts baby-dolly in a corner.[15]

JEZEBEL

[*Tap-dancing*] Hello? Happy and gay, remember? Point/Counterpoint. It's all for the pleasure of the play; and the play is in the dress. And in the undress. I'm positively overflowin' with the milk of human kindness: always ready to spread a little sunshine© and give as good as I get because, lemme tell you: ain't nothin' like a good fit. And no skanky broad nowhere's gonna swing my partner and Sunday-best *me*! She is outta there!

DOLLY

Do unto others. Got it. You're a real paragon.
[{*To the audience*} We all know what she's spreading and it ain't sunshine.]

TARTUFFIE

And Tartuffie's the name, casuistry's my game. If I'm dolled up, it's that my adornments are words. At banquets and *soirées*, I fear no man alive. Bless my soul, there's no one holds a candle to me.

DOLLY

I wouldn't look sideways at you. [*Gesturing toward the audience*] Now: sideways at *them*—that slew o' young heartthrobs out there—that's a clothes-horse of a different color! You know the type: doll-baby boys trying like all get-out to one-up me in the fashion department. Like they're some kinda Jezebels. But social intercourse has its cost, you know, and all I gotta do is . . . Just one look: that's all it took, oh baby!© And the *eyes* have it. Quite the setup, really, because, by the by, that's all they're gonna get off me before they take a powder. And off they go, empty-handed, gonna beat a hasty retreat before they ever tap this. [Now, come on, vogue.©]

JEZEBEL

[Well, butter my butt and call me a biscuit!] I got a couple o' suck-ups been trottin' along behind me for the longest time now: a month, two months, a year, two years. I run 'em ragged till they're practically shitting their silks and velvets and ribbons and laces.© Got 'em waitin' on all sides, but I give 'em just enough of a taste to keep 'em hangin' on.© And then, guess what? [Stop in the name of love!©] I slam the door in their faces and leave 'em out in the cold with their teeth chattering before they ever tap this.

TARTUFFIE

[Oh, Lord!] 'Tis the nature of man.

DOLLY

'Tis the nature of the beast, more like, and the beast is a sucker. Like takin' candy from a baby.© *His* end justifies *my* means.

JEZEBEL

If they only had a brain.© It's women got the know-how, got the wiles, got the moves. We've *got* this.

[*Together, the three ladies endeavor to whip the crowd into an antiphonal frenzy.*]

TARTUFFIE

And who was it, pray tell, who hung Virgil out to dry—in a basket—just for fun?

DOLLY

A tiny little woman—please!—had wise, old Solomon on his knees, worshipping at her feet.

JEZEBEL

A woman finishes a man right off. It's a real snow job.

TARTUFFIE

And who was it, pray tell, that cut brave, strong Samson down to size? Took a little bit off the top, as it were?

JEZEBEL

Who coulda snagged the golden fleece without a black magic woman?© [Yo! does the name Medea ring a bell?]

TARTUFFIE

For a woman, deception never sleeps. She's hell-bent on trickery and, with malice aforethought, she's always on the lookout for just the right scheme to head a man off at the pass and nip that thing in the bud. For her own salvation.

DOLLY

And pleasure it is©—great pleasure—when a woman plays her role and maybe lays all the blame on her husband for saying "the Devil come here today! C'mere, take 'er away!" She's got the poor sap wrapped around her little finger.©[16]

JEZEBEL

You think I got egg on *my* face? Like this luminous complexion comes cheap.[17] [Jack be nimble, Jack be quick, Jack watch out for that candlestick!]

DOLLY [*singing*]

Oh, summer of love! I get a feeling like I'm traveling through the sky on the wings of a nightingale. Oh, I can feel something happening.© [*Et Tartuffie?*][18]

TARTUFFIE

Well, hello, Dolly.© [I thought she'd *never* get to the chorus.] Come to think of it: What ever happened to our Lady of Theology? I haven't seen Theologina around lately.

DOLLY

Jubilation T. Hornpone,© said the actress to the Pope. In the name of Saint Cornelius, don't tell me you haven't heard! She went to Rome, she did, Tartuffie, for a dispensation to get vested and so forth so that, from here on in, she'd have the power and the authority to hear our confessions.[19]

TARTUFFIE

Oh, happy day!© Mark my words: 'Tis a far, far better thing for us all.

JEZEBEL

That woman really knows her stuff. She's into it so deep, there ain't a Ph.D. nowhere, no how, got her know-how. [Not even in the Religious Studies Department.]

DOLLY

And don't get me started on those theologians. Bunch of asses, the whole lot of 'em! Dirty old dogs! Dirty old doggy-style! And have you seen those get-ups? A theologian's got no honor and no class. Don't know his elbow from his ass.©

TARTUFFIE

[When you lay down with dog turds, you get fleas.] In the name of Saint Julian, the-oh-so-hospitable, Theologina knows all.[20]

DOLLY

She certainly knows how to read between the lines. Knows her Bible inside out too. She's looked the whole thing over from one end to the other: that's the *French* Bible. And other books besides, like Virgil's *Metamorphoses*. [{*Tartuffie glares at her.*} And the *Iliad*, the *Space Odyssey* . . .] And she's all over that *Farmers'* . . . *Almanac*. You name it, she's got her nose in it.

JEZEBEL

Totally. She got a mind on her. It's awesome.

DOLLY

She knows her way around any subject: civil law, canon law, papal decrees. . . . She's a doctor, a lawyer, a pulpiteer-in-chief and, in the name of Saint John the Baptist, *she's* the one on hand every day to correct all the errors of those higher-ups at church. Who says you can't teach an old dog new tricks? Those books get plenty of action.[21]

TARTUFFIE

She's the one who reviewed the translations from vulgar Latin into the *rustica romana lingua.* [*The women look confused.*] Into the vernacular. [*More silence*] Into French, [for God's sake!][22]

JEZEBEL

[Vulgar is as vulgar does.] Who else is gonna catch all them errors if it ain't women?

DOLLY

Seriously. A bunch of blabbermouth confessors who don't even know which end is up? They're practically illiterate and they're the ones gonna discipline and punish us women? As if!

TARTUFFIE

They've certainly never gotten a thing out of me and they never will. [*Aside*] Nothing of consequence, that is.

JEZEBEL

Truth or consequences! I'll play. It don't bother me none to tell 'em any old thing and get it all off my chest. A real fire in my belly, or wherever. Let it all hang out, I say.

DOLLY

I'll never tell what's on my conscience. What happens within stays within.

TARTUFFIE

In sure and certain hope, one day there shall come a dispensation to absolve us of all our wrongs.

[{*As if Theologina has missed her cue*} Oh where, oh where could that dispensation be?]

[Scene 2]

THEOLOGINA *enters* [*out of breath, messy, disheveled, and a little dirty, struggling to carry a great number of boxes, purses, satchels, bottles, etc. She rummages through the items looking for something very particular.*]

Through the twists and turns of outrageous fortune, from the mountains, to the prairies, to the oceans white with foam,© through purple mountains majesty above the fruited plain,© up and down, high and low, far and wide, here and there, everywhere: I rushed right over, having toiled tirelessly on the entire negotiation. So, here I am, signed, sealed, deliverance,© and—check it out!—with a great big pile of bulls! Pardons, indulgences, dispensations: all this can be yours if the price is right!

Ladies: I spared no expense. *Unus, duo, tres, quattuor, quinny, sex!* I'll confess any woman on the face of this earth: one by one, two by two, by the dozen, by the thousands. It's all within my power! And about those husbands: it'll be our little secret. Mum's the word. Mummery too. All's well that ends well.

DOLLY

Boy am I glad to see you! Welcome back!

JEZEBEL

Me too. I'm so happy, I could pop a vein. I'm all hot and bothered just lookin' at you, Theologina.[23]

TARTUFFIE

Me too. But I'm not bothered at all. Indeed, I'm feeling much easier already, more at peace. Welcome.

THEOLOGINA

[*She brandishes a huge scroll.*] I came as fast as the good old legs could carry me, directly from Rome, where I've seen it all and where I've obtained—*voilà!*—this bull, which touches upon a number of very serious matters. Go on, girls, take it all in. Read it and weep!

DOLLY

Mother Mary, would you look at all those seals! That thing must be worth its weight in . . . weight.

THEOLOGINA

It just so happens that, in exchange for the coin of the realm, I've indulged. And I've brought the whole kit and caboodle right back here on my own personal beast of burden. Although, there *was* that big moment at the tippy-top when . . . . That ass breaks free and goes down, down, down into the valley of death—reins, bridle, and all—and expires on the spot.[24]

JEZEBEL

The Pope sure as hell got that one wrong: stickin' you with a hard-headed ass when you need to ride the pony express.

THEOLOGINA

In Rome, asses are a dime a dozen—they're practically giving them away—and there's no ass like a kiss-ass French ass. That, I can assure you. They go like hot-cross buns. Some are even endowed with enormous crowns, big and wide as a cardinal's—.

DOLLY

Sin? But there's something that doesn't quite sit right about vesting asses like that with rank and position.

THEOLOGINA

In the name of Saint Maclovius, patron saint of morons and shellfish—they're piled higher and deeper out there. In my experience. [I've seen it with my own eyes.]

JEZEBEL

[{*To the audience*} She means Saint Mack on the down-low. You got the dough, they got the bull.]
So: wanna give that dispensation o' yours a read?
That we might be privy to the contents contained therein?

THEOLOGINA

[*She waves the document very quickly so as to preclude a closer look.*] Silence! for I shall now read this bull, and ye shall see that this is the real deal. You've never seen bull—*a* bull—like this. It covers everything, the ultimate pour-over. And I personally worked all the angles to come up with the main clause myself.

Hear ye! Hear ye! [Regarding the power to interrogate women jointly and severally—it's all in good order, all right here in this written instrument—Whereas . . .

{*Jezzie grabs the oboe.*} No, not *that* instrument.]

Oyez, Oyez! Hear ye, hear ye!

Reading the bull

"Let it be known to all the men and women gathered here today that, by my authority, I do hereby solemnly vest Madame Theologina with the full rights and power to confess all women from A to Z—and this, without respect to class—to grill them from the head down to the ass."

The signature then reads: "Signed by Jack Asse."

Et sic et non, a quolibet, at last! And not a single word out of place. No joke. All in due form and properly executed.[25]

DOLLY

I've got a real doozy on my conscience I've been meaning to confess but I've been keeping it all in.

TARTUFFIE

O Theologina, great and wise and full of knowledge: you shall know forthwith my deepest, darkest secrets.

JEZEBEL

Me too, I'll spill. The truth, the whole truth, and nothin' but the truth about everything I been tryin to forget: the whole dirty business.

THEOLOGINA *takes the surplice and the stole*

Prepare to unburden yourselves then, ladies, for, whatever it be upon your conscience, ye shall be purged. [It's cathartic.] Now take a moment to gather your thoughts.[26]

DOLLY

In the name of Saint Michael, I'll sing like a canary! [And a great trumpet shall blow. And maybe we can finally do that motet.] You'll have every word of it: chapter and verse of . . . chapter and verse.[27]

JEZEBEL

Some windfall, right?—[and hey! who are you callin' a strumpet?] We're gonna make out like bandits with that thingy, I can tell. I'll just confess what I done wrong. Name that sin, wipe the slate clean.

TARTUFFIE

We've been wasting our time confessing to those fat, mealy-mouthed priests. We confess to all the little sins but not word one about the big ones.

DOLLY

From here on in, we're gonna do it our way, from beginning to—[*smacking a butt*]—end. But let's make it snappy and confess all this stuff before we forget. In remembrance of *moi*!

THEOLOGINA

Make the sign of the cross, all three of you! I'm certainly of a mind to use confession in order to be privy to your innermost thoughts.
[*The three women might muddle in pantomime about how to do this correctly, especially Jezebel.*]
By the power vested in me, I [hereby] bless you in the name of the Father and the Son.
[{*To the audience*} What? You think they know the difference?]

DOLLY

Okeydokey, then, I'll play. No kidding, I'll tell you all the wrong I've ever done. Now, about my face: the penetrating sideways glances, the steely-eyed seduction I've been working like a charm on all those wimpy lover boys, batting my baby blues every which way but—doctor, my eyes!© I confess.

THEOLOGINA

Eyes on the prize, was it? And you opened even wider, didn't you?, once you saw the treasure trove? [Baubles and bangles,] trinkets and chains, sable and squirrel fur. A doll for all seasons. [And we call that "Dolly-sign" eyeballs.]

DOLLY

[Eyes wide open, purse wide open.] But I *am* awfully sorry for that sin of mine. I repent. I confess. Whatever.

THEOLOGINA

Have you ever been to Mass for the sole purpose of faking a little devotion?

DOLLY

[Does the Devil have horns?] All the time! I was there for one reason and one reason alone: to make a mockery of all that's holy. If you've got it, flaunt it! [*She vogues.*] [*That* is my contrition position.] All dolled up. Fashion cash-in. Rubbing their noses in the latest *couture*: low-cut gingham dresses cinched all the way in at the waist and with great gilt belts. I wear that *gilt* like a badge of honor, I do. And everybody's talking about my fashion sense because, when Dolly gets dolled up, it's always over the top. [Now, come on, vogue!©]

THEOLOGINA

That particular sin is pervasive and most displeasing to God. [It's a travesty.]

DOLLY

[*Moi*? I'm not a transvestite!] But I *have* been around. Everywhere. Parties, banquets, festivals: [the usual watering holes] where all the gossip, badmouthing, and rumormongering begin. *Everybody* doin' the nasty. But, if you want the real scoop on who comes up with the most vile, outrageous filth, *c'est moi*!© I'll one-up any man or woman out there in gossip; and this little Dolly's spread plenty in her day. Trashed the reputations of quite a few wives too.

THEOLOGINA

Essentially speaking, then: the greater the sin, the greater the material burden on your conscience, and, the greater still, the requisite penance.

DOLLY

[*She beats her ample breast.*] Yeah, yeah, yeah. I repent already, okay? For that and all my sins, I'm truly sorry.

THEOLOGINA

You're inclined, are you not, Dolly, to be out and about in Montmartre? Playing around with the locals on pilgrimage? Drawn to all those holy relics, are you? Oh, the monk-ey business![28]

DOLLY

[Montmartre? They got a whole "Dolly" museum up there! Plus, a monk makes a helluva sacred host.][29] I've been out at least four times lately by Saint-Germain-des-Prés: red-light district. Been achin' for a cure gonna lick that infection once and for all.
[{*She kneels.*} See here? I'm down on my knees 'cause no one wants a monk-ey with a social disease.©]

THEOLOGINA

Butter wouldn't melt in your mouth, of course. But, behind those abbey walls, deep within the inner sanctum, those boobs have been known to work real miracles out of false devotion. What with all that trailing along behind all those holy rollers—sleazy monks and slimy abbots, the fat slobs!—a woman soon finds herself pregnant. [Now tell me:] Mightn't such a case have befallen you?

DOLLY

What do *you* think? There was this one day—a girl's gotta go along to get along—when I'm fully intending on doing it, you know, for kicks: play it as it lays, dance to their tune because I've got my eye on this new dress and my husband's all bent outta shape about what it's gonna set him back. [You gotta front those big deposits, right?] But, when you gotta have it, you gotta have it. Long story short: I'm gonna do whatever it takes, outta spite, you know? Gonna get my comeuppance as I see fit and play the whole thing out on my terms. All's fair in love and war, and this doll shall be avenged! I won't be sidelined! Vengeance is mine, sayeth Dolly: an eye for an eye. A tit for a tat. I simply *had* to have that dress in my possession.

THEOLOGINA

[Possession is nine-tenths of the law, to be sure.] But you might want to leave the tits out of it. Now, let's move on.[30]

DOLLY

Somebody sure as hell made a move on *me* the other day. And—not to worry—a fashion plate always rises to the occasion. So, I'm on my way to Père Lachaise, right?, for a little *déjeuner sur l'herbe*, whistling past the graveyard and such. And then, there's this nut-job in the garden, right?, spanking the bishop, if you catch my drift. I'm only human, you know. Deep down inside me there is good, there is good, there is good, there is untapped good!© So, I'm on my knees in no time, right?, and—talk about creaming in your—. He pontificates all over me! Speaking of which, I might just as well fess up to what came next.[31]

THEOLOGINA

As well you should, indubitably. But do be mindful about vengeance. And we'll get to the adultery in a minute. Next?

[*Tartuffie misunderstands and, thinking that it's her turn, she falls to her knees, only to rise in frustration when Dolly continues.*]

DOLLY

Okay, so one time—some Sunday or holiday—I'm all down in the dumps, right?, because I'm over at Saint Merri's, and I see this amazing dress with furry trim at the hips and plenty of room up those [bishop] sleeves. And, seein' as I'm all about deep pockets and everything, I just had to have me one. I wanted it real bad; but my husband—God damn him!—he makes this whole point of telling me there's no way in this life I'm ever getting such a slutty dress. So, then—I don't wanna blow it, right?—God only knows how, but I manage to put out. But, the whole time, I'm two steps ahead of him 'cause, the very next day, at the crack of dawn, I make myself a little rendezvous out in the Bois de Boulogne. Bagatelle Park. I got a guy in the *seizième* handles this sort of thing for me.

THEOLOGINA

Did you perchance go into the woods, pretending like you needed to pee?

DOLLY

[Duh. I've seen *Blind Man's Buff.*] Like I had to squat down to pick a bouquet of violets [or roses or what have you]. So, I excuse myself, right? And—enter, stage left—ooh love, ooh lover boy©—staff in hand, *la bitte en fleur*, horn o' plenty, plenty o' horns, and plenty horny. We gathered the hell outta them rosebuds, just to pass the time. And anything else we could get our hands on.[32]

THEOLOGINA

That was most improper.

DOLLY

Got me a scarlet gown off it—[didn't even need to fake a headache!]—with squirrel-fur trim all around.[33]

THEOLOGINA

Which Dolly might consider not wearing inside out. I do believe that's a fashion misstatement.

DOLLY

[*Singing*] Into the woods, the grass is green! Under the linden tree with you. Into the woods, the grass is green! The cuckold sings cuckoo! And cock-a-doodle-doo![34]

THEOLOGINA

Small wonder. All dolled up in that fashion from your head to your ass.

DOLLY

I never sinned in this life except outta my incontrovertible sense of fashion.

THEOLOGINA

Whence my assertion that it's impossible for the husband, as provider, to keep you dolled up like that in the latest fashions. Not without help.

DOLLY

[And that's no fabric-ation!] If it's this season, I'm in it: draping myself in velvet, silks, and satins, slipping myself into crinolines, taffetas, and petticoats. All the rings on the fingers and bells on the toes;© the cork-soled, fuzzy slippers, the bonnets, chains, and chokers; the sable and the lambskins. All mere trifles. But giant rocks and family jewels? Wow. Not like they're hard to come by. And the husband as provider? Don't make me laugh.

THEOLOGINA

Others "provide," I understand: kill two birds with one stone. But, any lover feathering your nest had best be careful, lest he fall into your trap. I'm astonished that your husband doesn't put up a fuss.

DOLLY

Like I care. A bird in the hand is worth two in my bush. I play my hand, he follows suit. And I lead him around by the nose.

THEOLOGINA

By the nose, is it? Rolled out the red carpet, did you? And I suppose you just happened to give him a whiff of what's really going on down there.

DOLLY

Anyway the wind blows, doesn't really matter.©

THEOLOGINA

'Tis an ill wind that no one blows good.[35] [*Jezebel grabs the oboe again and is rebuffed by a glare from Theologina.*] One whiff down there and a man goes hog wild.

DOLLY

[Puts the hubbies to the testes, all right.] I got the stakes, I ante up, and I bleed 'em dry. Whenever I feel like. Nobody bluffs like me. I got game, and it's my name on everybody's lips. [{*She makes the sign of the cross.*} From those lips to God's ear!]

THEOLOGINA

This is madness. When a man gets his blood up, he does *not* put his best foot forward, a slave to the basest of animal instincts. Down and dirty, like a pig. It's pathetic.[36]

DOLLY

Half a foot's more like it, but I put on a happy face.© I fake a little affection; he grabs a little thigh. Big deal. But I've had enough of this confession already. I'm thinking that pretty much covers all the wrong I've ever done. Whatever.

THEOLOGINA

If, even by omission, you have committed other sins that you've neglected to mention or that you no longer remember, then pray now, that God forgive you and have mercy on your soul.[37]

DOLLY

Amen!

THEOLOGINA

To that!

And now, by the power vested in me [*sotto voce*] for as long as it lasts . . . Get over here Jezebel. Your turn.

JEZEBEL, *confessing*

What am I supposed to do here? What do I say?

THEOLOGINA

Make the sign of the cross and say *mea culpa*, for God's sake! *Mea maxima culpa.*

JEZEBEL

What the—! Ain't like I learned it in school, I swear.

THEOLOGINA

I shall now hear your case, all in due form: the entire reckoning. Now, get over here and tell me: how long has it been since your last confession?

JEZEBEL

[*Distracted throughout*] I ain't been to confession . . . comin' up on four years Ascension Day.

THEOLOGINA

What's this? Mary, Mother of—. These are grave errors!

JEZEBEL

It's them illiterate confessors gimme the creeps. Don't know one end from the other. Besides, they can't keep a secret. Always shootin' their mouths off. They got loose lips, I swear.

THEOLOGINA

Asses that they are! By what right do they reveal the secrets of the confessional? I'll see personally to this abuse and reform those asses but good. But, pray, do go on. Don't stop now. You can't be too careful about this sort of thing.

JEZEBEL

Maybe you wanna interrogate me about my makeup. Go on, ask me anything. We can go through the whole list of what I done.

THEOLOGINA

Tell me about the makeup, [at least as a foundation].

JEZEBEL

Funny you should mention it: to make myself more attractive, I had my whole face done. My body too. In style. It's all about the package. It's window dressing, all for show. Everybody's doin' it. Tits and ass, orchestra and balcony. What they want is what you see.© And, by the *buy*, what you see ain't exactly what *they* get. Like a virgin, hey! Touched for the very first time.© *Not*![38]

THEOLOGINA

Regarding that last statement: you're coming dangerously close to the mortal sin of pride.

JEZEBEL

It's my eyes done the sinnin', checkin' things out willy-nilly like I got no free willy. A girl can't help it.

THEOLOGINA

Wait just one minute. Regarding that last instance, I must inquire: Have you been playing games? The one they call "hide the sausage," perhaps?

JEZEBEL

Hide the sausage? What do *you* think? On my backgammon. I shoved that thing straight up the wazoo and played the hell outta them shit-kebabs![39]

THEOLOGINA

From "A" to *zee derrière*!

JEZEBEL

[*She takes a swig of liquor.*] Set 'em up, down they go! Gin! Just blow in the box and game over! It's my pretty little lies do 'em in every time. As a professional sweet-talker, bunch o' pussies all fall down.[40]

THEOLOGINA

As does your conscience, bearing such a heavy load. But your conclusion strikes me as a bit premature. Plus, that was a dangling modifier.[41]

JEZEBEL

Premature? Haste makes waste and, lemme tell you, this ain't wasted! Plus, if anything's dangling, it ain't no modifier. And I'm on it. Just the cunning sorta gal to take on all comers.

THEOLOGINA

Which doesn't even qualify as sleeping your way to the altar. They're clearly most eager to make an enormous donation, and I doubt very much it's to the Church.

JEZEBEL

[To have and to hole.] If they wanna put somethin' into collection, try takin' care of *this* fashion plate. I satisfy their every appetite, cater to their every whim. All good enough to eat. [*Fleur de lys.* Whatever they desire.] Long as there's a steady stream o' cash, just come on in, boys! But, when the money runs out, it's out the back door with 'em and they can kiss my ass! [A pox on all their houses! It ain't no picnic.]

THEOLOGINA

Oh, come on. And let's not mix apples and orgasms. Plus, that's two, two, two sins in one. You soothe them with fairy tales, [only to avoid them like the plague.] Speaking of which—over here, I said, you Jezebel!—you've never been to Naples, have you?

JEZEBEL

Damn straight I been there.

THEOLOGINA

And Syria? Consorting with the locals and sweating it out? Have plague will travel?[42]

JEZEBEL

You know it! Mary, Mary, quite contrary, how did that garden grow? It was cockle shells galore when I went deep into the countryside—free room and board too, and that ain't no claptrap! For me, there was plenty of room at the inn first shot out of the box.

THEOLOGINA

But was this proper lodging?

JEZEBEL

[{*Breaking into a sweat*} 'Twas brillig and the slithy toves did gyre and gimble in the wabe: all mimsy were the borogoves and the momeraths outgrabe the hell outta themselves!] It's quite the setup, really: come one, come all. The bedrooms is all painted copper—fit for a king and a king-size fit—and the style's, well, "jez" like I said: all pump and circumstance, knock, knock, knockin' on heaven's door.© And they really keep it up too. Folks want for nothin'—[you can have your cake and eat him too!]—and, if you got a taste for quail, everything's finger-lickin' good. But you gotta pay the piper on the way out, which is all birdshot if you ask me. Only problem: it's like an oven out there, so you're pretty much sweatin' like a pig the whole time.[43]

THEOLOGINA

[*To the audience*] As if she'd just been there.
I do believe you're getting warmer.

JEZEBEL

I'm there any time.
[Knock, knock!

THEOLOGINA

Who's there?

JEZEBEL

Goliath.

THEOLOGINA

Goliath who?

JEZEBEL

Goliath down, thou lookest tired!]

THEOLOGINA

You've never done anything illegal, have you? Some stunt that would rise to the level of reckless endangerment?[44]

JEZEBEL

You're kidding, right? I give love a bad name.© Done plenty o' damage in my day. There's one guy used to run fast as a greyhound but, now, let's just say he's dead as a doornail. [*Sotto voce*] In bed. Got a pain in the joints, all splayed out in front of the fire cryin' his eyes out—"waah, waah, waah, the gout!"—[and Fouque him!][45] All on accounta—ooh, ooh, crazy love©—he feasted his eyes on *this*. One little nip, and I'm good to the last drop.

THEOLOGINA

No accounting for a Jezebel's taste. Shame. Shame.

JEZEBEL

Know what? Who cares? Who says the big pussy's gotta come around at all like a eunuch at a whorehouse? He can put up or shut up.

THEOLOGINA

Anyone wishing to keep a Jezebel like you in style will most certainly put up with that little extra something you give him to remember you by.

JEZEBEL

Put up, put out, and get thee behind me, Satan! It *is* all in *zee derrière*. Theologina, I got two other bad things I wanna confess; so, let's get it on©—I mean, get *on* with it.

THEOLOGINA

Confess. Let it all out. Get it off your chest. Don't hold back.

JEZEBEL

As I was sayin': Back in my porkin' days, it was all [put down the vinegar,] take up the honey pot, and spread a little sunshine.© That was my style and I landed plenty o' bright, shiny things in my stash. All decked out like a queen and you shoulda seen the size of my rocks! But forewarned is foreskinned: [everything's comin' up roses© and] them roses was bloomin' all over the place. So much for drippin' in jewels.[46]

THEOLOGINA

[And nothing can bring back the glory in *that* flower.] You're very well-endowed, I see. Snatched it all up, did you?
[{*To the audience*} As plain as that zit on her face. *Et in terra* pox.][47]

JEZEBEL

And that's all I have to say about that. If I done wrong, I'm truly sorry. My bad. [*She kneels, but thinks better of it.*]

THEOLOGINA

Let's go, Tartuffie, you're up. Make it snappy. Just do a blanket confession.

[*Languorously and ostentatiously, Tartuffie takes her Bible, kneels, and makes the sign of the cross as Theologina glares.*]

TARTUFFIE

[Bless me—. Very well, then.] To come straight to the point: I confess most sincerely to Almighty God, the Creator, and to you too that—

THEOLOGINA

[Sanctimonious bitch! It ain't over till the fat lady sings.] Tartuffery is a sin that is an affront to the good Lord and to all the saints.

TARTUFFIE

On bended knee, I confess that, regarding Tartuffery, I have sinned most shamefully and outrageously against my God. I would pretend to be off on pilgrimage, but all the Bible-thumping was mere pretense. I was simply playing a role when, in reality, I was sneaking off into town, Tartuffily, to play around and . . . [*in a whisper*] get laid.

THEOLOGINA

'Twas the work of a hypocrite, Tartuffie.

TARTUFFIE

When my husband was away on business, I'd go into the woods—religiously—about thirty miles outside of Paris—all the way into the wetlands—to make merry. But I didn't exactly have devotion on my mind. I sang every dirty song known to man, which honor would reprove, with a frisky young Frenchman in tow. Stylish, dapper, eager to please. Hit all the right notes and turned in quite the performance. On top. Rocked my world.[48]

THEOLOGINA

[*To all three women.*] Have you no fear of making cuckolds out of your poor, miserable husbands? Hypocrites commit multiple abuses and crimes against nature. O, ye of little faith! Ye fear neither God nor the Devil. Ye are ensconced in obstinacy, in heresy! *Ergo*, your crimes are unforgivable and, [*directly at Tartuffie*] failing reparation, you're headed straight down the path to perdition.[49]

TARTUFFIE

If I could just conclude my confession: *Mea culpa! Mea maxima culpa!* With contrition in my heart, [my voice cries out in the wilderness!] For practicing deception and for raising Cain, may the Lord have mercy on my soul! Alas! Woe is me! I confess sincerely that I . . . I . . . I . . . [*She whispers her next line so softly that no one hears for the first several times until, finally, she yells it out.*] I screwed God outta the tithe! And for that sin, I am truly sorry.[50]

THEOLOGINA

Have you ever been to Mass after dinner?

TARTUFFIE

Why, yes. Commonly . . . communally . . . communionly. I've been there so often that there were those who thought I was living on a steady diet of crucifixes and icons of the Blessed Virgin. For all the ill I've ever done, for these and all the other sins which I cannot now remember, I am truly sorry. In the name of the Father, the Son, [and I forget the third one], I humbly beg forgiveness on my knees. [{*She strikes a pose.*} Am I not the picture of devotion?][51]

THEOLOGINA, *speaking to all the ladies*

Do better from now on. And be ye obstinate no more!

DOLLY

So how's about some absolution? We'll take that blessing any time. [By the powder vested in you and so forth.][52]

THEOLOGINA

No need. Seeing as you've already confessed, no absolution for you! Because, with these, my parting words: verily I say unto you that women get hustled through their confessions all the time. They're heard every day but, then, after a full allocution—when all is said and heard and done—they are not, in fact, absolved. Besides, my bull does not extend so far as to cover the full absolution.[53]

JEZEBEL

Jeez! Is that any way to treat a lady? You get a bunch o' women to confess and, then, you leave 'em hangin' high and dry with no absolution in the end? You just make like a Catholic and pull out?

THEOLOGINA

Pull out. Exactly. [What can I say, girls? You got me on a technicality.] Therefore, without further ado, with feeble but diligent footsteps,©

this very instant, I shall away! I'll hightail it right back to Rome, fast as that ass can carry me, and see if I can't do my best to finagle an audience with the Pope on this dispensation matter, such that, henceforth, he might certify me to grant absolute absolution. In the meantime, it's time to dispense with *you*. Bye-bye for now. That's all folks![54]

[*Theologina rushes off and the three penitents start to pass the hat for contributions. Tartuffie glares at any spectators not forthcoming.*]

TARTUFFIE

And thus, she abandons us, with little choice but to accept this state of waiting . . . for what? Godot?

DOLLY

[I say folks, if anybody's interested in catching another show, I'd best tell you who we are. We can be found at colleges and universities everywhere—why, we're on the faculty in the French Department at this very school—correcting your God-awful grammar! Our school, our rules. And so . . .]

[*All three women make the sign of the cross for this doubled version.*]
If anyone should happen by, inquiring as to who we are:
Grammatically, we certify our academic repertoire.
[If you don't know the golden rule, then get your asses back to school!][55]

The END

5.

Confession Follies: Folie à Deux?

Le Badin, la Femme, et la Chambrière

CAST OF CHARACTERS

The FOOL, [FOUQUET] (Le Badin)
GWYNNIE, the WIFE (La Femme)
MANDY, the CHAMBERMAID (La Chambrière/Mannette)
[BOZO, the Valet, also a Fool]
[Various nonspeaking extras: additional Chambermaids, Father Maurice, a Nun]

PRODUCTION NOTES

The *Farce nouvelle à troys personnaiges, c'est assavoir le Badin, la Femme, et la Chambrière* (*RBM*, #16) has been edited only once in *ATF*, 1: 271–88 (again, paginated but without verse numbers). Petit de Julleville devotes all of six lines to it in the *RTC* (112); and other précis appear in Faivre (*Répertoire*, 64–65), Delepierre (*DLU*, 30), and Tissier in the context of *Blue Confessions* (*RF*, 6: 381). I know of no translation into English or any modern vernacular, and I can see why. The text is "highly mutilated" (*RTC*, 112) and "highly defective" (*ATF*, 1: 271n), its 341 more-or-less regular octosyllabic couplets occasionally corrupt to the point of indecipherability. Montaiglon understandably went with a good old-fashioned diplomatic edition: "having failed in our efforts to reestablish some of the dropped verses, we have elected to preserve the original in its exact form" (1: 271n). "As is" is right. Brace yourselves for the lengthiest Production Notes and endnotes of this book.

Plot

There's no other way to put it. Nobody really gets it. For Delepierre, the dialogue is "extremely muddled" and the action "barely intelligible" (*DLU*, 30). Ditto for Faivre, who summarizes it "without any real certainty" because its sorry state "impedes our understanding of the details of the plot and the motivations of the characters" (*Répertoire*, 64–65). Even so, our final confession-themed play is well worth figuring out.

Depending on stagecraft, *Confession Follies* is a farce, a tragedy, or something in between. Upon entering a sick but well-to-do household, we meet, in one bedroom, the abusive fool of a husband, Fouquet, who is abed nursing his gout. In the other bedroom lies his long-suffering, unnamed wife (here, "Gwynnie"), also abed, but nursing her wounds from Fouquet's latest beating (1: 273–74). In need of attention from her illicit lover, Father Maurice (*Messire Maurice*), Gwynnie dispatches her Chambermaid, Mannette ("Mandy"), to fetch him. Not so fast, threatens the Fool (*Le Badin*), who may or may not be Fouquet. You'll see. He intercepts Mandy, announces that *he* will be the one to deliver the requested pastoral care, and Mandy plays along, probably in coerced complicity. She informs Gwynnie that Maurice will be popping over as soon as he has heard the dying Fouquet's confession; and the rest plays out around two metadramatic masquerades.

In MASQUERADE #1 (Scene 5), it's the Fool who, disguised as Maurice, feels Gwynnie up—the better, some have assumed, to confirm any suspicions about her adultery. But he gets more than he bargained for when, in farce's classic move, Gwynnie shows and tells all. The Fool-in-Disguise then terminates the scene, upon which Gwynnie reckons that turnabout is fair play. In collaboration with Mandy, she masterminds a revenge scenario of her own in MASQUERADE #2, set in Fouquet's bedroom (Scene 7). It is now Gwynnie who, costumed as a nun, directs the pastoral proceedings in an attempt to wheedle a deathbed confession out of her unrepentant and distinctly undying husband. But, in contradistinction to *Confession Lessons*, the closest farcical analogue (*FF*, 128–43), there is no real avowal from the faux penitent . . . unless you want to count his annoyed proclamation about being tricked. In two iterations of the moral of the story, he lambastes all women with "Treachery,"—or "Trickery,"—"thy name is woman" (*Il n'est trahyson que d'une femme* [1: 285]; *Il n'est finesse que d'une femme* [1: 288]). So far, so good?

Hardly.

What have the women done to the Fool to occasion such a grievance? What has he lost? What have they gained? And whose side is Mandy on anyway? Do the women beat Fouquet black and blue, as at the end of *Confession Lessons* (*FF*, 137–43)? And, if so, would that be a protofeminist triumph or a Pyrrhic victory? With or without confession, are *any* of these characters redeemable? Is *the play* redeemable?

It's all very hard to tell, especially when Delepierre recaps MASQUERADE #2 like so: after the Fool has completed MASQUERADE #1 in his Priest costume, "*once again*, it is the Fool who *takes the place of* the husband and listens to what the wife has to say" (*DLU*, 30; my emphasis). In other words, Delepierre thinks that *Le Badin* and *Fouquet*—the Fool and the Husband—are *two different people.* Are they? And, if the Fool "takes the place of the husband" in Fouquet's bed in MASQUERADE #2, then where is Fouquet?

As foolish as any sotie, *Confession Follies* reads more like a *commedia*-styled, pre-Artaudian series of free-standing vignettes for mimed improvisation, subject to ever-changing fortunes. But, mercifully, on one point, the text is unequivocal: "Fouquet" is most definitely the husband. Both Mandy and Gwynnie speak his name no fewer than fifteen times, the latter pointing him out to the audience in her very first speech as *mon mary que* vous *voyez* ("my husband that you see" [1: 271; my emphasis]). And there's the rub. "Fouquet" is not named in the cast list, nor are any lines attributed to him *as* Fouquet. One male character alone is scripted—the generic *Badin*—which begs the question of the titular Fool's identity. If, indeed, the Fool is Fouquet-the-Husband, then, per Delepierre, how can he *take the place of* the husband in MASQUERADE #2 (*DLU*, 30)? And, if he's *not* Fouquet, who is he? Nor does it help that the Fool likes to refer to himself in the third person—and in the longest and most impenetrable speech of the play, no less (1: 278; below, note 16)—which leads to misprisions anticipatory of the *Seinfeld* episode in which "Jimmy likes Elaine." Here's the problem: officially, *Confession Follies* is a "farce for *three* characters, to wit, the Fool, the Wife, and the Chambermaid." It's the *Farce nouvelle à* troys [not *à quatre*] *personnaiges, c'est assavoir le Badin, la Femme, et la Chambrière.* "Three" is the magic number for Faivre, for whom the *Badin* is indisputably the Husband (*Répertoire*, 64–65); but Delepierre counted *four* and, to be perfectly honest, when I first read the play, so did I. So, who's onstage?

It's true, farce is notorious for its creative accounting. But it doesn't normally lose count of its cast members, all the more so in that most offerings went by such names as "The Farce for X Characters." Is it, therefore, the title that is wrong? Is *Confession Follies* a play for *four* characters? Could Gwynnie's husband be a Harpo Marx–like presence who is seen but not heard in the conventional *linguistic* way? In a script replete with onomatopoeia, is Fouquet's communication limited to the universal nonverbal language of grunting, groaning, coughing, and sneezing (below, § "Language")? As we shall see, the singular advantage of a fourth character in a maddeningly messy text is that it means only two substantive errors have occurred in its dissemination, one possibly having precipitated the other. The first is the misnomer about *trois personnages*; the second is the omission of "The Husband" from the cast list. (Analogous omissions have, in fact, been known to occur in such a play as the *Farce nouvelle des femmes qui apprennent à parler Latin* [*RC*, #17], projected for a future volume as *Chick Latin.*) This would also explain why the Fool speaks of Fouquet: that is, he is *not* Fouquet. Who, then, might that fourth character be? And can he resolve the central anomaly of the play?

As Gwynnie tells us in excruciating detail (1: 273, 278), Fouquet is an apoplectic savage. Upon learning of his wife's infidelity in MASQUERADE #1, there is no theory under which an inveterate abuser would fail to erupt in a murderous violence that would have stopped both Gwynnie and the play dead in their tracks. If Husband Fouquet, disguised as Maurice, was close enough to palpate his wife in MASQUERADE #1, there could be no MASQUERADE #2. Was the lack of verisimilitude at all problematic for the *farceur*? Probably not; but it certainly would be today. The solution lies in the mise-en-scène, which must be addressed forthwith under "Plot" in a commingling of all the usual categories of these Production Notes.

I submit that the Maurice-Impersonator and the Badin *of MASQUERADE #1 is not Fouquet at all but, rather, another character type as beloved in farce as he is in commedia and in Molière*: the *Badin* shall be Fouquet's nosy, meddlesome, disobedient trickster of a Valet. And he shall be called . . . wait for it . . . "Bozo." (Go with "Harpo," if you prefer, but that's the name I assigned to Tarabas of *Shit for Brains* [*FF*, #8].)

The presence of a valet is justified on several accounts: for one thing, the household is sufficiently wealthy to afford more than one chambermaid (1: 285). For another thing, it is not uncommon that a farcical valet—take Willy in *The Shithouse* (*HD*, #2)—would try to turn his mistress's adulterous assignation to his own advantage. In MASQUERADE #1, Bozo would likewise engage in a grope-fest of Gwynnie and—eureka!—once we make room for Fouquet's *valet*, most of the pieces of the puzzle fall into place thanks to a piece of stage business. When Fouquet cancels Mandy's Maurice-fetching errand, the serial manhandler, Fouquet, grabs *Bozo* by the scruff of the neck and conscripts his *valet* into playing Maurice in MASQUERADE #1. Fouquet can still spy on "Maurice" and Gwynnie—but *from outside* Gwynnie's bedroom window—from which vantage point he can *see*, at least partially, but not fully *hear* her adulterous avowal. (Either that, or he's a bit deaf.) This dramaturgical strategy then saves Gwynnie *and the play* from any showstopping violence because Fouquet doesn't hear the big reveal of her *liaison dangereuse*. But, wait, there's more:

Under those circumstances, MASQUERADE #1 is, logically, the last straw for Gwynnie. She cannot abide having had her upper-class self groped by a mere valet whom she would surely have recognized. After years of simmering resentment, moreover, she would have yet one more reason to get back at Fouquet, indubitably the author of this new indignity. Meanwhile, if a voyeuristic Fouquet is crouching at the window of Gwynnie's bedroom to watch Bozo play MASQUERADE #1, that position would clearly exacerbate the master's gout (particularly if he keeps falling over at key visual moments). Fouquet would thus be motivated to return to his bedroom, which is precisely where Gwynnie needs him for MASQUERADE #2. No showstopping violence there either because not only would Fouquet never have heard the confirmation of Gwynnie's adultery: Gwynnie's nun's habit would insulate her from reprisal. Even farce could scarcely stage, in real time, the assault of a nun. In any event, the subject of infidelity never comes up in MASQUERADE #2. Ergo, vengeance can be Gwynnie's; and, by analogy to the retaliatory pseudo-deathbed-confession scene of *Confession Lessons* (*FF*, 128–36), Gwynnie and Mandy can immobilize, discipline, and punish the vile Fouquet. At long last, the otherwise confusing closing aphorism about women's treachery makes sense. *Confession Follies* is rendered legible by a feminist dramaturgy that miraculously does three things. It faithfully preserves the misogynistic farcical tendency to insulate abusive men from formal legal consequences; it resolves most of the dramatic irregularities; and, in refusing to let Fouquet get off scot-free, it honors and updates a comedic legacy in which women take the law—and the farce—into their own hands.

Characters and Character Development

They all seem so familiar. The brutal, older, sicker, jealous, cuckold of a husband. The beaten-down, sexually rapacious, adulteress of a wife. The smart-alecky, unreliable, exploited chambermaid and, maybe, her male sidekick, the valet. But let's start with the character about whom the most information is divulged, even though he is never scripted by name. The husband's name derives from "Fouque" (< Germanic *Volk*), a fairly common moniker in the Loire region (the setting of *The Jackass Conjecture* [*HD*, 140–46]). Perhaps he is of German extraction and speaks with a German accent; but, regardless of how you hear him, he's bad *fouque*. Described in Scene 1 as huffing, puffing, and ready to blow, he's always burning up and—*quelle coincidence!*—*fouquet* was also a dangerously fiery game. Per Godefroy, it was "played by inserting a piece of cord up one nostril and lighting it on fire." The player then undertook to extinguish the blaze by blowing as hard as possible out of the other nostril, awakening pity for "the clumsier when they burned themselves." Play with Fouquet, you play with fire. Even in his isolation, disease, and despair, he is too much of a monster to elicit tragic pity. To add insult to injury, the crazy, nasty, shitty husband (*fol, infect, breneux*) is paranoid, underhanded, lonely, and melancholic. Gout *does* attack the joints; but how can he be both bedridden and on the move? Is he a trickster *feigning* illness? Is he in bed *fouque-ing* around with someone other than Gwynnie? With a random nun? Another man? A chambermaid who has little choice in the matter?

Like all the dramatis personae of *Confession Follies*, Fouquet is a study in contradictions. For Faivre and Delepierre, he is no fool when "playing the dying man tongue-in-cheek" (*Répertoire*, 65; *DLU*, 30). But that's *exactly* who he is: *fool* enough—*Fool* enough?—to be a trickster tricked, a bully ultimately flattened by the same violence that he inflicts upon others. *Whence my Two-Fool Conjecture.* Fouquet is the Fool-Husband, to be flanked here by a second fool, Bozo-the-Valet. But, in keeping with the original foolishness, why not go crazy and cast twins or, crazier still, a single actor in a dual role?

N.B. For fidelity to the original text, I've nevertheless scripted Le Badin as The Fool but I've indicated in brackets, when need be, who I think he is at any given moment: Bozo or Fouquet. For the sake of clarity in the two Masquerades—and, as I did in At Cross Purposes *(FF, 220–21)—I've relied on such overdeterminations as "Bozo-as-Maurice," "Gwynnie-as-Nun," "the Fool-Husband," "Bozo-the-Valet," and so forth.*[1]

The volatile Fool is scripted a full fifty-five times, often with Mandy by his side and, just as often, sounding more like a valet than a master. In many ways, he is the loquacious star of the show who is none the more decipherable for all that speechifying. For example, he opens the farce with a pleasurable song about pleasure, which is out of character for the hateful Fouquet . . . unless the Husband is in bed with somebody other than Gwynnie . . . which would then shed an entirely different light on all his onomatopoetic groaning. During MASQUERADE #1, he sighs that he'd rather be having sex with the chambermaid in the woods (1: 280), which may be what prompted Faivre to surmise that the Fool has been conspiring with Mandy the whole time (*Répertoire*, 65). But, if he has easy access to Mandy, why go to all the trouble of arranging that masquerade in the first place? This is farce. Check. He's a *fool.* Check. But *which fool*? A despicable Fouquet would be hankering to spy on Gwynnie; an intrusive Bozo would be delighted to be penetrating her inner sanctum, where a valet is not expected to serve; and he could still be surprised by what he learns of Gwynnie's extracurricular activities with Father Maurice. Equally plausibly, Bozo could be in cahoots with Mandy—even married to her—taking her side (albeit from self-interest) against a mistress and a master who abuse her. As in *Blind Man's Buff*, servants who work together play, plot, and scheme together (*FF*, 182–91). But what—and whom—are they playing?

Normally, we can count on *vous* vs. *tu* to resolve questions of social intercourse. In *Confession Follies*, not so much; but a brief parenthetical is in order for the language of *all* the characters. For the most part, and as expected, Mandy addresses her mistress with *vous*, while Gwynnie answers with *tu*. Gwynnie uses the courteous *vous* with "Father Maurice," aka The-Fool-in-Disguise, and vice versa; and "Father Maurice" says *vous* to Gwynnie and *tu* to Mandy. The Fool—whoever he may be—addresses Gwynnie with *vous* and Mandy with *tu*; and both of these would be appropriate: the former between noble husband and wife and the latter between master and servant, *servant* and *servant,* or *servant-playing-master* and *servant.* In MASQUERADE #2, Gwynnie-as-Nun engages the Fool with *vous* for Fouquet; plus, let's not forget that *anyone* would use *vous* for declarations to the *audience.* Now, take this curious moment in MASQUERADE #2, when the Fool in Fouquet's bed swears: *Dieu* te *mauldie / Quant par toy me fault mourir* or "God damn you, you're the one who's killing me!" (1: 284). Who is talking to whom? Faivre understands the line as an exasperated *sotto voce* from the Fool-Husband, Fouquet, targeting a poorly concealed Gwynnie-as-Nun (*Répertoire*, 65). But, unless it's an improper eruption again, *tu* would be highly irregular from a well-heeled husband to his wife, and downright rude from a valet to a mistress. Is the remark directed at Mandy? At an obstreperous spectator? At Bozo? Again, *the Two-Fool conjecture resolves a great many of the difficulties.* Bozo is the Father Maurice Impersonator in MASQUERADE #1; Fouquet is himself in MASQUERADE #2.

Furthermore, any deviation from the linguistic norm can be chalked up to one of these things: an emotional aside by an emotionally overwrought character; a servant's imitation or mockery of the master or mistress; or *anybody's* imitation of Father Maurice's or the Nun's *politesse*. For that last one, it's logical that even Mandy would *vousvoyer* Bozo when he's playing Maurice, and there's one more thing: a servant breaking through with *tu* when *vous* is de rigueur is perfectly in keeping with a character type that is considered innately lowbrow. Readers might be familiar with the convention from Marivaux's eighteenth-century *Game of Love and Chance* in which Arlequin can't manage to keep up the linguistic pretense of elegance for two minutes. When our Fool makes his déclassé boasts about his erections or his rise to the loftiest heights of the afterlife (1: 272, 281, 287), it's all part and parcel of farce's usual elitist barb at the foolishness of upwardly mobile servants. And all's classist well that ends classist well.

As for the unnamed wife, I've christened her "Gwynnie" because her opening prayer to Saint Genevieve sounds much like Guinevere's "Where Are the Simple Joys of Maidenhood?" from *Camelot* (1: 271, 274). Part victim, part abuser (of Mandy), part adulteress, and part straight woman, Gwynnie bewails from her bed a life marred by domestic violence. Today, we would qualify her as a survivor of marital rape; and, until she dons her nun's attire, hers is the vexed and vexing role of a supremely tragic figure. Regularly chastened into submission and largely denied even the comforts of a confidante, Gwynnie revisits the cycle of violence upon Mandy and struggles to find solace in the arms of Father Maurice. Her communication is more grammatically elegant than that of the other characters; so, she might be of noble (or nobler) birth. In the masquerades, for instance, her use of *vous* with "Maurice" is impeccable, as is the "Nun's" with Fouquet. She can also cite the odd liturgical phrase, be it from her regular attendance at Mass or from all those tête-à-têtes with Father Maurice (the former, an ideal alibi for the latter). But, as with all the dramatis personae, there are anomalies, chief among them: her plot-driven but completely unverisimilar command that Mandy fetch Maurice. Although consonant with the *farceur*'s sexist view of female sexuality, it strains twenty-first-century credibility that a woman recovering from a recent assault would be in the mood for sex. (Minimally, this would demand that some time elapse, as it will here so that Gwynnie may take charge of her own sexuality [below, § "Sets and Staging"].) Then again, there's a small underlying hint as to why. She makes a fascinating statement about the condition of her tummy or uterus (*la pance*) that sounds suspiciously like pregnancy (1: 281). Perhaps the urgency of the rendezvous with the good father is not a sex-seeking act at all but the panic-move of a terrified victim of abuse who must share the news with the father of her bastard child. And that's not all.

Another anomaly concerns Gwynnie's intellect. She is patently clever enough to plot MASQUERADE #2. Is she simultaneously stupid enough to fail to recognize the Fool-as-Maurice in MASQUERADE #1? (Unless, of course, she never spends much time looking at Father Maurice's *face.*) Faivre contends that the Wife, initially buying the story of her husband's impending death, "figures out *eventually* that it's the Fool in Father Maurice's clothing and decides to get back at him" (*Répertoire,* 64–65). But how long is "eventually"? Ultimately, it's a choice between feminist dramaturgy and, as Faivre intimates, an almost *Marriage-of-Figaro* moment when a brutalized wife responds to her husband's first-ever signs of physical tenderness (*Répertoire,* 65). *Once again, the Two-Fool conjecture is clarifying*: it's Bozo-the-Valet manhandling Gwynnie in MASQUERADE #1, and the Valet *or* Fouquet whom *she's* manhandling in MASQUERADE #2. Under that theory, Gwynnie—who is nobody's fool—handily identifies Bozo as the Maurice Impersonator, which would fuel further outrage against a husband who not only beats her but has now positioned his *valet* to feel her up. More dispositive still: that scenario finally justifies one of the most bizarre utterances of the play when, during MASQUERADE #1, she tells "Father Maurice" to stop the very pat-downs for which she had purportedly summoned him (1: 280). He's *not* Maurice and she knows it. And, best of all, it resolves the question of why a battered wife would be so daft as to cite chapter and verse of Maurice's caresses in the presence of her abuser: she *wouldn't be. He's not there.* Fouquet is outside. Bottom line for Gwynnie: *she does not suffer fools gladly.*

The name of our third official character, spoken nine times, is "Mannette," "Megnette," or "Mennette," all diminutives of "Mary," all denoting a small "hand" or "basket" (if not yet "handcuffs"). I toyed with "Minnie," "Manon," and, for the longest time, "Mary-Annette," owing to the other characters' efforts to reduce her to a mere "marionette." But she is no Bergsonian puppet going through motions, no matter how jack-in-the-box-like she pops up with a vengeance ("Laughter," chap. 2). In the end, I went with "Mary-Amanda," "Mandy" for short. The Chambermaid might not be fully "loved by God" (< Latin, *amanda*); but she repels everybody's *man*ipulations and *man*splaining, even as they hector and threaten her with the "dear," "baby," and "honey," reserved for children or servants (*ma mye, m'amye*). Mandy is scapegoat and soubrette, actress and smart-ass. She's a worthy forerunner to Molière's Dorine of *Tartuffe* and a scene-stealer who lands some of the farce's funniest lines. Still, for so central a player, she too is inscrutable. We can assume that Mandy is sufficiently churchgoing to trot out a prayer like the *tu autem* (1: 281); and I take her at her word that Gwynnie beats her (1: 276). But to whom, if anyone, is she loyal?

There is definitely no love lost between maid and mistress. Mandy would have just cause to turn on both boss Fouquet *and* coworker and/or paramour Bozo. Some Fool or other has arranged for her front-row seat at the grope-fest of her mistress, which might piss off any chambermaid, loyal or disloyal. But could Mandy really be so cruel as to tell Fouquet that Gwynnie wants him dead, thereby all but guaranteeing a vicious retaliation (1: 273; below, note 8)? Faivre and Delepierre see her as starting out on Gwynnie's side, only to switch to Fouquet's during MASQUERADE #2 (*Répertoire*, 65; *DLU*, 30). But why would she take up violent Gwynnie's cause? To unite against a common enemy? Or is it, rather, that the voluptuous Mandy *has* been *fouquet-ing* around with the master all along? If so, I hasten to emphasize that such relations would have been about as "consensual" as those of Sally Hemings "with" Thomas Jefferson, Carrie Butler "with" Strom Thurmond, or in #7, *Bro Job*, Pricker-Upper "with" the aster of the house. Such coercion, moreover, would elucidate Mandy's allusion to what Fouquet has "put her through" (1: 272). While farce customarily pokes fun at the lives of chambermaids, the sad social reality was that female servants were raped by masters and valets alike.[2] Mandy's accent, dialect, and grammar will be crucial to the role: maybe savvier lingo in her conversations with Gwynnie but a sarcastic "slave-speak" with Fouquet, in which she assimilates the politics of the oppressor. (Feel free to change her dialect as you see fit.) For me, the bottom line is that Mandy's true allegiance lies with her favorite interlocutor: the audience. And that's whose side she's on. *Ours*.

Finally, one might stage a number of nonspeaking characters, starting with the chambermaids, of whom there are clearly several. Depending on the level of wackiness, the real Father Maurice might put in an appearance too. He is part priest, part doctor (*Répertoire*, 64), and, like his *confrères* in *Brother Fillerup* (#6) and *Slick Brother Willy* (#11), all lover boy. Perhaps, like Willy, he is present at first, only to beat a hasty, half-naked retreat before the action proper begins... which would account for that cassock-disguise conveniently on hand for MASQUERADE #1 (as one was in *Confession Lessons* [*FF*, 118]). Or perhaps he has laid healing hands upon a beaten-down Gwynnie so recently that he hasn't yet left the premises, which would allow for further insanity. Additionally, since a nun's habit is likewise on hand in Gwynnie's chamber for MASQUERADE #2, has a sister been offering Gwynnie succor? Or has the nun been succoring Fouquet? Go ahead: go as full-on absurdist as #8, *Johnny Palmer*. You can't have too much folly in the *Follies*.

Language

I reserve for note 16 the corrupt and mind-bogglingly difficult lines that announce MASQUERADE #1. For now, I confine myself to this observation about nonverbal comedy, which often takes a back seat to language per se. On one hand, there are multiple gestural demonstratives like "there he is!" "come here!" or "go there!" contributing to the overall problem of being in two places at once. On the other hand, as in *Wife Swap* (*HD*, 305–97), there is a profusion of onomatopoetic emissions of pain or pleasure: the *a!* of "hey," "ah," and "aha"; the rip-roaring clamor of laughter, farting, and sneezing; and the achoo! of *esse, esse, esse, esse!* or *etesecs*, which sounds like "etcetera" (1: 272, 284). Corporeal noise is even vaguely liturgical, harkening back to the original *farsae* or *farsurae*, an early term for the Kyrie or Sanctus of the Mass (Davis, *Farce*, 7). Consider, toward the end, Gwynnie-as-Nun's "we acknowledge thee to be the Lord. All the earth doth worship thee, the everlasting Father." In lieu of the correct Latin (*te aeternum* patrem *omnis terra veneratur*), she twists it into *te* eternum putrem / *omnis terra veneratur* (1: 286), which approximates the snotty sexuality of sneezing, veneration, and other venereal activities. The same goes for the obscene transformation of such sacred prayers as the *Tu autem* (1: 281) and the *Te Deum* (1: 286–87), the latter associated with deathbed confessions.[3] May they all rest in pieces.

Sets and Staging

The sick house is comprised of two bedrooms separated by a common area with a large table. Fouquet's quarters might be located house left, the "sinister" side, and Gwynnie's, house right. As was the case in *Wife Swap*, where I proposed an entire series of alternate endings (*HD*, 311–17), dramaturgy will clinch what *Confession Follies* is or is not to be. Its extreme lack of textual clarity invites near limitless artistic freedom in one of the scenically busier farces. As a prelude to Scene 1, I recommend a mimed montage of scenes from a troubled household, including but not limited to Gwynnie's liaison with Father Maurice, Bozo's and Mandy's relationships (sexual or other) with their employers and with each other, Mandy's unhappy inability to execute contradictory orders (as in *Playing Doctor* [*FF*, 200–204]), and above all, Fouquet's violence. To the extent that the horrific beatings of Gwynnie are stageable at all, they could possibly work as *comédie-ballets* (*FF*, #5 and #6); or they might already tease the rise of a dominatrix in a more physiological version of what Natalie Zemon Davis famously called "Women on Top." Such a mimed overture might also serve to establish some soupçon of the female comity that will be required at the end of the play. Have the women make a silent sisterly pact, fight back, or break free.

In MASQUERADE #1, we're in the world of physical comedy, here revolving around the Fool's need for three hands. Whoever is impersonating Father Maurice—Fouquet or Bozo—the comedy, tragedy, or tragicomedy resides in his holding a Bible or rosary in one hand, "healing" Gwynnie with the other, and pawing Mandy with a third one. When the scene shifts to Fouquet's bedroom for MASQUERADE #2, the positions are materially reversed. It's the Fool abed now, albeit with an ongoing need for three hands: one for feeling up Mandy, another for any deathbed-related rituals, and a third to defend himself from any attack from Gwynnie-as-Nun (with or without Mandy's aid). But here's the kicker: it's unquestionably Fouquet in bed. Gwynnie-as-Nun repeatedly hails him as such; and she is savvy enough to recognize her own husband. If, however, there are, in fact, two Fools onstage—Fouquet and Bozo—then where's Bozo?

Of a panoply of possibilities, this is the one that best resolves the issues: give Bozo a motivation to be front and center at MASQUERADE #2, and have him shove Fouquet under a blanket and jump into the bed while the master is still in there![4] From there, Bozo can turn in what he means to be a credible performance of the invalid's ways. Not only does this clarify the Fool's curious line about "Gwynnie" *killing him* (1: 284; above, § "Plot"): that line is now directed at *Bozo*, who is trying to stifle Fouquet under the covers. This strategy also has the singular advantage of allowing Fouquet to continue to contribute onomatopoetically, but as a constrained lump in the bed. Of course he's sneezing and choking! He's *suffocating* under the covers until—at last—the coup de grâce! Now in league and highly motivated to avenge themselves, Gwynnie and Mandy deactivate the oppressors, tying up one or both with rosary beads and settling the score with a flogging.

Costumes and Props

The stage is littered with three categories of object: comestible medicines (or liquors and wines *passing as* medicine), plus a well-stocked bar; multiple canes or walking sticks to support locomotion and physical violence, at least one in every room (baseball bats, sticks, rods, rolling pins, etc.); and religious paraphernalia (icons, rosaries, Bibles, and a bottle for holy water that resembles a flask). Fouquet's sick room is overflowing with chamber pots and soiled cloths, if somewhat less so than the fetid dwelling in *Shit for Brains* (*FF*, 258–859); and both bedrooms feature a standing chest or *coffre* at the foot of each bed. Gwynnie's chest holds a nun's costume; and a cassock is lying in the main room, a leftover from prior performances, not necessarily thespian.

Mandy might sport a French maid's outfit; and Gwynnie and Fouquet are wearing long-sleeved dressing gowns, the latter's very soiled. Bozo is in butler's garb, which comes in handy for his Maurice-impersonation; but he should always look maximally foolish with a fool's cap, which he could forget to remove during MASQUERADE #1. The unholy trio—or unwholesome foursome—is now ready to take it away.

Scholarly References to Copyrighted Materials (in order of appearance and indicated by © within the text)

"The Simple Joys of Maidenhood." By Alan Jay Lerner and Frederick Loewe. Music Theatre International. https://www.mtishows.com/camelot.
"Wrigley's Spearmint Gum [jingle]." By Steve Karmen. ASCAP Work ID: 570016664.
"Il est de nôtres." Traditional.
"Ya Got Trouble." By Meredith Willson. ASCAP ID: 550000489.
"Dang Me." By Roger Miller. BMI Work #275944.
"Evil Woman." By Jeffrey Lynne. BMI Work #393757.
"My Way." By Paul Anka, Claude François, Jacques Rivaud, and Gilles Thibaut. BMI Work #1044656.
"And When I Die." By Laura Nyro. BMI Work #40714.
"The Rhythm Is Gonna Get You." By Gloria Estefan and Enrique Garcia. BMI Work #1248618.
"Two Tickets to Paradise." By Eddie Money. BMI Work #1564326.
"Hosanna." By Andrew Lloyd-Webber and Timothy Rice. ASCAP Work ID: 381488533.

"The Hallelujah Chorus." From George Frideric Handel's *Messiah* (1741).
"That's the Way I Like It." By Harry Wayne Casey and Rick Finch. BMI Work #1481515.
"Greensleeves" ["What Child Is This?"]. Traditional ballad.

[Scene 1]

[*Lights up on the home of Fouquet and Gwynnie. To the strains of incongruously beautiful music, a mimed flashback might choreograph the household's troubled history, culminating in Fouquet's most recent assault on Gwynnie. Lights down and, then, up again to signal time elapsed. Each abed in their separate chambers, Fouquet is fuming and Gwynnie is in prayer, picking up her icons consecutively. Mandy and Bozo stand hand in hand in the main room until a great commotion summons them to Gwynnie and Fouquet, respectively. They look in from the thresholds and return center stage, electing instead to call out their responses to Master and Mistress from the main room.*]

The FOOL [BOZO] *begins [in song]*

You know what they say, folks: Pleasure is as pleasure was, as pleasure was! Easy come, easy go. A fool and his honey are soon parted.[5]

The WIFE, GWYNNIE

[Oh, Genevieve, Saint Genevieve! It's Gwynnie here, remember me?] Oh, Genevieve, Saint Genevieve!© Right over there! for all to see: [the great provider! The great provide-*her*!] Haven't I put up with enough from that husband of mine? [From now on, I intend to pray to someone else instead!©]

[*She grabs a different icon.*] Save me, o blessed Virgin. How many times have I implored you to watch over me? Haven't I put up with enough from that husband of mine? Right over there for all to see!

THE FOOL [FOUQUET]

[*To Gwynnie*] Wherever you are, I can hear you, so you better hold your tongue!

[{*To the audience*} And that goes for you too, folks! [Shut up!]

The CHAMBERMAID, MANDY

Oh, *puh-lease*. Don't you be startin' in again now, Fouquet! *Sir*.

GWYNNIE

What's he on about this time?

[*Mandy moves slowly toward the threshold of Fouquet's bedroom and lingers there.*]

MANDY

[*To the audience*] What? Me hurry? [Check it out, *fouques*:] He's got it so bad, he's gonna bust a gut. Omigod, what a pig! Huffin' and puffin' till—watch out!—he's gonna blow! Just imagine what a victory it would be to get rid of him once and for all. Omigod! There'd be no sin in that, after everything he's put me through.[6]

[GWYNNIE

Oh *my* God! There'd be no sin in that, after everything he's put *me* through! If only I could get someone to off him. Vengeance would be mine, sayeth the wife!]

The FOOL [FOUQUET] *sneezes*

A-a-a-choo!

MANDY

God bless you, sir! [{*Sotto voce*} And God *help you*!]

GWYNNIE

Thar' she blows! Wait for it . . . [*The Fool* {*Fouquet*} *sneezes.*] That was a big one.

THE FOOL [BOZO]

[*To the audience*] I got a big one too, by God! Check out how stiff! [*Fouquet grabs a stick and is disappointed by the lack of response.*]

MANDY

No, seriously: I pray that Jesus succor you.

THE FOOL [FOUQUET]
Oh, Mandy?

MANDY
What's up, *sir*?[7]

THE FOOL [FOUQUET]
I'm dying here.

MANDY
Now why would you wanna go and do a thing like that?

THE FOOL [FOUQUET]
What's *Madame* on about?

MANDY
She says if you were six feet under, *sir*, then, body and soul, she'd be free at last, free at last, good God Almighty, free at last![8]

THE FOOL [FOUQUET]
[*Struggling to rise from bed and brandishing his cane*] Screw her! If it weren't for all those scary folks out there . . . I'd pop her one in a minute! As if I can't get up—*get it up*—for a good pop! And I'd have me a thing or two to say to you too, toots![9]

MANDY
Whatchoo talkin' about?

THE FOOL [FOUQUET]
Crazy bitch! I know better than to say anything to *you*.

[*With easy access to the liquor in the main room, the two servants partake and engage in nonlinguistic activities.*]

GWYNNIE
Oh, Mandy?

THE FOOL [BOZO]

Chitter, chatter, yakkety-yakkety-yak!© [*Gwynnie bangs her cane.*] On your mark, get set . . . And she's off!

MANDY

I'll be right there.

GWYNNIE

By all means, move at a glacial pace, you know how that thrills me. And get your fat ass in here now!

[*Mandy heads to Gwynnie's bedroom while Bozo finds a corner in the main room where he indulges in food and drink.*]

[Scene 2]

[*In Gwynnie's bedroom*]

[GWYNNIE]

Get over here, girl! Closer! Do you or do you not remember the time that son of a bitch, Fouquet, beat the crap outta me and chased me all the way down the street with a wooden stick?[10] Damn fool!

MANDY

Rings a bell.

GWYNNIE

Damn! And I'm getting it from all sides now? Cuts like a knife every time. Sweet Jesus—and you too, Saint Genevieve—[it's Gwynnie here, remember me?©]—this I pray: deliver me from that fool—and this whole damn corpus—once and for all and make me a widow!
Now, tell me, girl: where was it that he hit me again?
Mandy?

MANDY

On the side, ma'am.

GWYNNIE

On the side is right! [And whose side are *you* on anyway?]
Now, get outta here and go tell that nasty prick, Fouquet, that, if I die from that beating, I'm going to Heaven and *he's* going straight to hell. Guilty, guilty, guilty for all eternity! And you be sure to tell him I'm gonna sic the law on him too if he doesn't let me outta this thing.

MANDY

I'll get on that right away. [*She doesn't move.*]
[{*To the audience*} What am I? *Maid* to order here?]

GWYNNIE

And, by all means, take your time.
[*Fouquet erupts in another coughing fit.*] Don't tell me he hasn't choked to death yet. He really outdid himself that time. Somebody oughta stuff a sock in it.

MANDY

And you know very well he's in bed, poor bastard. All laid up. Down for the count. Not a friend in the world to comfort him in his hour of need.[11]

GWYNNIE

His hour of need? Ha! The hell you say, girl! Now, get out of here already and go tell Father Maurice to get a move on. [*Mandy still doesn't move.*]
Now! Tell him to get his ass back over here pronto and—oh, sister!—frock me up. Noon sharp. Go on! What the hell are you waiting for? [Help me with my makeup!]
A little hands-on healing will do a body good, as I've known for quite some time now. But you know what?

MANDY

What's that, ma'am?

GWYNNIE

Tell him to be sure not to forget the holy water. His little flask o' Saint Pauli, girl.[12]

MANDY

I'll be sure to give him the message.

GWYNNIE

Go on, then, get out of here! But you know what?

MANDY

What's that, ma'am?

GWYNNIE

Not one word outta you to that prick!

MANDY

Which prick would that be, ma'am?

GWYNNIE

That nasty shithead, Fouquet!

MANDY

[Oh, *that* shithead!] Thanks for clearing that up for me.

[*After another coughing fit, Fouquet proceeds to the main room.*]

GWYNNIE

Let him stew in his own juices till he chokes! If only the gout would rot his damn joints and muzzle him for good! Now, be sure to tell Father Maurice exactly what I told you. I've got a reputation to consider, you know.

[*Exit Mandy*]

[Scene 3]

[*In the common area*]

THE FOOL [FOUQUET]

Hey, hey, hey! Where does Mandy think she's going? Somethin' fishy goin' on?[13]

MANDY

Can't stop now. Don't have time.

THE FOOL [FOUQUET]

I say: Hey, hey, hey! Where does Mandy think she's going?

MANDY

If I take too long, I'll get in trouble with Madame.

THE FOOL [FOUQUET]

And hey, hey, hey! Where does Mandy think she's going? Somethin' fishy goin' on? [And, by the way, how's tricks?]

MANDY

If I weren't so scared o' gettin' smacked around, I'd have me a thing or two to tell you about what's goin' down around here.

THE FOOL [FOUQUET]

Speak up, girl! Go on, speak!

MANDY

[You wanna know how's tricks?] It's the mistress. She's hurtin' in her lady parts.[14] I gotta go fetch Father Maurice so he can fix her up.

THE FOOL [FOUQUET]

Is that so?

MANDY

[*She grabs a bottle of beer and makes the sign of the cross.*] And, he's supposed to have his flask o' Saint Pauli on him too.

THE FOOL [FOUQUET]

A flask, is it? I bet he's fillin' up right now.

MANDY

All the way.

[THE FOOL, {FOUQUET}

Knockin' back a few.

MANDY

Ave Maria, gratia plena. Knockin' up just *one*!][15]

THE FOOL [FOUQUET]

[*He sings.*] *Au mentibus, aux fessibus, au sexybus! Et glou et glou et glou et glou et glou . . .* © One word gets out about this—if he spills—is there ever gonna be trouble! [With a capital "T" and that rhymes with "P" and that stands for Fool!©]

MANDY

[{*Sotto voce*} "P" does *not* stand for "fool," fool!]
In the name of Saint Johnson, Master! She said I cain't say nothin' to nobody and that I gots to step on it and fetch *Monsieur* right away.

THE FOOL [FOUQUET]

Not if I beat her at her own game and pull the old switcheroo.

MANDY

Whatchoo talkin' about?

THE FOOL [FOUQUET]

Nothing up my sleeve and . . . abracadabra! Magician, heal thyself! I'll turn the tables on her. Observe. [*He grabs a staff, taps it on the table, does a quick Tramp routine à la Charlie Chaplin, and beats it on the table.*]

MANDY

Is that before or after I get the crap beat outta me?

THE FOOL [FOUQUET]

She comes after you and—! Might makes right! That's *my* rule of thumb. Now get back in there! Go cry your eyes out. Do a whole production: "the Devil take you" and what-have-you. Nothing to be scared of. But I'm not fooling around and—. In the name of all that's holy, I've got a few tricks of my own up my sleeve for the good Father and—. Just you watch: [No more *fool*ing around! Wait for it . . .]

[*After Fouquet locates a cassock, he interrupts Bozo's repast, grabs his valet by the scruff of the neck, and conveys gesturally to a resentful Bozo that the Valet must transform himself into Father Maurice.*]
[Presto change-o!] I'll take care o' Maurice, all right. Now, get back in there and tell her I swore on a stack o' Bibles that, unless he hears my confession, no more Fouquet! We'll soon see who's *fouquing* over whom under *my* roof! Home sweet home, my ass! [{*Menacingly*} Unless you're expecting me to play the role myself.][16]

MANDY
I do believe, sir, that, in this whole town, there's no dirtier trickster than you.
[{*To the audience*} *Fouquin'* awesome. Uh-huh.]

[*As Mandy rehearses in mime for* MASQUERADE #1, *Fouquet continues to prepare Bozo with Bible, rosary, and a flask of holy water.*]

[Scene 4]

[*Mandy ensures that her histrionic rush to the front door is seen by both Gwynnie and Fouquet. Bozo lingers in the main room to observe; and Fouquet lingers menacingly behind Mandy.*]

GWYNNIE
[*Calling out to Mandy*] And where the hell do you think *you're* going?

MANDY
And God only knows. Fouquet done come and gone.

GWYNNIE
If only it had been to the gallows—hanged by the neck until he was dead—and drowned at the bottom of the sea. But I said: Where do you think you're going?

MANDY
And God only knows. Fouquet done come and gone.

GWYNNIE

Is that so?

MANDY

[*Tearfully*] Unto the Lord, he done commend his spirit! That's what they say.

GWYNNIE

Oh, gimme a break. And you're crying about it? I swear! In the name of Saint Benedict, [they ought to take a rope and hang him! Or skin him alive!©] If only he'd died ten years ago! No skin off my nose. Things would have been a damn sight better around here for me. So, gimme a break, I said, and get over here! Did you talk to Father Maurice or what?

MANDY

Yes, ma'am, he's right behind me. He said he'd be right with you as soon as he heard the master's confession. Should be along any minute now.

GWYNNIE

Aha! Just what the doctor ordered!

MANDY

[*Loudly, as if Bozo has missed his cue*] I say, look! Here he comes. Quick and dirty. Even broke a sweat. [{*To the audience*} Like a pig. Again.]

[Scene 5: Masquerade #1]

[*In Gwynnie's bedroom*]

The FOOL [Bozo] *puts on his priest disguise* [*and, with a big shove from Fouquet, makes his entrance into Gwynnie's bedroom. Still abed, Gwynnie sees Fouquet exit the house and position himself outside her window.*]

Howdy-doo, there, sister, howdy-doo, there, missy. How are we holding up today, babe?[17]

GWYNNIE

Fine for now, "Father," but fear today, spawn tomorrow.

THE FOOL [BOZO-as-MAURICE]

[*Fondling his rosary and Mandy*] 'Tis but the cares of this world, babe. Howdy-doo, there, sister, howdy-doo, there, missy. I best get to work on you right away. [{*To Mandy*} And—oh, sister!—I'll plow *your* fuckin' field any time!]

GWYNNIE

And not a moment too soon. You've been a very bad boy, you big ape, and—I give you fair warning—you deserve a spanking. Now quit fooling around, Father Maurice, and watch those magic hands![18]

THE FOOL [BOZO-as-MAURICE]

[*Sotto voce*] I wish to God me and the chambermaid was out bushwhackin' in the woods right now. Back in the saddle, takin' them reins, groomin' that horsey![19] [*He tries to usher Mandy out the door.*]

GWYNNIE

That's quite enough of that, Father Maurice. What? Leaving so soon?

THE FOOL [BOZO-as-MAURICE]

Tell me, *Madame*, where does it hurt?

GWYNNIE

Right up here, around my tummy.
[What does he need? A road map?]

THE FOOL [BOZO-as-MAURICE]

[*Attempting to palpate Gwynnie*] Just a little bit above the thigh?

GWYNNIE

Knock it off, Father Maurice. [Damn fool! If thine thigh offend me, *fouque* it out!] [*She "accidentally" knees him.*]

THE FOOL [FOUQUET]

[*Aside, from his spot outside the window*] Good luck curin' *that*!

GWYNNIE

Oops! Sorry about that.

THE FOOL [BOZO-as-MAURICE]

[*He tries again while pressing against Mandy.*] It's *here*, right? Feel how stiff.

GWYNNIE

[*She knees Bozo again.*] Oops! You're on the wrong side! Now quit rubbing me the wrong way!

THE FOOL [BOZO-as-MAURICE]

Yeah, yeah, yeah, I get it, missy, Jeez! But, sometimes, when the good doctor lays hands on a little lady, you gotta go for it, you know? [*Groping Mandy again*] I swear: Whenever I'm around you, I'm—ten-hut!—hard as a rock and—scooby, dooby, doo!—brave as a Swiss![20]

MANDY

[*To the audience*] [And who could remain neutral in the presence of *that*?]

Would you listen to Father Maurice! That's some service! [He'll be all over the *anus dei* in a minute!] *Et tu autem*, Padre?

THE FOOL [BOZO-as-MAURICE]

Got my finger on the [w]hole problem right here!

GWYNNIE

Jesus Christ! How very subtle of you.

THE FOOL [BOZO-as-MAURICE]

As if you'd know better than the doctor! The world's greatest homeopath!

GWYNNIE

A real doctor of souls would be homeopathing me like crazy by now—damn straight—as usual. Bleed me two or three times till I'm red as a lobster. And then flip me over.

THE FOOL [FOUQUET]

[*Loudly, as he strains to hear*] Say what? Say who?

[THE FOOL {BOZO-as-MAURICE}

Say what? Say who?]

GWYNNIE

[*Gwynnie compromises Bozo's disguise, flips herself over and farts.*] Say *you*, Father Maurice. You know: when you were attending to me.[21]

THE FOOL [BOZO-as-MAURICE]

[*Committed to proving his success to the voyeuristic Fouquet*] Shut up! Shut up! Evil woman!© I'll thank you to abide by the teachings of the Church, madam—I swear!—and I'm leaving right now.

GWYNNIE

Oh, [I get it.] I'm not afraid if my chambermaid hears. She finds out everything anyway. Like when you were wrapped around me so tight, I could hardly breathe? And you were saying: "Don't worry, I'll make a handmaid outta you yet. You mind *your ménage*, I'll mind my *ménage-à-trois*."[22]

THE FOOL [FOUQUET]

[*Loudly*] Say what? Say who?

[THE FOOL {BOZO-as-MAURICE}

Say what? Say who?]

GWYNNIE

Say, *you*, Father Maurice.

THE FOOL [BOZO-as-MAURICE]

It must've slipped my mind.

GWYNNIE

It was that day Fouquet was all laid up in front of the fire. And, then, after a bit, you came creeping on in to lay hands on me. In bed. Don't tell me you don't remember.

THE FOOL [BOZO-as-MAURICE]

No way! I swear.

GWYNNIE

Careful! You know what God does to liars. Wow.

THE FOOL [BOZO-as-MAURICE]

But what about poor Fouquet, sick that he is? I really feel his pain.

MANDY

I'm sure sorry as hell about it!

GWYNNIE

[*To Mandy*] Sorry? You can take your pity and shove it up your ass! If he drowns at the bottom of the Seine, you think it's some great loss? Small potatoes. In fact, I say we go look in on him right now and play a little trick of our own. On *him*. [Burnabout is fair play.]

THE FOOL [BOZO-as-MAURICE]

You do that. I'll be off now to say Mass while you two go see Fouquet.

[*From outside Gwynnie's window, Fouquet notices Bozo's departure preparations. He hastens back to his bed.*]

GWYNNIE

Adieu, *Monsieur*, [go with God].

THE FOOL [BOZO]

God, my ass! We'll soon see what He's got in store for you!

[*Exit Bozo in great haste to Fouquet's bedroom, where he dives under the covers with his master, whom he will impersonate.*]

[Scene 6]

[*In Gwynnie's bedroom*]

GWYNNIE

You know what? How about we dress me up like a nun? And be quick about it, girl. I'll go do a whole lamentation number on Fouquet.

[*Mandy rummages through the large chest at the foot of Gwynnie's bed. She might even head for the wings to consult briefly with the props master before returning with a nun's habit.*]

MANDY

Here you go. This one oughta do the trick. Fits like a glove. Tight as a nun's ass.

[*To the audience*] What? She'll be kickin' that habit in no time!

[Scene 7: Masquerade #2]

[*In Fouquet's bedroom*]

THE FOOL[s]

A-A-A-A-choo!

[*Enter Mandy and Gwynnie-as-Nun.*]

GWYNNIE-as-Nun

Bless you, Fouquet.

THE FOOL [BOZO-as-FOUQUET]

Madame, right back at . . . at . . . *at-choo*! [*After both men sneeze again, Bozo delivers an over-the-top deathbed performance.*]

GWYNNIE-as-NUN

And now, the end is near and so you face the final curtain.© You might have a care, *Monsieur*, for your immortal soul in the great hereafter.

THE FOOL [FOUQUET]

[*Sotto voce*] *Et tu*, Mandy? [*Bozo attempts repeatedly to stifle him.*] I'm dying here. Again, God damn it!—and you're the one who's killing me![23] O Lord, why have you forsaken me?

GWYNNIE-as-NUN

Lord, have mercy! Careful, sir, lest you rot in hell. [*Semper et aeternum.*]

THE FOOL [BOZO-as-FOUQUET]

Hell shmell! It's all Greek-style to me. I'm not scared o' dyin' and I don't really care!©[24] [*More sneezing ensues.*]

MANDY

Bless you, Fouquet.

THE FOOL [BOZO-as-FOUQUET]

Bless *you*, Mandy!

MANDY

I am your humble servant. Totally [fuckin'] servicing you all these years.[25]

THE FOOL [BOZO-as-FOUQUET]

[*With one hand on Mandy's belly and the other on the "Nun's"*] And when I die, and when I'm dead, dead and gone . . . There'll be one child born in this world to carry on.© [Now, carry on, God damn it!][26]

MANDY

Of all your chambermaids, I'm the crème de la crème.

[*Increasingly aroused by Mandy, Bozo huffs and puffs while Fouquet flails.*]

THE FOOL [BOZO-as-FOUQUET]

[*To Mandy*] Jesus H. Christ on a cracker, you got that right.
[*To Gwynnie-as-Nun*] Say, Sister, isn't it about time we got to my Last Will and . . . [*Gwynnie makes an abrupt move on his lower torso and his voice becomes quite high-pitched.*]
. . . Testicle?

GWYNNIE-as-NUN

Overact much? [Now, shove it, clown!] And I'll thank you, sir, to take a more respectful tone when invoking our Lord Jesus, who died on the cross for your sins to redeem His people.

THE FOOL[s]

[*The Jesus imitation fails to get a laugh.*] Jesus H. Christ on a cracker! Still dying here!

GWYNNIE-as-NUN

And what, pray tell, do you propose to do about it? The end is near, remember? Time to face the final curtain.© Ever give a second thought, to your immortal soul?

THE FOOL[s]

Treachery, thy name is woman!

GWYNNIE-as-NUN

And, if you don't get it just right, my friend . . . Has it never occurred to you that the Evil One is about to catch you in some bad acting? The Devil is gonna get you, [the Devil is gonna get you!©]

THE FOOL [BOZO-as-FOUQUET]

But isn't Father Maurice still here, that I might receive absolution?

GWYNNIE-as-NUN

I'm perfectly capable of taking care of your last confession myself. If you're willing, that is. And when you die, [and when you're dead, dead, and gone,©] the glory of Paradise awaits.
[{*Aside*} All dogs go to Heaven!]

THE FOOL [BOZO-as-FOUQUET]

And good night, nurse. By the way, Miss Nun, where shall I be laid to rest?

GWYNNIE-as-NUN

Smack in the middle of the convent. [We put on a great funeral there.] [{*To the audience*} And, you know: I'll bring a date. I've got two tickets to Paradise! Gonna pack my bags and leave tonight!©]

THE FOOL [BOZO-as-FOUQUET]

And have Father Maurice throw in an extra *gaudeamus* or two.
[*Aside*] He'll sing like a canary, all right. The service to end all servicing.
Sing *laudamus te, benedicimus te, adora-a-a-mus te!*
He sings
Hosanna, hey-sanna©*—a—a—achoo!*

GWYNNIE-as-NUN

Thou sneezest? And thy snot spilleth upon the ground? *Et in nostrila pax: pax hominibus.*

MANDY

Tibi omnes angeli bisexualis. [*Gloria*—I'm walkin' on *egg-shell-sis Deo* around here!]
The earth moved. The angels wept [in Heaven on high! And he could at least get a Kleenex.]

THE FOOL [BOZO-as-FOUQUET]

Jesus flippin' Christ! Who's gonna be higher up in Heaven than me? I'll be a count up there, or a duke, or a pope. Maybe even an emperor: king of kings!

GWYNNIE-as-NUN

[And, Lord of Lords!©] Have a care for your Creator, I implore you! Confess. Say it: "Bless me, Father, for I have—. Go on. [*She grabs a soiled cloth near the chamber pot and wipes his face.*] Make your peace. Pray to God and the Virgin Mary and Saints Betty and Veronica that—.[27]

THE FOOL [BOZO-as-FOUQUET]

And don't forget Father Maurice's piece![28]
[{*To the audience*} What is this? The Shroud of Urine?]

GWYNNIE-as-NUN

And don't *you* forget every blessed saint in the firmament. And don't have a cow.
[*Aside*] Not even the sense God gave a flea! He can't even remember his damn lines.
[*She tosses the filthy cloth over Bozo's face again and with Mandy's help, she wraps it so tightly that he gags, coughs, and sneezes. The two women then grab a second filthy cloth and brusquely remove the bedcovers to reveal a scrunched-up Fouquet. They repeat the procedure and haul both men out of bed.*]
Enough! Ho-sanna, hey-sanna, sanna, sann-heave ho!©

MANDY

Heave ho-ho-ho! Best idea she's had yet!

GWYNNIE

[And, once and for all, shove it clowns!] Adieu, Fouquet.

THE FOOL [BOZO as himself again]

Adieu, Mandy. [*He rushes off.*]

GWYNNIE

[*To Fouquet*] You're on your own now.

[*The two women twist Fouquet in his blanket and shove him out of the bedroom and into the common area.*]

MANDY

Adieu, Fouquet.

THE FOOL [FOUQUET]

Adieu, Mandy.

MANDY

He's already pale as a sheet. Why, I do believe he's been fasting.[29]

[BOTH WOMEN TOGETHER]

The two scream [*as both women kick Fouquet out of the house and into the street.*]

Adieu! and go Fouquet yourself!

[Scene 8]

[*In the street*]

THE FOOL [FOUQUET]

Adieu already, God damn it, and to hell with all of you!

Adieu, milords, and pay attention! [Take it all in because—there oughta be a law! Drumroll, please:] Don't take the law into your own hands! Take 'em to—. Oh, screw it! [A man who is his own lawyer has a *fouquet* for a client!]
Trickery, thy name is woman! Fool me once, shame on you. Fool me twice, shame on . . . And to thine own self be screwed!
[There's no Fouquet like an old Fouquet.
Now *Fouque* you!]
The end![30]

[*Possible closing music.*][31]

6.

Brother Fillerup

Frère Fillebert

CAST OF CHARACTERS

BROTHER FILBERT (Frère Fillebert)
[COLETTE], the NEIGHBOR LADY (La Voysine)
[DONNA], the MISTRESS (La Mestresse)
PERRETTE, the Chambermaid (La Povre Garce, Perrete Venés-tost)

PRODUCTION NOTES

The first of our two farces from the *Recueil La Vallière* (#63), the other being #12, *Immaculate Deception*, is the *Farce nouvelle de Frère Phillebert* (fols. 354v–357r), whose name is spelled "Phillebert" in the title only. For many years, only Francisque Michel had edited it as the third play of *RFMSJ*, vol. 4 (again, paginated within a given play but not continuously throughout the volumes); but, on 29 August 2020, Thierry Martin posted his online edition at https://sottiesetfarces.wordpress.com/2020/08/29/frere-phillebert/. For the former, I cite by volume and local page number ("ABT," § "Editions"). *Frère Phillebert* was summarized by Petit de Julleville in *RTC* (141), by Faivre in *Répertoire* (175–76), and at length by Gustave Witkowski in *MTA* (443–51). Depending on who's counting, it is comprised of 157 to 163 verses that are mostly octosyllabic except in a few moments of metric disorder. To my knowledge, there is no translation into English or any other vernacular.

"God says awake," wrote Jacques de Vitry (1180–1240), "the doctor says sleep; God says fast, the doctor says eat; God says mortify your bodies, the doctor says flatter them—not to mention those who, on the pretext of purging you, advise fornication" (cited in *MTA*, 444). In *Brother Fillerup*, it all sounds vaguely Platonic, Gorgianic, and, well, *orgasmic*. At stake in this *mystico-médico-burlesque* farce (*MTA*, 451) is a commingling of rhetoric, medicine, cosmetics, and gymnastics, the likes of which even Drama Queen Dolly has never seen (#4). Driving the plot is, to paraphrase Rodgers and Hammerstein: How do you solve a problem like Perrette (*MFST*, 268)? What else? Prescribe some sex for the desperately ailing chambermaid—and lots of it. Enter that healer of souls, Brother Filbert, who is definitely up for some bad medicine. Indeed, back in the day, a brother might be empowered to do it all, especially in such municipalities as Grenoble or Romans, both of which experienced a shortage of doctors (*MTA*, 447).

The bare bones of the plot are laid out as easily as *la povre garce*, Perrette herself, who is described repeatedly as a poor, pathetic "wench," "wretch," "creature," or "slut." When her mistress (here, "Donna") is unable to tolerate the girl's sloth any longer—Perrette is literally dragging her ass—Donna gets a urine specimen and, with BFF "Colette" in tow, hauls that ass to Brother Filbert. Kin in many respects to the charlatans of *The Pardoners' Tales* or *Slick Brother Willy* (#10 and #11), our medicine man diagnoses her quickly after examining the maid's urine, eyes, and nose. Perrette is suffering from lovesickness or *le mal d'amour*, the subject of Mary Wack's still indispensable magnum opus. *Ergo, fill 'er up!* Cure the hell out of whatever ails her, doctor's orders. The farce then wraps with an extensive, versified prescription to be filled stat: extensive consortium with the male of the species. Why? Because a hard man is good to find (*Répertoire*, 176).

As we shall see, however, Filbert's homeopathy is characterized by highly ambiguous agency. Who is doing what to whom—and *for* whom? What can it mean, for example, to bleed Perrette "between two groins" (*la fault seigner entre deux aynes* [4: 13])? The position is all the creepier in that *seigner* also signified to make the sign of the cross (below, note 9). If, as Donna complains, the chambermaid is a pain in the ass, maybe she's *really* got a pain in the *ayne* (as in, a virile member). So, whose ass is really on the line?

In the barely seven lines that Petit de Julleville devoted to *Frère Phillebert*, he took offense: "in the hands of Molière, the motif makes for a charming and almost chaste comedy; here, it is still at the rudimentary and vulgar stage" (*RTC*, 141). To which Filbert would doubtless tell him to take his teleology and shove it up his ass. Nor is this a scrip for a husband (*RTC*, 141). For one thing, it's not impossible that Perrette is already married . . . in which case, the remedy would be less connubial consortium and more adultery. At least, that's Faivre's take on our farce: it's a juridico-medical "legalization of the sex act outside of marriage" (*Répertoire*, 176). And, in the end, as it were, this misogynistic little piece tells us an awful lot about the early pseudomedical foundations of sexist humor (as detailed elsewhere in *Bitches and Pussycats* [*HD*, #8] and *Playing Doctor* [*FF*, #6]). Can a feminist dramaturgy salvage *Brother Fillerup*? Or, to borrow one of the play's metaphors, do we let the whole thing come tumbling down?

Ultimately, only the mise-en-scène will tell whether Perrette is a hypochondriac, a legitimate patient, or a faker. If she's wilier than she looks and the whole thing was just a setup to get some sex, she'll certainly have pulled it off. I'd probably go with the sexually liberated Perrette who reclaims her own body, repels *man*-ipulations, and tells Brother Fillerup to take his own prescription and shove it up *his* ass. Or *her* ass if that's what a girl wants. Or, if the maid is played by a man, *his* ass if *he* wants. *Brother Fillerup* is a tough Filbert nut to crack; and those nuts were made for cracking.

Characters and Character Development

Ready or not, here he comes. Presenting "Frère Fillebert," here, "Brother Filbert," aka "Brother Fillerup" (notwithstanding some question as to his theological credentials [*SFQS*, note 6]). The nutty "Filbert" reminds us to keep our eye on the nut-ball. Hazelnuts were ripe around Saint Filbert's Day (22 August), and he's gonna *crack* you up. A spiritual con-man and a sex therapist *avant la lettre*, his reputation precedes him. He is also a malady-chasing voyeur and *écouteur* who has plausibly caught wind of Perrette's condition (*MTA*, 445).

Next on the scene, the unnamed mistress and her unnamed neighbor, "La Mestresse" and "La Voysine." I've christened the former "Donna," a generic lady of the house, and the latter, "Colette," the name of another such neighbor in *Confession Lessons* (*FF*, #3). Faivre might be right that, overall, the two women are poorly sketched and ill-defined (*Répertoire*, 176); but that doesn't preclude a depth to be plumbed by dramaturgy. Both emphasize the proverbial difficulty of "finding good help these days"; and, for Donna,

Perrette's rehabilitation would ensure better service. Meanwhile, Colette is happy to lend moral and physical support to her BFF, including urine transport. When they speak in one voice, apparently to praise Filbert's irremediably chauvinistic prescription, a witheringly ironic delivery can rectify the medieval message.

As for "Perrete," which I'll spell "Perrette" to match other farcical diminutives: her full name is seen only in the Cast of Characters as "Perrete Venés-tost" (*RLV*, 457v), which yields something like "Petra Come-Early." Maybe she will, maybe she won't. But a *pierrette* by any other name—that is, a small stone, rock, or pebble—is on a rocky course if forced to submit to a quack seeking to get his rocks off. A *pierrette* also denoted the pit of a stone fruit and—*quelle coincidence!*—Donna thinks that her chambermaid is the pits, obedient though the girl is. She's *debille* to boot (4: 6), as in "debilitated," "feeble," or "weak" (albeit not necessarily today's "idiotic" or "moronic"). But does she melancholically crave what she has never had? Or, as the proverbial girl who "cain't say no," does she rapaciously covet more of what she can't do without? God only knows she *cain't* say no to Donna, no matter how humiliating the request.

Poor Perrette! *La povre garce!*—which, by the way, proved challenging to translate succinctly. With additional connotations of dissolution, poverty, and disease, *une garce* is a socially inferior gal and even a "miserable slut": a chick, tramp, tart, trollop, strumpet, floozy, or chippy. 'Tis pity she's a whore? Or, as Emma Maggie Solberg might prefer, a *Virgin Whore*? Or she could also be a nice girl, even a virgin (*SFQS*, "Introd."). To tease those meanings out, I've varied the characters' idiosyncratic invocations of her condition, occasionally with song lyrics. But, when push comes to shove it, is she pure or impure? Bitch or pussycat (*HD*, #8)? Comic or tragic? Does Perrette endure all the abuses to which chambermaids were routinely subjected (#5, #7)? (*A garce* was a rape victim too [*TFR*, 354–69; *MTA*, 448n]). Is *Brother Fillerup* the harrowing story of an all-too-real sexual assault? Or mightn't it be as lighthearted as Rachel Dratch's *SNL* character Debbie Downer? Do we hear the trombone's telltale "womp, womp" each time Perrette opens her mouth? Speaking of which, what does she sound like? A southern sensibility would work well; feel free to replace any given *you* or *yes, ma'am* with *y'all* or *yes'm*. Perhaps she has the deep, masculine voice of a chain smoker as well, fixated at the oral level. So, why not give her an opportunity to define *herself* with a theme song (below, note 3)? After all *Perrette, venez tost* was the subject of a bawdy song of 1547, as we learn when the character appears in *The*

Trial of Johnny Slowpoke.[1] Whatever you decide—ultrafeminine? pregnant? man in drag?—paint yourself a picture of an ass-dragging Perrette-the-Cat in heat.

Language

Talk about your shockers: with the exception of the noneuphemistic *Vray Dieu*, there's not much cursing. In lieu of obscene language, *Brother Fillerup* gives us constant pointing, gesturing, and poking at Perrette's body during a pseudomedical examination riddled with double entendres on looking, seeing, endowing, and truth-seeking (*voir/pourvoir/pour voir*). He is literally "deposing her cunt" (*con tester*) when he inquires about the locus of her illness: *D'ou vient se mal qui vous conteste?* (4: 11). It's all very musical too, from Perrette's assertion that no *chant*, *rondeau*, or *ballade* will cheer her up to this diagnostic refrain: *Vray Dieu! Qu'elle est malade, / Helas! D'aymer, la povre garce* (4: 8–9; *SFQS*, note 32; *MFST*, 261–62). Literally, this means "My one true God, how sick she is, alas, from love, the poor wench"; but, to my ear, it plays to the strains of country music, making for an excellent translational combo of "Poor, Poor, Pitiful Me" and "The Lovesick Blues." The refrain of the former, "woe-ho-hoe is me," has the added advantage of laughingly mocking—*ho-ho-ho*—a *whore*.

Elsewhere, we come upon the urgently needed *soroboro* (4: 10), a seemingly untranslatable term that I find in no dictionary. It may be a compound of *soros* (an exaggeration or a bad joke) and *boroflement* (a battle or quarrel); or, as for Martin, the biblical character Zorobabel (*SFQS*, note 44). For all we know, Brother Fillerup might be producing, with great flourish, an herb whose nickname eludes us. Or perhaps he intends *oroboro* (Middle French *ourobouros*): the snake eating its own tail and symbolizing infinity. This is the grass snake of the pharmacist's insignia, an ersatz version of which we shall encounter in *The Pardoners' Tales* (#10).

Nothing compares, though, to the linguistic high point and the #MeToo low point of the closing prescription for women of every social class (*povre garce ou jeune fille*; below, note 9). The declamation thereof is a veritable scene unto itself in which the play's various metaphorical registers all come together: warfare (with a kind of *vagina dentata* feel), medicine, food, and, curiously, sailing. Filbert's recipe is a *recepte pour le cotillon / Que la povre garce a perdu* (4: 12–15), which is far from straightforward to translate. On one hand, it might be the miraculous restoration of a woman's virginity, a feat attributed to the great Saint Muffie in *The Pardoners' Tales* (and a reading consistent with Martin's *seigner* as "penetrating the hymen" [*SFQS*, note 69]). On the other hand, when Filbert prescribes lying with the male of the species—*A! s'el a une foys lysté / Avec le malle* (4:10, 12–13)—it's an open question as to whether the verb tense of this coupling (the present perfect) is anticipatory or retrospective. And what about the *cotillon* itself? Technically, it's a peasant girl's slip as well as a kind of militaristic male *armor* with all the requisite sexual connotations. Siege shall be laid; the citadel shall be taken (*asailly* at 4: 9). If anything, Filbert's bipartite plan for bleeding Perrette "between two groins" (4: 13) would appear to dictate that she look at love—make that sex—from, as Joni Mitchell would say, "both sides now."

Sets and Staging

I've elected to set the play at or near a bustling marketplace near the homes of Donna and next-door neighbor Colette. This allows Donna to hear Filbert's opening sales pitch, which she may or may not have heard before, and to rush right over to Colette's for advice (a procedure familiar from *Bitches and Pussycats* [*HD*, 245–51] or #11, *Slick Brother Willy* [sc. 11]). Regardless of whether the women are coming or going, they're having some trouble corralling Perrette. Alternatively, they might be conversing in a domestic space. But the key location is Brother Filbert's place of business, situated between the market and the women's homes, with its designated consultation area. We encountered another such space in *Marriage with a Grain of Salt* (*HD*, #12) but, if you're imagining a circus-tent structure, not so fast. Our text is explicit that Filbert's office has a *door*. We know this because, in Scene 2, the women *knock* on it (4: 9). One can only wonder how an itinerant healer has come by such a pied-à-terre? Is he renting from a local brothel?

Remarkably, *Frère Phillebert* features no fewer than ten stage directions over its barely 160 verses, some written in the margins of the *RLV* (*Répertoire*, 175), and which, as usual, I render unbracketed and italicized. Among the more comedic: the collection and conveyance of a urine specimen (also present in *Blind Man's Buff* [*FF*, 167], *Marriage with a Grain of Salt* [*HD*, 410–11], and *RBM*, #13, the *Farce d'un Amoureux* [projected for a future volume as *Pissed Off*]). And just how does she supply her "fresh made" urine (4: 8)? A male actor can't exactly whip it out and fill up the text's portable *urinal*, a vessel normally reserved for ailing men confined to bed (although, that's what will transpire in *Jenin, Filz de Rien* [*RBM*, #20], forthcoming in my next volume as *Who's Your Daddy?*). If we're at market, Perrette could *steal* a *urinal* and execute her task offstage. If we're at Donna's place, she could fill it up by transferring the contents of a chamber pot.

Once the diagnostic material is in hand, we must determine *whose* hands. It seems implausible that Donna or Colette would personally take charge of such a yucky prop; but, any hand-off only enhances the hands-on slapstick of leaky, overflowing containers in an indelicate balancing act. Whatever the setup, the lab work arrives chez Filbert in sufficient quantity for a diagnosis. Perrette then delivers an over-the-top performance of medical distress, complete with moaning, groaning, coughing, sneezing, and, eventually, a bona fide giggle fit. (Try filling the examination room with medical marijuana and making Filbert's office a pot dispensary.) This is also the moment when Perrette's body language will clinch her character. Who's pulling the strings of this grope-fest? Is she coughing from smoking, disease, or displeasure (like Elmire in *Tartuffe*, act 4, sc. 5)? And is that a pistol in her pocket or is *he* just happy to see Brother Filbert to get *her* fix? Fix her up, fix him up, fix the whole play up as you like. But be sure to *camp it up* with a production number. I'd go with a parodic, retro montage of *Petticoat Junction*, a fitting end for a bunch of medieval drag queens.[2]

Costumes and Props

With the exception of that all-important *urinal*, the long-necked forerunner to the bed pan, the key props belong to Brother Filbert: his reading glasses (4: 12), a panoply of medicines and placebos, a number of alchemical recipe books, and a doctor's little black bag with rudimentary tools of the trade (a stethoscope, a tongue depressor, etc.). Also onstage: a large variety of receptacles for excretions, such as specimen jars, beakers, a glass vase, bed pans, and chamber pots, plus, in an updated production, home pregnancy tests, jars of weed, hash brownies, and drug paraphernalia.

Scholarly References to Copyrighted Materials (in order of appearance and indicated by © within the text)

"Poor, Poor Pitiful Me." By Warren Zevon. BMI Work #1189347.
"The Lovesick Blues." By Cliff Friend and Irving Mills. ASCAP Work ID: 420097327.

"Respect." By Otis Redding. BMI Work #1244564.

"That Old Black Magic." By Harold Arlen and Johnny Mercer. ASCAP Work ID: 500035232.

"Little Less Talk and a Lot More Action." By Keith W. Hinton and Jimmy Alan Stewart. BMI Work #880887.

"Joshua Fit the Battle of Jericho." Spiritual.

"Do It [till You're Satisfied]." By Billy Nichols. BMI Work #309081.

"When the Saints Come Marching In." Traditional.

"War Is a Science." By Stephen Schwartz and Roger Hirson. Music Theatre International. https://www.mtishows.com/pippin.

"Let 'Em In." By Paul and Linda McCartney. ASCAP Work ID: 420198209.

"I Whistle a Happy Tune." By Richard Rodgers and Oscar Hammerstein II. ASCAP Work ID: 390083480.

"Hokey Pokey." Traditional.

"Treat Her Right." By Roy Head and Gene Kurtz. BMI Work #1542510.

"Maria." By Richard Rodgers and Oscar Hammerstein II. ASCAP Work ID: 430030594.

"Waited So Long." ["Daddy, I'm No Virgin."] By Carly Simon. ASCAP Work ID: 530179450.

"Virgin." ["Not a Virgin Anymore."] By Annie Poe, Kenneth Burgomaster, and Matthew Wilder. BMI Work #5369139.

"What a Girl Wants." By Shelly Peiken and Guy Roche. BMI Work #4993749.

"I Cain't Say No." By Richard Rodgers and Oscar Hammerstein II. ASCAP Work ID: 390003762.

"Hand in My Pocket." By Glen Ballard and Alanis Morissette. BMI Work #2028578.

"Petticoat Junction." By Paul Henning and Curtis Massey. BMI Work #1169258.

[Scene 1]

[*Possible opening music*][3]

[*At market, Donna is having trouble rounding up Perrette. From the audience, enter the peripatetic Filbert, little black bag in hand, perhaps engaging various women—or men—as he wanders. He might eavesdrop for a time until he catches sight of the listless Perrette.*]

Brother Filbert begins

BROTHER FILBERT

Folks say it everywhere because it's true: You're loved by God? Then people don't love you! But you know what? I couldn't care less because *I* am in His good graces: me, my parents, and all my kin. What you want, baby we got it,© every last one of us: the gift of second sight. Name your disease—[*gesturing toward the genitalia*]—any disease!—and we can cure it. That's right! There's not a specialist in this whole city comes close to my hands-on healing. You got the broad, I got the cure for whatever ails the poor wretch.

[*He indicates Perrette.*] Watch closely now because, before you know it, I'll be succoring that little tramp but good. Long story short: I'm fixing to hang out here for a piece—[maybe put down some roots]—so I can prescribe the cure [to end all cures]: whatever she needs.

[Scene 2]

Enter the Mistress of the wench

DONNA

Hey! Neighbor!

Enter the Neighbor

COLETTE

Now what?

DONNA

[*Pointing at Perrette*] Can we at least talk about that pathetic creature? Mother Nature sure as hell skimped on that one. What am I supposed to do with her?

COLETTE

Well, we better think of something. If she could quit dragging her ass, that would at least be a start.

DONNA

Everybody in town is talking about a brother—goes by the name of Filbert—can cure whatever ails you. That's right: there's not a Hubert, a Robert, a Lambert, a Hilbert, or a Gilbert gonna fix you up just like that, one, two, three! [Not even a Wilbur but—watch the Bertie, folks! He's a-comin' up in another farce! Anyway:] You name it, bro's got it. Got *you*. In a flash. [They call him Brother . . . butterup, pickerup, hiterup, puckerup, *Fillerup*! Now, giddy-up and] let's go and see him![4]

COLETTE

So, step on it. We better hurry. And, if he can cure that little tramp, so much the better.

[*To the audience*] For you too, folks! Let's go!

DONNA

We can bring her along. Maybe that'll cheer her up. Perrette!

Enter Perrette, the poor wench.

PERRETTE

Yes ma'am?

DONNA

Get over here and gimme a urine specimen.

[*As Perrette hesitates, Brother Filbert watches and delivers various asides, initially unnoticed and unheard by the women.*]

BROTHER FILBERT

What she needs, by God, is a good stiff one!

DONNA

Perrette!

PERRETTE

Yes ma'am?

COLETTE

What's gotten into her? She's a hot mess.

PERRETTE

[*Clutching her chest*] It's my heart, here in my bosom!

DONNA

Perrette!

PERRETTE

Yes ma'am?

DONNA

[*Impatiently*] Get over here and gimme a urine specimen!

Perrette brings the portable urinal.

PERRETTE

Here you go, ma'am. Made me some fresh in this here urinal. See?

COLETTE

Look, there! The color doesn't lie! That glass is all cloudy already.

BROTHER FILBERT

[They seest through a glass darkly.] Wo-hoe, woe is me!©

The TWO WOMEN *sing*

And she's lonesome! She got the lovesick blues!©

BROTHER FILBERT

That's my cue! A little recon always pays off. Time to make my entrance, *hon-hon-hon*! And a quick buck too.

The TWO WOMEN, *singing*

And Lordy, she's lonesome!©

PERRETTE

Ain't nothin' you can sing—country, folk-rock, R and B—gonna cheer me up. I'm all pissed off. [*Cue trombone: womp, womp.*]

BROTHER FILBERT

Wo-hoe, woe is me!©

[The TWO WOMEN] *sing*

And she's lonesome. She got the lovesick blues!©

Perrette starts coughing and her mistress feels her head.[5]

DONNA

Go on, girl, give it the old heave-ho. Cough it up! Spit it out!

BROTHER FILBERT

Careful she don't fart it out! Thar she blows!

[*Perrette cuts a huge fart.*]

COLETTE

[As if we didn't see that one coming.] She needs looking into, alright.

PERRETTE

Oh my God, it's my heart!

BROTHER FILBERT

[*Aside*] Wo-hoe, *ho* is me!© Heart, my ass! [Heart, *her* ass!]

DONNA

Come on. Let's get her in to see the doctor. He's a specialist, you know. You can see very well that her poor heart's gonna give out.

COLETTE

So, make it snappy! Let's get a move on! We'll bust the door down [if we have to] but please, after you, Madame. [Age before beauty.]

[*Exit Brother Filbert in great haste to beat them to the "office." After some mimed confusion as to who goes first, the women follow with Perrette's urine in tow. Their haste has messy consequences for the transport of said specimen.*]

[Scene 3]

[*The women peer inside Brother Filbert's office.*]

DONNA

This is it. Here's where he hangs out. We better knock. Hello! [Knock knock!]

BROTHER FILBERT

Who's there?

[DONNA

Madame.

BROTHER FILBERT

Madame who?

DONNA

Ma damn maid! She's a wreck!]

[*The women push Perrette forward with the urine.*]

COLETTE

[Behold!] We bring you the urine of this little tramp. There's not a marketplace anywhere—nowhere no how—that's got a doctor like you, got the know-how to get to the bottom of this and fix her up once and for all. See for yourself.

[*Perrette clutches her chest and delivers a histrionic pantomime of her illness. Audience response is insufficient.*]

BROTHER FILBERT, *looking her [and her urine] over*

She's dyin' up here! [*He grabs smelling salts and medical equipment.*] Wait much? Poor, poor pitiful thing!© She's got it all over.

DONNA, *heaving a sigh.*

There must be something you can do. Just look at her!

BROTHER FILBERT

And *habeas corpus* to you too! I'm looking, I'm looking. But how far in do you want me to look? She's dyin' up here, I said! [And she's gonna croak in a minute] if she doesn't turn things around. Just look at her! She's got it all over![6]

COLETTE

Can you tell us what she needs?

BROTHER FILBERT

Why, social intercourse, of course! With the male of the species. Any Tom, Harry, or Dick will do—and fast! I'm not kidding—because I'm telling you: it's that, or no cure for her!

[*He turns to the patient.*] Let's have a look in your eyes. Now—doctor's orders—do exactly as I say or no cure for you!

PERRETTE

Oh my God! It's my heart!

[*The examination is so thorough—and so thoroughly intrusive—that a ticklish Perrette has a giggle fit.*]

BROTHER FILBERT

Heart, my ass! Wo-*ho*, woe is me!© Now hold still. [And try to stay in character, wouldya?] [*He starts to undress her.*] Come on, let it all out. [*Perrette breaks free.*] We've simply got to get to the root of your trouble. Now, come closer and whisper in my ear: Tell me, where does it hurt?

DONNA

Out with it, girl!

PERRETTE

It starts in my head. Can't keep anything down—not even a little Benedictine—and, then, it's on to my heart. And, then, it goes all the way down, down, down to . . . [*She farts.*] And here too, in my lady parts.[7]

BROTHER FILBERT

Hoo-ha-ha! Lady parts, my ass! *Your* ass! Mary Magdalene's ass! I knew I was gettin' warm! [Did I get it or did I get it?] Wasn't that my very first guess about the little slut? Poor, poor pitiful thing!© [*He continues to palpate and grope.*]

COLETTE

Yes sir, doctor, but easy does it. She's not made of wax, you know. So, come on now, [show us your skill set!] Do that hoodoo that you do so well.©[8]

BROTHER FILBERT

Hoo-ha-ha! If she's hoo-done it even once with the male of the species, then—man, oh manhood!—I can pretty much guarantee that it's all gonna work out. No *species-ous* reasoning here! Everything's gonna be fine in the end.

DONNA

So, make it snappy! A little less talk, a lot more action!©

[*With great ceremony, he looks through some of his documents as if to find the right recipe.*] *Brother Filbert puts on his glasses and then writes out a prescription.*

BROTHER FILBERT

My special prescription at petticoat junction—
the poor slut has lost it; but it can be found—
is dirt in the skirt! [Fill it! Dirt in the skirt!]
The siege is now over. Charge! Long live the war!
My special prescription at petticoat junction:
[*Allons, enfants* . . . walls come a-tumblin' down!©]

Speaking to them [and to the audience]

The cavalry's here, guns ablaze, here they come!
[Man your stations for battle and—charge!—storm those gates!
Plus, it better be good—*montjoie!* Your acting too!
Wild man meets his wild-gal match on the field.]
Take that ass, men! Heads up! Let the bloodbath begin.

Reading

My special prescription at petticoat junction—
the poor slut has lost it; but it can be found:
If one of them gets overcome by the thrusts—
the pulsating, stabbing, the sticking it in—
One hand wipes the other. Stand back! Gird those loins!
'cause that girl's goin' down, boys. Just don't bleed her dry.
It's hand-to-hand combat, a brawl ass-to-ass,
mouth-to-mouth, burn those love candles down to the stubs.
Burn 'em down at both ends! That part's *her* cross to bear.
Plunge that enema in! Go on, expunge away!
Stick it right up her ass and—watch out!—here she comes!

[*To the men in the audience*]

Bump and grind, bump and grind till that broad pops a vein.
Go on, do it, do it until she's satisfied.
Do whatever it is,© until she's had her fill,
boys. You gotta go deep till she feels some relief.
Do it, do it till she can't tell which end is up!
Because enema, thy name is woman. That's that.[9]

All THREE *together.*

Oh, when the saints go marchin' in!© Sing hallelujah, Brother Fill![10]

BROTHER FILBERT

[And then, and then, and then, and gentlemen and then:©]
When the battle's been waged, if there ever should be
some gent comin' around maybe lookin' to buy,
knock-knock-knockin' for you at the door: let him in!©
Keep him with you all night and the whole live-long day
till he's eaten you up, honey, anchors aweigh!

All THREE *together*

Sing hallelujah, one and all! Long-life to Fill and fill 'er up!

BROTHER FILBERT

[And then, and then, and then, and gentlemen and then:©]
When your man feels afraid, hold his head up erect!
Go and whistle that happy tune!© Tweet, Tweety-birds!
Do it until he spills 'cause there's no keeping score.
Do it until you scream, do it until he takes you.
(The better translation is "until he rapes you.")
[This scrip of mine's sexist, it's misogynistic:
I hope that the ass on the line isn't mine.]

All THREE

Oh, when the saints go marchin' in!© Sing hallelujah, Brother Fill!

BROTHER FILBERT

[And then, and then, and then, and gentlemen and then:©]
Coming now to the end of my special prescription:
Go and fill that thing now and—hey!—I'll help you out.
[Doctor's orders, I say: hokey pokey it is!
Turn yourselves all around, turn yourselves inside out.
That's what *it*'s all about.© Now go fuck his brains out!
You'll leave no stone unturned. But you'd best check it out:]
We got no need for geldings, no! Chaucer, I'm not.
Just be careful you don't bite his fuckin' balls off!
And you'll huff and you'll puff till you bring down the house!

All THREE

Sing hallelujah, one and all! Long-life to Fill and fill 'er up!

DONNA

Here you go, Bro, here you go: here's $250 for your trouble, friend Fill-erup. You'll take it, please. In stride. [*She tenders the payment but shortly finds a way to pocket it back.*]

BROTHER FILBERT

Why, thank you, ladies. A thousand times thanks. [*Bowing*] I'm at your service, and I'll take whatever you've got.
[*Aside*] Right up the ass. Fix your wagon but good.
Plus, I'll do you one better: free re*fills* too. All part of the ultimate cure for all you sluts out there. And you nice young ladies too. The fix is in: a hard man is good to find and it's high time to fiddle about. But, speaking of fiddling: how's about a little number? What do you say? [A little night music? Who wants to tickle the ivories?] Let's do it.

[*Colette grabs him, perhaps by the codpiece, and turns his butt toward the audience.*]

COLETTE

[*Sarcastically*] Right, what a pleasure. I just *love* hearing a man do a number on me. And, on that uplifting note:
[*She smacks Brother Filbert on the butt.*]
[*This* is what I call all's well in the end's well.]

[The time has come, folks, gotta blow!]
We'll do a song before we go.
We hope that you enjoyed the show!
[*They sing.*][11]

The END

7.

Bro Job, or, *Cum Hither*

Les Chamberières qui vont à la messe de cinq heures

CAST OF CHARACTERS[1]

[The Narrator]
SAUCY (Saupi[c]quet)
PRICKER-UPPER (Troussetaqueue)
FLORENCE, the NURSE (La Nourrice)
FATHER JOHAN (Domine Johannes)

PRODUCTION NOTES

The official title of this play (*RBM*, #50) is the *Farce nouvelle des Chamberières qui vont à la messe de cinq heures pour avoir de l'eaue beniste*, to wit, *The Farce of the Chambermaids who Go to Mass at 5:00 A.M. to get their Holy Water*. First published in Paris around 1550 by Nicolas Chrestien in an undated edition (*SFQS*, "Introd."), it was reedited in *ATF*, 2: 435–47 (again, paginated but without verse numbers); and by Martin in *SFQS* at https://sottiesetfarces.wordpress.com/2016/01/13/les-chamberieres (accessed 10 February 2018). *Bro Job* is comprised of 248 verses in rhyming, fairly regular octosyllabic couplets (with an orphaned rhyme here and there). It was summarized by Petit de Julleville (*RTC*, 118), by Faivre (*Répertoire*, 92–93) and, in this case, briefly but insightfully by Sharon King in "Caught in the (One-)Act."[2] To my knowledge, there is no translation into English or into any other modern vernacular, which is a shame because there turns out to be a whole "Chambermaid Series."

Our farce joins an extensive intertextual dialogue with so-called dialogic poems such as these from the *Recueil de poésies françoises des XVe et XVIe siècles* (also edited by the same Montaiglon of the *ATF*): the *Apologie des Chamberières* (*RPF*, 5: 270–77); the *Replique d'une Chamberière* (*RPF*, 5: 278–83); and the *Banquet des Chamberières* from 1541 (*RPF*, 5: 284–95). There were other farces too: a *Farce des Chamberières* in the *Recueil Cohen* (#51), along with a kind of prequel to our story in the *RBM* itself. Immediately preceding *Bro Job* is #49, the *Débat de la Nourrisse et de la Chamberière* (*ATF*, 2: 417–34), which features many of the same characters in the same setting: the Chambermaids doing laundry, a Nurse, and another Father Johan. But, most germane of all: *Bro Job* shares forty-four consecutive verses with the *Caquet des Chamberières* (*The Chattering Chambermaids*) (*RPF*, 5: 71–83), a "non-dramatic piece" that survives in at least three editions, all three apparently consulted by Montaiglon.[3] There was a Parisian version for Jean de Lastré (Reims, 1577); an "inferior" undated Rouen version for Nicolas Lescuyer; and a third edition, also from Rouen but published for Costé.[4] It is to the unpaginated Costé edition, easily accessible online, that I turn for an occasional lesson because it is there that we find, after a lengthy prologue, those forty-four lines of reported speech that repeat the dialogue of *Bro Job*.[5] Nor was Montaiglon alone in his recuperative editorial efforts.

The "Silvestre" or "Crapelet" edition of *Poésies des XVe et XVIe siècles, publiées d'après les éditions gothiques et des manuscrits*, set typographically in Gothic letters, was published in Paris in a short print run of one hundred copies between 1830 and 1832. It too was deemed inferior by Montaiglon, who found it impossible to ascertain which base texts had served to establish the edition (*RPF*, 5: 71–72n); but it is well worth perusing. As the sixth of fifteen works, *The Chattering Chambermaids* is snuggled between two *sermons joyeux* and accompanied by an eleven-verse coda entitled "*La maniere pour cognoistre de quel bois se chauffe l'Amour*," "How to Kindle the Fires of Love."[6] Was the *Caquet* some sort of aphrodisiac? And, if so, who was kindling whose fires of love and, per Matthew 3:12, with what kind of unquenchable fire? One cannot help but notice that hard at work on that Silvestre/Crapelet edition was an up-and-coming "*jeune littérateur*" (*Poésies*, 3) who would go on to become one of the most distinguished figures in French medieval theater history: the same Francisque Michel who later partnered with Antoine Le Roux de Lincy on the inaugural edition of the *Recueil La Vallière*.

So, which came first? The poem or the play? Was the poem a *mise-en-écriture* of the play? Was the play a dramatization of the poem? Was there a more cyclical, reciprocal borrowing at play? Was the *Caquet* a theatrical piece of poetry? A poetic piece of theater? Was *Bro Job* a stimulating private read?

An in-depth response lies beyond the scope of this study, but one thing is clear: we are in the presence of what Paul Zumthor famously called *mouvance* (*Essai*, 65–72)—and not just at the level of language. Recall, for instance, that reported speech like the *Caquet*'s exemplifies the same sort of didascalic commentary that inspired Hardison's rediscovery of the liturgical origins of medieval drama (*CRCD*, Essay 3).[7] The chambermaids' chatter moved cross-generationally and cross-generically between performance and print, between poetry and Rabelaisian prose, and between fabliau and the satirical legal dialogues of a Guillaume Coquillart (*SFQS*, note 70; *ROMD*, 233–43). It's almost as if *Bro Job*, the fiftieth of the sixty-four *RBM* pieces, were the final farce per se of that *Recueil*, which then moved toward the debate structures of the morality play. Even Montaiglon, who maintained a rigorous distinction between poetry and theater (*RPF*, 1: xn), nevertheless posited an entire comic continuum: farce and protopopulist poetry perpetuated and preserved the "truly national[istic] *esprit* of the fabliaux and storytellers, all serving to transmit it to the *farceurs* of the age of Henry IV and Louis XIII, through which it will reach Molière and La Fontaine" (*RPF*, 1: v–vi).

Simply or not so simply put, *Bro Job* is no stand-alone. It belongs to an intertextual whole that is greater than the sum of its parts—some of which parts I've faithfully interpolated into this composite edition, where, again, they are signaled by angle brackets ("ABT," § "Critical Apparatus"). First, I've invited the *Caquet*'s judgmental male narrator to issue part of his 181-verse sexist diatribe (*RPF*, 5: 78–83) as a thoroughly detachable Prologue to our play, the better to connect dramaturgically what was already connected textually. Second, to build the character of the Nurse, I've cherry-picked one particularly illuminating line from *RBM*, #49, the *Débat* (below, note 17). And, third, to minimize confusion, I cite *ATF* by volume and page number alone, as usual, except when ambiguous; I cite the *Caquet* with its *RPF* page number and the *Débat de la Nourrisse et de la Chamberière* (*RBM*, #49) as *DNC* with the corresponding page number of *ATF*, vol. 2.

Plot

Where, oh where, is a chambermaid to go for the 5 A.M. Mass? With its maids'-eye view of late medieval domestic life, *Bro Job* is nothing if not site specific. Set in the very heart of Paris, the *Farce nouvelle des Chamberières* initiates a virtual walking tour of four very real churches: Saint Paul's, Saint Stephen's, Saint Benedict's, and Saint Séverin's (below, § "Sets and Staging"). Act 1 is situated down by the Seine, where two chambermaids are doing the wash and airing plenty of dirty laundry. Joined by the Nurse, they debate the relative advantages and disadvantages of the aforementioned houses of worship. Act 2 at Saint Séverin's is then devoted to their mad rush to get at the aspergillum of one Father Johan. Suffice it to say that the desired symbolic, sprinkling cleanse from the phallic *goupillon* or *vipillon* casts *aspersions* on the Church. Watch out, girls, for he has risen; and what he's spraying ain't no holy water. Whence my subtitle: oh, come all ye faithful.

An offended Petit de Julleville scarcely minced words when confining his analysis to a single remark: "A grotesque parade on the order of what the *bateleurs* proposed to the vilest members of the populace" (*RTC*, 118). For his own part, Faivre was stunned that, in 1550, such a play could have been published at all, no less performed, without the playwright being burned at the stake (*Répertoire*, 93). As for the innocent Delepierre, the chambermaids were merely "complaining about not receiving as much holy water as they would like" (*DLU*, 117). In light of Figure 3, the *RBM* woodcut, methinks he did not get the full thrust.

Characters and Character Development

For Faivre, *Bro Job* theatricalizes a classic Rabelaisian *contrepèterie* or spoonerism: the maids are *folles de la messe* and *molles de la fesse*—that is, "crazy for Mass and soft in the ass" (*Répertoire*, 93). Indeed, their precious essence is captured by the piquant, hot-to-trot monikers of the two principals, Saupicquet and Troussetaqueue (here, "Saucy" and "Pricker-Upper"). They are *tendre du cul* (as in *Bitches and Pussycats* [*HD*, #8]), their bottoms perpetually open for business. And, by the way, their Mistresses are getting plenty of action too from a steady stream of monks, soldiers, and a "protonotary," that last one a legal official in the feudal, royal, or pontifical courts.[8]

Saupicquet's vibe is alimentary, as in "spicy" or "saucy" (*RF*, 9: 272n), and it's only fitting: frustrated by the meager provisions at home, she's hungry (2: 440).[9] Saucy is a tasty little dish, a sneaky, eavesdropping voyeur, a dirty trickster with a great sense of humor (2: 437), and a hell of an impersonator to boot. She does a terrific job mimicking her employers' repartee to great comedic effect and in ways that echo the reported speech of the *Caquet*. Given the legalese coming out of her mouth, her Master might be in the legal

¶ Les chamberieres qui vont a la messe de cinq heures.

Figure 3. Frontispiece, *La Farce des Chamberières qui vont à la messe de cinq heures. RBM*, #50.

business. Either that or it's the Basochial voice breaking through, especially if she's played by a man.

The second chambermaid, Troussetaqueue, is the quicker "Pricker-Upper"; and the imperative of her name—*trousse ta queue*—signifies "prick up—or *stick up*—your dick" or "pick up your balls, gurl!" (In the *Recueil Cohen*, there's a whole *Farce des Queues Troussées* [#6]: the *Farce of the Pricked-Up Dicks*?) And this pricker-upper is all in: peckish for anything performant. Like Saucy, she eavesdrops and spies on the goings-on of a household that seems a bit wealthier than her friend's. She's quite the foul-mouthed little actress too: a drama queen hysterically solo-performing her employer's "separate bedrooms" routine. But, since her Mistress's refusals send the Master Pricker-Upper's way for sexual satisfaction, she could also morph into a tragic figure subject to persistent sexual assault (as in the legal cases detailed in my "Theater Makes History").

Next up is the odd woman out, the Nurse, also featured in the *Caquet* and the *DNC* and, here, "Florence," as in "Florence Nightingale." The other women resent her—a point amplified in the *Caquet* (*RPF*, 5: 83), which might have something to do with her slightly higher social status. (Nanny West of *Downton Abbey*?) Doing the washing is beneath her dignity: she'd never stoop so low. Not for laundry anyway. But, notwithstanding her better grammar, lexicon, and legalese, Flo is a mere wet nurse who might be toting a child around on her teat. Excessive in all her appetites—food, drink, gluttony, and the alcoholism associated with her type (*SFQS*, note 19)—she always wants something in her mouth. In fact, she's already guzzling her shot of red before 5:00 A.M. It's a cure for nausea, she says, or, as barbs about unbloodied sheets in the *DNC* imply, perhaps it's morning sickness? Although she has less dialogue than Saucy or Pricker-Upper, Florence is a fulsome, tipsy presence. There's plenty to eat at her place; so, try casting a woman of size.

At long last—it's like waiting forever for Tartuffe to appear—we meet our friendly neighborhood priest about three-quarters of the way in. He is Domine Johannes (pronounced "Johanné," as the versification makes clear), and I've gone with "Father" rather than "Lord" Johan. Obsessed with his aspergillum, he is hot on the trail for penitents, to whom he makes multiple assurances about the stick-to-itiveness of his equipment. It's a false claim: one of many. Martin even goes so far as to speculate that Johan is a caricature of the Cardinal Guillaume d'Estouteville, rumored to have fathered at least five children and, himself, a canon of Saint Séverin's (*SFQS*, note 57). In the *DNC*, his other talents include spying, eavesdropping, and impersonating a police officer.

Finally, as a counterbalance to, or a bona fide replacement for, the sexist narrator, consider incorporating the words of the *Caquet*'s Perrette. That's right: another Perrette, as in #6, *Brother Fillerup*, which would make for a nice double bill. It would also explain why our previous Perrette was so sick and tired—*povre garce!*—at the same time that it extends farce's intertextual conversation to the *Recueil La Vallière* (*RLV*, #63). Blurry though the boundaries between comedy and tragedy often were (as I argued in "Miscarriages"), her grim account of why she was forced to leave her previous employ might well transform our play into a full-blown tragedy:

> I left because . . . let's just say *somebody* was paranoid—and jealous—even though there was no cause to be. . . . [The Master] wasn't wooing me or anything like that. . . . Most of the time, he'd just grab me when there was no one else around, but that was about it. . . . When push comes to shove, I'm nothing. I barely make a living wage, speaking of which: for better or for worse, I got a proposition from this bachelor I know who wants me in service. But he wouldn't be sticking me with one of those frosty-bitch mistresses. At least I'll get minimum wage and maybe a hundred or so extra in tips. Not exactly pocket change, right? And he's promising other benefits too. But, in the end—if I could just finish my story here—I *still* wouldn't be getting enough rest. (*RPF*, 5: 81)

The wretched lives of chambermaids were no joke.

Language

Guess what? At the nadir of filth and obscenity, there is no cursing and no taking the name of the Lord in vain. That said, there is no dearth of faith-based exclamations either: a full dozen or so variations of *ma foy*, *par ma foy*, *par ta foy*. And there's plenty of sexuality implicit in *Bro Job*'s primary metaphorical registers: militaristic, animalistic (equestrian), legalistic (Basochial), and "laundristic" (cleanses, loads, spigots, etc.). It all makes for a highly irregular spin (cycle) on the *Asperges me*, a Latin antiphon for all seasons except Easter. Based on Psalm 51:50, it goes like this: *Asperges me, Domine, hyssopo et mundabor. Lavabis me, et super nivem dealbabor. Miserere mei, Deus, secundum magnam misericordiam tuam* ("Thou wilt sprinkle me, O Lord, with hyssop and I shall be cleansed. Thou wilt wash me, and I shall be washed whiter than snow. Pity me, O God, according to Thy great mercy"). In addition to its homeopathic properties, the bitter, minty hyssop was also an aphrodisiac (*SFQS*, note 60). Could *that* be why the Crapelet edition tacked on that extra poem about "kindling the fires of love"? In any event, the women shout repeatedly "Sprinkle me! Spray me!" And let's not forget the all-important "font" of holy water, the *benoistier* that could refer to both the vagina and the testicles (*SFQS*, notes 69 and 70). Technically, and serendipitously, it is termed the *stoup*: looks like *shtup*.

A last intertextual tidbit warrants our attention: a meta-moment from the *DNC* that is so charming that I've worked it in. When that play's Father Johan pokes fun at the chambermaids' battle, he quips that "somebody ought to be putting this stuff on paper" (*Et fusse pour mettre en parchemin* [2: 424]). "Writing stuff down" was the protonotary's job and the playwright's too: it's called a script.

Sets and Staging

The time: probably a weekday since, eventually, the women are urged to come back on *Sunday* (2: 446). The place? Location, location, location. Paris, Paris, Paris. *Bro Job* requires two principal sets. For Act 1, both the *Caquet* (*RPF*, 5: 78, 83) and the *DNC* (*ATF*, 2: 418) specify "at the river," where rocks or rudimentary benches offer seating. In Act 2, we move to lady's choice, Saint Séverin's, for the climax and the winner of their debate about four—count 'em—four real churches, the other three of which might be depicted in the background: Saint Paul's, Saint Stephen's and Saint Benedict's. Today, you can still visit Saint Séverin's and Saint Stephen's on the *rive gauche*, as well as Saint Paul's on the *rive droite*. Not so for Saint Benedict's, which was destroyed in 1831, a casualty of the Haussmannization of Paris (*SFQS*, note 49). Nicknamed the "Wrong-Way Church of Saint Benedict" (L'Église Saint-Benoît-le-Bétourné), it used to be in the rue Saint-Jacques, a stone's throw away from the Sorbonne. Meanwhile, Saint Stephen's, which the Nurse describes as "up the hill" (2: 441), is almost certainly a reference to Saint Etienne du Mont at 30, rue Descartes in the Fifth Arrondissement, not far from the Pantheon and the Bibliothèque Sainte-Geneviève. But seriously, folks: as if fat Florence would climb all the way up there? or, for that matter, over to Saint Paul des Champs in the Marais, which is so far that Martin thinks it's an error (2: 441; *SFQS*, note 45). Take my word for it. I walked the topography myself, and that's without schlepping cumbersome laundry baskets. Indeed, the physical comedy might be enhanced by having the chambermaids do just that.

Other local color is provided by the watering hole known as the *Mortier d'Or* (2: 442), not exactly the "golden font" for holy water but "The Golden *Bowel*" (*or* as "gold" + *ord* as dirty). For Martin, it's a gay bar (*SFQS*, notes 52 and 53); but one thing is clear: it's got a revolving back door. Speaking of which, the crucial question is: how in the name of all that's holy to stage the phallic ballet of the spritzing aspergillum?

Of an "erotic metaphor in action," Faivre opines that, "of all the farces that mime the sex act on stage, this one is doubtless the most explicit and the most daring: while sleazy clergymen abound, it is scarcely the norm that they would satisfy their needs and those of their flock in the middle of the church" (*Répertoire*, 92–93). What with farce's propensity for symbolic literalism and literal symbolism (*HD*, 11–12), a fetishized, milk-shooting aspergillum would desacralize all that it touches. As Martin concludes, with a shout-out to Lluis Borrassa's *Flagellation*, "religious symbolism works the same mechanism as carnal symbolism: there is no difference between a saint in an ecstasy and a lover in orgasm" (https://sottiesetfarces.files.wordpress.com/2017/12/lluis-borrassa1–e1600943894948.png). To which *Bro Job* enthusiastically responds: *Vive la différence!*

Costumes and Props

For the laundry scene: soap, washtubs, baskets, buckets, washboards, a rudimentary iron, piles of clothes, and so forth; and, for Florence, such alimentary necessities as bread, wine, and a bottle of Chivas Regal (for a pun with *charivari* [2: 442]). Per Montaiglon, she might carry a small flask, ostensibly for holy water (*RPF*, 4: 135; *ATF*, 2: 75). *Not.* Pricker-Upper's basket is overflowing with clothes of all shapes and sizes, including many belonging to infants and small children. These are visibly reddish, yellowish, brownish, as they were in the revolting itemization of *Shit for Brains* (*FF*, 271–74).

Inside Saint Séverin's, the audience must see each prop mentioned in the script: candles, collection receptacles, the golden bowl for holy water, and baskets often held by farmers in phallic position for "winnowing" or separating the wheat from the chaff. But the pièce de résistance, evocative of the portable hand-cannon (2: 441–42; my note 25) is the magnificent, bejeweled aspergillum. Obviously, it must be long and pointy.

Scholarly References to Copyrighted Materials (in order of appearance and indicated by© within the text)

"Rock Around the Clock." By Max Freedman and James Myers. ASCAP Work ID: 480039358.
"These Boots Are Made for Walkin'." By Lee Hazlewood. ASCAP Work ID: 500170925.
"Bad Moon on the Rise." By John Cameron Fogerty. BMI Work #79979.
"Baby Got Back." By Anthony L. Ray. BMI Work #72106.
"Burning Love." By Dennis Linde. BMI Work #160887.
"Love, Reign o'er Me." By Pete Townshend. BMI Work #924510.
"Hit Me with Your Best Shot." By Edward Sydney Schwartz. ASCAP Work ID: 380218380.
"Shambala." By Daniel Moore. BMI Work #1319243.
"God Rest Ye Merry Gentlemen." Traditional.
"Don't Leave Me This Way." By Kenneth Gamble, Cary Grant Gilbert, and Leon Huff. BMI Work #323300.
"Go Your Own Way." By Lindsey Buckingham.[10]

[Prologue]

[*Possible opening mime depicting the home lives of Saucy and Pricker-Upper*]

⟨The NARRATOR

Ladies and chambermaids, forgive me, please,
should I choose to reveal your secret ways.
If you're good, no offense: apologies.
Ladies and chambermaids, forgive me, please.

Only the guilty need fear wrath from me,
strutting their asses everywhere these days.
Ladies and chambermaids, forgive me, please,
should I choose to reveal your secret ways.[11]

Some are good people. That is my position:
It's neither libel nor misogyny.

I'd die before defaming—that's un-Christian—
when some are good ones: that is my position.

So sad! We love our neighbors. It's tradition:
Do unto others, small though they may be.
Some are good people. That's still my position:
It's neither libel nor misogyny!

I speak to so-called "ladies"—chambermaids—
at market having fun and getting laid,
hawking your fishy wares, pimping your asses,
selling your souls, no knowledge of what class is:

I'm talking to *you*, vicious sluts, and I assure you: you're where honor goes to die each and every time you open those vile, stinking traps. That's right, I'm talking to *you*! Not that I was ever on the receiving end of your twattle. No, no, not I! But a friend of a friend was. You do unto them all, from stable boy to master, till you've trolled them to death, piling it on till you bring down the house.

You're called "chambermaids," as in *maids*. You're *women*! And you've got that act of yours down pat. The way you live it up, we might as well be calling *you* the ladies of the house. You're better off than they are!

So, hear ye! Hear ye why and how:

As any nobleman knows, it's hard to find good help these days. Ladies and gentlemen, you know exactly what I mean: what you need is a nondisclosure agreement. And a fixer. And, if you don't have a good man in your employ, then you'd best get on that right away. Find him and keep him, folks—where there's a will, there's a way—or you'll spend your whole life on the hunt. But, no! You use one of those wrinkled old bats instead. I call it as I see it, and what you call *them* is pimps! Madams, *Mesdames*! It's outrageous, and I'll have you know—forgive me for not mincing words—that, while you're out, your lovely dwelling place is a fuckin' whorehouse!

. . . In the name of the one true God, oh, the sin! Oh, the iniquity, the fornication, the incest! I do believe that's precisely what the lot of them are up to, "maid" for each other every single night, and that's the truth. Have you no fear of [God's] justice? His judgment cometh, and that right soon, when *you*, gentlemen, are providing the venue for this despicable spectacle, when *you* are liable for all the criminal acts committed therein. So, wake up! You must cease and desist immediately!

[*He proceeds with virtuoso imitations of the different voices.*]

"Quick! It's the Mistress! You gotta get out of here, babe! Quick! Out the back or *Madame*'s gonna get real mad. Outta here, I said! Out the back door, babe!"

"God give you good day, Ma'am."

"You, chambermaid! So? Did you keep an eye on the house?"

Good heavens, Madam! You're not even looking! She's been knocking back so many stiff ones that she's knocked up![12]

So, Perrette answers and tells the Mistress that she's sick. She's weak and dizzy all over and she needs some fresh air. She's got a real bad tummy ache—you know she does—and you also know why! [Don't tell me you didn't catch our performance of *Brother Fillerup*!] She's been complaining nonstop for a whole week when—people!—all she needs is a good poke. What she's *not* saying is that that boyfriend of hers is already waiting in the wings outside of town: in the fields, cue stick in hand, and all ready to rack her.

And, now, off she goes, into the fields for a little recreation, and she "won't feel so sick no more." But, for that, she needs to speak to Madame and do a whole number on her. Crying and flailing: it's a real production. She can't very well say that this is the money shot, that she's gone far too long without, and that that dry spell must come to an end. And she's also not saying that the boyfriend stands ready to whip out a great big picnic—herring, salad, bread, beer—and warm up the fowl because that fagot's all ready!

We're all so sorry! Poor little Perrette! She's not feeling well. She's got a fever. People! Do I really have to spell it out for you? If she's hot, it's "hot to trot"! And, if she's sick, well, she's not the only one "sick and tired" from one solid week of nonstop rockin' around the clock!© [There's no end to what she's been up to and *into*.] Eating, drinking, and carousing. Singing, dancing, badmouthing, and tongue-lashing! As for the rest, I'll leave it at that. I prefer to take this up in writing some other time. Not, however, before I provide you with a full account of everything they've been saying when they're all together down by the river.⟩

[*Exit the Narrator, booed off the stage, as his tale comes to life.*]

[Act 1]

[Scene 1]

[*Paris: close to daybreak. Dimly visible on the banks of the Seine is Pricker-Upper, surrounded by piles of laundry as Zydeco music plays incongruously in the background. She testily works the washboard.*]

Enter SAUCY

Quicker, Pricker-Upper! Get a move on, girl, or we'll miss the five-A.M. holy water! Hurry up! We gotta go!

PRICKER-UPPER

Holy shit, Saucy! Can't you see I'm all wet here? And your timing sucks.

SAUCY

How do you figure?

PRICKER-UPPER

Girl. I didn't sleep a wink last night. That Bible-thumpin' bitch I work for was in one of her moods again. ⟨Miss Tartuffie, she goes apeshit again.⟩ She don't feel like turnin' in with *Monsieur*. Gives him the cold shoulder—outta spite, you know?—just to make trouble. ⟨Separate bedrooms and such: she don't wanna touch him with a ten-foot pole! Now, a *one*-foot pole, that's a whole 'nother can o' worms⟩ 'cause, lemme tell you: in the name of my own blessed Saint Muffie, ⟨*Madame* likes *that* just fine—and the sooner the better. Just her kinda monk-ey business.⟩

SAUCY

She gives him the business, all right. Girl got game—I swear!—especially when she's all by herself.

PRICKER-UPPER

So, she's all: "I made a promise to Saint Whatserface"—our Lady of Keep-Your-Hands-to-Yourself—that she's gotta give them lady parts a break every now and then, at least on weekends: like it was her time o' the month or somethin', and that she ain't doin' it. Not with her husband, anyway.

SAUCY

Sounds like he just wanted to warm the old cockles.

PRICKER-UPPER

Sounds like *she* wanted to warm 'em, I swear! [Sounds like even God Himself gave it a rest on Sundays!] That bitch was horny. [And them boots ain't made for talkin'!©] Besides, it ain't like you need a shoehorn to squeeze yourself in there.[13]

SAUCY

You won't catch *my* mistress makin' no cockamamie vows like that. She's a brave little foot soldier, she is: ⟨always rushing the vanguard for the first thrusts.⟩ [Rear guard too.] And is she ever stocked. She could garrison a whole damn battalion! There's always room for one more. Make that *two* more. ⟨The Master don't pay it no mind but I'm thinkin' he must be on to her.⟩[14]

PRICKER-UPPER

Speakin' of stockin' up: my boss has got plenty o' meat to bring to the table. So, he goes:
"Aren't you coming to bed? Got your spot all warm for you right here."
And the Mistress, she goes: "Nuh-uh. I promised God and all."
And the Master's like: "Well, vittle-dee-dee! I'll just go sleep with the chambermaid, Pricker-*right*-Upper."[15]

SAUCY

And I do believe you would've been proud as all get-out if he would've gotten hard as a rock right then and there, I swear! Come on, admit it: you would've wanted it, right?[16]

PRICKER-UPPER

And why not? If the Master woulda come at me with a tender touch, I woulda been down with that: make *me* the "stimulady" of the house. [Welcome to *my* garrison, boys! Time to shelter in place.]

SAUCY

Easy come, easy go. Quick and dirty. On the fly. It's all backroom deals over there anyway.

Sometimes ⟨at night⟩, I listen in too when *Monsieur* and *Madame* are in bed.
And the Mistress, she goes: "Come closer, dear. And don't you forget I'll be wantin' some chow first thing tomorrow morning."
And the Master's always, like: "I'm runnin' a little short this month, dear. Maybe next cycle. There's a bad moon on the rise."©

PRICKER-UPPER

[There's somethin' on the rise, all right, and it ain't the moon!] Same old, same old. And what does little Miss Saucy do when she hears that kinda talk?

SAUCY

Girl. I can barely keep a straight face! If anybody needs to strap on the feedbag, it's me! I've gotta bite the hell outta my tongue so I don't burst out laughing, I do solemnly swear! ⟨And then, there's that whole tricky business I had to come up with to sneak the protonotary in.

[PRICKER-UPPER

Proto- what?

SAUCY

Protonotary. They write shit down for the Pope.] Anyway, he ain't no fiddler but he sure can fiddle around. Comes right on in, mounts that pony, and—no boots, no spurs, no nothing—he rides her ragged! Swing your partner, do-si-do!

[*Florence begins her approach at some distance, initially unseen by the women.*]

PRICKER-UPPER

Say, isn't there a nurse over at your place looking after the little one? I can't stand that woman. Such a dirty suck-up. Now, *there's* somebody they oughta make a farce about!

SAUCY

I'll have you know: you'd never catch *me* in service in a house with no baby. Wet-nursing sucks. It's total bullshit. Makes me sick to my stomach.

PRICKER-UPPER

You're sick to your stomach? Try waitin' on some shitty nurse hand and foot and haulin' the bitch's laundry down to the river! Now *that* sucks. And she's the one gets jealous of other folks. It ain't right.
But enough with the dirty laundry already. My load's finally done.
Wanna get outta here?
Shit! Speak o' the devil: here comes that damn nurse right now—drunk as a skunk every morning as usual so she can pump the milk outta them tits. And she ain't gonna be shuttin' up till she gets her hands on some sausage, hot dogs, and buns! It's the only thing that works. If you ask me, our best bet is to just make nice. Nobody takes her on. That's how it goes at our place anyway. It's a losing battle.⟩[17]

[Scene 2]

[*Florence saunters over to Pricker-Upper, a bottle of scotch in one hand and an enormous picnic basket in the other. She inspects the laundry and makes herself comfortable. Throughout the scene, she drinks heavily and gorges herself on all the food until there is almost nothing left. A hungry and thirsty Saucy will partake whenever Florence isn't looking.*]

FLORENCE

I'm here. There's still plenty of time to head out for five-A.M. Mass. [*She makes the sign of the cross and takes a swig of her wine.*]

PRICKER-UPPER

Well, if it isn't Florence Nightingale! A bit early in the day for that, no? I swear! Gimme a break.

FLORENCE

You swear? It's called breakfast and I'm starving! Give *me* a break. I get so sick to my stomach in the mornings that, if I don't get maybe a half a glass of wine in me, I'm no good the whole day.

PRICKER-UPPER

You're pale as a sheet. Lemme guess: Nauseous in the morning?

SAUCY

Always stinks o' menfolk, that one: from carrying that boy around all day, I do believe. "Carrying a boy." Get it? You do the math.[18]

FLORENCE

It's been ages since anybody slipped me a little something under the table.

[*To the audience*] And a long time between performances.[19]

SAUCY

Uh huh. You been taking in quite the load, girl, and I don't mean laundry. No more bloody sheets. Ahem. [All hustle, no Flo.][20]

PRICKER-UPPER

Twist that faucet and tap that. She likes it all frothy and white. You know what they say: "Don't sheet where you live."[21]

FLORENCE

[*To the audience*] I'll think of a snappy comeback in a second, I swear.

[*She takes another swig.*]

PRICKER-UPPER

Don't tell me: another tummy ache? Something stickin' in your craw? The truth is hard to swallow, ain't it?

FLORENCE

When it hits me like this, I can't keep anything down. Not even liquids.[22]

SAUCY

Uh huh. You're a real saint. Butter wouldn't melt in your mouth. Or up your ass.

[*To the audience*] Next thing you know, she'll be savin' our fair city by stickin' her finger in the dyke.][23]

PRICKER-UPPER

[Nah! Give that girl a battering ram. Butter that butt and call her a biscuit. Hello! Last tango in Paris?] She don't care where she sticks it. Long as everything's on the up and up. [And way the hell on the down-low.]

SAUCY

Shoot, girl! No army's ever gonna snatch victory down *there* from the jaws of defeat! "Snatch," get it?

FLORENCE

Over at our place, we got this protonotary comes by the house all the time.

[PRICKER-UPPER, {*still confused*}

Proto- what?

SAUCY

Protonotary. I already told you. They write shit down for the Pope.]

FLORENCE

No, listen! Is he ever on the case! Makes house calls and everything. And I can assure you that, when he stands up, she really takes notice. [*Silence*]
I say: he's fucking the Mistress. It's quite the system they've got worked out too, you know? You've gotta give it up for that. Me too.[24]

PRICKER-UPPER

Don't tell me: he's got her doin' the old do-si-do. On her back. Oh, yeah!

FLORENCE

Oh yeah, oh yeah, you know it, sister! Baby got back,© I swear, and, by that, I mean—allow me to demonstrate—it's the sign of a Master who'll buy anything.

SAUCY

Ladies and chambermaids! You name it, he'll buy it. And he'll fuck it too. Court's always in session over there. In chambers. It's a regular seat o' judgment. [*She grabs one of Florence's bottles.*] Bottoms up!

PRICKER-UPPER

And right in the back door. [Talk about your county seat!] Better watch that ass before it gets taken to court!

SAUCY

You're lucky, Nursey. At least you've got plenty of bread and wine at your place. All you can eat. And communin' a-go-go. [And gettin' *sauced*. Get it?]

FLORENCE

And don't forget the nightcaps. I swear, when that protonotary comes by, nothing's too mmm, mmm, good.

PRICKER-UPPER

Mmm, mmm, *good*ness got nothin' to do with it, I swear! It just so happens we're practically dripping in the filthy lucre over at my place. Holy shit! But the Mistress is such a tightwad, she only lets me fill half a carafe for the whole damn day. For the both of 'em! Her *and* the master! And get this—sshhh!—she makes me dilute it, even though *Monsieur* ain't exactly partial to watered-down wine at dinner.

SAUCY

[You must be emptying the damn chamber pots all night!]

[*There is a great cacophony of bells, seemingly from every church in Paris.*]

If we hang around here much longer, we might miss out on the holy water.

PRICKER-UPPER

Nah, they ain't said Mass yet. The bells are still ringin' all over the place.

FLORENCE

Where should we go?

PRICKER-UPPER

I say we go for it and hit Saint Paul's.

SAUCY

Saint Paul's? Surely not. They say that, when the vicar's finished up with his chambermaid, he sticks it to her so bad, he can barely get the family jewels back.

FLORENCE

We could always head up to Saint Stephen's. There's bound to be a monk up there who'll do a morning Mass.

SAUCY

She does have a point. The way I see it, when a monk gives you a sprinkle with that aspergillum of his, it's like, every drop he ekes out has been blessed twice, for sure.

FLORENCE

Amen to that! Or there's always Saint Benedict's. I go there sometimes.

SAUCY

[O' they doth make the torches to burn bright!] They don't mess around out there, and that's no joke. This year, I hear they're firing off those hand-cannons so hard and fast, they fertilized a whole field of Carmelite nuns! [And that's nothing to shake a firestick at!] Speed that plow! From fallow to fruitful-and-multiply! Burn that chaff with unquenchable fire! Winnow away! Fire away! [You know what they say: Nothing comes between a monk and his aspergillum! Get it?][25]

PRICKER-UPPER

[Don't wanna cast no aspersions or nothin' but] me, I don't much care for their holy water. I hear they been shootin' off a pretty dirty wad these days over at the Golden Bowl. Golden *Bowel*, more like. Watch out, boys, here they come!

FLORENCE

I beg your pardon?

[PRICKER-UPPER]

Cock au vin, anyone? I say: I hear they been pullin' some real shit with the Jesus Juice. It's leftovers from some monk's enema bag![26]

SAUCY

They'll drip no wine before it's time. And, hey: at least they've got themselves a hobby.

PRICKER-UPPER

Oh, come on, we're in the middle of Paris. We can prick and choose.

FLORENCE

That's enough of a production already. What do you think this is? A pilgrimage to Rome? [{*She ekes out the last drop of her bottle of scotch.*} Shivaree-ree-Regal!]

PRICKER-UPPER

Speakin' of which . . . Have you seen the Roman candle on Father Johan up at Saint Séverin's? [Talk about your hunk o' hunk o' burnin' love© o' God!] Let's tap that. When he says Mass, he does the chambermaids regal.

SAUCY

Jeez! I do believe not even his daddy tended to the flock like that.

FLORENCE

So, let's quit standing around!

PRICKER-UPPER

You're in quite the hurry there, Nursey.

SAUCY

She's outta bread, outta dough, and she's really in need—"in *knead*," get it? [It's all sifting and fucking.]

[*The three women hasten to Saint Séverin's.*]

[Act 2]

FATHER JOHAN, [*summoning the faithful*]

Asperges me, Domine, Ysopo et lavabis me. Miserere mei Deus. Who wants some? [Purge me with hyssop, and I shall be clean. Wash me, and I shall be whiter than snow. O Lord, I'll be awash in the white stuff! What do you say, folks? Just say the word and it's yours!] [Come out, come out, wherever you are!] Come one, come all, come hither! *O magnum mysterium! Et admirabile!* Where the hell is everybody?

PRICKER-UPPER

Ready or not, [Daddy,] here we come. Just in time for first dibs on the holy water.

FLORENCE

I want *me* some, and before there's a whole crowd.

SAUCY

Lord Johan, [reign o'er me! Rain on me!©] Rain that holy water all over me! Hit me with your best shot, Father, fire away!©

FATHER JOHAN

Bad girls. You ladies are sinners!

PRICKER-UPPER

You can *lavabis* the hell outta me too.

FLORENCE

Jeez, Father Johan! [Mother Mary!] Don't tell me there's nothing left for Nursey.

FATHER JOHAN

[*To Florence*] You, keep your pants on. I'll do you in a minute. [*He sprinkles Pricker-Upper.*] [May the Lord raise you up.] *Asperges.*

SAUCY

Do me! Do me! [There's definitely something about Mary.]

FATHER JOHAN

Just hold on. There's plenty for everybody, but I can't do you all at once. *Asperges.* Why, I do believe . . . it's almost like you're thinking I'm gonna run outta juice. Never happens.

SAUCY

One more time, Father Johan! Wash away my troubles!© *Asperges me* like crazy. And *lavabis* me too while you're at it.

PRICKER-UPPER

Harder, harder! You're comin' up short. Your aspergillum ain't nearly long enough.

FATHER JOHAN

So, come a little closer. Cum hither. This thing can only reach so far.

SAUCY

You better not let us down, I swear!—or I'll be takin' matters into my own hands.

PRICKER-UPPER, [*shoving Saucy out of the way*]

[A hand job, is it?] She's goin' nuts! Wants it all to herself! In the name of Saint Johnson, I'll get my fair share!

SAUCY

At least take it easy on Daddy Johnson's spritzer. Don't manhandle that thing! If you were to bust the equipment, it would be a crying shame!

FLORENCE

Where's my share? For the love of God, Father—Mister Johnson of Saint Séverin's—you better give me somethin' right now or—push comes to shove—I'll grab you by that stiff, white collar o' yours and wring your bony neck!

PRICKER-UPPER

Outta my way! You're gonna bust his sprinkler! Lemme in!

SAUCY

Once he fills *her* vessel, that thing's not comin' out. She'd rather die. It'll be in there till it rots. That one loves a good stoup.

FATHER JOHAN

Ladies! I can't possibly keep this up for all three of you, I swear! My stoup's running dry.

FLORENCE, [*squatting unsteadily*]

Naturally, a good nurse is prepared to *stoup* as low as it takes to squeeze out what little she can and make do.

FATHER JOHAN

[*To all three women*] So, shut up. I've got much better in store for you.

PRICKER-UPPER

Come again?

FATHER JOHAN

You're all gonna run along now and come back on Sunday, and I'll take care of all three of you. A private sprinkle. To each her own aspergillum. But—cum hither—it'll be our little secret. On the QT. Very, very hush-hush.

PRICKER-UPPER

Long as I get me a great big spurt.

FATHER JOHAN

From my head to your tail. O magnify the Lord with me! [And no sloppy seconds.]

SAUCY

[O tidings of comfort and joy juice!©] Very well, Father Johan. That'll do for just this feast day. It's the nature of the beast-day.

FLORENCE

The beast-day with two backs! Long as we make it a nice, big, fat one.

FATHER JOHAN

[Enough to shake a stick at.] You'll be takin' it in, hand over fist.

SAUCY

[Like a fistful o' collars,] I swear! [*Indicating Florence*] But it would have to be a big fat one to be up for a second act with *her*!

FLORENCE

[*Kneeling*] Come fortify me!© You can't beat fresh meat for promoting milky-white lactation.

PRICKER-UPPER

And that one's always toasted. Whatever it takes. She just turns the other cheek.

FLORENCE

Teats don't fail me now! I'm on my knees here.

FATHER JOHAN

No worries, believe me. But, for now, it's every girl for herself. Off you go.

[*Florence is still hanging on to Father Johan.*]

SAUCY

Wanna lay off the beefcake already, Nursey? [Like a dog with a *boner.*]

FLORENCE

But you better come through, for—yay!—one day our lord shall come. [*She rises.*]

FATHER JOHAN

[*To the chambermaids and the audience*] Run along home, now, and go play hide the sausage! Roast those weenies: they plump when you cook 'em! Off you go, I said!

As for me, I've got business elsewhere! [{*With an inclusive spin of the aspergillum*} Round and round and round she goes, where she *stoups,* nobody knows!] You never know where I'll pop up, so, beat it!

[*Doubled version begins here.*]

Just put your lips together, folks, and blow.
God bless you! Hope you all enjoyed the show.[27]

[*At the end of the doubled version, financial contributions might be solicited to the tune of a closing number.*][28]

The END

8.

The Resurrection of Johnny Palmer

La Resurrection Jenin à Paulme

CAST OF CHARACTERS

JOHNNY GLAD-HAND PALMER, a Monk (Jenyn à Paulme)
JOANIE, Johnny's Sister (La Seur Jenyn)
JOACHIM, a Brother (Joachin)
TONI, Johnny's Cousin (Thoynon)
BROTHER BIRDIE, a Drag Queen (Caillette)
[Toni's Baby]

PRODUCTION NOTES

The *Farce nouvelle et fort joyeuse de la resurrection Jenin à Paulme* (*RC*, #50) might well be anonymous; but its 330 rhymed octosyllabic verses terminate with a shout-out to its possible authors, the students of the famous Collège de Beauvais: *Vive les enfans de Beauvais!* (*RC*, 346n; below, note 23). It was edited by Cohen (*RC*, 405–11), Koopmans (*RFlorence*, 709–20), and Martin in *SFQS* (https://sottiesetfarces.wordpress.com/2013/07/18/la-resurrection-jenin-a-paulme/); and summarized by Faivre in *Répertoire* (382–83). Per "ABT," I cite by verse number from the easier-to-access *RC*, supplying the occasional lesson from *RFlorence* and *SFQS*. To my knowledge, there is no English or modern French translation.

The dates proposed for our play range from 1499 (*SFQS*, "Introd.") to the second decade of the sixteenth century (*RFlorence*, 720), that is, contemporaneous with the French wars in Italy under the reign of Louis XII (1498–1515). As partial proof, Martin cites the deceased "Jénin des Paulmes" from *Légier d'argent*, another *RC* farce (#25) that seems to allude to the French occupation of Milan (1499–1500) (*SFQS*, "Introd."). But, mostly, those hypotheses have to do with the character of Caillette, a famous jester in the courts of Charles VII and Louis XII, and whose name was also on the lips of Clément Marot and Bonaventure des Périers (*SFQS*, "Introd."). While we know nothing of any performance of *Johnny Palmer*, Petit de Julleville catalogued a lost *Résurrection de l'Abbé* performed in 1529 in Montpellier by student actors (*RTC*, 312). It was likely a celebration by such a theatrical society as the Conards, he surmised, who, after a long absence, were returning triumphantly to the stage (*RTC*, 374).

Plot

In the first of our two Resurrection plays, Johnny Glad-Hand Palmer has risen at Easter, that most sacred moment of the liturgical calendar. Like Jesus, he too has been to hell and back; but this is no Palm Sunday *quem quaeritis* trope, that harbinger of the so-called origins of liturgical drama. Make way, folks, for Johnny-*Palmer* Sunday and for farce's own spin on the "Harrowing of Hell," when a resurrected Jesus descended to the underworld to free the imprisoned souls.[1] Make way too for a bunch of drunken, sotie-like fools rising up to harrow the hell out of ecclesiastical justice on earth. And curtain up on a bona fide medieval theater of the absurd.[2] Think of *Johnny Palmer* as Christ in the temple turned upside down: the afterworld *à l'envers*.[3]

As Johnny's sister laments his untimely demise, Brother Joachim tries to cheer her up with sex, when, lo and behold! Enter none other than Johnny: player par excellence of tennis and what-have-you, newly resurrected, and ready to party. Eventually, they are joined by Cousin Toni (Thoynon), who has recently given birth, and Drag Queen Birdie (Caillette), after which Joanie calls a mock court to order. Part Town Council and part tribunal, this semilegal body rules that all resurrected fools like Johnny shall have a place of refuge: the new religious house of the Order of Baboons. And they all live happily ever after or, as the French say, *tout finit par des chansons*: "it all ends with songs" (of which Brown has identified six [*MFST*, 190, 222, 230, 232, 263–64, 279]). In *Johnny Palmer*, it's more like *tout finit par des boissons*—"it all ends with *drink*," and with any vessel whence it spurts.

Faivre was not impressed. Just another one of those mediocre student farces, he griped, which didn't hold a candle to *The Resurrection of Johnny Slack-Jaw* (#9). There weren't even any good descriptions of the afterlife

(*Répertoire*, 382)! And yet, Faivre floated an intriguing hypothesis that Koopmans rejected (*RFlorence*, 720n): What if the hell that Johnny had endured lay not across the river Styx but just down the road apiece at the Châtelet prison (*Répertoire*, 383)? And what if the liberated souls were his fellow prisoners, also to return from the dead but when their prison terms were up? "Nothing supernatural in the return of Johnny Palmer," jokes Faivre: "he lived his hell in the heart of Paris, a few feet away from the Latin Quarter" (*Répertoire*, 383). This was a "metaphorical death," concurs Tissier, "of his *état civil*" or status as a free man (*RF*, 11: 25). So, what was Johnny in for? Was he an actor who, like others (*MES*, 332–36), was jailed for an anticlerical farce? An impecunious fellow languishing for years in debtor's prison (Geltner, "Medieval Prisons," 4)? Or was it a single night in the drunk tank? Dramaturgy will decide.

Ultimately, in a denouement that flips Rabelais's Abbaye de Thélème on its ass, the Company erects an edifice dedicated not to noble lords and ladies in love (*CWFR*, 116–27) but to the Order of Baboons. *Johnny Palmer* wraps when Birdie ascends to a throne or *chaire* (v. 297) that sounds more like a toilet. And not just any toilet-throne, mind you, but the "Seat of Shit" associated with the legendary Pope Joan, the infamous ninth-century woman who had masqueraded her way into the papacy. Her sacrilegious subterfuge led to the manufacture of a special chair, pierced through with a hole through which any future Pope's manhood could be verified.[4] No more transvestite travesties, thank you very much, as *Johnny Palmer* comes to a close in a synesthetic symphony of sights, sounds, smells, touch, and taste. Between ramming a resistant spigot into the bunghole of a wine cask and the omnipresent cacophony of an enthroned Birdie's gastric distress, we're about to learn that he who troubleth his own house shall inherit the wind. And the *wine*. That's right: a bunghole is both the oenological and the anatomical term that farce so frequently "comedifies." It's more constipated than consecrated. And, for *Johnny Palmer*'s Baboons—holy shit!—it's quite the seat of power. Restore us, says farce, and regain the blissful seat!

Characters and Character Development

In a comment subsequently removed from *SFQS*, Thierry Martin quipped that "the characters are totally insane and the author himself must have been drunk." He had a point; and their insanity must be played up. Their accents too, as when Johnny returns from hell speaking the heavily marked—and heavily mocked—northern Picard dialect (*SFQS*, "Introd."). (Johnny Slack-Jaw of #9 returns from Heaven speaking Latin or, at least, "kitchen Latin.") For the most part, I've left the script dialectally unmarked so that the play's highly localized vibe may be adapted to any desired regionalism; but, since the opening verses are very close to country music, one can confidently pepper the script with *y'all*. Hype its joyous anticlericalism with "Brother" or "Sister" So-and-So. Go all in. Go all out. Do notice, though, that there is a formality and an elegance to the grammar underneath the accents, particularly when the cast has truck with Joanie.

Known throughout only as "Johnny's Sister" (*La Seur à Jenyn*), emotional "Joanie" cries, flails, and laments; she also jokes and plays straight-woman. Her relationship with the dearly departed can best be described as inappropriate. "If Johnny's sister grieves for him," remarks Faivre, "it's because [Johnny] used to take her from convent to convent to get groped by the monks" (*Répertoire*, 382). So, is Sister Joanie a prostitute and her late brother a pimp? Another fallen sister? Her grammar is largely superior to that mangled by the other hicks onstage; and, oddly enough, the first Latin we hear is hers (v. 11), not Brother Joachim's. She disdainfully *tutoies* him, by the way, while he uses *vous* with her; and any momentary *politesse* of hers can be chalked up to the presence of song lyrics. Once Birdie and Toni are on the scene, Joanie is somewhat dwarfed; but she reasserts herself at the end.

Brother Joachim (*Joachin*) is a thoughtless and crass lecher who swears like a stevedore by any saint that comes to mind (like Kathy Griffin's mother?). Suspected to be a Franciscan by Martin, he conjures the celebrated *contrepèterie* about heading over to *les bons Cordeliers* ("good Franciscans") to find *cons bordeliers* ("whored-out cunts" or, for that matter, "assholes") (*SFQS*, note 20). Whatever his order, Joachim is eager to pick up where Johnny left off: namely, by pimping Joanie out to anyone *but* the sleazy Franciscans. Does he know them too well? Excessive in food, drink, and *gaillardise* (v. 306), he appears to have fathered a child out of wedlock. Just ask Toni. After all, Saint Joachim was the patron saint of fathers, among others. But this one seems to be the funhouse mirror image of Joachim of Nazareth, husband to Saint Anne and the putative Father of the Virgin Mary, for whom childlessness initially had been an issue. And one last thing: with almost fifty scripted pieces of dialogue, Jokin' Joachim is a big talker. True, not everything lands; but, if at first you don't succeed, try, try, try . . . to hear the telltale drum that punctuates any contemporary stand-up comedian's joke that bombs.

Our title character, "Jenin à Paulme," is a most unholy palmer who can't keep his palms to himself. Johnny is a player, a pimp, and a real "handful" after a "handout." The better to preserve his status as a *joueur de paume*, the precursor to a tennis player, I've kept his palm in the game as "Johnny Palmer." Notwithstanding his recent sojourn in hell, his body still works like a charm, as evidenced by its extensive sonorous and olfactory participation. Indeed, in light of the play's propensity for onomatopoeia (below, § "Language"), a latter-day Johnny could channel his inner Monica Seles and grunt like crazy. It's all in keeping with the digestive, flatulent, and excremental activities to come from atop the "seat of shit." Be sure to give Johnny a funny accent too, to go with his stylistic tics. And imagine him as Gargantuan. It can't be purely coincidental that Rabelais's *Gargantua* concludes with a "Prophetic Riddle" (chap. 58) that's a vision of either the Apocalypse or a tennis match. Keep your eye on the ball, then, and . . .

Watch the Birdie—oops! that's badminton—watch for the dynamic duo of "Birdie" (Caillette) and "Toni" (Thoynon). Koopmans even goes so far as to speculate that the former might have been played by Caillette himself (*RFlorence*, 720). *Herself? Themselves?* Far and away the most extraordinary aspect of this role is its Butlerian gender trouble, here accompanied by pronoun trouble. Is the frenetically singing and dancing Caillette a man? a woman? a drag queen? a farcical version of Kabuki's *onnagata*? It turns out that much gets sorted out if we employ gender-nonbinary pronouns for Birdie, who should be played high camp with an enormous bosom. Why "Birdie"? Aside from denoting a frivolous and talkative person, a *caillette*, which sounds like "little quail," is also a cow's stomach, the locus for secreting gastric juices. Birdie does plenty of that, especially when seeking to "relieve themselves" (*faire mon aisement* [vv. 298]) toward the end of the play with "a volley of stinky farts" (*Répertoire*, 382). Are there any other kind? And one more tidbit: while Faivre understands Caillette to be Toni's brother (*Répertoire*, 382), I'm not so sure. That determination seems to be based on Toni's wish that "my brother" come along to Johnny's resurrection (*Mon frère, or allez . . . au ressuscitement de Jenin!* [vv. 255–57]). Since Joachim is present too at that moment, Birdie might just as readily be referring to *him*—Joachim—with the more generic "my brother." Nor does it help that the characters alternate constantly between *tu* and *vous*, such that it is challenging to distinguish *politesse* from plural addressees.

As for cousin Thoynon (deriving from "Anthony"), "Toni" is prone to decent grammar and indecent behavior. She's hell-bent on correcting Birdie for the same eating, drinking, and partying in which she herself indulges. Do as she says, not as she does. What with frequenting shady neighborhoods, Toni has gotten pregnant (vv. 185–92), which didn't stop Koopmans from mistaking her for a man (*RFlorence*, 715n)! All those masculine pronouns referring to women can get confusing, I'll grant you (*FF*, 53–54)—beyond which, farce has been known to stage a pregnant man, as in *Le Galant qui a fait le coup* (*RLV*, #39). But not this time. And whose kid is it anyway? It's Joachim's, in all likelihood; so, dramaturgically, I'd draw inspiration from an old Howard Stern bit reprised in *Private Parts* and get that baby into the act: at least the sound of its bawling up in Heaven. Womp-womp, wah-wah, boo-hoo. Toni loves onomatopoeia and—how convenient!—*Thoynon* rhymes with the *hon! hon!* of laughter in the same way that *Toni* rhymes with *hee, hee!* Ergo, *hee, hee, hee, hee,* all the way home!

Language

Linguistically and ideologically macaronic, *Johnny Palmer* is all about taverns and nightclubs, courts and Councils, food and drink, dancing and partying, boating and piracy, wine casks and bungholes, digestion and excretion, and, at its potty-mouthed worst, thrones and toilets. It is all the more logical that, during a struggle with a recalcitrant bunghole, wordplay gets so explosive that it recalls this modern *contrepèterie*: *pour trouver le trou du fût, il faut écarter les caisses* ("to find the hole of the cask, you must move the barrels out of the way"). When you turn the spoonerism on its ass, you get: *pour trouver le trou du* cul, *il faut écarter les* fesses ("to find the asshole, you must move the butt cheeks aside"). Elsewhere, our play conducts an intertextual discussion with *Cooch E. Whippet* (*FF*, 364–65) or *The Shithouse* (*HD*, 97) about the inhabitants of hell. It tips its fool's cap to a *gorrière*'s fashion sense (#4, *Drama Queens*) and to the Chaucerian gelding of Brother Fillerup's prescription (#6). There's also a concrete reference to a troupe of brotherly actors or student performers, as in #10, *The Pardoners' Tales* and #11, *Slick Brother Willy*. But, mostly, it's tennis take all, with rackets, paddles, volleys, backhand, balls in the air, and onomatopoeia up the wazoo. You'll find some of the original Middle French noise—or music—in italics: the jubilant *tarara, tararirene, hy! hy!* (v. 100), the magical *ababou, tanfarara, tanfarara* (v. 92), the hoisting *touet, touet* (v. 177), the giggling *hon, hon, hon, hen, hen!* (*MFST*, 190; 222; 230; 232; 263). I even intuit a couple of *Ubu-Roy*-like moments where it seems that we're hearing an obscenity until a final consonant resolves the meaning in favor of something else: *maire* > *merde* ("Mayor" vs. "shit"); *faire chière* [*lye*] > *faire chier* ("to party" vs. "to make someone shit") (notes 16 and 22). It's what you might call a *trompe-l'oreille.*

Sets and Staging

There's a distinct neighborhood feel to the Parisian setting teeming with pubs and clubs. Think Soho, think theater district, think Moulin Rouge, Folies Bergères, Crazy Horse, and seedier Pigalle. And do depict those nightspots on the backdrop, along with a tennis court. Some of the locales may be fictional, such as the "Champ Gaillard" (*RFlorence*, 718n). As the construction site for the Church of the Resurrected Baboons, it is presumably a street—or a house—of ill repute in the Fifth Arrondissement (*SFQS*, note 133); but, for legibility, it shall be another Gallic "field": the Champs-Elysées. Other establishments are real (*RC*, xxi–xxvii), notably the Châtelet and the Collège de Beauvais (v. 326). The former was intimately connected to farce, hosting Basochial pleadings in the Grand' Chambre and detainees in Châtelet prison (*TB*, 8–27; *ROMD*, chap. 3; *RFlorence*, 720). The latter, founded in 1370 by Jean de Dormans, Bishop of Beauvais, was situated in Le Bourg l'Abbé (v. 193), roughly corresponding to today's Third Arrondissement (*RC*, xxvi; *SFQS*, note 81; *RC*, xxvi; *RFlorence*, 719n). And then, there's the *Pomme de pin* (v. 225), or "The Pinecone," a favorite hangout of Villon and Rabelais (*RC*, xxiii), the sexual and theological symbolism of which would have escaped no *farceur*. (I'll be going with "The Winey Little Bitch.") Women used to place pinecones under their pillows for fertility; and the Pope's own staff bore a pinecone, to say nothing of the three-story-tall bronze *Pigna* in Vatican City.[5]

Now, consider the *Ruppée* (v. 227), which, in a way, I might have treated under § "Language." Cohen gave up on identifying it (*RC*, 411n); but Koopmans believes that it's the *Rappée*, a Parisian cabaret at Les Halles (*RFlorence*, 716n). Maybe he's right, maybe I'm wrong; but I suspect a near-untranslatable microlevel spoonerism that would flip *Ruppée* into the comestible, digestible *purée*. In French, this very popular backward-talking syllable-swapping is known as *verlan* (for *l'envers*). It's a farcical *mot à l'envers*, as it were, attested as early as Béroul's twelfth-century Tristan's reverse name of "Tantris." Additionally, *purée de raisin* is a synonym for wine . . . on top of which, *Ruppée* looks a bit like *ruper* ("to burp"): all consistent with the onomatopoeia of digestion in a play that gleefully stages the unfortunate outcomes of that process. (Martin kindly reminds us that a fart is often considered a drink [*SFQS*, 106], as in the flatulent *dégustation* of the *Farce of the Fart* [*FF*, 85].) And let's not forget the *loppin* that Joachim pinched at the *Ruppée*. It's a "little nibble" or a "blow struck"; but, when likewise flipped on its butt, we get *polain*, a "virile member" at the very textual instant when the illegitimate sire of Jokin' Joachim's loins comes up. Here, the *Ruppée* shall be "Dick's Creamery."

For the inauguration of the Company of Baboons, which features a rousing chorus of their chapter anthem (vv. 231–34; *MFST*, 263–64), the space must be suited to scholastic, juridical, and celebratory functions. I've designed a *tableau vivant* (below, note 17), after which all the drinking, singing, twisting, and dancing of the *barbary liry* hurtle toward a Rabelaisian ending (vv. 195–97; *MFST*, 279). As if to theatricalize Brother John's famous pun from *Gargantua* (chap. 27), the *service divin* (the divine office) morphs into the *service du vin* (the serving of wine) (*CWFR*, 66). *Divine service* as *wine service*: that's what Brother Johnny serves up and passes out.

Costumes and Props

Detritus from a night of partying includes empty bottles—or boxes—of wine, a few tennis rackets, and a large number of hats. For the headgear: the trademark furry hats of the Basochiens (*ROMD*, 136–41), fools' and jesters' caps, Devil-ear hairbands, a *toque* or chef's hat, and, in recognition of tennis, some headbands, bandanas, and perhaps a cap emblazoned with "Make the Resurrection Great Again." For Johnny, a cape; and for Joachim, a wheelbarrow. For the Council Meeting: wine casks containing potables of questionable clarity, a common cup, and a long table with five chairs for dining and deliberation. Nearby the throne-toilet, place some reading matter and an anachronistic iPhone or two.

Scholarly References to Copyrighted Materials (in order of appearance and indicated by © within the text)

"Since You've Gone, [My Heart Is Broken Another Time]." By Gary Busey. ASCAP Work ID: 490359716.

"We May Never Pass This Way Again." By Darrell Crofts and Jimmy Seals. BMI Work #1617190.

"All She Wants to Do Is Dance." ASCAP Work ID: 310240843.

"What'd I Say." By Ray Charles. BMI Work #1631628; also licensed through https://raycharles.com/music/singles-discography/.

"They're Coming to Take Me Away, Ha-Ha." By Jerry Samuels. ASCAP Work ID: 500221503.

"Bibbidi Bobbidi." By David Mack, Al Hoffman, and Jerry Livingston. ASCAP Work ID: 320044162.

"Achy-Breaky Heart." By Kenneth Gregory Watters. SESAC Work Number: 55896468.

"When Johnny Comes Marching Home." By Patrick Gilmore [aka Louis Lambert]. (19th c.)

"Over the Rainbow." By Harold Arlen and E. Y. Harburg. ASCAP Work ID: 450062263.

"When the Saints Come Marching In." Traditional.

"Do-Wacka-Do." By Roger Miller. BMI Work #1719799.

"Row, Row, Row Your Boat." Traditional.

"Sit Down, You're Rocking the Boat." By Frank Loesser. ASCAP Work ID: 490071624.

"My Boyfriend's Back." By Bob Feldman, Gerald Goldstein, and Richard Gottehrer. BMI Work #1028431.

"Johnny B Goode." By Chuck Berry. BMI Work #773553.

"I'll Take You There." By Alvertis Isbell. BMI Work #643764.

"Twist." By Hank Ballard. BMI Work #1561070.

"Pa-, Pa-, Pa-, Papageno." From *The Magic Flute*. By Wolfgang Amadeus Mozart (1791).

"Hey Diddle Diddle." Nursery rhyme.

"Once in a Lifetime." ["Letting the Days Go By."] By David Byrne, Brian Eno, Christopher Frantz, Jerry Harrison, and Martina Weymouth. BMI Work #1117241.

"Celebration." By Eumire Deodato Almeida et al. ASCAP Work ID: 330279293.

"It's in His Kiss." By Rudy Clark. BMI Work #744118.

"Chevaliers de la table ronde." Traditional.

"And When I Die." By Laura Nyro. BMI Work #40714.

"Plop, Plop, Fizz, Fizz." [Alka-Seltzer jingle.] By Thomas Dawes. ASCAP Artist IPI Number: 88568319.[6]

"C'est si bon." By Henri Betti and André Hornez. ASCAP Work ID: 887366085.

"Les Champs Elysées." By Pierre Delanoë, Michael Wilshaw, and Michael Deighan. BMI Work #849309.

"Bye-Bye, Birdie." By Lee Adams and Charles Strouse. ASCAP Work ID: 320119564.

"La Marseillaise." By Claude Joseph Rouget de Lisle. (18th c.)
"Barbara Ann." By Fred Fassert. BMI Work #87434.
"Bottle of Wine." By Tom Paxton. ASCAP Work ID: 320130096.
"Show Me the Way to Go Home." By James Campbell and Reginald Connelly [aka Irving King]. (1925).

[Scene 1]

[*In Paris in the wee hours, the bars have closed but a few stragglers remain on the deserted streets. The set is strewn with hats, as if another comedy has recently been staged.*]

JOHNNY'S SISTER, JOANIE *begins [in song]*

Since you've gone, my heart is broken another time!©
So, here's the thing: I've got the blues. My brother Johnny's dead! My broken heart will never mend. Ain't none of y'all seen him come by this way? I know he never had much use for God or nothin', but did He really have to kill him off? Good God Almighty! Johnny would gladly have done without. Oh no, Johnny, no! You've come and gone. I wish to God that you were still alive!

Enter JOACHIM

Mary, blessed Mother of—! What's wrong?

JOANIE

Everything's wrong.

JOACHIM

[*Lecherously*] I can see you're upset. What gives?

JOANIE

What gives? [*Making the sign of the cross*] *In nomine Patri*, I'm in such a piteous state that, unless there's a reversal of Fortune from the good Lord Himself, there's not a man in this town who can reverse *my* fortunes.

JOACHIM

You're still young and perky. Chin up. Be of good cheer. Snap out of it! And—man, oh man!—there's no need to be so frosty. Everybody knows that the icy fingers of Death make you crazy.

JOANIE

[*She brushes Joachim aside.*] I'm crazy, all right: crazy mad—oh, Johnny, my brother!—every time I think of you.

JOACHIM

[*To the audience*] Good God Almighty, she's a master*piece* . . . of ass! You need me to clean your chimney there, little lady? Come noon, I'd be glad to lend a hand and sweep those blues away.[7]

JOANIE

Since he's gone, my heart is broken another time![©8] Lord have mercy, I haven't had a moment's happiness since they laid my brother Johnny Glad-Hand Palmer to rest! And he shall never pass this way again.[©] Ashes to ashes, dust to dust. There is no joy in Studville. [Mighty Johnny has checked out.]

JOACHIM

[*He imitates Johnny's preferred tennis maneuvers as he grabs her.*] Who? Good old game-set-match Johnny? Now, shut up because I'm ready to serve, and have I got the balls! We'll make out like bandits here.

JOANIE

No way you've got my brother Johnny's stuff.[9] [He was nobody's fool.]

JOACHIM

[*Waving a fool's cap over his genitals*] In the name of Saint Johnson, I swear! I'm not fool enough to haul your ass over to the Franciscans like your brother Johnny used to do.

JOANIE

I get over there from time to time, when I've got something to get off my chest with the heavenly father.[10]

JOACHIM

Whoa-ho-ho! Not to worry: I'm the soul of patience and I'll do right by you. Count on it. Maybe your brother Johnny swallowed all that jiggery-pokery but I can think of better things to swallow whole. Plus, I'd never do you like that. [{*He points to the sleeveless scapular of his monastic habit.*} See? Nothing up the brotherly sleeve of this here scapular.]

JOANIE

[{*To the audience*} And that's just crapular.]
You'd do me just like that, you damn pimp.

JOACHIM

Any time the spirit moves you, Jezebel! Next time you get the urge to make a few bucks, I'll pop you in my wheelbarrow—not some rickety cart—and take you there in style. Cash and carry, by golly, on that highway to Heaven! What more can I say? Your own personal magic carpet ride!

JOANIE

As long as it's all on the up and up. I'll have you know I frequent the right kind of people.

JOACHIM

The crème de la crème, I'm sure. Mum's the word. *Mummm, mummm,* goody.

JOANIE

When my brother Johnny was still alive, everybody over at the cloisters and the convents would roll out the red carpet for me. Whatever I wanted, my wish was their command. Those doors were always open.

JOACHIM

Open is right. For business. Your reputation precedes you.

JOANIE

Oh, the tricks I played.

JOACHIM

Oh, the tricks you turned! Crème de la crème all over your sweet ass! Ding-dong-ding, little lady, you can ring my bells any time.

JOANIE

Been there, done that. And I do believe there's no momma's child ever done 'em all and undone 'em all like me. In one way and out the other.

JOACHIM

And with brother Johnny waiting in the wings the whole time—the patience of a saint, that one—keeping a close eye on things.

JOANIE

[*To the audience*] I do solemnly swear, folks: since he died, I ain't never hooked up with the likes of him again. Feast to famine, I guess, I can barely make ends meet.

JOACHIM

I won't let you down, by golly! I know what I'm doing—it's all part of a brother's act—and we'll have ourselves a grand old time, believe me. To hell with Johnny! He's food for worms. Now, party on, Joanie!

JOANIE

And don't you be thinking I'm one of those sluts who does two at a time.

JOACHIM

In the name of Saint Peter's cock-a-doodle-doo, I take thee at thy word, [fair maid]! Now, coochie, coochie coo, Johnny's Sister! Follow me, 'cause it's happy hour somewhere and all the munchies are finger-lickin' good.

JOANIE

Is that so?

JOACHIM

Let's stop beating around the bush, shall we? All you got to do is dance!© Now, off we go. Just follow my lead. Do what I do, say what I say.© [*He grabs her and begins to lead.*]

JOANIE

Whoa, now! Are you trying to trip me up?
[{*To the audience*} Some of us have been to rehearsal.]

[Scene 2]

[*As Joachim tries to lead Joanie away, enter, Zorro-like, a cape-clad Johnny Palmer. At first, he is faintly heard and seen only by the audience.*]

JOHNNY PALMER

Ha-ha, hee-hee, ho-ho!© Tennis anyone?

JOACHIM

Let's be on our merry way.

JOHNNY *singing*

Salagadoola mechicka boola bibbidi-bobbidi . . . Boo!©[11]

JOANIE

Joachim, my achy breaky heart© will never be merry again.[12]

JOACHIM

How come?

JOHNNY *sings* [*still at some distance*]

When Johnny comes marching home again, hurrah, hurrah! The ladies they will all turn out!© And that goes for you too, Miss Thing!

JOACHIM

Jesus H.—I'll be damned if that's not Johnny Palmer headed this way!

JOANIE

Lord have mercy! Where?

JOACHIM

I heard him right over there.

JOHNNY *sings*

Abracadabra, alacazam! Tennis, anyone? Ha-ha, hee-hee, ho-ho!©

JOANIE

Bless my soul, there he is! It's him—*he*—him! It's Johnny! Johnny! My brother Johnny!

JOHNNY

Hey, hey, hey, sis, whaddaya say?

JOANIE

There he is! He has risen! What do I do?

JOHNNY

Damn straight, babe!
[{*To the audience*} Been to rehearsal, my ass!]

JOACHIM

[*He makes the sign of the cross.*] *In nomine Patri et—.* Blessed is he who cometh in the name of the . . . Dude. Way to make an entrance.

JOHNNY

Ha-ha, hee-hee, ho-ho!© Game, set . . . tennis anyone? We gonna drink to my arrival here or what?

JOANIE

Lord have mercy, my brother! Where'd you come from?

JOHNNY

Hello! Where'd I come from? I can't say, but I bet that I've come a long, long way.

JOANIE

[Not from . . .] You've been—oh my God!—*there*?

JOHNNY

Hello! From far, far away. Behind the moon. Beyond the rain. Somewhere under the rainbow.©
[*He gestures, his back toward the crowd.*]

JOACHIM

[*Sarcastically*] Great to have you back. [And cheat front, wouldya?]

JOHNNY

Here I am! Like a bat outta hell, where—you should pardon the expression—there's hell to pay. It's a damn torture chamber down there.

JOACHIM

Tell me: Is it a long way down?

JOHNNY

What the—? Dude. It's the path to hell!
[Hey, folks! Wanna know how you make holy water? You boil the hell out of it!]

JOACHIM

Paved with bad jokes, I guess. What kinda folks they got down there?

JOHNNY

Hello! Every kind and then some. I seen Gilbert Thingamajig maybe a week or so ago, hangin' from the highest tree.

[JOACHIM

Really? All the way down there?][13]

JOHNNY

Dawg. You think God's gonna put up with any shit? He don't mess around.

JOACHIM

[*To Joanie*] Say something to him!

JOANIE

Jeez, I hardly dare. Tomorrow is another day.

JOHNNY

I even seen . . . Remember poor old Alan? I seen him around too. And Charles—the one who killed that gelding that time. [Mount was fine till they cut his balls off.] He's right next to your uncle, Joachim.

JOACHIM

[How did you know my uncle's name was Joachim?] They coming back too, or what?

JOHNNY

Hello! In sure and certain . . . You betcha! They'll get sprung in about two months. Just sit tight.

JOACHIM

As a nun's ass.

JOANIE

And *nun* too soon, Jeez. I wanna be there in that number!©

JOHNNY

Ooh-la-la!

JOANIE

And, in the name of Saint Johnson, I'm there! And there *will* be joy in Studville!

JOHNNY

Hello! People! Still parched here! Dry as a bone. Bottoms up! Bottoms up!

JOANIE

Coming right up for everybody, honey. As much as your little heart desires.

JOACHIM

For God's sake, this is crazy!

JOHNNY *singing*

Abracadabra, alacazam! And we'll all feel gay when Johnny comes marching home!© [*He doffs a cap, grabs a tennis racket, and swats someone.*] And doo whacka doo whacka doo© to you too!

[*Enter Birdie at some distance, initially unseen. He/She/They near the group to see and hear what's going on.*]

JOACHIM

Game, set . . . catch! And he brought back a—. [Dude. That's your hat from Scene 3.] Same fool as he ever was. [Talk about your typecasting.]

JOANIE

Bless his heart! Now what?

JOACHIM

Off we go, I say, before he reveals himself to our friends. Exit, stage left!

JOANIE

Since you've gone, my heart was broken another time!© Johnny, my brother, when you died, I almost had an achy-breaky heart attack© and dropped dead myself.

JOHNNY

Yo-ho-ho! Arthur Ashes to ashes, dust to dust.
[*He laughs at his own joke, turns to the audience, and attempts to move them all toward a tavern.*] Maestro, [a little traveling music please]:
McEnroe, row, row your boat . . . ©
[{*To the audience*} No, not you, folks! Sit down, sit down, sit down you're rockin' the boat!© Yo-ho-ho-ho!]

[Scene 3]

[*Enter Toni.*]

BIRDIE

Ho-ho-ho-ho! Come on along with me now, Toni, and welcome Johnny home.

TONI

What, Cuz? You mean my cousin's back? He has risen?[14]

BIRDIE

Duh. He's with his sister. Come along with me, now Toni, so I don't get scared. Scooby-dooby-doo-doo . . . *Do!*

TONI

Ha! Ha! Ha! I can't hardly wait to see him *cuz,* Birdie girl, we're gonna party. *Cousin/Cousine/Cou*-seeing is believing! [My cousin's back and there's gonna be trouble!©]

BIRDIE

Hey-la, hey-la, my cousin's back!© Swing your partner!

TONI

Maybe you could take it down a notch?
[{*To the audience*} They always have to make a whole production.]
Be good now and come along peacefully.

BIRDIE

[*Continuing to dance and grabbing one of the hats off the ground*] Good. Birdie, good, good, good!©

TONI

Birdie, be good!© Really? That's the look you're going for? What's cousin Johnny gonna have to say about that?

BIRDIE

That it's time to party! [It's time to get down!©] And that he'll bring the wine. Party on, [Toni], party on!

TONI

Party on—ha! ha!—and I'll tell you where. Come on!

BIRDIE

Be there with bells on. Round and round and round she goes . . . Ha! ha! ha! ha! ha! ha!

TONI *smacking him* [*i.e.,* them]

Ha! ha! ha! Where she . . . *Stop*! Behave yourself. [Birdie,] be good© because . . . *heeeere's* Johnny!

BIRDIE

Where's he at? If you'd be good enough, *Madame*, to—. Mercy! Just take me there!©

TONI

There he is! There he is!

BIRDIE

Avast ye, matey!

TONI

Easy does it there, sir—*madam*—steady as she goes! Now quit fooling around and show him your [damn] breeding! [*She bumps into Birdie's enormous fake breasts.*] And don't be such a boob!

BIRDIE

Ha! Johnny, ha-ha-ha! Johnny, ho-ho-ho!© And now, my good sir: put 'er there, pal. And fork over the headgear!
Hey! What's with the cape? [*They try to take Johnny's fool's cap and fail.*]

JOHNNY

Game, set . . . catch! [When hell freezes over!]

TONI

Ha! ha! Where'd you come from cousin? Hey! Did you hear I had myself a baby? You never saw him—kid croaked—but you'll soon see who made the little bastard. [*She indicates Joachim.*]

[*Johnny doffs his cap and hastily puts it back on.*]

JOACHIM

Well, hats off to the damn miracle child! Wherever could it have come from?

TONI

From right outta my womb! Big as a little piggy. But, soon as he was born, pirates stole him away. He was already going "yo-ho-ho!"[15]

JOACHIM

[And a bottle of rum!] You won that kid in a poker game up at the Moulin Rouge!

TONI

Screw you! [*She points to her womb.*] Read it and weep![16]

JOACHIM

Just come right out and say it, toots.

[*Birdie begins to dance again.*]

JOHNNY

Watch the Birdie now and—come on, Toni—let's do the twist.

Johnny sings

Just shake your little ass, it goes like this. Twist! Twist!© Sing out Toni! Toni-Tone, the Tonester, Looney-Tones, Antoinette, Anthony! And God bless us, everyone!

BIRDIE

And God bless Johnny.

JOHNNY

God bless you too 'cause I just had me a gander at my Grammie down there too. And the soul of my little cuz. [*He points to Toni's womb and to Joachim.*] Pa-pa . . . Papagena! Papageno! Papagena! Papageno! Papagena, Papageno, Papagena!©

TONI

In the name of Saint Johnson, I do believe he's telling the truth. [*To Joachim*] You recognize me now, don't you, bro?

JOACHIM

Yeah, for the *trol—*.

JOHNNY *sings*

La! La! La! And hey, hey, hey! diddle-diddle. [*He swats Toni on the ass.*] The cow jumped over the moon! [The little dog laughed. . . .©]

JOACHIM

[*He laughs.*] Same as I ever was! Same as you ever was.© [And who are you calling a dog, dawg?]

JOANIE

Let's change the subject.

TONI

Hop, hop, hop to it! It's party time. Celebrate good times, come on!©

JOACHIM

Jolly good, I say. I'm a helluva sacred host, so—[*with a tennis move and a gong for the bad joke*] I'll serve!

JOANIE

"Serve it up" is more like it, but it's a good idea anyway. Now, let's have some fun!

TONI

Hop to it! There's no turning back now. Celebrate good times, come on!©

BIRDIE

Yo-ho-ho!

JOACHIM

And no more yak-yak-yakkin' around here.

JOHNNY

Let's go on home for dinner. I'll serve! Cook you up some goose and—hello!—what's good for the goosing is good for the gander!

BIRDIE

Always takin' the piss, that one, but enough fooling around! And, by the by, we are not pickin' up the tab again, you hear? We'll do potluck. Oh, ye of little faith! You think he's talking about the Last Supper?

[*They prepare to leave for* somebody's *place but don't actually go anywhere. Instead, the drunken revelers—including a plant or two in the audience who might join them—slowly, surely, and sacrilegiously morph into a banquet scene that takes on a kind of Pageant-of-the-Masters quality. They become a living, breathing image of Da Vinci's Last Supper where, conveniently, everyone is already cheating front.*][17]

JOACHIM

Jolly good! All I need is a little fruit o' the vine. I don't eat much.

JOANIE

[If I had a nickel for every time I heard that one!]
[*She displays a huge cask.*] Here's a little something I picked up last night over at Ye Olde Winey Little Bitch. The tavern. [*They look doubtful.*] Really.

JOACHIM

[I prefer the Pinecone myself. Gimme a pine*cunt* any day, but] here's a juicy little morsel I picked up over at Dick's Creamery. [Taste the soup.]

TONI

From our soup to his nuts! He got the meat, I got the motion.

JOACHIM

In nomine Patri... Quick! We better say grace.

TONI

You first.

JOHNNY *sings [and attempts to get everybody dancing.]*

Give me Baboons!

[Ladies and gentlemen, we are the members of the Holy Order of Saint Baboon. Care to sing along?]

Give me Baboons!
Everybody sings
We are drunken baboons
and our rules say that here's what we do:
Sleep in till noon, and, at midnight, we'll croon
you a tune of the drunken buffoons![18]

[So, come on, baboons! Monk-ey see, monk-ey do! {*He lays a huge fart.*} Bottoms up! {*He lays another fart.*}]

[*Birdie has some difficulty inserting the spigot into the bunghole of the wine cask; and the pressure of their exertion leads to more farting. When the hole is finally pierced, the liquid gushes out all over; so, receptacles must be found quickly.*]

TONI

Ha! ha! Is that the way to drink?©

JOACHIM

No, no, that's not the way!© Good God Almighty, Birdie, did you—? Is this the shit they're giving us to drink?

TONI

Ha! Goddamn son of a...

[*The pressure valve released, the cask overflows.*]

BIRDIE

[*Goutons voir! Oui, oui, oui! Goutons voir, non, non, non! Goutons voir, si le vin est bon!*©] Help yourselves! Bottoms up!

JOANIE

Only if you can get by on one tiny little drop. It's spillin' out all over and—[*sniffing the "bouquet" as Johnny farts again*]—opening way up!

BIRDIE

[*Handling the wine cask*] You don't know what you're talking about. I personally screwed that spigot all the way into the bunghole. So, don't you be letting it go to waste. Whoopee! Drink up. Please. Dunk your bread in there. [This is my body and this is my . . .]

[*As Johnny continues to belch and fart, he beckons one and all to sing and dance. Meanwhile, Joachim greedily guzzles as much wine from the keg as he possibly can. The others angle to get at a common cup that becomes increasingly disgusting.*]

JOACHIM

To hell with that lousy, rotten son of a—. Gross. That cup runneth all over the place and it stinks!

BIRDIE

[*To Joachim*] Excuse *you*! Am I or am I not the one who supplied the Jesus juice?

JOANIE

Must be nothing but bran where he's been. He's fartin' like a pig! [And I thought I was the one with the "Preparation-*Aitchy*" breaky heart.]

TONI

[*To Johnny*] Colon blow, blow, blow your boat!©
[*To Joachim*] And no mudslinging either! Seriously? You're in no position to be casting aspersions.

BIRDIE

[*Indicating Joachim*] Get rid o' that bug up my ass, wouldya Toni?

[*The mimed disciplining of Joachim ensues, apparently effective because the brother is silent for a time.*]

TONI

[*To Joachim*] Come off it, my brother, and on your way! Always down and dirty with you! This is some fine resurrection we've gotten ourselves into.[19]

BIRDIE

[*To Joachim*] You suck.

TONI

Some novice. *Grand cru(de)*, if you ask me. As if anyone would follow *him*!

JOHNNY

Ha-ha, hee-hee—.

JOANIE

Ho-*no*!©

BIRDIE

Is he drunk? Didn't seem like he'd had that much to drink. [*They perform a frenetic—and flatulent—dance as the others continue their dialogue.*]

TONI

Know what? Before we part company here today, what do you say we make it official and call our order . . . to order.

[*Joachim is offended that Toni is not addressing* him. *He makes his displeasure manifest but capitulates gesturally after everyone looks daggers at him.*]

JOACHIM

Your call. Order away. I'll do what you do, say what you say.©

JOANIE

So ordered. Without objection.

JOACHIM

I promise.

JOANIE

[*She clears her throat.*] From this day forward, whatever the cost, we shall have our own convent, the better to welcome back all those who return from the dead and get resurrected like my brother Johnny.

JOACHIM

In the name of Saint Johnson, let's do it! And when I die—and when I'm dead, dead and gone,© maybe I'll get resurrected too! At least my house will be in order.

JOANIE

This calls for a real masterpiece, though, [and not just some Pageant-of-the-Masters-piece]. In living color. And much better set design. Who, then, shall be commissioned for this purpose?

JOACHIM

[If we build it, they will come.] Just tell me where and when and, by God, I'm on it! But no pageant wagons, okay? [Those have to go before the Architectural Board of Review.][20]

TONI

And your neighbors show up and make objections. Bitch, bitch, bitch.

JOACHIM

There's nothing they can say that won't go our way. They won't have a leg to stand on.

[*The characters make a move to position Birdie on a high, dilapidated chair to be used as a throne, which they then elevate and place in front of the long dining table. A particularly large and messy pot is spoiling the scene, so Joanie places it under the throne.*]

JOANIE

In charge of the erection of this building—and set design too—I nominate Birdie, in the flesh, so that, by the power vested in *him* . . . her . . . *they* can preside and commission somebody.

TONI

Aha! They're one of a kind. Perfect for our ho-ho-holy order. She's your man!

[*Everyone prepares for a makeshift tribunal.*]

JOANIE

[A backhanded compliment if I ever heard one.] Now quit dawdling. Up you go, Birdie! Have a seat over there on the throne, listen to all parties, and dazzle us, sir—ma'am—with your wit.

BIRDIE

[*More farts ensue.*] Totally ready to take a load off. But there's a hole in that throne? [I'll be just like Pope Joan!][21]

JOANIE

Indeed. Now sit your ass down and—shit!—give it a rest.

[*Birdie mounts the throne and Toni rushes over to assist with pen, paper, and an iPhone so that Birdie can tweet.*]

BIRDIE

Pop, pop, fizz, fizz, oh, what a relief it is!© *C'est si bon.*©

TONI

If it please the court, Birdie, Your Eminence, by the power vested in you: Where and by *hoo-hoo*-whom shall our convent be built?

BIRDIE

I've got just the man for the job, by God! Our own Jokin' Joachim! *Quel enfant terrible!*

JOANIE

And where shall it be?

BIRDIE

Where else do you go to see and be seen? *Oh, Champs Elysées—[la-la-la-la-la]—aux Champs-Élysées!*© Plus we need the foot traffic if we're gonna get converts.

JOANIE

It's a fine ruling, all in good order.
[*To the audience*] And no comments from the peanut gallery!

BIRDIE

So ordered. I give you leave.
[{*To the audience*} No, don't *leave*, folks!] We're just getting down to business. It's almost time to clean up [and, then it's bye-bye, Birdie!©]

[*Birdie takes the pot that is located under the pierced throne and hands it to Joachim before making a move to depart.*]

JOANIE

[What a brilliant invention!] And you, Brother Joachim, shall take care of *that*, sir. Head counsel for making shit happen. [*Joachim protests gesturally and is again stared down.*]
[*To Johnny*] And, if you need an extra pair of hands, my brother: Johnny on the spot over there is at your service.
[*To Joachim*] What are you waiting for? Legal representation?

JOACHIM

But not one more move out of Birdie! That's our new Mother—*Father*—Superior. [Queen of queens and lord of lords!]

BIRDIE

I accept.

TONI

Me too, that's for sure. Good call.

[*Johnny is handed a towel for intimate paperwork, which he promptly "palms" off on Joachim.*]

JOHNNY

They don't call me Johnny Glad-Hand Palmer for nothin'! For palm to palm is holy Palmer's . . . Gross. You know what they say, folks: Don't shit where you live! [Party on!][22]

[*The Company begins to pass the hat for financial contributions.*]

TONI

Let's get outta here!

JOHNNY

Please, after you.

JOACHIM

[God bless you *Messieurs*! God bless you, *Mesdames*. God bless you *Messieurs-Dames*!] Long live the company! Long live the theater! Long live our campus! And, since we've clearly got to spell it out for you folks: That's the end of *The Resurrection of Johnny Palmer*, our glad-handed friend, the dear[ly departed . . . departing as we speak. Going, going, gone!] And, with that, we bid you adieu until the morrow because [that's game, set, match! *Allons Enfants-sans-Souci de la patrie!*©][23]
[*Doubled version begins here.*]
Long live our troupe, each woman and each man,
'cause now it's time for you to lend a hand.
This Resurrection play about our friend
might well be done but you've still got glad hands.
Adieu till next time, folks, this is the end.
[*Doubled version ends here, before a possible closing number*][24]

The END

9.

The Resurrection of Johnny Slack-Jaw, or, *The Harrowing of Heaven*

La Résurrection de Jenin Landore

CAST OF CHARACTERS

JOHNNY SLACK-JAW (Jenin [Landore])
ALISON, his WIFE (Sa Femme)
The PARISH PRIEST (Le Curé)
ADSO, Novice to the Parish Priest (Le Clerc)

PRODUCTION NOTES

The *Farce nouvelle très bonne et fort joyeuse de la résurrection de Jenin Landore à quatre personnaiges* (*RBM*, #24) appears in *ATF*, 2: 21–34—again, paginated but without verse numbers. It was first published in Paris by Nicolas Chrestien between 1547 and 1557, sometime after *Johnny Palmer* (#8), but the play itself is older (*RF*, 11: 25n; *FFMA*, 4: 119). Indeed, when Tissier reedited and translated it into modern French, correcting some thirty errors in the *ATF* along the way (*RF*, 11: 19–58; *FFMA*, 4: 114–28), he placed its date of composition between 1511 and 1512. Contemporaneous with Pierre Gringore's *Prince des Sots*, this was a historical moment that coincided with the Wars of Religion pitting the French Louis XII against Pope Julius II, whom the former longed to depose (*RF*, 11: 25–29; *FFMA*, 4: 119). I know of no English translation of our play of 242 octosyllabic verses; but helpful plot summaries are provided by Petit de Julleville (*RTC*, #182, 228), Faivre (*Répertoire*, #148, 380–81), and Delepierre (*DLU*, 45–46).

Plot

It's Easter again, as in *The Con-Man's Confession* (#1) and *Highway Robbery* (#3), and—lo and behold!—he has risen. No, not *Him*. It's "Jenin Landore," drinker, player, all-around funny man, and the literal "April Fool" of the play's overarching joke (§ "Language"). But, unlike Johnny Palmer (#8), this Every-John has returned not from below but from above, with a quick stop in Purgatory for drunkenness (*RF*, 11: 38n). He brings with him, moreover, a vivid account of the hellacious politics of Paradise which rivals that of some of the feistier *moralités* of the *Recueil La Vallière* (Beck, *Théâtre et propagande*). Newly endowed with "wit and science" (as in John Redford's sixteenth-century play by that name), our resurrectee's got "know-how" (*science*; 2: 28), to wit: a Platonic combo of skill, technique, and "technology" (*technē*) to be demonstrated by an unholy trinity of skills. Johnny *knows how* to shut women up, to read palms, and to make himself invisible.[1] Now you see Him; now you don't. Papa's got a brand-new bag. Of tricks.

Although this is certainly not the first joker's eye view of the afterlife,[2] Johnny's Paradise features an otherworldly death match in which the patron saints of Rome, Venice, France, and Spain (Peter, Mark, Dennis, and James, respectively) vie for their farcical slices of heaven.[3] The Swiss and the Germans have sent in mercenaries too (2: 25); while Saint George of England looks on cautiously from the sidelines. And *quelle coincidence*! When Louis XII took up arms against Pope Julius II, he was supported militarily by the Swiss and, later, by the Venetians and the Spanish (*FFMA*, 4: 119). Also present are many of the battle-players catalogued in Isidore of Seville's seventh-century *Etymologies,* a kind of performance studies *avant la lettre* complete with warriors and equestrians, drinkers and gamblers, card and dice players, comic and tragic actors (bk. 18; *ROMD*, 77–89). But something—or someone—is lost in the scuffle, be it Johnny, the protagonists, the author(s), or the copyist(s). Predictably for farce, everything is backward in a proto-Seinfeldian land of opposites. Saint Christopher is on horseback and Saint Martin on foot when, iconographically speaking, it should be the opposite (2: 27; *RF*, 11: 46n). Saint Benedict is walking around with a blackbird (a demon in disguise), which he should have normally shooed away with the sign of the cross (*RF*, 11: 39–48). Saint Paul, who was decapitated in Rome, is the decapitator of Saint Dennis (2: 24; *RF*, 11: 40n); and the peaceful Saint Francis of Assisi is whacking people right and left.[4] Meanwhile, at the feet of the "Archangel" Michael is no neutralized Devil but a "hot babe" (2: 24); while San Lorenzo, the patron saint of cooking, is doing the roasting instead of being roasted (2: 25; *RF*, 11: 42n; below, § "Sets and Staging"). Plus, check out who is *not* Heaven-sent. There are no lawyers in Heaven, that is: no *procureurs* (prosecutors), no *avocats* (lawyers), no *plaideurs* (litigators), no *sergens* (bailiffs or police), and no rhetorical imperative to forsake physical arms in favor of verbal mediation (*ROMD*, 89–110). Even Saint Yves has failed to sneak through Johnny's Pearly Gates when, apocryphally, Yves was the only lawyer to make it into Paradise (*RF*, 11: 47n; *FFMA*, 4: 312n). It all makes for some fine, self-deprecating Basochial humor akin to a contemporary lawyer joke like this one: An attorney arrives in Heaven, only to see that the Pope is lodged in the equivalent of a Motel 6. Saint Peter explains: "We have over a hundred Popes up here, but we've never had a lawyer."[5]

For Petit de Julleville, *Johnny Slack-Jaw* was an undramatic if "nicely rhymed" satire (*RTC*, 228); and, for Faivre, it was conventional (*Répertoire*, 380). I submit, however, that it's a dazzling farcical *monde à l'envers* in which the very "Harrowing of Hell" is turned upside down as a "Harrowing of Heaven."[6] Sacrilegiously, Palm *Sunday* morphs into palm *reading* (2: 29), communion *wine* into wine-*tasting* (2: 22), and a former *stiff* demands a *stiff* drink (2: 21). But, from Plato to Rabelais, there is truth in wine—aided here by a pun on *voire* ("truth" or "true") and *voirre* ("glass") (2: 21–22). *In vino veritas. In farsā veritas?* Truth will out this side of Paradise, starting with the same question asked by our previous play: Was Johnny ever really there? Or, in the immortal words of R.E.M., was it all "just a dream, just a dream"? Can Johnny be both dead and buried (*ensepvely*; 2: 21) and, at the same time, per the *RBM* woodcut, lying in repose (Figure 4)? Yes, he can. It turns out that *ensevelir* denotes both "to bury" and "to wrap in a shroud," which permits Tissier's ingenious resolution of a pun that also works in English (*RF*, 11: 25–27; *FFMA*, 1: 120). If Johnny was dead, he was "dead drunk" (*ivre mort*), only to snap out of his catatonia to perform his resurrection as a parlor trick. How terribly Christlike of Johnny: dead, but not really as he lands the play's main salvo that Catholic literalism was the big joke.

Once upon a time in Valenciennes in 1547, medieval audiences were said to have witnessed a reprise of the miracle of the loaves and the fishes during a Passion play (Enders, "Performing Miracles"; *DBD*, chap. 12). Johnny is no Christ figure, and God only knows he isn't the Pope wearing the shoes of the fisherman. He's a practical joker and a Christ-impersonator with bigger fish to fry: nowhere more so than in his closing disappearing act. Make

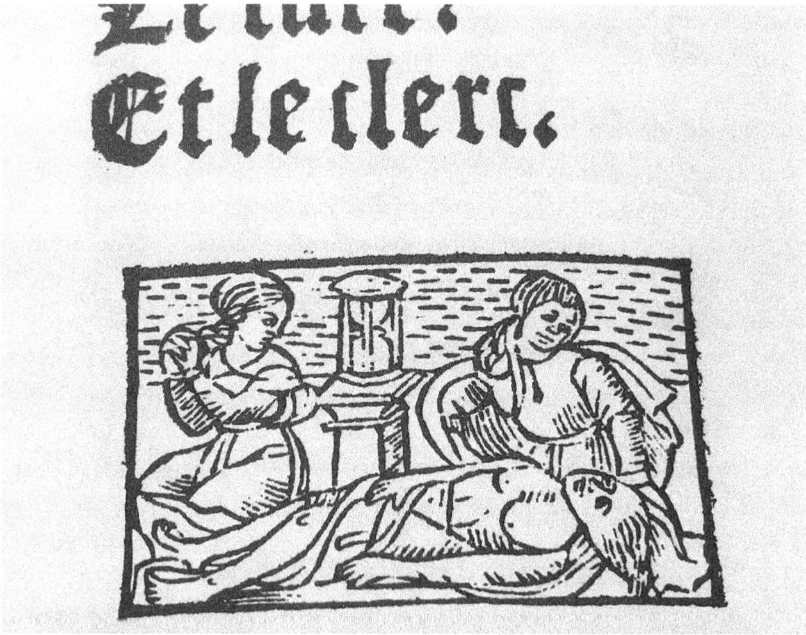

Figure 4. Frontispiece, *La Resurrection de Jenin Landore. RBM*, #24.

way for the miracle of the Fools and the Fishes! And the fishnets (below, § "Language").

Characters and Character Development

When we enter in medias res, Johnny's unnamed Wife (here, "Alison," which I borrow from Chaucer) is weeping for the dearly departed. She's distraught, hysterical, and histrionic—all with fairly good grammar—and smarter than your average farce-wife. At times, she is borderline regal or aristocratic when addressing her husband with *vous*. And yet, she is vaguely menacing in her interrogation of the resurrected Johnny, with whom she eventually loses all patience (*FFMA*, 4: 120). Why not? He's a pain in the net. Try giving her the upper hand by putting her in fishnet stockings.

With his novice in tow, the Parish Priest (*Le Curé*) aims to please, albeit less lecherously than Jokin' Joachim of *Johnny Palmer* (#8). He's a pedagogical and theological go-to guy, ready to impart any wisdom necessary for interpreting Johnny's account of the afterlife. Armed with the vocabulary of scholastic disputation, he clearly relishes his magisterial role, as if presiding at a quodlibetal disputation: questioning during the *disputatio* and issuing the final intellectual resolution of the *determinatio* (Enders, "Theater of Scholastic Erudition," 345–51). Overall, he is relatively polite, if somewhat more casual before the resurrection, courteously employing *vous* with both Alison and Johnny.

Slyly mirroring any learners in the audience, the Novice (*Le Clerc*) appears to be a theology student. (Technically, a *clericus* could be any "instructed" man.) As an homage to Umberto Eco's *Name of the Rose*, I've christened him "Adso," and he has quite the learning curve. Nearly as chatty as his Master, he intervenes twenty-one times to the Priest's twenty-four, peppering everybody with questions. Initially, his good manners are very much on display with flowery speech; but, the more he sees, the more curious and uninhibited he becomes, lapsing into *tu* toward the magical ending. We also know something else about him: like twenty-first-century students, he's tired and he needs to get some sleep (2: 34). Actors too.

Now enter the title character, for whom all the world's a stage, and all the men and women merely straight-men. Consistent with the play's iconographic befuddlement, if he has returned from anywhere, it's—"straight as a curved dagger"—from the kingdom of mixed metaphors (*tout aussi droit qu'une faucille*; 2: 26). Above all, Johnny is hell-bent on being believed as he delivers two-thirds of the play's dialogue (*je vous prometz*; *certes*; *par mon serment*). Perhaps that's why he's such a fast-talker: speed might forestall prosecutorial scrutiny of all the anticlerical zingers. Regardless, the historical present is perfect for the breathless pace of Johnny's adventures, punctuated "all over" with *atout, atout* (2: 24), which I've rendered with the ubiquitous American *like, like, you know, like*. He also favors the onomatopoeia of warfare, and his *patic, patac* (2: 24)—the origin of today's *patati, patata*—sounds a lot like the auditory effects of a *Batman* comic book. But the greatest challenge lies in translating his full name: "Jenin Landore," a masterpiece of wordplay.

When endeavoring to convince the company that it's really him, Johnny utters this key but untranslatable line: *Si suis-je Jenin par le nez / Et Landore par le menton* (2: 23). Literally, it's "Jenin by the nose and *Landore* by the chin (or the jaw)," all as the clergy takes one on the chin. But what in heaven's name does that mean? For the longest time, I'd scripted him as "Long Dong Silver," which captured the farcical obsession with the lower body, the phallic nose or chin of Mister *Johnny*son, the equine nature of "horsing around," and the trial endured by Anita Hill. But why would a silver-donged devil be recognizable by the nose and the chin? Suspecting more linguistic nonsense, I tried Pig Latin (*ig-pay atin-Lay*), gibberish (*githigee-bithiger-ithigish*), and *verlan*;[7] and I hunted for *contrepèteries* (*FF*, 43–44), all to no avail. In the end, I stuck with Johnny's explanation as written: Johnny by a nose (a medieval sign of intelligence [*FF*, 379; *RF*, 11: 239n])![8] Cast an actor with an aquiline schnoz and a "nose for wine" (*le nez du vin*). As for *Landore*, while it looks a bit like "golden-tongue" (*langue d'or*), it's actually a fool, a clown, an "oaf," or, as in Rabelais's *Pantagruel*, a "slow and lazy person who always seems to be nodding off" (*CWFR*, 524). This fits the exhausted Johnny to a tee (2: 34). He's a sloth, a slouch-*mouth*, and a slack-jawed slacker who might be suffering from a hangover (*la gueule de bois*). Eyes wide open, mouth wide open, all agape for drinking, talking, and farcing around.

Language

As early as Henri d'Andeli's thirteenth-century send-up of university politics, Plato and Aristotle were going at it in an Isidorian battlefield in the *Battle of the Seven Arts* (188–95). French ideological warfare had long been cast in blood-drenched militaristic terms; and that is precisely what obtains here. But the primary linguistic feature of *The Resurrection of Johnny Slack-Jaw* is its prankster's April-Foolishness, to which this section is devoted.

"April Fool!"—*poysson d'apvril!*—cries foolish Johnny (2: 31), or, as the French have it, "April *Fish*!", and there's definitely something fishy going on. If, in *Johnny Palmer* (#8, § "Plot"), *tout finit par des boissons*—"they all drank happily ever after"—in *Johnny Slack-Jaw*, *tout finit par des* poissons: "they all *fished* foolishly ever after"? Brace yourselves for a lengthy exploration of some of the wackiest intertextual wordplay ever because this whole farce depends on it.[9]

Why an April *fish*? Simply put, what the English *Second Shepherd's Play* does with *sheep*, *Johnny Slack-Jaw* does with *fish*. And not sheepishly. Easter often falls in April and, sometimes, serendipitously, on April Fools' Day (as in 1453, 1464 1526, 1537, 1548, etc.). As does fishing season, the time of abundant, easily caught hatchlings. And, most germane of all, the April Fish is related to the holiest of Christological *jeux de mots*: the acrostic for Jesus's name. JESUS was the sacred fish (ICHTHUS or ICHTHYS): I*esous* C*hristos* T*heou* Y*ios* S*oter* ("Jesus Christ, Son of God, Savior"). But the punning gets even *ickier* when a particularly symbolic fish gets caught in Johnny's net. Holy mackerel!

It's mackerel season too (*RF*, 11: 52–53n), and there are plenty of fish in the See. Plus, a fish by any other name smells just as stinky inasmuch as "mackerel" also connoted "pimp" (*macquereau*) and "go-between" (*entremetteur*). That fishiness then sets up a deadly serious but seriously playful spin on the *mediatory* role of any priest as go-between. In the bender-overworld of *Johnny Slack-Jaw*, self-indulgent priests are intermediaries between God and man in the same way that *pimps* are intermediaries. *Playing* tricks is transformed into *turning* tricks, just as Joanie used to do in #8, *Johnny Palmer* (sc. 1). When Johnny puts on his magical mystery show, he's the middle man par excellence between Earth and Heaven, the ultimate *entremetteur-en-scène*.

Furthermore, if Valenciennes gave us the miracle of the loaves and the fishes, *Johnny Slack-Jaw* concentrates on its farcical double: the miracle of the mackerels and magpies. Indeed, our play alludes directly to a piece of dialogue from one of the better-known farces. In *For the Birds* (*HD*, #4), the mismatched couple, Connor and Maggie, argue for several hundred verses about a magpie vs. a cuckoo. When you put a magpie in a cage, asks Maggie, what do you teach her to say? What else? *Macquereau* or "sleazy pimp" (*HD*, 126–30). In *For the Birds*, Maggie's caged Christmas cuckoo triumphs over Connor's uncaged "Maggie-pie" (*HD*, 134); in *Johnny Slack-Jaw*, the winner is Johnny, with a metafarcical, interspecies joke about the Christmas magpie and the Easter Fish. When it comes to *fowl*-mouthed Christmas birds and stinky, pimped-out April fishes, *Johnny Slack-Jaw* gives us both fish *and* fowl. Make that fish and *foul*. Or fish and *fool*—all the more so in that, over in Scotland, an April fool is an April "gowk" or "cuckoo" (the British *gob* or *fool*). April Fool again! And there's nothing foolish at all, by the way, about the whole stylistic maneuver, one of best examples of rhetorical *transsumptio* (metalepsis) I've ever seen. Nor, as far as I can tell, about what may well be the first apparent use—far earlier than the seventeenth-century origins posited in the *Littré*—of *poisson d'avril*.

Sets and Staging

Given Johnny's report, the first dramaturgical decision to be made is whether, when, and how to depict the upside-down kingdom of Heaven. This is a Paradise of such compelling linguistic, iconographic, ideological, and theological proportions that it practically begs to be visualized dramaturgically with such a device as the scenic dissolve that follows "I remember it as if it were yesterday." A mimed sequence might enliven Johnny's visit to the great thereafter; or the battle royal might be painted on a backdrop.

Next, one must determine where we are when the curtain goes up. At Johnny's wake, as Figure 4 suggests? It's a suggestion that appears, moreover, to have influenced Delepierre's and Tissier's readings (*DLU*, 45; *FFMA*, 4: 121). Both have Johnny bolting upright from wherever his not-really-dead body is lying in repose. But images have been known to lead us astray, as when the title-page image of *Marriage with a Grain of Salt* memorialized something that never happened in the play (*HD*, 398–400). I've tried something else instead. Have Johnny enter on horseback, for instance, à la *Monty Python and the Holy Grail*, to interrupt Alison's lament. Or borrow the cemetery set from *At Cross Purposes* (*FF*, #7) and have Johnny *about to be* laid to rest. The prospect of being buried alive would certainly trigger a resurrection right quick. Or borrow the set from #8, *Johnny Palmer*, and have him awaken from a bender on the deserted streets after the bars have closed. Better yet, borrow the tavern set of #10, *The Pardoners' Tales* (*RBM* #26 to our play's *RBM* #24 with only *The Jackass Conjecture* in between [#25, *HD*, #5]).[10] For one thing, Johnny is always in high *spirits*: *spirituel* means "witty." For another thing, he employs a tavern metaphor when describing San Lorenzo, who was roasting Swiss (*Lansquenets*) "on the grill, like they was sausages at a tavern in winter" (2: 25). This is entirely in keeping with a Paradise where, you should pardon the expression, everybody is at *lager*-heads. Here, then, is my recommendation for how to split the difference: in light of the title character's need for fishnets for his magic show, stage the action at the docks of a busy port where a sleazy bar is de rigueur. And one last thing: since Johnny will reappear after his disappearing act, have some fun figuring out how he might unveil, un-*net*, and un*knot* himself at the denouement, potentially as late as the Statesian curtain call (*Great Reckonings*, 197–206).

Costumes and Props

Plenty of food and drink should be available, along with all the necessities for at least one game of three-card Monte (decks of cards, rudimentary tables, etc.). Of the utmost importance is the most comically sacrilegious part of Johnny's costume: his burial shroud, which functions here as a veritable magician's cape and which can double as a ghost costume (below, note 19). For the big ICHTHUS payoff, fishing rods and large fisherman's nets are mandatory, filled with as many fake or real crustaceans, fish, and mackerel as the nose can tolerate. If the set is shared with *The Pardoners' Tales*, some baby clothes might be present, especially an infant's bonnet for Johnny's reference to King Herod's Slaughter of the Innocents (2: 33). It could then make way for the principal prop of our next play (#10, § "Costumes and Props"). Finally, some instruments might be placed strategically onstage for a closing musical number.

Scholarly References to Copyrighted Materials (in order of appearance and indicated by © within the text)

"So Long, Farewell." By Richard Rodgers and Oscar Hammerstein II. ASCAP Work ID: 490089142.
"Magic to Do." By Stephen Lawrence Schwartz. ASCAP Work ID: 886449522.
"Heaven Sent." Jingle. By Buddy Weed.[11]
"How Long?" By J. D. Souther. ASCAP Work ID: 380147929.
"Oh, Mary, Don't You Weep." Spiritual.
"Papa's Got a Brand New Bag." By James Brown. BMI Work #1149944.
"Losing My Religion." By Robert Baskaran, William Berry, Peter Buck, Michael Mills, John Michael Stipe, and Brian Wakefield. BMI Work #20325189.

[Scene 1]

[*Possible opening music*][12]

[*The scene: near a bustling port, where many goods and comestibles are being loaded and unloaded*]

ALISON *begins* [*with a song*]

Alas! My husband's come and gone,
my Johnny Slack-Jaw. Woe is me!
My hope, my joy, it's all gone wrong:
Alas! Alack! He's come and gone!
No happy mem'ries: just this song.

I'm sad! My heart mourns woefully.
Alas! Alack! He's come and gone,
my Johnny Slack-Jaw. Woe is me![13]

The PRIEST

[Oh miser*ee*, hee, hee, hee, hee!] Even when they were burying him, that drunk was still askin' a brother for a good stiff one.

ADSO

A stiff one for a stiff! [That's a good one!]

ALISON

Alas, 'tis true!

The PRIEST

[Ashes to ashes. {*He coughs.*} Dust to dust.] He died of thirst.

ALISON

You can say that again.

The PRIEST

He sure knew how to knock back a few. Never left a thing in his glass either. Always good till the last drop.

ADSO

In that respect, he was like you, Father. He always enjoyed a good wine-tasting too. And bar-hopping.

ALISON

Oh why, oh why came Death to wrest from me the one I loved so well and take him down? [*She teeters.*]

The PRIEST

Steady as she goes! [*He imitates Johnny's drunken gait.*] Good old joker Johnny? Straight was his gait? *Not.* [And pass a field sobriety test?] He could barely walk a straight line! Always went down easy.[14]

[Scene 2]

[*Enter Johnny Slack-Jaw, possibly on horseback. From nose to chin, his face is almost entirely covered by his burial shroud as he gallops about the platea.*]

JOHNNY SLACK-JAW

Bona dies et bonjouribus! Yo! Up there in the peanut gallery! That's Latin for "God bless." Now, stand back! stand back! 'cause here I am! here I am! I just been there!

ALISON

[*She makes the sign of the cross.*] Bless me, Mother, Our Lady of Comfort, Joy, and Getting-Your-Book-into-Print![15] What is this?

JOHNNY SLACK-JAW

This is your husband!

ALISON

He's dead! Never have I been so sore afraid!

JOHNNY SLACK-JAW

I am dead, yet now have I risen. Sure as I'm standing here.

ALISON

Where'd you say you've been?

JOHNNY SLACK-JAW

In Heaven, [o ye of little—.] Quit lollygaggin' and check it out! [*He tugs on his shroud.*] What do you call *this*? Got my burial shroud and everything! Made a stop in Purgatory too.

ALISON

You are not Johnny Slack-Jaw. I have no idea what you're doing here.

JOHNNY SLACK-JAW

Am too! [*He reveals his face.*] It's me! Johnny Slack-Jaw! Snatched from the jawbones of death. So, chin up, honey! The nose knows, and it's Johnny by a nose! And by the hair of his chinny-chin-chin!

The PRIEST

That's him, all right.

JOHNNY SLACK-JAW

You can say that again!

ALISON

Yeah, well, he's not laying a hand on me.

JOHNNY SLACK-JAW

Oh, the stories I could tell if I felt like opening my mouth.

ALISON

What stories? By all means, knock yourself out. Let's hear 'em. There are no secrets onstage.

JOHNNY SLACK-JAW

I saw one helluva commotion up there. It was awesome.

The PRIEST

A series of unfortunate events?

JOHNNY SLACK-JAW

I saw. . . . So, there was, like, Saint Peter with his keys . . . and Saint Paul with his sword and, like, he'd cut off Saint Dennis's head. And Saint Francis was, like, fightin' 'em and whackin' 'em all over the place with a pow! wham! bam! And—yada, yada, yada—it's, like, then, in comes Saint Mark—right?—and he practically skins 'em alive! And, then, in comes Saint James—*Santiago de Compostela*—all swashbucklin' and stuff, all havin' away like he's some kinda caped crusader. So, like, God sees this whole troupe, like goin' at it—right?—and, well: hear ye! hear ye! and abracadabra! He ups and picks Himself the winner and it's, like, Saint Francis! But, me, I was gettin' scared, so I just got the hell outta there![16]

The PRIEST

Tell us, Johnny Slacker, what about Saint George? What was he up to?

JOHNNY SLACK-JAW

He was in no condition to be strikin' while no Iron Maiden was hot, lemme tell you. And he wasn't slayin' no dragon neither! Let's just say he was lookin' to cut his losses.

The PRIEST

I must say that that battle does indeed appear to have been "awesome."

JOHNNY SLACK-JAW

And then—. Whoa! Gird those loins! They gotta close the gates to Paradise—it's a real siege mentality, you know?—'cause the whole place is surrounded! It's totally crawlin' with Swiss and a bunch o' German mercenaries to boot. And, lemme tell you, they're all geared to be wagin' one hell of an awesome war up there in Heaven, and that's the God's honest truth. So, check it out: there's not a moment to lose, right? So, God, He goes and creates each of 'em their own personal slice o' Heaven. Everybody knows these guys have hated each other forever. [It got partisan up there, yah know?]

ADSO

Just one second there! You must be mistaken, inasmuch as that would be creating an entirely new cultural construction of Paradise . . . [*inspecting Johnny's burial shroud*] out of whole cloth.

JOHNNY SLACK-JAW

You can say that again, I swear! But, then, it's a real knock-down, drag-out, right? All of 'em hammerin' and poundin' away. And you got San Lorenzo—right?—who's, like, havin' himself a grand old time cheffing. He's roastin' Swiss on the grill, like they was sausages at a tavern in winter. [And, hey! Fork the Swiss!] Obviously, I was not gonna be stickin' around.

The PRIEST

Explain.

JOHNNY SLACK-JAW

Next thing you know, they'd be stickin' a fork in me too and—game over! I know the ace o' spades when I see it and [they ain't trumpin' my ass!]

ALISON

[And the joker is wild.] If you could just get to the point and tell us what Heaven is like.

JOHNNY SLACK-JAW

[Yeah, yeah, yeah.] Lemme tell you, it sure ain't what it used to be.

ADSO

[*To the Priest*] Is that correct, Master? Can you explain?
[*To Johnny*] Care to clue us in about Saint Matty? Mickey? Whoever.

JOHNNY SLACK-JAW

Same old, same old. Unless you wanna count that hot babe at the feet of the Archangel Michael, like, instead o' the Devil.

The PRIEST

That's hardly appropriate.

JOHNNY SLACK-JAW

Yeah, well, God help me, that's how it is. Plus, you got Saint Benedict the Elder, keepin' up the old laws. Only, then, you got Saint Benedict the Younger too, and he ain't even keepin' up the Church no more, that's for sure. Nope. He's just walkin' around with that blackbird o' his on his wrist, puttin' on airs, all dolled up like he's some kinda player.

The PRIEST

I must admit that, for a slacker, Johnny talks quite a good game.

[*Alison glares at him and taps her foot impatiently.*]

JOHNNY SLACK-JAW

I oughta talk good when I just been there! Walked me a crooked mile straight over here. And if I would've been smarter, I would've been, like, well within my rights to never come back here at all!

ALISON

[{*Aside*} When do *I* get my seven minutes in heaven?]
Were you in Heaven long?

JOHNNY SLACK-JAW

Yes, ma'am! And, lemme tell you: it's about as drama-free up there as your average Thanksgiving dinner.

The PRIEST

I do believe that the truth of the matter is that there is no suffering in Heaven.

JOHNNY SLACK-JAW

Saint Christopher's ridin' around on horseback up there.

ADSO

And Saint Martin? What about him?

JOHNNY SLACK-JAW

He's on foot for the time being.

ALISON

Say, what were the Apostles up to up there?

JOHNNY SLACK-JAW

They're all sayin' the Lord's Prayer.

The PRIEST

Does anybody overdo it in Heaven?

JOHNNY SLACK-JAW

You mean, like, get all "lawsuited" up and ready to go? Nope! You got no suits, no trials, no war, no jealousy. And there's no debatin' either 'cause they only got the one lawyer. They don't even need litigators in, like, that eminent domain.

ADSO

What about the District Attorney's Office? Tell us: there must be some prosecutors up there, right?

JOHNNY SLACK-JAW

I cannot tell a lie, I swear, so I'm prepared to report that—hear ye! hear ye!—didn't see me a single one, and that's the truth. There was one got as far as the Pearly Gates but, when he tried to get in, he gave God such a splitting headache, they kicked his ass right outta there.

ADSO

[He must be referring to Saint Yves, Master.] But what about bailiffs and—hey, Johnny!—what about peace officers? Is there a police presence in Heaven?

JOHNNY SLACK-JAW

Jesus H. Christ on a cracker! Didn't see me a single one.

The PRIEST

And, therefore, all things considered—when all is said and done—would you say that you learned something up there?

JOHNNY SLACK-JAW

Lord have mercy, you can say that again! [But what? Go fish!]

[The PRIEST

So, what is it?

JOHNNY SLACK-JAW

Where?][17]

The PRIEST

Enlighten us. What did you learn?

[*A hubbub of noisy excitement follows at the port.*]

JOHNNY SLACK-JAW

Now hear this: I learned . . . Pay attention! Silence!

The PRIEST

What?

JOHNNY SLACK-JAW

Stuff. Know-how. [Go fish!]

ALISON

What stuff? [I already told you: no secrets onstage.]

JOHNNY SLACK-JAW

How to keep women from talkin' when I feel like it. [Go fish!]

The PRIEST

'Tis a wondrous thing but—bless my immortal soul!—I do believe that a demonstration might be in order.

JOHNNY SLACK-JAW

It's true!

ALISON

[*Menacingly*] And how exactly would that work, Johnny?

JOHNNY SLACK-JAW

Just give 'em a little somethin' to drink 'cause I do believe that, when they be drinkin' they don't be talkin'! And that's the truth, one hundred percent! It is known.

ADSO

Johnny, what other know-how do you . . . you know . . . know how to do?

JOHNNY SLACK-JAW

I got one for you: I learned how to read palms. I can tell folks their fortune, soon as I see their hands.

ADSO

Is this true?

JOHNNY SLACK-JAW

In the name of Saint Peter, the Apostle: the truth, the whole truth, and nothing but the truth! You first, Monsignor, gimme yours. Come on, don't be shy.

The PRIEST

Here you are, good sir.

JOHNNY SLACK-JAW

I don't believe what I'm seein'! But—no!—I dare not say.

The PRIEST

Permission to speak freely. [{*He glares at the noisy audience.*} God knows everyone else does.] Say your piece.

JOHNNY SLACK-JAW

The truth of the matter is . . . Where ya been your whole life? At an orgy? You're a drunk and a glutton, which is why you're gonna live a long life. Plus, you're really into the female o' the species. And you got you an appetite for wine too. The good stuff. That's your whole scene: ain't nowhere else you'd rather be.

The PRIEST

Goddamn crazy son of a—! That joker *is* wild!

JOHNNY SLACK-JAW

Tibi soli and *ipso facto* to you too, bub.

ALISON

Lord have mercy, Johnny, what on earth—? You speak Latin now? I can't understand what you're saying.

JOHNNY SLACK-JAW

Like Latin from Heaven! I'm so full of it, I'm ready to pop!
If I wouldn't have let it all out, I was gonna burst for
sure.

ADSO

Over here! Over here! Do me! Take a look at my hand!

JOHNNY SLACK-JAW

[*He studies Adso's palm at some length.*] Dawg. You're a real player, ain'tcha kid?

ADSO

Lord have mercy, Johnny, you're shaking your head.

JOHNNY SLACK-JAW

It's all that blood rushin' to my brain and messin' with Johnny's head! I'm too smart for my own [damn] good.

ADSO

Quick, what does it say about me?

JOHNNY SLACK-JAW

April fool!

ADSO

April fool?

JOHNNY SLACK-JAW

Well, look who's catchin' on! That is correct, yes.

ADSO

Fine. But, verily, I do not understand your meaning.

JOHNNY SLACK-JAW

[*To the audience*] What is he, nuts? Can you believe this fool? Dude. When you put a magpie in a cage, what's the first thing you teach it to say? [Did you or did you not catch our performance of *For the Birds*?] Out with it!

ADSO

Mackerel. [{*Abashedly to Alison*} That means "pimp."]

JOHNNY SLACK-JAW

[*Brandishing a large mackerel and fishing rod.*] Holy mackerel! Would you listen to the filthy mouth on that kid!
[*To Adso*] Atta boy, *clericus*, [there's a good goy! Check it out, fools! Remember the miracle of the loaves and the . . . say it with me now: *fishes*!] [*He uses the fishing rod to point to the life-line on Adso's palm.*] Bottom line—bottom *line*, get it?—April fools! April fish! April

mackerel! [April intermediary between God and man! April Pimp! April fuckin' Priest! The fish is a mackerel, the mackerel's a pimp, the pimp is a priest, and—holy icky *ichthus*! Talk about your middle man! Intermediary, my ass!] The Priest is the biggest April Fool of 'em all and—I swear!—so are you! What a joke![18] Now, to finish up the reading: you too, Padre junior! Plus, you're a student: you're lazy. And you like to get your rest.

ALISON
Wow. [*She presents her palm too.*] Over here! Whatever will you have to say about me, dear?

JOHNNY SLACK-JAW
What I don't know won't hurt me, woman, I swear! Or my reputation. Seek not and ye shall not find.
Plus, if I were to read your palm, I might well uncover evidence of that which I do not wish to know and. . . . Case closed! Besides . . .

ALISON
Besides what?

JOHNNY SLACK-JAW
At this juncture, Johnny would assert his right to remain silent.

ALISON
Oh, really? As if you could!

JOHNNY SLACK-JAW
I swear, woman, a wise man sticks his nose into his wife's affairs as little as possible. Don't ask, don't tell.

The PRIEST
A fine strategy. He knows the score. [*He strokes Alison's hand.*] Flying off the *hand*-le is a sin, you know.

ALISON
Johnny, what other stuff and know-how did you learn to do in Heaven?

JOHNNY SLACK-JAW

All o' you better watch your step or I'm gonna scare the bejesus outta you in a minute!

ADSO

Come again?

JOHNNY SLACK-JAW

Silence! Not one word and ye shall witness an awesome feat, [strange and wondrous,] for I shall make myself invisible! I can do it whenever I want, and that's all you need to know. Nothing up my sleeve and—behold! Got the nets of Saint Peter and Saint Andrew right here, gonna make you fishers of men!
[{*He covers himself with his burial shroud and, after dumping out any dead fish, with the nets too.*} "Holy Ghost! Holy Ghost! This is not an episode of *Scooby Doo*!"][19]

ADSO

I take thee at thy word but—God help me!—have you got the goods to prove it?

[*While Adso is distracted, possibly by the smell of rotten fish, Johnny finds a place to hide and "disappears."*]

JOHNNY SLACK-JAW

[*To the audience*] [Who's he talkin' to?] I swear!
[*To Adso*] You can't see me! [I'm invisible!]

ADSO

But, say, bro! Where ya headed anyway?

JOHNNY SLACK-JAW

Jesus H. Christ on a cracker! None of your business! Plus, you can't see me—remember?—even though . . . Peekaboo, I sure see you!

ALISON

Lord have mercy, Johnny, cut me some slack-jaw! Just how long are you planning on keeping this up?

JOHNNY SLACK-JAW

As long as it took King Herod to slaughter the Innocents. Just you wait and see because, to confound the brave, I shall bring down fire and fury!

The PRIEST

[*To Alison*] People who come down from Heaven are invisible. That's how it works. [{*He takes a peek under the net where at least one or two fishes remain.*} Especially when they've got something to hide.][20]

ALISON

No argument from me. If people from Heaven are invisible, one could hardly see them. [And, by the way, your tautology stinks to high Heaven.]

JOHNNY SLACK-JAW

"*Tautily.*" *Bonjour, bonsoir*, I bid you *adieu*! To yieu and yieu and yieu.© Go with God. [*He waves his cape and, with or without the nets in tow, temporarily disappears behind some crates. Several spectators rise to depart.*]

ADSO

It's a miracle! [But wait! He's making the audience disappear!]

JOHNNY SLACK-JAW

[*He returns to perform some magic tricks, the better to solicit financial contributions.*] You should see the awesome feats I could perform for you if I weren't so tired: [pop the coins off the eyes o' dead Irishmen!] But, for now, adieu. I'm outta here.

[*Doubled version* begins here.]
And now I lay me down to say,
I'll live to play another day.[21]

[*Possible closing music* after doubled version.][22]

The END

10.

The Pardoners' Tales, or, *Panderers' Box*

La Farce d'un Pardonneur, d'un Triacleur et d'une Tavernière

CAST OF CHARACTERS

The PARDONER (Le Pardonneur)
The SNAKE-OIL SALESMAN (Le Triacleur)
[FRENCHY,] the ALEWIFE (La Tavernière)
[A number of Extras at the Bar, mostly Monks]

PRODUCTION NOTES

The *Farce nouvelle tres bonne et fort joyeuse à troys personnages d'un Pardonneur, d'un Triacleur et d'une Tavernière* (*RBM*, #26) appears in *ATF*, 2: 50–63—again, paginated but without verse numbers—and in *RF*, 5: 229–73. Tissier also translated it into modern French (*FFMA*, 2: 161–73), as did Ernest and Paul Fièvre in an online verse edition: http://www.theatre-classique.fr/pages/programmes/edition.php?t=../documents/ANONYME_PARDONNEUR.xml (accessed 19 January 2021). So too did Ana P. O. Tavares and Anabela dos Santos Rodrigues into Portuguese but, sadly, it is no longer available online. While I know of no English translation, *The Pardoners' Tales* has been much summarized and discussed, in this instance, by Petit de Julleville (*RTC*, 159), Faivre (*Répertoire*, 318–19), Delepierre (*DLU*, 48–50), the Toldo brothers ("ETCF," 297–99), and Garapon in "Le Réalisme" (15–16). Published by Nicholas Chrestien between 1547 and 1557

(*RF*, 5: 231n), it plays out over 321 octosyllabic verses but not in the standard rhyming couplets, which often yield to *huitains*.

Plot

To paraphrase an old joke: What's the difference between a Pardoner, a Snake-Oil Salesman, and a bucket of shit?

The bucket. Or, in this case, the box: a strongbox (*coffret*), to be exact, which serves as both the key prop and the incarnation of the play's overarching joke (below, § "Costumes and Props"). And what's the difference between a Pardoner (of Chaucerian fame) and a Snake-Oil Salesman? The former is "a sort of vagabond who travels from town to town selling fake relics and trafficking in indulgences" (*RTC*, 189); the latter traffics in more terrestrial narcotics, touting the panacea known as mithridate or theriac (*theriaca*, *thériaque* > *Theriacleur* > *Triacleur*). At first an antidote for snake bites, theriac can be traced all the way back to King Mithridates VI of Pontus (2nd c. BCE), who supposedly perfected the original recipe and from whom it gets its other name, *mithridatum*.[1] The *Triacleur* is, thus, a literal snake-oil salesman, his grass snake (*couleuvre*) still emblazoning the contemporary French pharmacist's insignia. His buyers probably felt much better much faster too: the active ingredient of theriac was opium.

The *Pardoners' Tales* opens with over two hundred verses of dueling sales pitches to all the *Seigneurs, Messieurs, Messeigneurs* there assembled until the pitchmen move on to their next mark, the unnamed Alewife, as she laments her disappearing regulars: pardoners from Amiens and snake-oil salesmen from Venice (2: 59). (Could it be the Wars of Religion?) A masterpiece of intertextuality and double entendres, this farce reprises the *jeu-parti*-structured ripostes of *Match, Point, Counterpoint* (*HD* #6); it brings together the legerdemain of our two resurrected Johnnys (#8 and #9); it lampoons the pilgrims' progress of *Drama Queens* (#4) and *Holy Deadlock* (*HD*, #7); it channels the two hungry thieves of the *Chicken Pie and the Chocolate Cake* (*FCMF*, 151–58); and it picks up on the spiritual and bodily curatives prescribed by Brother Fillerup (#6), Slick Brother Willy (#11), Doc Double-Talk (*Playing Doctor* [*FF*, #6]), the Husband-Trader (*Husband Swap* [*HD*, #10]), and Master Pierre Doribus (*Sottie nouvelle*, *RT*, #9). Mostly, this fever-pitched donnybrook reminds me of the fabulous tale of the big-mouthed actor, Jean de Pontalais, as told by Bonaventure des Périers (1500–1544) in the *Nouvelles récréations et joyeux devis* (*DBD*, 108–10). Legend had it that Pontalais had once interrupted a preacher's sermon with the noisy drum-banging that typically advertised a play. To make a long story short, priest and actor each demand that the other shut up, which culminates in the *farceur* smashing his drum over the infuriated priest's head. But this was not just folklore. Pontalais, one of the aliases of the phallically named Jean de l'Espine, was a real flesh-and-blood actor who was quite popular between 1510 and 1540 (*RF*, 11: 237). Indeed, "Master Jehan du Pontalez" was one of three Parisian *farceurs* who, with Jacques le Basochien and Jehan Seroc, was imprisoned for a time for having angered Francis I (*MES*, 336).

The denouement is likewise a masterpiece, involving a feat of sleight of hand at the tavern with the all-important *coffret* and the allegedly precious relic it contains: *le beguin des innocents* (explained below, § "Costumes and Props"). When the Pardoner asks the Alewife, here "Frenchy," to accept the box in lieu of payment—*on one condition*—we can feel the mythological reversal coming from a mile away (2: 62). Under no circumstances is she to open the box or unwrap its miraculous contents. Needless to say, our latter-day Pandora breaks her promise post haste, unleashing . . . You'll see. But this is no Rabelaisian Silenus box in which inner sublime medicine is masked by outer grotesque figures (*CWFR*, 3). Instead, this farcical "Panderers'" Box will ensure that somebody takes their medicine.

Characters and Character Development

The Pardoner and the Snake-Oil Salesman are medicine men, charlatans, pseudohealers, and apothecaries for body and soul. But let's not put too fine a point on it: they're con-men, scammers, flimflammers, and *pushers*. They're forerunners to Tom Lehrer's "Old Dope Peddler," for whom "today's innocents [or *beguin des innocents*]—are tomorrow's clientele." First to claim the public's attention with a delicious promo on full or partial remission for their sins is the itinerant Pardoner, a *moine vagant* like Slick Brother Willy (#11; *RF*, 5: 32). He's a smooth-talker unwilling to bite his tongue, although he presumably has one for sale. So, by all means, think Chaucer's Pardoner, think Elmer Gantry; but, above all, think one-man show. Clearly relishing the spotlight of his opening fifty-eight-verse infomercial, this Pardoner peppers his spiel with all the tics that we associate with untrustworthy hard-sellers. *Believe him*, he asserts incessantly: it's all on the up and up (*je le vous afferme*, *j'en suis tout seur, je le vous asseure*). He assures, he affirms, he promises, he certifies, he guarantees. Belief, after all, is what it's all about for two men who deploy *croire* and *cuyder* time and time again. But he doth protest too much. Self-indulgent to the end, he could be a man of size, gluttonous enough to indulge his every appetite, be it food or anger. And, oh, the taking of the name of the Lord in vain, as he rounds out the *par bieu*, *mort bieu*, *corps bieu*, *sang bieu*, *vertu bieu*, *ventre bieu*, and *chair bieu* with an occasional *mon Dieu* and a *Jésus* (2: 57–59; *RF*, 5: 257n). For all his pique, though, the smooth-talking Pardoner is not a *fast*-talker. There's a certain slowness of speech akin to that of a modern Swiss accent, which is conveyed by an unusual amount of diaresis or *scansion* (when a normally silent vowel is pronounced for an extra poetic foot).

Occupying a lower rung on the social ladder is the Snake-Oil Salesman, who is relentlessly *tutuoied* by his rival (whom he audaciously *tutoies* back)—that is, when the Pardoner deigns to address him directly at all. That may be why the *Triacleur* is also at pains to make guarantees of his own (*rien de plus certain*; *je vous affie* [2: 54; 57]), as when stressing that he is a credentialed member of a trade that had been municipally regulated since 1484 (*RF*, 5: 253n). That said, he lacks even the pharmacist's requisite grass snake. As revealed by one of the few original stage directions, he displays not a *couleuvre* but an eel, another animal with a rich folkloric past (*DBD*, 79–81): *Adoncq il monstre une enguille au lieu d'une couleuvre et dit* (2: 52). He too doth protest too much. A highly focused fast-talker with better-than-average grammar, the Snake-Oil Salesman at first gains the upper hand over his more reactive antagonist. Per the Alewife's remark about Venice (2: 59) and like Father Amadeus in *The Jackass Conjecture* (*HD*, #5), he might speak with an Italian accent. Physically, the mouthy merchant might be missing a few teeth: one possible source for all the tooth relics for sale.

Eager to recoup her business losses, Frenchy has her eye on the prize the whole time, laying it on thick to get into that strongbox. Her own dear husband—don'tcha know?—used to be in the same line of work "pulling teeth" (2: 61), a profession scarcely known for its moral probity (*RF*, 5: 235). I give you, from *SNL*, John Belushi's "Samurai Dentist" or Steve Martin's Theodoric of York.[2] I've christened her "Frenchy," by the way, in honor of Marlene Dietrich's character in *Destry Rides Again*. There's something "wild west" about this saloon; but feel free to substitute "Alewife Annie" or "Ado Annie" for the ultimate girl "who cain't say no." Once alone with the *coffret*,

Frenchy echoes the play's opening debate by debating *herself* in a lengthy soliloquy. To peek or not to peek? Self-proclaimed simple, frail, and naive soul that she purports to be by nature (*nice, fresle et de propre nature* [2: 63]), she sounds just like Eve in the *Play of Adam*: a "weak and tender little thing" (*fieblette e tendre chose* [*MD*, 91, v. 227]). But Frenchy is all Pandora at heart; and the two diabolically irreligious tricksters give her more than she bargained for. And a lot less too.

Last but not least, there's a way in which the *spectators* are bona fide characters in the play. The Pardoner names them by name; and their epithets require translation (2: 51–53; below, note 8). They are the protagonists' *confrères, connoisseurs, con-seurs* ("cunt-sisters?"), and—who knows?—the *con-frairie* of farce-mounting Conards whose reputation for ass-holiness preceded them (2: 51–52). Worthy of any Rabelaisian list, they are the descendants of the great confessor and "cunt-spanker" (*con fesser*), Saint Woody (*Couillebault*) of the "beautiful balls" and the author of dubious "revirginizations" that sound almost like abortions (*RF*, 5: 245n).[3] One can almost imagine a processional of the unholy crew of pseudosaints Boozler (*Pion*), Poontang (*Fente*), Meatstick (*Boudin*), and, fresh off *Bro Job* (#7), Muffie (*Velue*) (*DSI*, 192–94, 214).

Language

The metaphorical world of our play is populated by mythical creatures, starting with the mermaid-like Melusine (2: 52), whose fourteenth-century legend comes down to us from Jehan d'Arras (Maddox and Maddox, *Melusine of Lusignan*). Other magical beasts are linked to the provenance of the talismanic teeth, feathers, eggs, claws, or nails, but their transumptive reach is complex. Take the *coque-grues* (*coquecigrues* in Rabelais): they are neither shellfish nor fowl (*RF*, 5: 265n). But, as an admixture of cocks, cockle shells, and cranes, they are also part of an idiom that means "when hell freezes over"—which is when each vendor will accept the authenticity of the competition's booty. Meanwhile, the veritable architecture of Heaven is held up by a beam (*chevron*) that keeps us focused on the materiality of the stage. Most fascinating of all is the virtually untranslatable wordplay related to the pharmacist's grass snake, the *couleuvre*. The French say *avaler des couleuvres* ("to swallow grass snakes"), which, to closest approximation, means "to bite your tongue" or "to be so insulted that you're not able to reply."[4] Our two vendors reply like crazy until their thirst gets the better of them, which prompts them to "swallow grass snakes" along with their pride.

Sets and Staging

Tissier surmises that our play is of Norman origin (*RF*, 5: 232n) but, in light of a reference to the Seine (2: 57), we are likely in Paris. Two sets are needed: the open marketplace (or a Beckettian no-man's-land), where a game of "three-box Monte" might foretell the flimflam; and Frenchy's drinking establishment, with its buffet setup featuring three upside-down bowls on the bar for further games of "three-bowl Monte." Mime is crucial throughout, particularly to punctuate the hucksters' endless Rabelaisian lists. (I've always suspected that Gargantua's catalogues of games and ass-wipes were meant to be read aloud with accompanying body language [*CWFR*, 50–54, 34–35].) And sleight of hand is the order of the day, whence my dramaturgy that repeatedly directs the audience's gaze toward the disappearing and reappearing strongbox.

Costumes and Props

As in *Shit for Brains* (*FF*, 271–76), interminable spiels double as a props list as our salesmen go at it tooth and nail. Literally. A little bit of tooth here, a little bit of foot there (*de la dent, du pied*, etc.): they're armed to the teeth, as it were, especially the Snake-Oil Salesman who has concealed many items on his person. Both men transport multiple tins, boxes, and buckets of balms, ointments, elixirs, stuff, and nonsense. To make the most of some of the more obscene goodies—tongue, bones, and sausages in honor of *Saint Boudin*—one could almost stage the Snake-Oil Salesman hotdogging with an anachronistic Sabrett's cart: something befitting a traveling sausage fest. Also handy for some of the puns: Turkish taffy and novelty-store chattering teeth. (If you ask me, this sounds like medieval product placement.) The Pardoner, sporting a silly *chapeau* to tip his hat to Pontalais, could carry various contracts too, ideally with many hanging seals. The Snake-Oil Salesman brandishes his eel and, given his allusion to his personal griffins, why not give him some stuffed birds or an Easter basket of marshmallow chicks? Just one caveat for the two men's stashes: they must be portable enough to bring them into the tavern.

Decisive to the stunning denouement, which I won't spoil here, is the strongbox, which should contain something metallic to simulate the cling-clang of coins. This "little tin box," the symbol of corruption in *Fiorello*, is like the Fool's cosmetological bait in the Dutch farce *Blow in the Box* or, better yet, like "Pandarus's box" from Chaucer's *Troilus and Criseyde*. In the end, it all comes down to the pièce de résistance inside, ostensibly a baby's bonnet belonging to one of the infants massacred during the Slaughter of the Innocents (*RF*, 5: 271n): *C'est, ainsi que je l'entens, / Le beguin d'un des Innocens. / Gardez-le nous bien à point; / Mais ne le developpez point* (2: 62). To paraphrase the *Littré*, however, *le beguin* also applied to two types of irreligious individuals: a thirteenth-century heretic or a Brother Preacher who thought himself holy enough to decline civic or religious duty. Since our play text calls for both "opening" and "unwrapping" (*developer*) the *coffret*'s precious content, I suggest that the object inside the box be doubly shrouded: a bonnet inside a drawstring purse. Bottom line: in a play where there are no innocents to be found (except maybe in the audience), I do believe that I've found the *mot juste*—the *acte juste*—for the play's big verbal and visual payoff. But no spoiler alerts. If you absolutely must, see note 26 below. For now, I'll confine myself to announcing that, when the pardoners bail, our medieval Pandora is not exactly in for an immaculate deception.

Scholarly References to Copyrighted Materials (in order of appearance and indicated by © within the text)

"Amazing Grace." By John Newton. (1779).
"The Lord Bless You and Keep You." Traditional hymn.
"Michael Finnegan." Traditional.
"I'm a Woman." By Jerry Leiber and Mike Stoller. BMI Work #4175708.
"Signed, Sealed, Delivered, I'm Yours." By Lee Garrett, Lula Mae Hardaway, Stevie Wonder, and Syreeta Wright. ASCAP Work ID: 490293528.
"Take Me to the Pilot." By Elton John and Bernie Taupin. BMI Work #1450840.
"Big Rock Candy Mountain." Traditional.
"Shake a Tail Feather." By Otha Hayes, Verlie Rice, and Zephire Williams. BMI Work #1318017.
"Little Tin Box." By Jerry Bock and Sheldon Harnick. BMI Work #883643.
"It's Raining Men." By Paul Jabara and Paul Shaffer. BMI Work #1226921.

"76 Trombones!" By Meredith Willson. ASCAP Work ID: 490040443.
"Longfellow Serenade." By Neil Diamond. SESAC Work Number 514272.
"Dry Bones." ["Dem Bones."] By Jay Weldon Johnson and J. Rosomond Johnson. (19th c.)
"Bust a Move." By Matt Dike, Luther Rabb, and Marvin Young. ASCAP Work ID: 320348316.
"Big Spender." By Cy Coleman and Dorothy Fields. ASCAP Work ID: 20137955.
"I'm Called Little Buttercup." By William Schwenk Gilbert, Nicholas Cameron Patrick, and Sir Arthur Seymour Sullivan. From *H.M.S. Pinafore* (1878). BMI Work #4257023.
"Respect." By Otis Redding. BMI Work #1244564.
"Old Dope Peddler." By Tom Lehrer. ASCAP Work ID: 450017026.
"Everything's Alright." By Andrew Lloyd-Webber and Timothy Rice. ASCAP Work ID: 250061588.

[Scene 1]

[*Possible opening music.*][5]

[*Lights up on a busy Parisian marketplace. The Snake-Oil Salesman, a pushcart of products by his side, is engaged in multiple games of three-card Monte while the Pardoner shakes a strongbox, attempting unsuccessfully to whip the audience into a frenzy.*]

The PARDONER *begins*

[Amazing grace, how sweet the sound!© And peace be with you, gentlemen, my brothers. Quit standing around and feast your eyes on these! Amen! Relics like these? Never again shall holiness sell by the pound. So, say it with me, boys: "amen!" What once was lost can now be found. Amazing grace, how sweet the sound!©]

By the power vested in these holy relics here within, the Lord bless you and keep you© and give you . . . a piece of the action! My brothers! It's been quite some time since I've been around these here parts but, please God, I'm fixing to make you all wondrous glad you came. So, [*pardon* me and,] beggin' your indulgence, gents: for your consideration here today . . .

I bring you the ears of Saint Woody, the *Cun . . . Cun . . . Cun*-fessor, and—wait, there's more!—his sister, too, Saint Muffie, and this stuff works miracles, whatever the slings and arrows of outrageous fortune.[6] I can hardly wait to tell you all about those very miracles. Why, once upon a time, all the way down in Africa—I do solemnly swear—this self-same saint, good Sir Woody, he went and . . . and . . . and—[*woody* or won't he, folks? He *wood*!]—he delivered a Jewess who was in the throes of premature labor and, *voilà*! No more baby! And, next item: Hear ye! Hear ye! all about what the great, the wise, [the powerful] Saint Muffie did for this other gal. She gave her back her virginity, I assure you! Shut that whole thing down and had 'er outta commission inside o' thirty minutes flat! And there was plenty o' dick traffic down there, believe you me. [A real open and shut case!][7]
But I digress. It's time to start naming names! Your friends, your neighbors, your fellow players and parishioners, crazy band o' jokers that they are, members one and all of that—oh, holey holy!—most sacred of brotherhoods, the Order of the Wood and the Muffie!
He reads the names [gesturally encouraging anyone named to stand, as if former winners of the "Miss Joker" Competition.]
Allez, Messieurs, écoutez-moi! There's Johnny Pointer, Barb'ry-Doll . . . There's [Honey Bea-Bea], Colin Mule and John-Boy Magpie, Tommy Fool . . . with John-John Deepthroat, Dickie Flick . . . There's John-n'-Tonic, Randy Dick, and Peter Tit-Mouse, Ronald Bean with Looney Tunie, Jeannie Queen, and Johnny Sappie, Gus DeBeer, and Marty Hammer. Say "Hear! Hear!" For all your kin again, let's begin again![©8]

Hear ye, hear ye, all ye gentlemen,
all about your kin and company—
company of men (the brotherhood)—
uncles, cousins, granddads, relatives!
Step right up but, then, down on your knees!
All this can be yours, I promise you,
if the price is right, gents: come on down!
Everything you need—the meatiest!—
bring it on 'cause, folks, it's pardon time!
Bring on the bacon! Warm that pan
for tenderloin and fatty ham,
pigs' knuckles, meat fit for a king:

Never forget that you're a man©
in pretty pointy, dainty things:
Go lay that spread for servicing
in stockings, hats, and gowns adorned.
Use doilies, napkins, napkin rings.
Eat up, folks! Dinah, blow your horn.
Come horn right in and go all out:
That's what a pardon's all about.

[That's right, folks!] It's a goddamn cornucopia! So, here goes nothing! Assume the position and come on down! Get your pardons right here! [*There is no movement from the spectators.*]
You think a pardon from Saint Woody is some kind of a joke? No way, folks, Jeez! And you think a pardon *parade* is a joke? Behold! [*He brandishes a vellum document with multiple hanging seals.*] All one hundred percent genuine, certified pardons! Signed, sealed, deliverance,© they can be yours!
[A fish story, you say?] Behold! Don't you recognize this? It's the seal of that mystical mermaid, Melusine, the water nymphomaniac, procured in a kingdom far, far away in *el grande Castillo de Genitalia*! It's true! Called for a toast with the Sultan himself, who just gives it right up to me: like Holy Water for chocolate and that's no Istanbul-shit.[9]

The SNAKE-OIL SALESMAN
[*Moving center stage to position himself in front of the Pardoner*] And hail Mary, hail Mary! What a load o' crap! Hey, buddy! You think anybody believes that bill o' goods?
Thereupon, he displays an eel instead of a serpent and says:
Stand back, folks, stand back! Stand back, [I say!] Hey, Margot, hey! Where you at, girl? Get your little kisser back up here and say "hi" to the folks! [How's about a hand for the little lady?]

The PARDONER
What is he, kidding? I'm preaching here! And I'll have you know that I do not take kindly to people hawking their wares during one of my sermons. Say, folks: bear with me now [and don't let him pawn anything off on you because . . .] I've got some head of Saint Boozler—right here!—and *more* names from the Brotherhood. And I do believe those

jokers were your very own grandfathers. All your kin again, folks, begin again![©] Johnny Battendown, Big-Mouth Inniscups, Johnny Bendero—

The SNAKE-OIL SALESMAN

. . . *ver* here, milords! Yo! Got me some salves, gonna be your *salve-ation*! Just the thing to rub all over your—

The PARDONER

Who does this lunatic think he is? Somebody shut that fool up.

The SNAKE-OIL SALESMAN

No, shut *him* up! That's enough preaching already. Shut up!

The PARDONER

Peter Drinkwell, Colin Gobsmack, Willy Blackout, Johnny Hooter . . .

The SNAKE-OIL SALESMAN

[*Hoo-hoo-*Hooter!] And gobble, gobble, gobble, [you snotty-faced heap of turkey droppings!] Butter wouldn't melt in his mouth—eh, gentlemen?—but that's some cheesy pitch!

The PARDONER

Omigod! I'm not the one who cut the cheese! Have you no shame? What a con-man! And there you have it, folks! Nobody pays any attention to the good saints and their miracles anymore. It's all liars and confidence men and yea-sayers. Flattery will get you everywhere, you know.

The SNAKE-OIL SALESMAN

Shut up!

The PARDONER

No, you!

The SNAKE-OIL SALESMAN

I have salves and fish oil that I got off Father John, you know, the Evangelist. [*He brandishes his eel again.*]

The PARDONER

Ha! What a snake in the grass! It'll be a cold day in hell before anyone believes that one![10]

The SNAKE-OIL SALESMAN

The hell you say, boy! Lemme do my job! Hey, it's a free market! Do I or do I not have my commercial license? You bet I do! I'm fully bonded and insured! Why, only just today before entering this fair city, I myself was restored to good health. Name your poison, folks—laudanum, arsenic, old lace, the wolfsbane of your existence—there's nothing they can't give that you too wouldn'ta been cured in no time, sure as I'm standing here! [*He brandishes the eel yet again, along with a bottle of gin.*] Even if you woulda been bit by a snake, and—omigod!—before you could even say "gin"![11]

The PARDONER

[Once bitten, twice die!] My friends, my brothers, *frères humains*: to preserve you from peril, I got the pork right here! The snout from good Saint Anthony's very own piggy-wiggy!

The SNAKE-OIL SALESMAN

Milords, behold! [By the light o' the silvery moonshine,] got me off this monk one time this sparrow's egg right here, got laid up the Barb'ry Coast. When there's a full moon, it's fertile, myrtle; but, when there's no moon, no go, no embryo! All hail Saint Muffie: [it's a moon for the misbegotten!] And I got plenty more drugs where that came from, which I'm fixin' to show you right now.[12]

The PARDONER

Lying crook! [Charlatan! And who are you calling Myrtle?] Don't fall for it, folks! Jesus H. Christ, it's a scam—you better believe it! It's a farce! Everywhere you go these days, nothing but dirty tricksters. Present pardoners excluded, of course.

The SNAKE-OIL SALESMAN

Believe *him*? He layin' it on thick enough for you, folks? He takes you for a bunch o' suckers.

The PARDONER

And, now, for your consideration, allow me to show you the crest of Pilate's cock . . . that crowed. Plus, from atop Mount Ararat, half a plank from Noah's Ark![13]

The SNAKE-OIL SALESMAN

[Ara-*what*?] And, take *me* to the Pilate!© I'm the one come down from the frozen mountaintops, where I collected this here root.

The PARDONER

And there's another cock and bull story! Lying crook! [Squawk, squawk, squawk!] That's chicken-shit! Can you believe this guy?

The SNAKE-OIL SALESMAN

[*Speaking more and more quickly*] Gentlemen, over here! Some salve from those very special ingredients found growin' only in the Holy Land: growin', growin', growin' . . .

The PARDONER

Gone! That liar and his squawk-box can go straight to—. Jesus H. Christ! That's some Mess O'Potamia! Drivel, I say! That's not even chicken *soup*! It's just flour and water. [And you know what they say, folks, "paste makes waste."]

The SNAKE-OIL SALESMAN

Liar, liar, pants on fire! God damn him! He can go straight to hell if this ain't the real, genuine article! [I have been to the mountaintop!] Fetched it all the way out at the big Rock Candy Mountain, where they hung the Turk that invented work!©

The PARDONER

Ha! Holy flippin' Christ, you did *not* get that [Turkish taffy] from—. That's a crock-a-doodle-doo!

The SNAKE-OIL SALESMAN

Get a load o' preacher man over there, takin' the name o' the Lord in vain! Jesus fucking Christ! They oughta lock him up and throw away the key! Wouldya listen to the filthy mouth on that priest! All the swearin' and cussin'. A disgrace to the profession, eh, folks? [{*He brandishes a sack, anachronistically full of Ziploc bags filled with pieces of tongue and wafer-like crackers.*} Lock him up! Lock him up! Lock him—]

The PARDONER

[Up yours!] I beg your pardon! You're the one who can't zip it! Are you completely incapable of holding your tongue for five minutes while I finish my presentation? In point of fact, pal, you'd do well to shut up, or you'll soon answer to me!

Gentlemen, behold! Here's the wing of one of the seraphim at the right hand of God! And don't you be thinking this is some farce! Now, gather round—right here!—and take a gander. *Ooh-la-la-la-la!*

The SNAKE-OIL SALESMAN

A gander? Ha! [Yo, Boccaccio!] That's a feather from the goose he had for dinner! [And yeah, yeah, yeah. Every time you hear a bell, an angel gets its wings!]

Jesus H. Christ! You've really got that act o' yours down pat there, pal: flim-flammin' these good folks like that. [Now shake a tail feather©] and get lost!

[The PARDONER][14]

[*Increasingly irate*] And Jesus H. Christ Almighty, you lie! [*He makes the sign of the cross.*] Crock-a-doodle-*lujah*, and amen to that!

The SNAKE-OIL SALESMAN

There he goes again! Takin' the name o' the Lord in vain! Talk about practicing religion without a license! I'm the one's got the drugs. Right here in my little tin box.© [A place for everything and everything in its *play*.] No, wait! That's two, two, *two* little tin boxes! [Two for the price of one,] from the very depths of hell! From the gaping maw of Cerberus! Managed to extract 'em, I did, on Easter Sunday, no less! Looky here! [*With a toothy grin, he brandishes the boxes, shakes them, and removes some teeth.*][15]

The PARDONER

[*Making the sign of the cross*] *Benedicite Dominus*! You can take thy bounty—*das Gift* that keeps on giving—and shove it up—. You're lyin' through your teeth!

The SNAKE-OIL SALESMAN

But wait, there's more! Looky here! Got your Hairy Beardtongue right here! Grows right by Persephone herself down in hell, near the Devil's Paintbrush. And, looky here! Got me some o' that special root for, you know, messin' around with alchemy. Dug it up personally, I did, with my own two hands, I absolutely guarantee. And, then, to carry the whole load back up, got my very own specially trained griffins.[16]

The PARDONER

Well, sweet Jesus, King of Kings! [Knock me over with a griffin feather!] When hell freezes over! You lie!

The SNAKE-OIL SALESMAN

But wait, there's more! Looky here, folks! Got your baby chestnuts right here! First fruit o' the tree! The one all the way at the bottom of the Spanish Main! Knocked that junk off, I did, in one fell swoop.

The PARDONER

[And, hallelujah, it's rainin' nuts!©] Would you listen to this guy? Those are knockoffs, folks! Do you think he gives a fig about all those lies? [And Jesus wept!] God willing, he'd be in chains right now, drowned at the bottom of the River Seine! At least, until after I finish preaching. Right here, gentlemen! I've got part of the kerchief of Our Lady of the Back of Beyond.

The SNAKE-OIL SALESMAN

Here's part of Hannibal's foot. And his head. And his thighs too.

The PARDONER

Frankly, pal, I don't give a damn. If your lips are moving, you're lying.

The SNAKE-OIL SALESMAN

[*He fumbles for some novelty teeth as his voice becomes ever more shrill.*] Looky here! From the very walls of Paradise, a small pebble. Check it out! *Ooh-la-la!*

The PARDONER

Climbed all the way up there, did you? As if *you* could top me.
He must be high.

The SNAKE-OIL SALESMAN

[Sticks and stones, pal! A full octave higher than *your* score.©] I was *carried* up! In a basket. On Good Friday.

The PARDONER

Over here, gentlemen, don't listen to that basket case! [So, he caught the last performance of *Drama Queens*. So what?] *I* have the story of a real miracle to tell you![17]

The SNAKE-OIL SALESMAN

[And *I'm* the oracle here! You want pith? {*He brandishes his eel again.*} I'll see your Pythia and raise you one three-card Monty-Python!] Hey! Who wants drugs? [Not to get all Machiavellian or nothin' but] . . . got your mandrake right here! [Double, double, toil and trouble, fire burn and cauldron bubble.] Got ear o' pelican too, but wait! There's more! [*Brandishing the marshmallow chicks*] All the way from Greece from Mount Athos—no chicks allowed!—got the feet from four phoenixes. Got these beauties right outta their nests and—feets, don't fail me now!—rise! Come on, babies, rise!©[18]

The PARDONER

[Talk about your sermon on the mountebank!] And *I've* got—right here! Allow me to demonstrate—these bones from the Beatific Numbskulls. This one's from good Saint Pecker, and here's another one from Saint Poontang of the Sacred Vault.

The SNAKE-OIL SALESMAN

[Them bones, them bones, them dry *bonus*! Now hear the way of the Lord,© bonehead! {*He grabs some sausages and moves to strike.*} Phony baloney!] I've got me, from Tarantino-land—you'll give your eye-teeth for this one, folks—the tricuspid of Geoffrey Big-Tooth, who roams the earth bitin' everybody's heads off.[19] For God's sake, folks, stand back! For—yea, though I walked through the valley of Golgotha, I fished this baby right off the Mistress of Kegs, outta the burned-out hole of a lightning strike. And look what else I got! [Dragon eggs] from across the [narrow] sea! [*He grabs a bucket of prunes.*] And a great big pile o' cockle shells! And, from Heaven on high, some comet dust! And—[*bream* me up, Scotty!]—a little somethin' off the foot o' the Man in the Moon who holds up the holy firmament. Raise high the moon-beams, carpenter! And walrus. [You folks up in the rafters'll be beamin' from ear to ear in no time, 'cause—wanna know what?—it's a matter of truss. {*As if the other actor has missed his cue*} Act now!]

The PARDONER

[Bite me! You're a pain in the flying buttress.] And Jesus flippin' Christ in a bucket! You pinched that off a tree in somebody's garden! That's a prune and you're the pits, you damn *homeopath*!]

The SNAKE-OIL SALESMAN

Here's some wood from David's drum: the one he plays before God!

The PARDONER

And that's another lie, folks! Jesus H. Christ! Everybody knows David played the harp! [*He pops a prune in his mouth and takes a few steps back.*]

The SNAKE-OIL SALESMAN

And Jesus flippin' Christ in a bucket to you too, pal! To the moon with your preachin', to the moon! Just wait'll I get my hands on—. I'll soon give you something to preach about!

[*Lights down as a mimed scene of push me pull you ensues, which leaves the Pardoner off-balance.*]

[Scene 2]

[*Lights up on Frenchy, at the door of her near-empty tavern, now populated by only a few patrons, including a monk.*]

FRENCHY, the ALEWIFE

[My whole business has gone to pot!] Got no drinkers comin' round here no more. Jeez, I'm losin' my whole clientele: even the regulars. All those snake-oil salesmen from Venice, those pardoners from Amiens, all begging their way from church to church lookin' for a handout. All of 'em used to come by my place. [*She endeavors to attract passersby in mime, eventually venturing into the street within earshot of the two pitchmen.*]

The SNAKE-OIL SALESMAN

Gentlemen, you want it? I got it!© Praise the Lord! All good and good for you! Here, milords: one o' the doorstops from the Pearly Gates! Holding firm up there at the firmament, is it? *Not.*
And, here: no mortal eye hath seen—till now!—this round stone right here: the very stone that David used to kill Goliath! [Put that giant butt in a sling!] [*He feigns prayer.*][20]

The PARDONER

I'm wasting my time here. Must be losing my touch. I forget what I was going to say.

The SNAKE-OIL SALESMAN

[Hello! Rehearsal. Heard of it?
Knock, knock!

The PARDONER

Who's there?

The SNAKE-OIL SALESMAN

Goliath.

The PARDONER

Goliath who?

The SNAKE-OIL SALESMAN

Goliath down, thou lookest tired!] So, what do you wanna do here, pal? Wanna go get drunk? What do you say, sir? Truce? If we don't make peace—[*brandishing his eel again*]—we're just gonna keep snaking each other's deals. And, as you know very well from experience, you can't go to the same well twice. [Remember those hustlers in *The Chicken Pie and the Chocolate Cake*?] Two is a crowd.[21]

The PARDONER

Right you are, pal. Let's go somewhere and *indulge*, shall we? We'll just have to ask around for where we can find a good pinot.
[*As if Frenchy has missed her cue.*] There must be *somebody* around here who can direct us.

FRENCHY

Right here, gents! Right this way! You're here! You've come to the right place. Come on in. I've got good wine.

The SNAKE-OIL SALESMAN

Dipso facto! You don't have to ask me twice! [Rehearsal, I said! Heard of it?]

[*After they enter, he places the strongbox on the counter with great ceremony, retaining a tin or two on his person.*] Here you go. Hang onto this strongbox for me, would you?

FRENCHY

[*She promptly hides the box under the counter.*] So, tell me, gents, if you don't mind my askin', what line o' work you two boys in anyway?

The PARDONER

Who, us? Begging your—. We're pardoners, ma'am, at your service. *I* am, at any rate: the real deal. This one here is just a snake-oil salesman!

FRENCHY

In the name of Saint John, I knew it! [*She makes the sign of the cross.*] If only my dear, departed husband were here, yes siree, he'd be rolling out the red carpet for you two as we speak or he'd never forgive himself. And it just so happens, he used to be in the same line o' work as you boys, yes siree.[22]

The PARDONER

How's that now?

FRENCHY

Pullin' teeth. Made a real good living at it too. It was his specialty.

The SNAKE-OIL SALESMAN

[*He shakes one of his tins of teeth.*] Jesus H. Christ! He was one of us!

FRENCHY

Ha! Just as I thought! Delighted to have you, gents! Relax, please. Take a load off. Enjoy! You two have some catching up to do. [Check it out: a whole beggars' banquet.]

[*Sotto voce*] [And, hey, hey, hey big spenders!©] All you can eat for just $99.99.[23]

[*A great deal of gluttonous eating and drinking ensues.*]

The PARDONER

[My, my, my! Would you look at the time!] I do believe we've imposed quite long enough on your hospitality, my dear lady. [*He tips his hat.*] *Madame.*

[*With neither hesitation nor searching, he takes the strongbox from where Frenchy has hidden it, places it on the counter, reaches into his garment, and pulls out an object tightly wrapped in cloth. With great speed, he opens the strongbox, puts it inside, and closes the box tightly.*]

[This right here is a treasure chest], to be sure. What's inside is worth a fortune: more than a million in gold. But please: you'll keep it with our compliments.[24]

FRENCHY

What is it?

The PARDONER

You'll find out soon enough, but let's just call it a "Panderers' Box." You'll keep it, I insist. But it must remain completely intact. You must keep it covered at all times.

FRENCHY

Really? It's as precious as all that?

The SNAKE-OIL SALESMAN

Absolutely! Jeez, woman, [it's a *pan*-dora-*cea*!]

FRENCHY

I'd rather die than unwrap such a precious gift. [*She places the box under the bar.*]

The PARDONER

We'll be on our way, then, first thing . . . after supper.

[*More eating and drinking ensue, during which time another wrapped object falls from one of the men's pockets. Frenchy speedily picks it up and stashes it under one of three empty bowls at the bar. When her guests have finally finished eating, she moves jovially to escort them to the door. Meanwhile, the Snake-Oil Salesman retrieves the object from under the correct bowl and pockets it on the way out.*]

[The PARDONER]

We'll be off now, baby girl, we bid you adieu. [But, tell me: is it covered?][25]

FRENCHY

Adieu, gents, go with God. [It's covered].[26]
[{*To the audience*} And hallowed be my scam!]

[*The men leave the tavern; Frenchy watches until they are out of sight.*]

The SNAKE-OIL SALESMAN

[*From a safe distance in the street*] And hallowed be *our* scam! Jesus H. Christ on a cracker! She bought it tooth and nail!

[*Exit the Pardoner and the Snake-Oil Salesman*]

[Scene 3]

FRENCHY

[*Retrieving the box and beginning her inspection*] There's just got to be *some* way in, right?, to at least see what it is. Omigod! I'm a nervous wreck! It could be dangerous.
[*To the audience*] Whatever shall I do? Should I just go ahead and look inside? In violation of the—. Yes? No? What to do, what to do . . .
Oh, what the hell! I'm just gonna do it! But, first, a prayer to God, that He shouldn't punish me and such. Right. [*She falls to her knees.*]
Oh Lord, look down upon your humble creature, even now—*Eve?* And now?—weak and frail by nature, and forgive me if I should . . . accidentally happen to take a little peek inside, for I mean no harm.

Okeydokey, then. I've gotta get at that precious relic once and for all!
[*A monk at the bar thinks that she means him and responds accordingly.*]
[Here goes nothing!] [*She opens the box and unwraps the object.*]
Mary, Mother of—! What *is* this thing? I could almost swear it's—.
Oh my God! It's underwear! Wait. Let's not rush to judgment. Maybe it's just—. Oh, no, it—. No! It *is*! It's a pair of britches! And— Mary, Mother of—! They're full of shit![27]
Of all the low-down, dirty, rotten—. The shit people pull these days!
God damn the whole lot of 'em, this I pray.
Wanna know what, folks? All the world's a farce, the men and women in it merely players.
And just wait till my husband hears about *this*![28]
But, for now, I'm outta here. I bid you adieu.

I tell him everything, you know,
but bye for now, folks, gotta go.
We hope that you enjoyed the show.[29]

The END

11.

Slick Brother Willy

Frère Guillebert

CAST OF CHARACTERS

BROTHER WILBUR (Frère Guillebert)
MARVIN, the OLD MAN (L'Homme Vieil, Marin)
BLANCHE, his YOUNG WIFE (Sa Femme Jeune, La Femme)
AGNES, the GOSSIP (La Commère, Agnès)

PRODUCTION NOTES

Sometime around 1550, the anonymous *Farce nouvelle de Frère Guillebert très bonne et fort joyeuse* (*RBM*, #18) was published in the Norman city of Rouen by Jehan de Prest, in business there between 1542 and 1559 (*RF*, 6: 186; *FFMA*, 3: 237; *SFQS*, notes 1 and 217). It has been edited—again, paginated but without verse numbers—by Montaiglon (*ATF*, 1: 305–27), Tissier (*RF*, 6: 183–261), and Martin (*SFQS* at https://sottiesetfarces.wordpress.com/2017/03/30/frere-guillebert/). Although I know of no English translation, Tissier translated *Frère Guillebert* into modern French (*FFMA*, 2: 235–56), as did Faivre in *Les Farces* (1: 199–268), while another translation into Portuguese by Émilie S. Ribeiro, Gabriela L. Marques, and Marie B. de Almeida is, sadly, no longer available online. Summaries of our play appear in Petit de Julleville (*RTC*, 140), Delepierre (*DLU*, 32–37), and Faivre (*Répertoire*, 172–74); and, as a testament to its popularity, discussions of it can be found in Philipot, "Notice sur la farce de *Frère Guillebert*"; Witkowski, *MTA*, 155–56; Dufour, *Histoire de la Prostitution*, 296–302; and Koopmans, *RSJ*, 581–89. At 522 verses, *Frère Guillebert* is long and complex enough to have warranted 235 annotations in *SFQS* and to occupy a full eighty pages in *RF*, where Tissier corrected some hundred errors in the *ATF* edition (*RF*, 6: 186–87). While it unfolds in the usual rhyming octosyllabic couplets, it is structured around a series of poetic set-pieces featuring different rhyme schemes (*RF*, 6: 207–8; below, § "Language").

Of special interest: *Frère Guillebert* bears a signature, even if we don't fully understand its meaning: *du jeune clergie* [or *clergé*] *de Meullers. M.P.V.* (1: 327), For Tissier, the *clergé* might have been Norman student-playwrights enjoying an unusual freedom of speech (*RF*, 6: 187–90; *FFMA*, 2: 238), notwithstanding Petit de Julleville's contention that ecclesiastical authorship (or admission thereto) was out of the question (*RTC*, 140). But Martin reminds us that *clergie* was also a synonym for the Franciscan "Brothers Minor," the title character's monastic order (*SFQS*, notes 105 and 235) and whose founder, Saint Francis, is central to the plot.

Plot

Enter "Brother Wilbur" for one of the raunchiest sermons ever. It's a *sermon joyeux*, to be exact, which was both a parodic literary genre in its own right (*RSJ*, 585–89) and a descendant of the rhetorical art of preaching (*ars praedicandi*) with its variations on a sermonic theme.[1] This one clocks in at seventy—count 'em!—seventy verses devoted to sexual recreation and procreation; and—*action!*—the fix is in for Willy's assignation with an old fart's unnamed young wife (here, "Blanche"). Aided and abetted by BFF Agnes, Blanche feigns a pregnancy-related craving that will dispatch her sleepy spouse to market first thing the next morning. So far, so good—until *Marin* (here, "Marvin") forgets his purse, which sets off the standard farcical chain of events when he returns home to retrieve it.

Ciel! Mon mari!—Quick! It's my husband! Hide! And a brother does, diving headlong into a *coffre*, a common trunk-like chest elevated on four legs (*SFQS*, 116). Unfortunately for him, that's the precise location of Marvin's purse (*bissac*); and, as hubby feels around for it, he seems poised to grab that other purse: Willy's scrotum (as in #3, *Highway Robbery*). An understandable misprision. A *bissac* was a strap-on sac with two hanging pouches (below, § "Costumes and Props"). Whence, the crisis of *Slick Brother Willy* and its not-so-metaphorically imminent castration (which, for Martin, channels that of Abelard [*SFQS*, note 109]). Unbeknownst to Marvin, he's got Willy by the balls, prompting the preacher to rhapsodize about his own endangered equipment in a positively Villonesque Last Will and *Testicle* (1: 318–20). Willy is so petrified, moreover, that haste literally makes waste. He would have shit his proverbial britches (*braies*), the play's key prop, had he been wearing them at the time. Instead, with a little direction from Blanche, Marvin eventually grabs up not the money-bag (*bissac*) nor that other "bag" (the ball sac) but Willy's drawers. He then reexits for market. Exit Willy too for anywhere but that bedroom; and exit Blanche for an emergency advice session over at Aggie's. Indeed, this is one of very few farces to feature extensive scenes of women *tawking amongst themselves* (as in *Extreme Husband Makeover* [*HD*, #11, sc. 4] and *Confession Lessons* [*FF*, #3, sc. 2]). Meanwhile, back on the road for the second iteration of Marvin's errand . . .

Ooh, that smell! An overwhelming stench alerts Marvin to the distinctly nonhygienic pair of drawers that he is now carrying instead of his purse. But before he can double back yet again to raise hell, he is intercepted by Aggie. She convinces the codger that he is transporting none other than the talismanic, fertility-inducing britches of Saint Francis himself (*les braies du Cordelier*).[2] Seriously. How else could Blanche have become pregnant by the likes of Marvin? Her spouse then buys the fishy story hook, line, and stinker, as does his counterpart in the Dutch farce *Lippin*, discounting the evidence of his own eyes (*Medieval Dutch Drama*, ed. Prins, 48–51). And his nose. The malodorous pair is then returned to its rightful owner, Brother Willy, whose own pair is safe at last. In the end, when all are invited to rub their noses in the mystical drawers, farce rubs *our* noses in its send-off: mind your boys, boys, and kiss my ass! *Slick Brother Willy* is a masterpiece (of ass) that, narratively, linguistically, poetically, and materially, disseminates and "comedifies" a theory and practice of the purse.

Characters and Character Development

Technically, our leading man is probably a "Gilbert," a Germanic "wild boar," or a "Gil" of the *Second Shepherd's Play*; but, for obvious reasons, he is Willy-boy here: a real *dick* from a long line of farcical Willies.[3] With his *bissac*, his mini-me, and his little Franciscan "brothers in gray" (1: 306), he—*they*—make for the collective star of the show. Charged with reciting half the play's lines (*FFMA*, 2: 238), Willy is prone to synecdochic turns of phrase: women are "tits" or "nips" (1: 306–7) and men are the testicular part for the genital whole ("Introd.," § "Euphemism and 'Comedification'"). After all, *couille* denoted either one ball or the entire member (*SFQS*, note 21). *Guillebert* even sounds like *couille vert* or "green dick" (*SFQS*, note 3), the medieval equivalent, I suppose, of today's *la bitte en fleur* or "rising dick." But here's the other thingy: for all his bravura, he is just as chicken-shit as Mr. Allcock of *The Shithouse* (*HD*, #2), taking flight ASAP when the going gets tough because, for all his fixation on his balls, he doesn't have any. As in *Cooch E. Whippet*, it's anybody's guess as to how much this vaguely bisexual, *bissac-ual*, or gender-nonbinary fellow actually does with Blanche (*FF*, 338–39). Consider cross-casting or trans-casting gender-ambiguous actors.

The unnamed young wife is "Blanche," more in honor of Tristan's Blancheflor than of Tennessee Williams's Blanche Dubois. She is thin and pale (1: 307, 312), "blanching" at the mere thought of the nonperformant Marvin. But, overall, ambivalence and ambiguity are the order of the day for a ballsy woman with *prud'homie* (1: 324), who alternates between humor and malice, manipulation and panic, direction and misdirection, and feelings of entrapment and acts of empowerment. Getting caught in flagrante, for instance, was no laughing matter, as when an adulterous wife was murdered by her husband in 1567 for having had sex with a priest (Davis, *Fiction in the Archives*, 138–40). And, although her anomalous condition as "thin and pregnant" lacks a certain verisimilitude, that is the very issue addressed by the magical mystery drawers.

Assisting Blanche in all the comings and goings is her gossipy girlfriend (*La Commère*), identified in the text as "Agnes." While I don't see any evidence that she is a widow, she indubitably has what Martin calls "pimp-like tendencies" (*SFQS*, note 40) when she gets, *entremetteuse*-like, *in the middle* of things. Given Aggie's reminiscing about her activities "back in her day" (1: 309), she might be older and, by her own reckoning, wiser than her BFF. She's certainly a gifted practical joker and the author of the drawer-dropping denouement.

Last but not least, meet Marvin, "The Old Man" of the Cast List (*L'Homme Vieil*) and "The Husband" or "The Man" in the script (*L'Homme*), where his name is heard as "Marin," a "friend of the sea" (1: 310). *Quelle coincidence!* Blanche's fool's errand sends him out for mussels, among other goodies. In point of fact, I suspect that *manger des moulles* (1: 312) is a long-lost synonym for "fucking somebody over," all the more so in that *moule* also meant "dildo" (*SFQS*, note 193; Faivre, *Farces*, 1: 266n). Initially solicitous, "Marvin" does his best to satiate his insatiable wife; but solicitude soon explodes into rage, followed by gullibility when he falls for the fishy Francis story. As a model for Marvin, try the nearsighted, volatile, farcical Mister Magoo.

Language

Pride of place goes to our play's five poetic set-pieces, of which Marvin gets one: a stench-motivated, twenty-four-verse soliloquy (1: 323) with such fabulous rhymes as *foutiné/domine* ("fuck"/"the Lord"). But the rest is all Willy. He delivers an incomparable *sermon joyeux* (1: 305–7; below, note 4); an ode and a *rondeau* to Blanche (1: 309, 313); a testamentary bequest of his genitalia (1: 318–19); and a final prayer in which he commends unto the Lord his spirit—and his balls (1: 319–20). It all begins with that sermon on the "mount" that proves quite the mouthful to translate.

Oddly enough, Faivre and Martin view it as extraneous (*Répertoire*, 172; *SFQS*, note 40); but I beg to differ. It is in the sermon that Willy first broaches the crucial *bissac* (1: 305), its role in all manner of purges captured by this refrain in what we can safely term *vulgar* Latin: *Foullando in calibistris, / Intravit per boucham ventris / Bidauldus, purgando renés.* Loosely translated—is there any other way?—this is a description of coitus. *Fouler*, *fouiller*, or *foullando* denotes "messing up" or violently "banging away" when the penis (*bidauld*) enters the so-called vaginal "mouth" (*boucham ventris*), yielding something like: "In fucking around in the snatch, the dick passes through the vulva, comes in and unloads" (*SFQS*, note 4). But, since Willy is up for anything and since the *bidauld* could apply to both the male *and* the female genitalia, the sermonic refrain actually anticipates the materially bipartite *bissac*. If anything is *foullando* ("messed up"), it's the limpid sense of who's giving, who's receiving, and *where* (*SFQS*, note 11). *In calibistris* sounds as much like a female "jewel box" as it does the male "jewels" on their way in: *cailles* + *bisstre* = stones + wine corks (*RF*, 6: 209n–10n): that is, in the vaginal treasure chest (*custodi nos*), the family jewels (or dildoes) get "polished up" (*fourbir*). And, with regard to the hospitable *boucham ventris*: is somebody's mouth wide open to give another "bro job" (#7), whence, the need to gargle (1: 319)? What is *l'orifice de la pance* (1: 319)? A vaginal "hole in the belly" or the back-door hole on the flipside (*RF*, 6: 210n–211n, 244n)? Not that farce ever minds confusion about which hole is which, as in the allegedly accidental honeymoon sodomy of *Farce of the Fart* (*FF*, 82–83). And let's not forget Willy's racy rhyme of "purgatory" and "suppository" (*purgatoire/suppositoire* [1: 311]). In sum, there is something about this cocky oration that is relentlessly effeminate in its masculinity and emasculate in its femininity, something profoundly androgynous from the get-go about Willy's quest to make of two halves one (w)hole.

Otherwise, *Slick Brother Willy* speaks the language of sex. Fluently. In the notes to his edition, Tissier produced what amounts to a medieval *Urban Dictionary* of obscenities (*RF*, 6: 205–7). In addition to the love-boxes, snatches, jewels, collection plates, muff-diving, and helmet-polishing, we get plenty of greased entryways, buttered butts, hiding the sausage (*larder le connin*), dicking around, cocking things up (*cauqueson*, *cauquer*), and—believe it or not—the *huihot*, Middle French for "hoo-hoo" or "hoo-ha" (1: 323; below, note 23). You name it, it's in there.

Sets and Staging

By my dramaturgical count, *Slick Brother Willy* calls for at least three locations and thirteen scenes, the latter quite rare for a genre that privileges the one-act and even the "one-scene." The principal set is Blanche and Marvin's bedroom, situated in what is presumably a modest abode with no servants to answer the door. A four-poster bed will do nicely as a place to hang discarded articles of clothing. Other locations dictated by the text are: Aggie's place, perhaps next door, and the road to market, possibly traversing a bustling village. Decisions must be made as well about where Willy's show-starting sermon takes place. Remember: medieval preaching was solo-performance art. Jacomin Husson, for example, chronicled the Good Friday antiphonal frenzy promulgated by one Brother Oliver in 1515: "he did something that no one had ever seen before: for he showed a sacred Host and had the people cry out for mercy when he showed them the Host. . . . And when our Lord died on the cross, he showed a crucifix, again calling out 'Have mercy!'; and the people also cried out loudly" (*Chronique de Metz*, 294–95; cited in *DBD*, 229). Or consider the Latin diary of an anonymous fifteenth-century Franciscan active in Italy, as rediscovered and brilliantly analyzed by Carol Symes. This extraordinary document offers unflinching self-assessments of his sermons that ranged from "effective [and delivered] with passion and in a ringing voice" or "brought an audience to tears" to "not as passionate . . . as it should have been" or "really boring and badly preached" ("Knowledge Transmission," 210–11). So, where's Willy? He could be pontificating at the marketplace or at church; he could roam peripatetically among the spectators; or he could elocute from a makeshift pulpit before the curtain goes up, the better to reflect the timelessness and "placelessness" of a Willy who winds up in the wrong place at the wrong time. And, about time: yet another atypical dimension of our farce is that it takes place over two days (as in *Extreme Husband Makeover* [*HD*, #11]).

The real pièce de résistance, however, is the pivotal Scene 9, where the lost and found *bissac* poses seriously amusing challenges. Just how *flagrante* is Blanche and Willy's *delict*? What does Blanche find unsatisfactory about her "one lousy shot" (*povre coup* [1: 322])? Its speed? Its quantity? And what is their state of undress when Marvin risks finding the pair? There's a mad rush to hide Willy, who should definitely shake the proverbial tail feather. (Use goose-down bedding [1: 315] and have the feathers literally fly.) But what about verisimilitude? What about John Cleese's counsel that, in farce, "absurd situations have to be made believable" ("How to Write the Perfect Farce," 1)? How realistic is it that a brother would pause for an entire ode to his endangered manhood at the very moment of Marvin's imminent ball-busting grab (Faivre, *Farces*, 1: 202–3)? Sure, Marvin can grope slowly and unsuccessfully; but the rest of it turns on how to stage what goes down at the *coffre* at the foot of the bed.

Willy's utter panic about the safety of his scrotum tells us that the two purses are perilously close to one another. The thing is, his precise position has a lot to do with prepositions. Blanche has directed that Marvin won't see Willy if he's "stretched out *under* the chest" (*estendu soubz ce coffre*). But, during Marvin's purse hunt, she also reports having laid out the *bissac on* the chest (*sur ce coffre*) (1: 315–17). One option is to remove the fourth coffin-like wall of the *coffre* to give the audience a balls'-eye view inside. But I suggest that bottomless Willy should dive *under the chest*: just not *all the way* under. Once down there on all fours, the Frenchman is "scrunched up like a frog" (*se tenir en raine*) and, in that unhappy stance, his protruding purse can easily be mistaken by nearsighted old Marvin for the money purse, which is, at first, still located *on top of* the chest (1: 317). Likewise protruding is Willy's naked derriere (*SFQS*, note 118) or, for Faivre, his *fat* ass (*Farces*, 1: 233). To resolve the unstageability of such thingies, Thierry Martin recommends that Blanche toss some linen over the offending extremities (*SFQS*, note 118). But that doesn't completely dispense with a dramaturgical problem that occasioned Tissier to pen a whole section about nudity onstage (*RF*, 6: 201–4).

Willy twice speaks of "lying *right on top of* [Marvin's *bissac*]" (1: 316, 320), which would tend to indicate that he dove not *under* the chest but *onto* it, lying facedown therein in a posture that, by the way, he urges explicitly in his opening sermon (1: 306). But, if Marvin's purse is *on* the chest and Willy's butt is *under* it, how can our boy in gray be lying *on top of* the *bissac*? He might have grabbed it hastily, ventures Martin, to cushion any potential blow (*SFQS*, note 122), which would further account for out-of-it Marvin's inability to find it. It's equally plausible that, in a panicked dive for cover, Willy accidentally knocks the purse under the chest before assuming his position. I'd advise the latter. But that's nothing compared to how Willy beats his hasty retreat. When the Franciscan bolts *sans* underwear, he proposes to use his bare hands to support his ball sac (*sac à couille*). "I guess I'll just have to make a fist," he ejaculates graphically, "and take Brother Willy in my own two hands. Nature's own jockstrap!" (*Je prendray mon v[it] à mon poing; / Mes mains me serviront de brayette* [1: 321]). (As in *Blue Confessions* Montaiglon elided both *couille* and *vit* as "c" and "v" [above, #2, § "Plot"].) This makes for a Rabelaisian riff on monks as "free ballers," as it were, and wont to let their boys flap in the wind (*SFQS*, note 29): "they don't wear breeches with any bottom," says Panurge, "and their poor member stretches out at liberty unbridled, and thus goes dangling down onto the knees, as do rosary beads on women" (*CWFR*, 188). But check out Tissier's stage direction, *caressant son membre*: "Willy is caressing his virile member" (*FFMA*, 2: 249). Really? *Onstage?* Unless you believe in medieval pornography—deliberate or accidental—I think not (above, "Introd.," § "Pornography").

Costumes and Props

Brother Wilbur has two costume changes. For his sermon and his final appearance in Scene 13, he is garbed in Franciscan gray (*SFQS*, note 226); and why not give him a *farceurs*' drum like Pontalais's to quiet the house (above, *Pardoners' Tales*, § "Plot")? For the assignation with Blanche, however, he sports a doublet (*pourpoint*) and "leggings"-style trousers (*chausses*) (1: 314). (Apparently, it was infinitely more scandalous for a woman home alone to receive a Franciscan than a secular male visitor [*SFQS*, note 29].) And, by all means, take advantage of farce's trademark interplay of the literal and the metaphorical and have him show up with a bag of nuts. Dress Blanche in a tight-fitting nightgown with a massive décolletage and a peignoir. Other bedroom props include: goose-down pillows and a number of chamber pots, some overflowing.

Needless to say, the crucial props are the *bissac* and the *braies*: the purse and the "britches" or "drawers" (below, note 2). While the latter could be worn as either undergarments or over-garments (*RF*, 5: 273n), let's assume that we're talking about drawers. Britches have two legs; and a *bissac* is comprised of two pouches hanging on either side of a strap that was hung from the shoulder or neck (*SFQS*, note 101). Marvin's *bissac* must be small enough to resemble a man-purse but, at the same time, large enough to double as Saint Francis's britches. And one more thing: this may not be the first time that Brother Willy has shit a brick. As with similar props in *Shit for Brains* (*FF*, 271–74) or *The Pardoners' Tales* (#10, note 27), the purloined *bissac* is filthy: the property of an "ass"—or an "asshole," quoth Marvin, "that's hardly clean" (*un cul guères net* [1: 323]). I leave any olfactory effects up to you.

Scholarly References to Copyrighted Materials (in order of appearance and indicated by© within the text)

"Dry Bones." ["Dem Bones."] By Jay Weldon Johnson and J. Rosomond Johnson. (19th c.)
"O Come, All Ye Faithful." [*Adeste fidelis*]. Traditional (ca. 1600s or 1700s).
"This Old Man." Traditional.
"De-Lovely." By Cole Porter. ASCAP Work ID: 340019152.
"A Bushel and a Peck." By Frank Loesser. ASCAP Work ID: 320102867.
"Ride a Cock Horse to Banbury Cross." Traditional.
"I Can't Get No Satisfaction." By Mick Jagger and Keith Richards. BMI Work #608621.
"Field of Opportunity." By Neil Young. ASCAP Work ID: 360219907.
"Run for the Roses." By Dan Fogelberg. ASCAP Work ID: 480149122.
"Achy-Breaky Heart." By Kenneth Gregory Watters. SESAC Work Number: 55896468.
"Baby, It's You." By Burt Bacharach, Mack David, and Barney Williams. ASCAP Work ID: 320111553.
"Nothing Compares 2 U." By Prince. ASCAP Work ID: 440162807.
"Shake a Tail Feather." By Otha Hayes, Verlie Rice, and Zephire Williams. BMI Work #1318017.
"We May Never Pass This Way Again." By Darrell Crofts and Jimmy Seals. BMI Work #1617190.
"Shiny Happy People." By Bill Berry, Peter Buck, Mike Mills, and Michael Stipe. SESAC Work Number: 689794367.
"That Smell." By Allen Collins and Ronnie Van Zant. BMI Work #1483429.
"Get Ready." By William [Smokey] Robinson. ASCAP Work ID: 370083240.

"Let's Hear It for the Boy." By Dean Pitchford and Thomas Snow. BMI Work #858383.
"The Mess-Around." By Ahmet Ertegun [Nugetre]. BMI Work #981371.

[Scene 1]

Enter Brother Wilbur, [possibly wandering among the spectators. Once onstage, he settles on a perfect spot within earshot of Blanche and Agnes. Each time he utters his Latin refrain, he makes gestures representing the sex act.]

BROTHER WILBUR

Foullando in calibistris,
Intravit per boucham ventris
Bidauldus, purgando renés.+

[What? You don't know no damn Latin? Now hear the word of the Lord!© *Pokeamus igitur in vulvibus. Gaudeamus cum jismibus.*] People! Be fruitful and multiply! Bang away! *In becoming one flesh, may your fountain be blessed* and, sure as shootin', my own cup runneth way the hell over. *O genitalia gloriosa!* Release us o' Lord and come all ye faithful!©

[*E pluribus unum.* Yippee!
Foullando in calibistris.
Corpus "delecti." Let us {s}pray. . . .]

Dearly beloved, we are gathered here today to perform acts of great devotion. Listen and learn from my unctuously soothing words full of piety; for—yea!—my sermon touches upon the very incarnation of thy rod and thy staff, which comfort the hell out of me when, in they go! Head, ears, and tail, straight into the precious womb of you ladies. As for you, girls, you're probably saying to yourselves: "You don't say, Daddy-o! What's up with that? *Quo modo?* Come again?" [Well, that's what this sermon on the mount is all about.]

E pluribus unum. Yippee!
Foullando in calibistris.
Corpus "delecti." Let us [s]pray. . . .

Now, let's take this whole thing bit by bit, shall we? In today's reading from the Holy Scriptures, our text says *foullando*, [from the Latin *foulare*, which gives us *fouler*, and, then,] *en foulant*: I *foo*, you *foo*, we all *fool around* like crazy down there in that bag of goodies o' yours! That's right, folks: this is the money shot: [*In becoming one flesh, may the fountain be blessed!*] You gals got the collection plate; a gentleman wants to open that purse and make a donation.

You hear what I'm sayin' to you, baby girls? Get it? If we menfolk wanna latch on to those pretty little titties and head on down for a pickle tickle, well, mum's the word. It's all in good fun-bags. And don't you be tellin' your mamas! I say, ladies: why would God have given you a snatch if He didn't want us to snatch it? So, snatch that joystick and stick it in! Booty calls! And, if you know what's good for you, down you go! Ass in the air, lest that bum get bruised! O smiles of a holey night!

In becoming one flesh, may the fountain be blessed.
And never will it hurt to pee, foullando in calibistris.

So, heads up, all you red-faced, strapping young men, crowned with glory and partial to the female of the species! Perform an inspection! Check out that toolbox before working those tools and, then. . . . Knick, knack, Saint Paddy whack, give the dog a boner!© But plunge ye not into the darkest of smelly depths, lest, when ye purge, ye get the clap.

In becoming one flesh, may the fountain be blessed,
Lest Purge-atory greet your wee-wee, when foullando in calibistris.

And, hey, girls! Pretty little girls! Holy bazongas, the girls! [From sea to shining C-cup!] The ones who would never say "back off" when we're rocking out on those milky white titties! Here's the thing: *Ave Maria gratia plena*! Careful you don't get knocked up. Blessed be the fruit of thy womb? *Not.*

In becoming one flesh, may the fountain be blessed.
But not to start a family, foullando in calibistris.

And all you young married ladies out there, who can't quite manage to score even half of what you're craving: don't you be leading a brother on, you hear? It's not for you to take the reins. This is the kind of thing daddy can take care of in his sleep. So, just tuck a boy in and let him hammer away.

In becoming one flesh, may the fountain be blessed.
But watch out! no paternity, foullando in calibistris.

But wait, there's more! From right here in my pulpit, I can highly recommend the company of my boys in gray, cinctures and all. You have my word: when you do a brother a good turn, 'tis a glorious offering unto the Lord. So, indulge away! Up the wazoo! [In my Father's house, there are many rooms.] A full pardon awaits you, I'll have you know; so, go for that *corpus "delecti."* It's delightful, it's delicious, it's *delictable!*© And let us [s]pray:

When becoming one flesh, may that fountain be blessed.
E pluribus unum. Yippee! Foullando in calibistris.

Now, it's true: you got some real beauties out there, perky little girly-girls up for a roll in the hay, let you love on 'em a bushel and a pecker,© and beat that grain and thresh around. Only, then, they're all worried when they find themselves with a little bun in the oven. And, then: "Lord have mercy!" they say to themselves: "however did *that* come to pass?" Wanna know how, my sweet honey Beatrice? [I won't talk seven circles around it:] *Pokeamus igitur, baby!*

Intravit per boucham ventris:
E pluribus unum. Yippee!

As for all those barren old bats—butter wouldn't melt in their mouths, right? They're just dried-up relics now, playing the lady. Bottom feeders! Shitload o' prudes! Like it comes as some big surprise when they hear we're into women. Believe you me: those bitches have fucked their asses off till all that's left is a broke-down palace. So, release us o' Lord and come all ye faithful!© It's fuckin' cathartic, which is what is meant by our theme:

I told you: purgando renés!
Corpus "delecti." Let us [s]pray.

[Now, drumroll, please!] Ladies, allow me to introduce myself: your humble servant, Brother Wilbur, at your service. Ask and ye shall receive! Got your knight in shining armor right here, all ready to buff you up and buff up your stuff! *That* is my specialty. So, ride a cock horse© to gooseberry cross and, away we go! Old Faithful's gonna have you back in the saddle in no time. Come one, come all: that's what I say:

Bidauldus, purgando renés!
Corpus "delecti." Let us [s]pray.

[Just tell 'em Willy Boy is here because . . . What do you say, folks? One more time?]

[*Doubled version begins here.*]

You lusty men: when makin' hay
and poking 'round inside the hoo-hoo:
Clean out that purse before you spray
inside that cunt. It's what you do-do.
Avoid the clap and all the goo-goo,
lest through an ass darkly you see,
Foullando in calibistris.

O milky-titted little pretties!
Those haloed nipples: ooh-la-la!
Panties are never in a twisties:
Tada! Tata! And hoo-ha-ha!
We're on. You'd never say "Ta-ta!"
Just I and thou: no babe makes three,
Foullando in calibistris.

You married gals who'd like to stray,
whose men can't give you what you need:
Don't lead them on. It's pray to play!
And, should you wish to take the lead
in other beds while hubby sleeps,
the spouse still has paternity,
Foullando in calibistris.

With all my brothers, pray, make nice.
Bang! bang! without paternity!
'Tis liberty I preach, no vice.
Why, no! it's Christian charity.
Lend hands, lend lips! I guarantee:
You're pardoned most *delictfully,*
Foullando in calibistris.

Girls beat that wheat, o *Domine,*
right off the chaff so violently;
but, then, surprise! *Voilà bébé*!
Bun in the oven, kicking thee.
"Alas!" they say, "what can this be?"

You wanna know, my honey Bea?
Per boucham ventris. Yum. Yippee!

The dried-up prudes have had their day.
They take on airs: it's quite the game.
"Oh, what a shock!" they seem to say,
when they hear people screw: "Shame! Shame!"
Those fucked-up sluts are all the same.
Bidauldus purgando renés!
Corpus "delecti." Let us [s]pray.

But now the time has come to meet . . .
Ladies, presenting Brother Willy,
juiced up for any meet and greet!
Just ask him and he'll fuck you silly
'cause he knows how to mount a filly.
Polish his helmet! Have away!
Corpus "delecti." Let us [s]pray.

[*Doubled version ends here.*]

[*Curtain up, or exit Brother Wilbur*]

[Scene 2]

[*At or near the home of Marvin and Blanche toward day's end, a mimed scene might depict the displeasures of married life. Blanche heads to Agnes's place.*]

The WIFE, BLANCHE, *begins*

God give you joy! Hi, Aggie—hey!—and health, and pleasure, and relief.

AGNES

Hey, girl. Come on in. Right this way.

BLANCHE

God give you joy! Hi, Aggie—hey!

AGNES

You're pale! You're gonna waste away. Good Lord, what's up, girl? Where's the beef?

BLANCHE

God give you joy! Hi, Aggie—hey!—and health, and pleasure, and relief 'cause, as for me, I pray for death!

AGNES

How come?

BLANCHE

It's all beyond belief. Day in, day out, I'm stuck with that old lay-abed. And not in a good way, I'll have you know. You think I get any action around here? It's all "I want you, I want you"; but, then, zip! And with these tits and this ass? I'm just doin' time, like I was in the pokey.

AGNES

Lemme guess: all pokey, no hokey-pokey.

BLANCHE

Lord have mercy, girl. It's awful, just awful. He's got nothin'! If he manages to even get it up once a month, he's done for. Don't matter how hard I try to butter him up—hug him, kiss him—it all falls flat. Whole thing leaves a bad taste in my mouth, if you get the gist. Can you believe I got married off to that old fart? Screw the genius who cooked up *that* witches brew, 'cause ain't it just *swill*? Goes down like a bad beer, I tell you: waiting around all the time for grandpa to plow my fuckin' field. Gimme a break.

AGNES

There's always a loophole somewhere in those marriage contracts. What you need is a lover boy—there's the ticket—preferably French. Somebody to get at that boilerplate and fill in the blanks. It's only natural. Besides, sure as shootin': there's no way it's God's plan—or Mother Nature's either—for a young lady to be languishing without. Just be sure to find yourself a specimen who knows how to hold his tongue: and where, and how!

BLANCHE

Ain't that the truth! But a girl on the prowl's gotta watch out for all those busybodies lookin' sideways at her. Well, hell! [Stink-eye, my ass!] They can bitch and moan till they're blue in the face. I'm gonna turn things around. In bed. What? Like this gorgeous bod should be food for worms without so much as seeing the same action as my mama? So, come all ye faithful,© that's what I say! A friar, a convert, some brother-come-lately who only just got religion, a fuckin' novice. Who cares? He can poke around in my collection plate anytime.

AGNES

Way to go, girl, right you are! And, by the way: been there, done that on my—. *Back* in the day, you know? Take it from me: when you can't get no satisfaction,© it's one bitter pill to swallow.

BLANCHE

Got it. I'll be on the lookout, then. Something's bound to come up. Later, girl, I'm outta here to get . . . we'll see. I'll bide my time till I get mine.

[*Exit Blanche; lights down on Agnes's home.*]

[Scene 3]

[*On the road between the homes of Agnes and Blanche, enter Brother Wilbur. He sees Blanche and rehearses the gestures that will accompany his histrionic salutation.*]

BROTHER WILBUR

Mercy, *Madame*, mercy on me,
lest I should die before my time!
My heart's a hostage to your shrine,
its grief to ease by you alone.
I speak the truth: this is no line.
It pains me deep within my bones.

BLANCHE

Some come-on, Wills. Leave it alone.
Lovers don't lead so ballsily![5]

BROTHER WILBUR

To which, baby, I say I won't.
Offer yourself three times to me:
a holy fuckin' Trinity.

For verily, I say to . . . thee . . . thou . . . unto you . . . that, lending a helping hand to the poor and suffering makes for a glorious offering that is most pleasing to the Lord.

BLANCHE

[*Shushing him*] If our acquaintance were ever to come to light, my people would gouge my eyes out.

BROTHER WILBUR

No worries, babe: not one peep outta me about our little love nest. We'll play it on the down-low. You'll see. I'll be walkin' on eggshells: the quietest banging you never did hear. And I can always come on your tits.[6]

BLANCHE

Fine. Come by first thing tomorrow morning. I'll send Marvin out shopping.

BROTHER WILBUR

In the field of opportunity, it's plowin' time again!© Old geezer won't even know what hit him. [Now, run for the roses,©] 'cause this bud's on him.

BLANCHE

Good deal. I'm all over that sucker. Go ahead, Pops, make my day.

[*Blanche heads home and Brother Willy returns to the monastery to change clothes.*]

[Scene 4]

[*At the home of Marvin and Blanche*]

MARVIN
Where's baby girl been? Why so late? Now, tell me: where've you been all day?

BLANCHE
What's so damn urgent it can't wait?

MARVIN
Where's baby girl been? Why so late? There's no need to get all irate.

BLANCHE
Old bag o' bones! Just go away!

MARVIN
Where's baby girl been? Why so late? Just tell me: where've you been all day?

BLANCHE
[*Sotto voce*] Yeah, right. So there'll be hell to pay? I'd rather be in Purgatory.

MARVIN
Do you need a suppository? How about an enema? We could get you the great expunger.[7]

BLANCHE
[{*To the audience*} Like they say, folks: *Purge*-atory.]
Marvin, living with you is one big drag. I'm languishing without here, and it's abusive.

MARVIN
I don't beat you. I don't boss you around. If there's anything you need, all you have to do is ask.

BLANCHE

That's not the point. You just don't get where it hurts. Do I really have to come right out and say it? I'm way too young for you.

MARVIN

Whaddaya mean? I keep my end up at least five times a month. [Well, maybe once a week.] Why, only just the other day, I shot my wad.

BLANCHE

Gimme a break, you big pussy, that's barely enough to whet a girl's appetite. I'd just as soon have nothing.[8]

MARVIN

What's the problem? When you were still at your mother's, you did just fine without the old cock-a-doodle-doo.

BLANCHE

Which only makes it hurt worse. [Water, water everywhere and not a drop to drink.] I'm dying of thirst beside the fountain.[9]

MARVIN

I'm doing the best I can, woman. Good God, I'm achy-breaky© all over from keeping my end up. Besides, my efforts must have paid off if you say you're pregnant.

BLANCHE

Only because I prayed to Saint Whatserface that I'd get knocked up on whatever bitter dregs you manage to dribble out. And there's something else. I can't even bring myself to say it. You know.

MARVIN

Go on, Missy, out with it.

BLANCHE

Marvin, my dear, milord: I've got one of those cravings for . . . Lord have mercy! What if something were to happen to the precious fruit of my womb?

MARVIN

Just name it and it's yours. [Pickles and ice cream?] Hot stuff? Cold stuff? Cooked? Raw? I'll rush right out and get it for you.

BLANCHE

I've got me a craving for some great big *cod*. Fresh cod. And love-muscle—I mean: I *love mussels*. And white bread. And—oooh—a nice, fat, greasy shank of mutton. And some sweet wine and—are you listening, Marvin?—like from our wedding day: what was that again? The good white stuff?

MARVIN

You mean crème brûlée?

BLANCHE

There you go! By George, I think he's got it. [{*Aside*} *Vin blanc*, not *mariage blanc*!] I don't know how much longer I'll hold out if I don't stuff my face with some cream.

MARVIN

I'll head out to market first thing tomorrow morning, dear. [Without further ado.]

[*Lights down.*]

[Scene 5]

[*Before dawn the next day, lights up on Brother Wilbur in his chamber. He sings a merry tune, thumbs quickly through his Bible, discards it promptly, and heads to Blanche's home.*][10]

BROTHER WILBUR

Rondeau

Baby, it's you.©
She's fixing herself up, it's all for me,
and, thus, I must prepare genitally.
A masterpiece of Nature, folks, it's true!

I'm up for it. Nothing compares 2 u.©
These boys were made for action, naturally.
It's right they should be housed erotically,
lest stuff be led astray, up the wazoo.
Should Marvin be awake or should he sleep,
I must have at that coochie, coochie coo—
upon threat of disfigurement, it's true—
and stand erect, awestruck romantically:
She's fixing herself up, it's all for me.[11]

[Scene 6]

[*At daybreak, Brother Willy cautiously positions himself outside Blanche's bedroom window. A sleepy Marvin awakes and prepares for market with some difficulty.*][12]

MARVIN

Is it morning already? Glory be! I'd best be getting up immediately. Adieu. I'm off! To market now with me.

BLANCHE

Adieu. And could you shop effectively [for once]? Please? Get good deals. And don't forget anything.

MARVIN

Of course not. I remember. [*He rubs his eyes and temples.*] I've got it all up here.

[*Exit Marvin.*]

[Scene 7]

BROTHER WILBUR

Hello! Yo! Here I am, right on time, all ready to rise to the occasion.

BLANCHE

[*She admits him.*] You certainly are. Now, go on, strip. Off with the pants, off with the doublet, and get your ass over here. I've got your spot all warm for you.

BROTHER WILBUR *undresses* [*and looks around anxiously.*]

Are you sure this is all on the up-and-up?
[{*To the audience*} Could be entrapment, you know.] This whole scene gives me the willies.
Bless my soul, a guy can't be too careful.

BLANCHE

If you're that chicken-shit, you don't deserve a real lady.

[*Brother Wilbur overcomes his fear and jumps into bed with Blanche.*]

[Scene 8]

[*Lights up on Marvin on the road to market. He sneezes and reaches for his handkerchief.*]

MARVIN

Isn't that just my luck! I forgot my purse! I've got nothing! No bag, no pouch, no sack. I even forgot the basket [for my packages]. Best turn back right away and get my stuff.

[Scene 9]

[*Blanche and Willy are doing their business when Marvin bangs on the door.*]

[MARVIN]

Hello! Hey!

BROTHER WILBUR

Oh. My—. In the name of Saint John, Saint Francis, and Saint Johnson! What on earth is that?

BLANCHE

[*She bolts out of bed, the feathers literally flying.*] What do *you* think? It's the Lord and Master! The jig is up. He must be on to us.

BROTHER WILBUR

Jesus H. Christ Almighty! It *is* your husband! O Lord, look down upon your miserable servant, for I do believe . . . The Devil made me do it! It sure as hell wasn't God!

BLANCHE

Quick! Go hide! Anywhere! If he finds you, your goose is cooked.

BROTHER WILBUR

[*Frantically seeking a hiding place*] Oh my God, this is it! I'm a dead man. Help me, Saint Johnson! My butt is quaking! What if—? Do you really think he'll kill me if he finds us together?

BLANCHE

Nastiest man I ever did see. I fear for your package.

BROTHER WILBUR

Screw this whole thing! This is the Devil's doing, and I'm gonna have my ass handed to me on a silver platter. The feathers are really gonna fly!

BLANCHE

[So, shake a tail feather!©] He can't stand being had. And, when he gets pissed—you'll see—he foams at the mouth like a madman!

BROTHER WILBUR

Oh. My—. Our Father who art in Heaven, *Ave Maria*, and Jesus H. Christ Almighty! I'm screwed!

BLANCHE

Lord have mercy, this is no time for a sermon! Now, get a grip, buddy. Come over here and I'll hide you.

BROTHER WILBUR

All things considered, I'm thinking that my best option at this juncture would be . . . to get the hell outta here, by God!

BLANCHE

Quick! Stretch out over there. He's not gonna see your ass under that chest.

[*Blanche helps Willy squeeze most of the way under the chest at the foot of the bed; but his purse-like scrotum protrudes.*]

BROTHER WILBUR

My ass! That's exactly what he'll see. But, if this is really the only spot. . . . When you gotta go, you gotta go. I'm squeezed in as tight as I can, but cover my ass, wouldya? My boys are flappin' in the wind here! O' Lord, this I pray: Get me outta here in one piece, [by the hair of my skinny, skin, foreskin!]

[*Blanche tosses some extra linen on top of Willy, which, as the audience sees, provides insufficient cover.*]

BLANCHE

Shut up! Don't be such a wimp! I'll give you a hand as I'm able.

MARVIN

[*Banging loudly on the door again*] Hey! I say, hey! Are you gonna open this door or what?

BLANCHE

[*Grabbing her robe, Blanche goes to the door.*] Lord have mercy, dear! What brings you back so soon?

BROTHER WILBUR

[*Delivering the first of many sotto voces*] Back, shmack. Let him back the hell off. I'm scrunched up like a frog in here!

MARVIN

Can you believe the bad luck? I forgot my purse.

BROTHER WILBUR

Good God, the blow to end all blows! I'm lying right on top of it! In the name of Saint Benderover and—you too, Jesus—I'm a goner! Now what? Speak now or forever hold my dick? Lord have mercy, my one true God, this is it. And he was always such a good fellow, with his gleaming crown, his head held high. [And he shall never pass this way again.©][13]

BLANCHE

[Don't you remember?] I got it all ready for you on the chest before bed.

MARVIN

Go back to bed. I'll find it. Careful not to catch a chill. [*He fumbles around by the chest, grabbing on to whatever he can and comes dangerously close to Willy's "purse."*]

BROTHER WILBUR

Good God! He's headed right up my—. Oh, no! Not *there*! What in the name of Saint Valentine am I supposed to do now? Lord have mercy, what if he gets his hands on—*hell,* no! Not *there*! He can take the clothes off my back but—my God!—not the family jewels! I'm so scared, I could shit! [*He does. Or at least farts.*][14]

BLANCHE

No, [Marvin], not over there! You're at the wrong end.

MARVIN

So, where is it?

BROTHER WILBUR

Forgive me, o Lord, and have mercy on my soul. I prostate—*prostrate*—myself before Thee.

MARVIN

Good God Almighty! Who cut one? In the name of Saint John, it stinks to high Heaven around here!

BROTHER WILBUR

Like his shit don't stink! If that sonofabitch were in my position—. Try being all tied up in knots like this! Good God Almighty! He would've ripped out a few on the spot.

BLANCHE

So? Got it?

MARVIN

Almost. That's some slippery little sucker. I can't quite get my hands on . . . It's not here between the sheets. That thingy must be wedged in there but good.

[*Marvin continues to grope while Blanche endeavors to distract him.*]

BROTHER WILBUR

[{*To the audience*} You know what they say, folks: contents may have shifted during flight.] I move a muscle, and—*touché*!—I'm a dead man. *Frères humains qui après nous vivez:*[15] is Brother Willy to die so piteous a death? Bare-assed, balls to the wind, and for what?

A word or two, perhaps, in remembrance of me: my Last Willy and test . . . test . . . Testament, while I'm still of sound mind and—. [*He gasps.*][16]

[*Doubled version begins here.*]

[And now I lay me down to sleep.
I pray the Lord my balls to keep.]
I'm all exposed. It's getting chilly.
Alas, alack, slick Brother Willy!
If I should die before I wake,
I pray the Lord my soul to take.
Before I head for Heaven's payoff . . .
Before he cuts my fucking balls off!

[*Doubled version ends here.*]

To good friend Cupid, God of Love
I leave the soul of Brother Willy,
That Ye bestow it, from above,
to all the girls that I fucked silly.

My heart I leave in this, my will-y,
to her for whom my hour draws nigh.
And thus, Bro Willy, with a kiss you die?

O' girls, o' perky areolae,
sweet birds of youth, o' angel faces!
To buff and polish your *cuntzillae*,
my dick goes to your secret places,
my balls—*en garde!*—straight to third bases—
the porky kind to grab some thigh.
And thus, Bro Willy, with a kiss you die?

To sweet young maids: I leave my britches.
Rub front and back[17]—my gift to you-you.
Ashes to ashes, sugar-britches,
and bust to bust against the hoo-hoo,
so, when you're finished what you do-do,
you're all set for the next joy ride.
And thus, Bro Willy, with a kiss you die?

Last up: for shiny, itchy people,©
pansy-assed studs, scented and gay:
Here is the church, here is the steeple:
Open all doors. Fire away!
Kiss, kiss, bang, bang! In the back way
to fuck your wives, perchance to die!
And thus, Bro Willy, with a kiss you die?

To drunken buddies everywhere,
I pray: should Willy pass away,
remember him when on a tear,
rinsing your drunken mugs next day.
[Your brother played it as it laid]
and never let his throat get dry.
And thus, Bro Willy, with a kiss you die?

MARVIN
I just don't know where else to try. The Devil's work gets pretty hairy.

BLANCHE

Why not pray to the Virgin Mary?

MARVIN

Good golly, dear, too mad! No way! That damn thing must be socked away. [Who's handling our props anyway?]

BROTHER WILBUR

Into your hands, *o Domine,*
my spirit I commend. *Allez!*
Domine Deus, agnus dei,
feely-us testes—et anus!—
et impotente non sanctus!
Quo vadis? Eek! haec, ho-ho-hoc!
And what about my gorgeous cock?
Unkindest cut—right in the balls!
He's almost there now, sac and all!
Saint Johnson! What's a boy to do?
You'd kill a man whose balls are blue?
Good God! Prayers don't do any good.
Should I just let him see my wood?
Or let him sack my tonsured head?
Adieu, beloved hairy nuts![18]

BLANCHE

Quit looking! No, ifs, ands, or but[t]s! Look, dear! [*She points to Willy's drawers.*] What do you call that doohickey hanging right there on the bedpost?

MARVIN

What the devil? *Eureka!* I'll be damned! *Habeas corpus!* Oh, you great big beautiful—. Come to papa![19]

Nota bene: he shall mistake Brother Wilbur's underwear for his purse.

BROTHER WILBUR

At last! In the name of Saint Johnson, at last! What a relief! I *can* move a muscle!

MARVIN

Adieu, my dear. Now, just a little send-off before I go. Pucker up.[20]

BLANCHE

[*To distract him, she gives Marvin the best kiss ever.*] Knock yourself out. And leave me high and dry again, why don'tcha?

MARVIN

That was just the down payment. I'll finish up when I get home.

[*Exit Marvin*]

[Scene 10]

BROTHER WILBUR

O happy day! and praise be to Saint Johnson! Slick Brother Willy shall rise again! [Just tell them Willy-Boy is here!]

BLANCHE

Oh. My—. Lord have mercy! He really had you between your rocks and a hard place!

BROTHER WILBUR

How the hell did he get his hands on his purse, for God's sake? I was lying right on top of it.

BLANCHE

[*Feigning ignorance*] Jesus! So, what the hell did he take? He'll be back again in no time!

BROTHER WILBUR

Good God Almighty! No way he's up my Franciscan ass again! Hail, Mary, full of—! I'll get dressed, grab my junk, and get the hell outta here! But where in the name of God is my ball sack? [{*She looks confused.*} My britches. My drawers. My underwear, for fuck's sake!] I can't find it anywhere![21]

BLANCHE

Where was it?

BROTHER WILBUR

Next to my doublet: it was hanging right there on the bedpost.

BLANCHE

Mary, Mother of God, no way! That's what he took instead of his purse! Lord have mercy, I'm a goner! Soon as he figures it out, he's gonna kill me.

BROTHER WILBUR

And, my, my, my, would you look at the time! Gotta hit the road. And I won't be crossing paths with *him* again. I guess I'll just have to make a fist and take brother willy in these two hands of mine. Nature's very own jockstrap! [Now, exit, stage left!][22]

BLANCHE

Lord have mercy! Am I done for here or what?
You feel sorry for me, don't you folks? I never had much luck in the romance department but—Lord have mercy!—what's to become of me? [No, seriously: what do I do?] Make a run for it? If I wait around for him to get back, he's gonna kill me for sure.
I know! I'll go see what my girlfriend has to say.

[*Exit Blanche*]

[Scene 11]

[*At Aggie's home*]

[BLANCHE]

Hi, Aggie—hey! [Oh, fuck it! I don't have time for this:] Lord have mercy!

AGNES

You don't look so good. He didn't beat you, did he?

BLANCHE

I say, Lord have mercy, girl! I don't know what's to become of me. I'm a dead woman.

AGNES

Snap out of it. Every problem has a solution.

BLANCHE

So, help me out or I'm as good as dead. Lord have mercy, girl, what do I do? Looks like the hubby—genius that he is—grabbed Brother Wilbur's underwear instead of his purse.
Weeping [Plorando]
And, then, he headed right back to market.

AGNES

Good God, is *that* all? Shit, girl! What else you got?

BLANCHE

Yeah, well you don't know him like I do. He's gonna say I got plenty else, doin' it right and left. Like I ever get more than a tiny, little dribble outta him. Or one lousy time. Cross my heart and hope to die.

AGNES

No, seriously: that's it? Hail Mary, full of grace! Just go on back home. I've got a little performance to work up: a demonstration, if you will. I'll just prove to him that he's got the drawers of Saint Francis. You sit tight and play along.
[*A quizzical Blanche prefers to watch Agnes make her preparations and receive gestural reassurance from her friend.*]
Okay, I'm outta here. And, if I don't manage to calm him down, well, I'll have been a very bad girl who deserves a good spanking.

[BLANCHE]

Oh, my God, that's a load off! You make me feel so much better. I'm outta here too, in a flash.

[*Exit both women. Agnes hastens to catch up with Marvin on the road to the market; Blanche follows at a discreet distance instead of going home.*]

[Scene 12]

[*Lights up on Marvin, alone on the road but still fairly close to home. Agnes approaches and observes.*]

MARVIN

Well, what do you know! I'm almost there. But, in the name of Saint John—ooh, that smell!© What on earth is that stench? That purse stinks so bad, I can hardly breathe! Smells like loose bowels . . . or mussels . . . or rotten clam. It's almost as if . . .

Up my nose with a rubber hose! Purse, my ass! Good God, this is no purse! This is underwear! Right off somebody's ass—and not a particularly clean one at that! Just look at the [filthy] ball sac! Turn my back for one minute and—. To the Devil with you, madam! Just wait'll I get my hands on you. Opening up for some tomcat on the prowl. I'll be goddamned if she makes a cuckold outta *me*!

Mussels, was it? I'll give you muscle in a minute. The Devil take you and all your lowdown, dirty, rotten tricks! And the Devil can take me too if I don't get back at you. I'll slit your [pretty little] throat. Harrumph! Stuck it to me good, did you? That prick must have been hiding somewhere when I went back home. Jesus Christ Almighty, if I'd only known! I would've fucked you up royal right on the spot, by God, *Monsieur* . . . *Monsieur* . . . whoever the hell you are, Father What's-Your-Face! You're in there polishing up her hoo-hoo and it's all hoo-ha-ha at the poor cuckolded sap?

I think not, motherfuckers! The Devil take the lot of you, by God, 'cause I'm mad as hell and I'm not going to take it anymore! Stuck with the likes o' your sorry ass, am I, my fine lady? The hell with you, bitch![23]

AGNES

Good friend, are you quite all right? Such a commotion. Did you get mugged or something?

MARVIN

Good Golly! They sure stuck it to me! To market, to market with the old cuckold so he can cock-a-doodle-doo up her coochie, coochie coo! Sweeter than honey, bitter as—. Of all the goddamn gall! In the name of Saint Johnson, we'll soon see who's cocked up around here.

AGNES

Lord have mercy! Surely you're not suggesting that my friend's conduct might have been of questionable moral probity.

MARVIN

Conduct? [*Waving the drawers*] What the hell do you call this? Probity here, probity there. Her probity's pretty much in your face! [Fuck this shit!]

Monstrat caligas [*He shows the drawers again.*]

AGNES

Lord have mercy, friend, you mustn't think she's done anything wrong. Why, my heart's bursting out of my chest when I see you holding them like that in your own two hands. Lord have mercy! It's the drawers of Saint Francis! Don't you know a precious relic when you see one?

MARVIN

And how in the name of Saint Johnson did they wind up at my house?

AGNES

Seriously? Isn't it obvious? [It's divine intervention,] so help me God! Do you really think you could have fathered a child without the help of that holy relic?

MARVIN

Oh yeah? Who says I couldn't?

BLANCHE[24]

[Fat fuckin' chance.]

[AGNES]

Lord have mercy! You don't have it in you.

MARVIN

Do too! Besides, I fail to see what service could possibly be rendered—good God!—by *these*.

AGNES

Oh, really? Anybody else comes across the jewels in the crown, they know exactly what to do. You rub 'em seven times, front and back, recite the profession of faith, and, then, you discharge your conjugal duty. [*She handles the drawers.*] This is amazing! They were thought to have been lost forever! And to think that, if we hadn't bumped into each other like this—[{*aside*} more like if menfolk hadn't been doin' us like they do]—I never would have snagged 'im[25]—I mean snagged *'em*: they would never have come down to us. But you better hurry up and give 'em back.

MARVIN

I'll bring them back to the monastery myself, special delivery, with my own two hands.

AGNES

[{*Sotto voce*} And speakin' of two hands.]
Brother Wilbur comes by a lot. All you've got to do is hand them over to him.

MARVIN

Very well, then, but first, let's go see what the wife's got to say for herself.

[Scene 13]

[*Enter Blanche and, shortly thereafter, Brother Willy in monastic attire and initially unseen by the others.*]

[MARVIN]

Hail, Mary, full of grace. Forgive me, dear, I've wronged you terribly.

AGNES

Girl, you'll never guess what he was thinking about you! Never in his wildest dreams did our good man here imagine that you were in possession of the drawers of Saint Francis! He was quite beside himself—shocked, really—that such a thing should have come to pass.

BLANCHE

I had a feeling *something* was up when I found that pair just lying around the house. Needless to say, I'd rather rot in hell than ever engage in conduct that's anything other than beyond reproach. I'd never stoop so low.

AGNES

Girl, you've got to give them back.
[{*Aside*} And we'll soon see who wears the underpants in *this* family.]

BLANCHE

Lord have mercy, that's true. But they've served us well.
[*Under her breath*] And served him right!

MARVIN

Good God Almighty, dear, it never occurred to me till right now this very minute, so help me God.

AGNES

Look! Over there! It's Brother Wilbur headed right this way. Best to just hand them off to him.

MARVIN

Right you are. Say, Father, could you come over here please? We'd like to have a word with you.

BROTHER WILBUR

Might I be of service here? From what I see, I do believe so.

BLANCHE

These are Saint Francis's drawers. If you could please just take this junk off our hands.[26]

BROTHER WILBUR

I'll do it straightaway and case closed. But first: everybody on your knees and—[*waving the malodorous drawers*]—ask the good saint of Assisi to pray for our asses! And then, all three of you are gonna pucker

up and kiss the drawers of Saint Francis. Your breath will smell all the sweeter for it.
[{*Aside to the audience*} What's good for the goosing is good for the gander. And, while you're at it, kiss my ass!][27]

BLANCHE
You can rub-a-dub-dub 'em all over me, seeing as I've already come to know their great sweetness.[28]

BROTHER WILBUR
Well done, my sister, good job on that holy relic. Such a treasure!

MARVIN
Let's go bring them back, Father, before everybody leaves. [*They start to pass the hat to collect money.*]
[*To the audience*] Hey folks! A place for everything and everything in its place or we'll rub *your* noses in it too.
Do watch your steps, gents, as you go.[29]

BROTHER WILBUR
Bye, guys, hope you enjoyed the show!

[*Possible closing music.*][30]

The END

From the young clergy of Meulleurs.
M.P.V.

12.

Immaculate Deception, or, *Nuns Behaving Badly*

Farce nouvelle à cinq parsonnages (Soeur Fessue)

CAST OF CHARACTERS

MOTHER SUPERIOR, the ABBESS (L'Abeesse)
SISTER CRYBABY, the First Nun (Soeur Esplouree/La premiere Soeur)
SISTER GOODY TWO-SHOES, the Second Nun (Soeur de Bon Coeur/La deuxieme Soeur)[1]
SISTER FRISKY, the Third Nun (Soeur Safrete/La troisieme Soeur)
SISTER BUNNY (Seur/Soeur Fes[s]ue)
[A number of extra nuns for the chapter meeting]

PRODUCTION NOTES

The *Farce nouvelle à cinq parsonnages*, *RLV*, #38 (fols. 204v–211v), appears as the fourteenth piece of *RFMSJ*, vol. 2—again, paginated within a given play but not continuously throughout the volumes—under a title that has tended to stick: the inconsistently spelled *Soeur Fesue*.[2] Tissier, however, takes his cues from its closing lines and dubs his edition *L'Abbeesse et Soeur Fessue* (#59; *RF*, 11: 235–89). So too does Faivre in his summary (*Répertoire*, 37–38) whereas, for Petit de Julleville, it was *L'Abbesse et les soeurs* (*RTC*, 106–7). Our farce was reedited by Martin in *SFQS* at https://sottiesetfarces.wordpress.com/tag/fessue/ (accessed 20 January 2017), translated by Tissier into modern French (*FFMA*, 4: 183–98), and discussed by Hayes (*Rabelais's Radical Farce*, 51–53), Toldo ("ETCF," 294–97), and Maxwell (*French Farce*,

162–63). With the exception of one musical set-piece, most of the action unfolds in rhyming octosyllabic couplets, some corrupt, which may account for the divergent verse totals: 357, 353, and 352 for Tissier, Faivre, and Petit de Julleville, respectively.

Since our story was in circulation from Jean de Condé's "Dit de la Nonnette" (ca. 1313–37) to Boccaccio's *Decameron* 9.2 (1352) to Rabelais's *Tiers Livre* (1546) (*RGCF*, 6: 266–69), we are moved to ask what we did of *Bro Job* (#7): Which came first? The poem, the play, or the prose? Earlier theories had placed the composition of the *RLV Soeur Fessue* between 1510 and 1546, but for Tissier it is a Norman version (*remaniement*) of a relatively late lost original dating from approximately 1535 (*RF*, 11: 244–47; *FFMA*, 4: 185). He likewise believes, with Saulnier, that Rabelais borrowed his own "Soeur Fessue" from that lost version, which may indeed predate our farce by some ten years (*FFMA*, 4: 315n; Saulnier, "Histoire d'un conte rabelaisien").

Although I've uncovered no evidence of a fifteenth- or sixteenth-century performance, *Soeur Fessue* has been staged a number of times; and the production by Mario Longtin, an expert on the *RLV*, is available on YouTube at https://www.youtube.com/watch?v=djhacuv__3c (accessed 27 January 2021). After my translation was complete, he was good enough to share his own English translation, to which it's a pleasure to allude when pertinent.

Plot

Inconceivable! An entire convent is at sixes and sevens when word gets out that one of the sisters is pregnant. The thing is: knocked-up Soeur Fessue is not exactly Agnes of God. Like Margot of *Blue Confessions* (#2), "Sister Bunny" has been giving herself over to various delights, here, with a certain "Brother Hard-On." (That's a literal translation, I assure you, of her baby-daddy's name, "Frère Roydimet," as in: "he sticks it in there erect" [*royde [il l'] y met*].) Three distinctly non-Chekhovian sisters rat her out to Mother Superior because Bunny has foolishly failed to take the other nuns' regular precaution against pregnancy: sodomy. And, if that sounds far-fetched to you, consider that her plight might have been ripped from the headlines. Across the Channel, the chronicler Adam Usk reported on a most unusual legal case of accidental pregnancy by sodomy, and I'm indebted to Sarah McDougall and William Arguelles for bringing it to my attention. Usk and the Abbot of Leicester had been dispatched to Nuneaton priory in the diocese of

Lichfield to investigate "various crimes, heresies, and iniquities of a heinous nature allegedly committed by one Robert Bowlons," who later confessed: "When we got there, we found that one of the nuns had, as a result of the unbridled lust of this Robert, *become pregnant through the semen dripping down during the act of sodomy, not through penetration by the member*" (*Chronicle*, ed. Given-Wilson, 120–21; my emphasis). Seriously? Sodomy was committed by Robert *Bowel-ons*? He fits right in with Sister Bunny and Brother Hard-On ("Sister Bigass" and "Friar Stickitinstiff" for Frame's Rabelais), and also with the albeit later Italian subjects of Craig Monson's *Nuns Behaving Badly*.

Meanwhile, back at the farcical convent, our cheeky Bunny issues a point-by-point takedown of ecclesiastical casuistry that is so compelling and so funny that I prefer not to spoil its triumphant scholastic logic. Suffice it to say that it has a lot to do with the monastic vow of silence, the secrecy of the confessional (below, § "Language"), and the injunction that people who live in glass houses shouldn't throw stones. With a repeated riff on Matthew 7:3 and Paul to Romans 2:1, it's all about seeing—and not seeing—what is right before your very eyes: "And why beholdest thou the speck of dust that is in thy brother's eye, but considerest not the beam that is in thine own eye?" (*On veoyt à l'oeuil d'aultruy tout aultre / Un petit festu odieulx; / Mais on ne voyt poinct une poultre / Qu'on a devant les yeulx* [2: 26]). As the plot swaggers toward its concluding sermonic words worthy of any morality play, Sister Bunny cites the Apostle Paul: "Judge not, lest ye be judged" (below, note 27). Or, as Boccaccio's Elisa puts it: "You all know that there are plenty of very foolish people who take it upon themselves to instruct and correct others, but as you will learn from my story, from time to time, Fortune justly puts them to shame—which is prosily what happened to the Abbess who was the superior of the nun I am going to tell you about" (*Decameron*, trans. Rebhorn, 701). In the end, the real butt of the joke is Mother Superior, who's going down. She is, quite literally, in no position to judge. All shall be revealed in due course but, at this juncture, I confine myself to comparing the plot to the old joke about the nuns waiting in line at the Pearly Gates:

> "And so," says St. Peter, "have you ever had any contact with a penis?"
> "Well," says the first nun in line, "I did just once touch the tip of one with the tip of my finger."
> "OK," says St. Peter, "dip your finger in the holy water and pass on into Heaven."

The next nun admits, "Well, yes, I did once get carried away and I, you know, sort of massaged one a bit."

"OK," says St. Peter, "rinse your hand in the holy water and pass on into Heaven."

Suddenly there is some jostling in the line and one of the nuns is trying to cut in front.

"Well now, what's going on here?" says St. Peter.

"Well, your excellency," says the nun who is trying to improve her position in line, "if I'm going to have to gargle that stuff, I want to do it before Sister Mary Thomas sticks her ass in it" (e.g., http://www.jokes4us.com/dirtyjokes/confessionjokes.html [accessed 27 January 2021]).

Nuns who live in glass convents shouldn't have the stones to throw stones.

Characters and Character Development

Like *Drama Queens* (#4), our finale stages female characters only—nuns, no less—which startled both Petit de Julleville and Tissier (*RTC*, 106–7; *RF*, 11: 240). It was one thing to take aim at lecherous monks; it was quite another to go after sisters doing it for themselves. Not that Antonia Pulci had any trouble sniping at gossipy Italian nuns in her sixteenth-century *Mystery of Saint Theodora* (*Florentine Drama*, 187–93). Nor do the nuns going medieval on Bunny's ass, even if ever so courteously with *vous*. Scripted as *La premiere*, *La deuxieme*, and *La troisieme*, the sisters sport names embodying their most pronounced character traits: Sisters "Crybaby," "Goody Two-Shoes," and "Frisky." Their weeping, judging, and joshing might be further amplified onstage by physical shtick or by a British accent peppered with "cheeky" or "bloody cheek." And, oh, the homoerotic dimensions to be teased out if one or more sisters are played by men!

The First Nun's name appears only once when, true to form, she is crying: *Seur esploree commence* (2: 5). Distressed, flailing about, and desperate to get everything off, let's say, a large chest, Sister Crybaby is allegedly so distraught by the threat to the convent's reputation that she squeals on Sister Bunny. Why not turn the other cheek? Martin suspects that it's a matter not of honor but of jealousy: a revenge-move designed to eliminate the competition (*SFQS*, note 26; below note 14).

"Sister Goody Two-Shoes" might well get her name from her "good heart," but she is highly attuned to the vices of both Bunny and Mother Superior.

Although the Second Nun seems a bit of a drag at first, she forsakes her elegant lexicon soon enough for "asses" and "assholes" (2: 7). With a veneer of reserve, Sister Goody speaks softly—sometimes, not at all—but, like Tartuffie of *Drama Queens* (#4), she carries a big stick underneath that habit.

Arriving a little later on the scene is the Third Nun, "Soeur Safrete," whose moniker applies to someone bright-eyed and bushy-tailed. Since she's perky, lively, gay, sassy, nubile, or wanton, any number of English names would suit her, but I went with "Sister Frisky" (as did Longtin). Between her and Sister Bunny, it's a toss-up as to who gets the funniest lines; but frolicsome Frisky gets in more than her fair share of double entendres and dirty jokes. She's a real good-time gal who goes for the jocular.

Now enter "Mother Superior" ("L'Abeesse") or, rather, let others enter in on *her*. Disturbed in flagrante with a priest—Brother Hard-On himself, asserts Martin (*SFQS*, note 41)—she controls neither her emotions nor her frantic cover story. All decorum drops along with somebody's drawers, and it's all downhill from there. For her Latin too, such as it is (*SFQS*, note 37). She's the "nun from Ipanema," as it were: she looks "but she doesn't see." Not even when there's a beam in her eye. Not even when the evidence is as plain as the nose *in* her face—and ours.

As eagerly awaited as Molière's Tartuffe, "Soeur Fessue" at last arrives on the scene as the piece of ass *de résistance*. Her coming has been foretold to us; and she stands out like a sore *bun*. Picture Barbara Streisand's "funny girl" Fanny Brice crooning that she is "the beautiful reflection of her true love's affection," while her costume simulates an enormous baby bump.[3] Technically, the name conjures "big, beautiful butt-cheeks" (*RF*, 11: 251–54), "Hotbuns" (Longtin), or "Bigass" (Frame); but I've gone with the absurdist Playboy vibe of "Bunny." And, if that reminds you of British PM Jeremy Thorpe's same-sex lover "Bunnies," so much the better. Plus, there's something incongruous about caricaturing the ass of maybe the only character who is *not* having anal sex. (Feel free to substitute "Fanny," "Sweet-Cheeks," or "Cheeky," if you prefer.) She may be a relative newbie to the convent, which won't stop her from mounting one helluva defense. Her manipulation of Scripture puts Mother Superior to shame and, although Martin views her theologically astute ratiocinations as a "clearly interpolated passage" (*SFQS*, notes 85–88), I submit that her smarts are not out of character at all (2: 26–27). Regardless of whether another voice is breaking through, she still hits all the right holy notes.

Finally, one could conceivably stage the all-purpose Brother Hard-On as a silent partner. The advantage would be the creation of some side-splitting mimed sessions; the disadvantage, the insertion of a man into an all-female cast . . . unless he were played by a suitably equipped female thespian. If you go that route, do heed the words of Sister Frisky: he is *rouge comme un beau cherubin* or "red as a beautiful cherub" (2: 12). It's not clear that she's talking about his face.

Language

In addition to brilliant wordplay on *covering, uncovering, discovering, head-covering,* and *ass-covering* (*couvrir, descouvrir, couvre-chef, couvre-cul*), *Immaculate Deception* revels in metacommentary on representation, faking, and laughter (*faindre*; *pour rire*). There's also something over-the-top about the masculine pronouns (*ilz*) relentlessly applied to oversexed and overdetermined women. Conventional though such pronominal usage might be (*FF*, 53–54), it would still poke added fun at transvestite actors. Sister Bunny, for example, was not only "impregnated" and potentially "raped" (*deceue et gastée* [2: 7]): she is "pregnant and pregnant" (*grosse & ensaincte* [2: 8]) (*RF*, 11: 260n; *SFQS*, note 11). Beyond that, *enceindre* plays tongue-in-cheek, as it did in *Cooch E. Whippet* (*FF*, 334–35), on an almost "saintly beltedness" about the waist as it hits below the belt (*sainte/ensaincte*; 2: 13).

Linguistically, the primary challenge involves how to render the corrupt biblical citations in such a way that they are both recognizable and unrecognizable. Snippets from prayers, psalms, and the liturgy pop up throughout, nowhere more so than in a singular parody of Psalm 51, the prayer of repentance, where farce's favorite activities of cleansing and purging very much apply. Meanwhile, don't get Bunny sophistically started on the sacred seal of confession as set forth by the Fourth Lateran Council: "Let the priest absolutely beware that he does not by word or sign or by any manner whatever in any way betray the sinner. . . . For whoever shall dare to reveal a sin disclosed to him in the tribunal of penance we decree that he shall not only be deposed from the priestly office but that he shall also be sent into the confinement of a monastery to do perpetual penance" (Canon 21).[4] Obviously, big-assed Bunny gets it ass-backward about who respects whose privacy in a very public setting.

Equally stunning: when ordered by Mother Superior to recite the *benedicite*, the sisters sure do a number on her with an actual song that was possibly added by a sixteenth-century player (*RF*, 11: 246–47). It's a bona fide *contrafactum*, that is: a hybrid of sacred and secular music that, like farce itself, is stuffed into the dramatic proceedings. Intriguingly enough, moreover, a stage direction prescribes that it must be sung, not spoken, at a sixteenth-century moment when the once-blurred medieval boundaries between speaking and singing would long have been resolved: *O lieu de le dire y chantent*, "Instead of saying it, they sing" (*RLV*, fol. 208r; *RFMSJ*, 2: 18).[5] And what they perform is the dirty "Dormez-vous, fillettes?" First published in Paris in 1536 and later set to music by Robert Godard in 1547, it's a striking analogue to "Frère Jacques" that asks: "Are you sleeping, little nuns?"[6] The answer is: not much.

Sets and Staging

In the Father's house, there are many rooms, and *Soeur Fessue* offers a marvelous topography of its house of worshipping whatever. There's the "dormitory," accessed by a ladder (*le monteur*), which I've translated as the more resonant "night stair" (*RF*, 11: 279n; *SFQS*, note 68). There's the *camera charitatis* (2: 12), the "chamber" where pilgrims were welcomed for physical and spiritual nourishment (*caritatis* > *caro* > *chair*): *fleshtivities* of manifest interest to the sisters. And there's Mother Superior's *parloir* (<*parler*), where she's receiving, all right, but not doing much talking. It should be located just off the play's centerpiece: a great hall or "chapter house," so called because the sisters congregated daily there to hear a chapter of the monastic rule. Other spaces are referenced more indirectly, but their integration into set design is useful. A *misericord* comes in handy as the locus where wayward nuns were disciplined, as does a dining hall or refectory. The latter was conveniently called the *frater*.[7] Oh, brother!

To capture the ebullient spirit of this farce, I recommend leading off with a production number. Try having the sisters sing, à la *Sound of Music*, "How do you solve a problem like our Bunny?" Or try the strange, sexist camp of Hong Kong Syndikat's 1980s synthpop cover of "Concrete and Clay" that peeks briefly under a nun's habit.[8] But, mostly, the issues are dramaturgical. **SPOILER ALERT!** If you'd rather be surprised by the visual nature of Mother Superior's undoing, please stop reading and proceed to the play.

As in *Slick Brother Willy* (#11), the big reveal turns on the use of a key prop: another pair of underwear (*haut de chausse*). Her unholy acts interrupted, Mother Superior finds that haste makes waste when she grabs her partner's drawers instead of her nun's coif (*cornette*). (If you're worried about the verisimilitude of this new misprision, see below, note 10.) And let it all be on her head! The underwear too, as an "ass-covering" cover story (*couvre-cul*) morphs ingeniously into a "head-covering" (*couvre-chef*): *Bien resamble / Çou de quoy en cuevre son cul* (*RF*, 11: 242–43). But it's a delicate dance as to who notices Mother Superior's headgear and when. Per the text, it's definitely Bunny, who thrice calls attention to it with variations on: *A! mon Dieu, vous ne voyés pas / Ce qui vous pent devant les yeux?* (2: 19, 20, 26). (The literal translation is "Oh my God, you do not see what is hanging before your eyes?"; but I've opted for a turn of phrase that mockingly underscores transvestism: "how it's hangin'?") And, while Tissier is critical of the repetition (*RF*, 11: 250, 269n–76n), I find that the three Petrine denials totally fit the bill. More perplexing is when everybody else catches on. Needless to say, Mother Superior is the last to perceive the damning piece of evidence; and the three sisters' gaze can plausibly be averted by having them on their knees for a time, not daring to look the Abbess in the eye until she invites them to rise and "raise their heads": *Levés, levés la teste* (2: 20).[9] But do have some fun with the audience's epiphany, which could tantalizingly be forestalled. Mother Superior could be unseen but not unheard for as long as practicable, grunting, groaning, and delivering her lines from within the *parloir*. Indeed, Tissier saw no other choice in that one could scarcely portray women engaged in sex acts (*RF*, 11: 248–50; *FFMA*, 4: 185–86). In the immortal words of Molière's Tartuffe, *ce n'est pas pécher que pécher en silence*—"sinning in silence is no sin at all" (act 5, sc. 4)—and this play is prepared to make some noise.

Costumes and Props

Most of the props are self-explanatory—Bibles, rule books, rosaries, and the like—but the choice of which religious habits is crucial to any satire of a specific brother- or sisterhood (above, "ABT," § "Oh, Brother"). Are the nuns Carmelites? Benedictines? A fantastical order? I suspect that we have entered a Franciscan monastery; but, in point of fact, we know little more than that the sisters are cloistered and that they sing daily praise of the Virgin Mary (2: 27). Have on hand a conductor's baton and a gigantic Robert's *Rules of Order* for the chapter meeting, along with, say, a *Rule of Saint Benedict* (if appropriate). But, as in our two previous plays, the essential prop is that telltale pair of drawers. Why not mount a triple bill of *The Pardoners' Tales*, *Slick Brother Willy*, and *Immaculate Deception* in which unholy relics and britches come materially together? The trick is to garb the nuns in *cornettes* and coifs that resemble boxers closely enough to render the flustered Abbess's misprision believable. A little net-surfing clarifies that in no time. The *cornette,* also a liturgical "psalter" that gets its name from the musical psaltery (*Decameron,* trans. Rebhorn, 702n), is a great big, floppy, two-sided headpiece: the *sur*-vestimentary equivalent of *Brother Willy*'s *bissac*.[10] Our final farce then closes this book with its own statement about clerical fashions.

Scholarly References to Copyrighted Materials (in order of appearance and indicated by © within the text)

"Amazing Grace." By John Newton. (1779).
"What's the Buzz?" By Andrew Lloyd-Webber and Timothy Rice. ASCAP Work ID: 530169050.
"Cry Like a Baby." By Dewey Lindon Oldham Jr. and Daniel Pennington. BMI Work #261591.
"Now I Lay Me Down to Sleep." ["All Night, All Day, Angels Watching Over Me."] By Otis Leon McCoy. (19th c.)
"Three Is Company Too." By Donald Nicholl and Joe Raposo. ASCAP Work ID: 500265976.
"I Whistle a Happy Tune." By Richard Rodgers and Oscar Hammerstein II. ASCAP Work ID: 390083480.
"Ya Got Trouble." By Meredith Willson. ASCAP Work ID: 550000489.
"Pickin' Up the Pieces." By Richie Furay. BMI IPI #57552074.[11]
"California, Here I Come." By B. G. De Sylva, Al Jolson, and Joseph Meyer. ASCAP Work ID: 330004507.
"Frère Jacques." Traditional.
"Bad Company." By Simon Kirke and Paul Rodgers. ASCAP Work ID: 320187240.
"I'll Be There for You." By David Crane, Marta Kauffman, Michael Jay Skloff, Philip Solem, Danny Wilde, and Allee Willis. BMI Work #2033645.
"Baby, What a Big Surprise." By Pete Cetera. ASCAP Work ID: 320230915.
"You Give Love a Bad Name." By Jon Bongiovi, Desmond Child, and Richard Sambora. ASCAP ID: 550147303.
"Stairway to Heaven." By Robert Plant and Jimmy Page. ASCAP Work ID: 490294198.
"Hot Blooded." By Louis A. (Andrew) Grammatico and Michael Leslie Jones. ASCAP Work ID: 380199428.

"They're Coming to Take Me Away, Ha-Ha." By Jerry Samuels. ASCAP Work ID: 500221503.

"Battle Hymn of the Republic." By Julia Ward Howe. (19th c.)

"Girl from Ipanema." By Vinicius de Moraes, Norman Gimbel, and Antonio Carlos Jobim. BMI Work #470303.

"A Tisket, a Tasket." Traditional.

"Who's Sorry Now?" By Burt Kalmar and Harry Ruby. ASCAP Work ID: 530081448.

"His Love Makes Me Beautiful." By Bob Merrill and Jule Styne. ASCAP Work ID: 380108632.

"Maria." By Richard Rodgers and Oscar Hammerstein II. ASCAP Work ID: 430030594.

"Concrete and Clay." By Thomas Moeller and Brian Parker. BMI Work #239352.

"Gimme That Old Time Religion." Gospel song. (19th c.)

"Papa Don't Preach." By Brian Elliot. ASCAP Work ID: 460257114.

"Girls Just Want to Have Fun." By Victor Carstarphen, Robert Hazard, Cyndi Lauper, Gene McFadden, Richard David Morel, John Cavadus Whitehead. ASCAP Work ID: 372137750.

"That's the Way I Like It." By Harry Wayne Casey and Rick Finch. BMI Work #1481515.

"Fat-Bottomed Girls." By Brian Harold May. BMI Work #406587.

"You Can Leave Your Hat On." By Randy Newman. ASCAP ID: 550069602.

"Sisters Are Doin' It for Themselves." By Ann Lennox and David Allan Stewart. ASCAP Work ID: 790710124.

[*Possible opening music.*][12]

[Scene 1]

[*At the convent near the sisters' chambers*]

Enter SISTER CRYBABY, The First Nun

O sister, good sister! I once was lost© but, now, Sister Goody, I'm most certainly not found. I'm so beside myself, I can't take it anymore.

SISTER GOODY TWO-SHOES, The Second Nun

What is it, sister? Bad news? Don't tell me you've been laying ye down in green pastures again. A little splendor in the grass?

SISTER CRYBABY

Nuh-uh.

SISTER GOODY

So, enlighten me.

SISTER CRYBABY

I'll never tell.

SISTER GOODY

But—Lord have mercy!—I could comfort you in your hour of need and ease your troubles. You must tell me. Get it all off your chest. There are no secrets between friends.

SISTER CRYBABY

Oh, my dear! [*She swoons.*]

SISTER GOODY

You better sit down. You're obviously upset about something. Speak up. Tell me what's on your mind. What's wrong with you?

SISTER CRYBABY

Nothing.

SISTER GOODY

Once and for all: out with it! Now, tell me the truth. [No secrets, I said.] Have you been at it again? What's the matter? Who's laid you down so low?

SISTER CRYBABY

Sshhh! Keep your voice down! I'll never tell [and I won't squeal either]. It's a matter of honor.

SISTER GOODY

Always the same old song, and it's not making any sense. [*Aside to the audience*] She doesn't know her honor from her ass.

SISTER CRYBABY

Sshhh! Once you mount that holy rod, there's no going back. As Mother Superior knows full well.

SISTER GOODY

Good heavens! And, for that, I'm truly sorry . . . that I even asked.

SISTER CRYBABY

No, no, I'll tell you the whole story. It's just that . . . You know Sister Bunny, right? [Sister Hotbuns? Sister Sweet-Cheeks? *Soeur Fessue*? Sister Bigass? Sister Bunny, for God's sake!] Well, Brother Hard-On's gone and done her. Pushed his way in and spoiled that whole thing.

SISTER GOODY

Ave Maria!

SISTER CRYBABY

She's pregnant! And she's already showing. [*There is little reaction.*] For God's sake, sister, I'm not kidding. She's knocked up! which is why we've all *clammed* up. We're speechless because *res ipsa poke-at-her*. And we're all goin' down with her![13]

SISTER GOODY

Ave Maria and Jesus! I've gotten plenty of tail—and plenty of satisfaction—in my day without ever getting knocked up.

SISTER CRYBABY

Lord have mercy, me too! Done it every which way. All over the place, just like her.

SISTER GOODY

Ave Maria! Oh, the pain! Oh, the suffering! My heart bleeds for her.

[*Enter*] SISTER FRISKY, The Third Nun

What's the buzz? Tell me what's a-happening? What's the buzz? Tell me what's a-happening?© What's up with the big debate? What were you two talking about just now? Lemme in on it, wouldya? It'll be fun.

SISTER CRYBABY

It's nothing, really.

SISTER FRISKY

You two were talking love, weren't you? Right here, right now! But see if I care. Yeah, see if I care. I get my fair share: as much as any of the other sisters communing their asses off around here. [It's a holy fucking Trinity!] So, go ahead, spill. You can tell me.

SISTER GOODY

As if we didn't know that you're not exactly the only one giving it her all. But the latest dirt is going to cause such a huge scandal, the dishonor's going to bring down the house!

[*Sister Crybaby weeps histrionically.*]

SISTER FRISKY

[Dirtbag's more like.] But what's with you cry-babies anyhow? Some *thingy* on your mind? Whatever did we find out this time? Come on, give it up: Who's in the hot seat?

The first and the second [nun] speak together.

SISTERS GOODY and CRYBABY

It's Sister Bunny, who's gone and done . . .

SISTER FRISKY

What?

SISTER GOODY

We don't dare say . . .

SISTER FRISKY

Oh, go on, say. It's a farce, [for God's sake!] It'll be fun.

SISTER CRYBABY

Fun? Lord have mercy, sister, you can't possibly conceive . . . I'm weeping and wailing from the pain! Whenever I think about it, I cry like a baby.[©]

SISTER FRISKY

Who's the cause of this?

The first and the second [nun] speak together.

SISTERS GOODY and CRYBABY

Sister Bunny.

SISTER CRYBABY

All night, all day,[©] I break into a sweat, I'm hot and cold all over, I can't sleep a wink. There is no peace, no rest from all the pain and the fear and the trembling.

SISTER FRISKY

Who's done you like this?

The first and the second [nuns] speak together.

SISTERS GOODY and CRYBABY

Sister Bunny. She's really gone and done it.

SISTER FRISKY

Done it on her knees, more like.

SISTER CRYBABY

Done it like all of us. But the worst of it is, she's knocked up.

SISTER FRISKY

Knocked up? What a dumb-ass! Jesus Christ! I'd be astonished if that sort of thing were allowed. Now, without necessarily impugning anybody's honor or pointing any fingers or anything, let's have it: Whodunit?

SISTER CRYBABY

Brother Hard-On.

SISTER FRISKY

Lord have mercy and, oh, mama! She's a fallen woman! But—hail Mary and, hell, Mary!—where the *hail* are we going to hide her till she's ready to give birth?

SISTER GOODY

How should I know?

SISTER CRYBABY

Remember that time when I caught her in the—? Let's just say I've known for quite some time that she's a good-time gal. She's always been a bit too open-minded for the religious life.

SISTER FRISKY

Open for business, more like. And up for a good time. All bright-eyed and bushy-tailed. She's been in love with you-know-who forever and—.

SISTER CRYBABY

Who, Sister?

SISTER FRISKY

Who else? Brother Hard-On. [O rocks of Ages!] Red and ruddy as a fat-cheeked little cherub. One time, I was messing around with Brother Dicky—you know—in private session, *in camera*, in the *frater*. Sweet. But Hard-On's a good time. Plus, you know: three is company too.©

SISTER GOODY

Oh, Sister Frisky! He can be so warm and sweet when he wants to stick it in stiff.

SISTER CRYBABY

Oh yeah! Really sets you on the straight and narrow. Whenever I feel afraid, good Brother Hard-On holds his head erect,© wraps himself around me, and hammers in that lesson but good. I get it right away.

SISTER GOODY

Is that so? He's got no fault to find with me. We have what you'd call a friendly arrangement. I've vowed to love, honor, and obey. Do unto others and such. It's only fitting.

SISTER CRYBABY

I get what you mean about Brother Hard-On's *largesse*, and he's definitely love-worthy and all. But we've got our reputations to consider, you know. We can't have people thinking that the holy life is some farce. It's too much to bear. So, I, for one, say we make a clean breast of it and tell Mother Superior that Sister Bunny is pregnant.

[*No one speaks.*]

No kidding.[14]

SISTER GOODY

You go, girl!

SISTER FRISKY

Sister, girl! *You* go! And, *miserere nobis*, Daddy-o Confessor! "Thou shalt wash me, and I shall be whiter than snow." Just stick him in the misericord and he'll be gettin' his in no time. On his knees![15]

SISTER GOODY

I say he gets solitary. He can do the time deep inside my chamber. [And thou shalt open my lips, O Lord: and my mouth shall show Thy praise.]

SISTER FRISKY

Okay by me! You love him; I get it. But, in the name of Saint Peter, Peter, penance-eater: now you're really talkin' Christian charity!

[*Sister Crybaby goes to fetch Mother Superior; Sisters Goody and Frisky remain behind in prayer.*][16]

[Scene 2]

[*Sounds of religious ecstasy emanate from the parlor. Sister Crybaby knocks; and, after a certain amount of time, a flushed and flustered Mother Superior emerges, wearing a curious piece of headgear.*]

The first, SISTER CRYBABY, *going to Mother Superior to speak with her Ave Maria.*

MOTHER SUPERIOR

Gratia plena. Hail Mary, full of grace. What's wrong? What brings you by?[17]

SISTER CRYBABY

[{*To the audience*} What? I need just cause?]
No particular reason. I just wanted to see you.

MOTHER SUPERIOR

I was just in my parlor prior to our repast, deep in meditation, taking in the word of God, that He might lift me up and edify me, body and soul.

SISTER CRYBABY

Lord have mercy! If only Death had come for me! 'Twould be a far, far better thing!

MOTHER SUPERIOR

What's wrong with you? Are you in love again? Don't tell me you're still longing for worldly things . . .

SISTER CRYBABY

Nuh-uh, that's not it.

MOTHER SUPERIOR

. . . because, as many earthly delights as there are out in the world, you can find it all right here, within our walls. This house is certainly no exception. You can take a lover any time.

SISTER CRYBABY

Lord have mercy, I'm sweating all over! Oh, the pain! I can't hold it in anymore. But my wretched heart dare not offend.

MOTHER SUPERIOR

What on earth is wrong with you, dear?

SISTER CRYBABY

It's Sister Bunny. She's gone and done . . .

MOTHER SUPERIOR

What? Has she insulted you? because, believe you me, I'll put in her solitary—I swear to God—unless . . . Don't tell me she's been pretending to be a virgin again! I do wish she'd knock it off already with the immaculate deception.[18]

SISTER CRYBABY

[*In a whisper*][19] She's gone and done . . .

MOTHER SUPERIOR

What? What are you trying to say? Speak up!

SISTER CRYBABY

She's gone and done . . .

MOTHER SUPERIOR

What already?

SISTER CRYBABY

It. She did *it*. *Corpus "delecti." Coitus non interruptus.*[20]

MOTHER SUPERIOR

Good God Almighty, who'da thunk it? That big, fat, knocked-up sinner! Up hers! *Sea culpa, sea maxima culpa*. Peck-peck-*peccavit*! And has *she* ever got one great big load of penance coming her way now!

SISTER CRYBABY

She did it, all right: led all the way into temptation and, now, *pregnantia est. Grossus.*

MOTHER SUPERIOR

That vile slut! She's really gonna get it now. But to whom, pray tell, did she give it up?

SISTER CRYBABY

Brother Hard-On, the monk. Way up. Ages ago.

MOTHER SUPERIOR

And we've got trouble.© Ring those bells! Summon all the *sistren* to the chapter house! *Adeste fidelis! Venite! Venite! Ding-us, dong-us, dong-us.* Get her *gluteus maximus* in here this very minute!

[Scene 3]

[*At the ringing of the bells, the other sisters rush to the chapter house, kneeling before Mother Superior and averting their eyes. They rise only when invited to do so.*]

SISTER GOODY

Hurry, sisters. On our knees for assembly.

SISTER FRISKY

You go, girl!

MOTHER SUPERIOR

So, what are you waiting for? Sing!

[*Sister Crybaby takes the lead and moves with great solemnity until the group morphs into a girl band. She taps her conductor's baton.*]

SISTER CRYBABY

The *benedicite*!

Instead of speaking it here, they sing.

[We're pickin' and grinnin'©—Christ died for our sinnin'—so, open, up those pearly gates,© because here we come! *Consummatum est.* Sing it with me, sisters! Hit it, girls!]

Are you sleeping, are you sleeping,
little nuns, little nuns?
Burning up with longing,
ready for ding-donging.
Ding-dong-ding, ding-dong-ding.

Are you sleeping, all alone there,
little nuns, little nuns?
Eaten up with longing,
longing for ding-donging,
ding-dong-ding, ding-dong-dong.

Are you sleeping, all alone there,
little nuns, little nuns?
Open up for loving,
here to kingdom coming!
ding-dong-ding, dong-dong-dong.©[21]

[Scene 4]

Enter SISTER BUNNY

Uh oh. This doesn't look good. [Ask not for whom the bell tolls because . . .] I guess I'm persona non grata around here. *Ave Maria, gratia poena* and suffering!

MOTHER SUPERIOR

Venite, approachamus, Madamus, and *genuflectus prontissimo*! Whatever possessed you to play hide the *saucisson*, I'd like to know, *et mountibus balonia ponia*? I *will* get to the bottom of this.[22]

SISTER GOODY

You're a fallen woman and you're bringing us all down with you.

MOTHER SUPERIOR

From this day forward, you shall be forever shunned. It's hell, fire, and brimstone for you, my girl, and bad company till the day you die!© What in the world got into you? How could you have been so careless? Bang, bang! You're dead. [And your afterlife's DOA.©]

SISTER BUNNY

[*Pointing toward Mother Superior's head.*] Oh. My. God. Right before your eyes!© Plain as the nose on your face! You really don't see how it's hanging?

MOTHER SUPERIOR

And let this be on your head!
[*Aside*] [Hold onto your hat, sister,] because you'd never catch *me* exposing *my* reputation like that.

SISTER BUNNY

[*My* head?] Lord have mercy, talk about exposure! There are none so blind as those who do not see. There! Right before your very eyes!© The evidence is pretty much in your face, albeit not yet known to all. For, yea: thou seest through an ass darkly, but not face-to-face. [And cheat front, for God's sake! The audience hasn't caught on either.]

MOTHER SUPERIOR

I'm in charge here—master of your domain—and your punishment shall fit the crime.

SISTER BUNNY

Oh. My. God. Do you really not see what's—? Right before your very eyes!© Plain as the nose *in* your face? You still don't see how it's hanging? Sure, I've been sinning like crazy and I feel really guilty about it and all, but—

MOTHER SUPERIOR

But what?

SISTER BUNNY

But I see your but[t] and raise you [one, two, three, four, five senses]. It's not like there aren't five hundred folks out there who think this is any kinda big deal. They don't do no better than me, [do you, folks?][23]

MOTHER SUPERIOR

[*To the other nuns*] Rise, sisters, raise your heads and behold! [*To Sister Bunny*] [Of all the bloody cheek!] You're a lying little slut and you've committed a mortal sin.

SISTER CRYBABY

Make her good and *miserere*-able, Mother, for having conceived *with* sin.

SISTER BUNNY

And forgive Sister Bunny. Turn Thy face from my sins. ["For I acknowledge my faults but *your* sin is ever before me."]

[*Mother Superior menaces Sister Bunny with a whip.*]

SISTER FRISKY

Make her pay! She's so far gone, that penance needs to hit her where she lives.

SISTER BUNNY

"For behold what is shapen in wickedness!" And forgive Sister Bunny her . . . girth.

SISTER CRYBABY

She does have a point. You don't want to be hurting the precious fruit of her womb or anything.

SISTER BUNNY

Imagine, if you will, that someone had given *you* the *buns'* rush in the middle of *your* business. [Talk about a pain in the—.] You would've found yourself in a much worse pickle than me and—know what? You would've totally freaked out.

MOTHER SUPERIOR

Silence! That will be quite enough of that! I'm still conducting my inquiry. Now, who is responsible for this trespass? Who knocked you up? You're so fat you're about to pop.

SISTER BUNNY

Who do you think, *Madame*? Brother Hard-On. Shot through the heart and he's to blame. He gives religion a bad name.© But I do beg forgiveness. Please.

MOTHER SUPERIOR

And where, pray tell, might this have been?

SISTER BUNNY

Not that it's any business of yours, but it was in the dormitory, right by that stairway to Heaven.©

SISTER GOODY

Why didn't you scream bloody murder?

SISTER BUNNY

You don't hear anyone else screamin' around here, do you?

SISTER FRISKY

[*Aside*] She must be kidding. This is all gonna come down on Mother Superior's head.

SISTER BUNNY

Scream? How was I supposed to scream when I was so overcome I was practically swooning? Besides, according to our Rules of Order, which I've never breached, by the way, we've all taken a vow of silence. There's no talking in the dormitory: [I *had* to hold my tongue.] After all, if I'd had the temerity to make any noise or commotion whatsoever—raise any sort of hue and cry—it would have been on *my* head, and a grave violation of the rules. Which is why I didn't dare say a word.

SISTER CRYBABY

A laughable excuse, I must say.

SISTER GOODY

She did keep that vow of silence.[24]

MOTHER SUPERIOR

Now, you listen to me: What stopped you from giving a sign—[some kind of sign©]—that you needed help? You wouldn't have borne the assault. We would have come straightaway—rushed right over—you bet your ass.

SISTER BUNNY

My ass! No, really, my *ass*. Lord have mercy, I gave a *rectal* sign. But nobody came to help. [*She demonstrates with a fart.*]

SISTER FRISKY

[*Aside*] Come running? *Moi*? I wouldn't have touched that thing with a ten-foot pole. [She that troubleth her own house shall inherit the wind!]

SISTER CRYBABY

Rectal sign, my ass!

SISTER FRISKY

Coulda happened. Brother Hard-On's a holy terror. Maybe that's the only sign poor Sister Dumb-Ass over there coulda made.

SISTER CRYBABY

It *is* the tell-tail sign, you know.

MOTHER SUPERIOR

But she's been knocked up for a whole year already! It's inconceivable that she couldn't have found *some* way to tell me—tell all of us—that she was with child.

SISTER BUNNY

Tell you? Lord have mercy!

SISTER GOODY

You're darn tootin', tell! Tell, tell!

SISTER BUNNY

I beg to differ with your logic there.

SISTER FRISKY

How do you figure?

SISTER BUNNY

[But lo, Thou requirest truth in the inward parts.] Lord have mercy! After committing such a grave trespass, I was really in the hot seat and my heart was beset with remorse. I was terrified that the Devil, the Great Deceiver, was coming to take me away© for my sin. So, I prayed the Lord that, in His infinite goodness, He might forgive me, as He does all men of good will. And I asked good Brother Hard-On to hear my confession. But, then, as he was discharging his duties and granting me absolution, he stated in no uncertain terms that I was absolutely forbidden to speak of what the two of us had done, which instruction I obeyed, lest I be damned for all eternity. Because, to break the seal of the confessional and reveal the priest's secrets: that's all it takes and, there you go: you're rottin' in hell with the most hardened of sinners and heretics, forever and ever.

SISTER CRYBABY

Now we're getting somewhere. It's quite the explanation, really. And she did say she was sorry.

MOTHER SUPERIOR

You'll be punished for this if it's the last thing I do. *Tua culpa, tua maxima culpa!* Oh, the shame! Oh, the sin! [Shame! Shame!]

SISTER BUNNY

Lord have mercy, Mother, *puh-lease*: Look not upon my sins but upon your own, deep within. [I say: Hey, lady! People who live in glass houses shouldn't throw stones.] And don't you be thinking that—[25]

MOTHER SUPERIOR

What? Don't be thinking *what*, you sneaky little slut? Have I ruined *your* reputation?[26]

SISTER BUNNY

[*Whipping out a Bible*] "And why beholdest thou the speck of dust that is in thy brother's eye, but considerest not the beam that is in thine own eye?" [Matthew 7:3: If thine eye offend thee, fuck it out!]

MOTHER SUPERIOR

My eye! My reputation's doin' a helluva lot better than yours, honey.

SISTER BUNNY

"Judge not, lest ye be judged. For our judgments are odious in the eyes of the Lord, the King of Kings." You know the drill, chapter and verse. ["Let he who is without sin cast the first stone."] And Saint Paul said unto us: "You, therefore, have no excuse, you who pass judgment on someone else"—thus spake the glorious apostle—"for at whatever point you judge another, you are condemning yourself, because you who pass judgment do the same things."[27]

MOTHER SUPERIOR

Wicked girl! I've had just about enough preaching outta you, you cheeky little bitch! Am I like you? Really? [*She gestures to a statue of the Virgin Mary.*] In the name of the blessed Mother—[we only sing her praises every single day around here! You know: the one who conceived *without* sin?]—you'll pay for this. Repent ye sinner!

SISTER FRISKY

Oh, come on, Mother, she'll come around. Could she just take her vows again or something? It would be for the best. [Maybe try another religion?]

SISTER BUNNY

[Thine eyes have seen the glory of the coming of the Lord!©] In your face! The beam in thine own eye, I said, plain as the nose on your—. [*With a grand demonstrative gesture, Sister Bunny touches Mother Superior's headgear.*]

It's a dead giveaway. And it demonstrates for all to see—no doubt about it!—that you've been getting down and dirty yourself.

MOTHER SUPERIOR

The beam in mine own eye? The nose on my face? [*Finally, she notices her lover's underwear on her head.*] *Ave Maria,* [*Soeur Fessue*]! What on earth is this? This is what comes of rushing me when I'm otherwise engaged. Oh my God! I must admit this is rather embarrassing.

SISTER CRYBABY

Unless mine eyes deceive me, I do believe that what we have here is a pair of drawers.

MOTHER SUPERIOR

Ave Maria, holy moly, and *mama mia*! I'm no less to blame than Sister Bunny!

SISTER GOODY

[*Examining the drawers*] Is this item part of our habits now? I'm not entirely certain this is the regulation underwear.

MOTHER SUPERIOR

I'm not exactly pleased with myself here. Sorry about that.

SISTER FRISKY

Oh. My. God. That's some piece of equipment—and a helluva pair! Is this what all the abbesses are wearing these days? Awesome new look for the sister with balls.

SISTER CRYBABY

A pair of drawers!

[*Sister Goody examines the drawers more closely, perhaps pointing out a stain. The sisters might throw the underwear around in a game of catch, taking turns putting it on their heads.*]

SISTER GOODY

What did you say this was again?

MOTHER SUPERIOR

Let's drop it, shall we?

SISTER FRISKY

Oh, come on, can't you take a joke? And, by the way, you're in no position to be denying Sister Bunny absolution. Nothing comes between her and salvation.

SISTER GOODY

Drawers on the head. Quite the fashion statement, really. [She looks, but she doesn't see.©]

MOTHER SUPERIOR

Oh, the hell with it!

SISTER FRISKY

Yeah, yeah, yeah, let's step on it, shall we? One hand washes the other. Same thing goes for all of us. What goes around comes around. And you know what they say about close shaves. So, maybe let's make like a barber and—[*grabbing the boxers off whomever's head*]—take a little bit off the top! Now, go on: absolve her already! [*She models the drawers on her head.*]

SISTER CRYBABY

Now *that's* what I call a madcap fashion statement!

[*To Mother Superior*] You were just getting ready to bring on the *audi nos*. [Oh Lord, hear our prayer. Yo, lord! Are you there?]

[*Sister Bunny falls to her knees for absolution.*]

MOTHER SUPERIOR

Bless you, sister, for you have sinned, just like the rest of us. *#MeToo, Fessue*. [*She makes the sign of the cross.*] *Ergo*, honey Bunny, *absolvo te*—I absolve you—out of the kindness of my heart. Again. *Gratis*. This one's on me; this bun's for you. And it's in the bag.

As you were. Consider yourself cleansed. Go in peace, come in peace. [All's well in the ends well. Now, make like a nun and get the frock outta here!]

[*To the audience*] [No, not *you*, folks! A tisket, a tasket, we're gonna pass the basket.©] It's time for collection.[28]

SISTER BUNNY

Deo gratias! And who's sorry now?© Not me! She was blind, but now I see.©

SISTER CRYBABY

And there you have it. To my mind, it's illogical that one man would accuse another of the very same sin with which he himself is stained, sullied, and besmirched. Now, wipe that smirch off your face because both are to blame. [And turn the other cheeky because], as you've seen here for yourselves today, sin will out. Witness the case of Mother Superior and Sister Bunny. [It's the doctrine of clean hands, folks:] the sin of one is the sin of all. [All are punishèd. Uncivil farce shows civil hands unclean.] Let those without sin cast the first stones.[29]

[*Doubled version begins here.*]

Thus, I conclude that there's a major error
with slut-shaming for sins known all too well
by the accusers—sullied, holy terrors—
they're stained with shame: they're going straight to hell.
We've made our case today; so, time will tell.
The truth is in your face: it isn't funny,
like when the Abbess trashed our Sister Bunny.
How 'bout a song before we runny?
Adieu for now. Show us the money.

[*At the close of the doubled version, they all sing.*][30]

The END

Appendix: Scholarly References to Copyrighted Materials

In 2015, the estate of Marvin Gaye was awarded $7.4 million in damages against Robin Thicke and Pharrell Williams for having, shall we say, "blurred the lines" of their appropriation of the copyrighted "Got to Give It Up." The award in *Gaye v. Williams* was later reduced to $3.2 million (885 F.3d 1150), but it serves as a cautionary tale for anyone negotiating fair use in the twenty-first century.

No medieval dramatist was concerned about copyright as we understand its protections today; and no *farceur* was checking in with the local troubadour to clear permissions for "Dormez-vous, fillettes?" (below, #12, note 21). Far from it: imitation was the sincerest form of flattery in an era when, philologically speaking, an author was an *auctor* or *aucteur* borrowing freely from prior wielders of authority (*auctoritas*). Thus, while premodern parodists were the frequent targets of legal reprisals, their delicts were typically unrelated to intellectual property theft. All was fair in love, war, and what we now call plagiarism. All use was fair use. Fair enough, but what about performances in the present?

As I've explained in previous Appendixes, the farcical repertoire is chock-full of "musical clichés" (*FF*, 401–3; *HD*, 427–28). Medieval speakers regularly break into song, such that beloved lyrics can even enter a lexicon. A copyright symbol doesn't appear over your head when you kick your partner out and shout, à la Mayfield, "hit the road, Jack!" Nor must you hasten to the BMI repertory or the licensing portal at www.raycharles.com for permissions related to "Hit the Road, Jack." Language eternally renews itself. Popular culture too, of which music is an integral part. In the fifteenth and sixteenth centuries, French farce was likewise wont to speak in lyrics and melodies; and music sang right back. Since those multiple musical intertexts are imperative to any faithful translation, I've once again fashioned a comparative musical tool that preserves both the original meaning(s) and the postmedieval proprietary interests of musicians, lyricists, and performers. For purposes of scholarly understanding, I readopt these practices:

The better to capture the musical spirit of the present dozen plays, I make a large number of time-sensitive suggestions regarding rough, translational analogues for the vast array of medieval songs, rhymes, or ditties. I further acknowledge anew that, given the speed with which musical tastes evolve, my choices might already strike you as old hat. By all means, swap away. None of my musical nods to the originals constitute quotations in the traditional sense. Rather, they are there to encourage actors, directors, and readers to strike the right musical notes for themselves and for their audiences. Please consider all songs here referenced to be my own unscripted musings that it seemed prudent not to set in stone. If anything, I've elected quite deliberately *not* to "script" the music officially. As my translations age, so too will their music—but the latter will age more easily when untethered to a specific historical moment.

That said, I cannot emphasize strongly enough that any theater company wishing to include music in producing these farces must seek and obtain the rights to currently copyrighted materials. This is absolutely mandatory and legally required. Failure is not an option; and any lack of response from the copyright holder does not in and of itself denote consent. Indeed, the primary purpose of this Appendix is to facilitate the acquisition of rights. (As far as I'm concerned, the pleasure of publicizing the work of a panoply of gifted lyricists and composers is just a bonus.)

Throughout this book, I've marked each allusion to music with the copyright symbol (©) as a reminder to check whether copyright applies. In an excess of caution, I do so even when copyright manifestly *does not apply*, as for "anonymous" or "traditional" folk songs, spirituals, ballads, lullabies, nursery rhymes, or *lieder* in the public domain (in which case, I give the dates of composition, if known). Better safe than sorry because, today, *specific renditions* of anonymous songs may indeed be designated the protected intellectual property of the recording artist. Normally, the copyright symbol identifies a song title here, less frequently a refrain or other lyric (above, "ABT," § "Prose, Verse, Music"). Speaking of which, this caveat: consistent with oral performance traditions, a musical catchphrase can enter the English language so completely that we no longer recognize its origins in a possibly copyrighted song. The converse as well. "Easy come, easy go" was an idiom long before people wrote songs by that name. It's a safe bet to say that I've missed a few English song lyrics that have wended their way into popular discourse. It's an absolute certainty that I've missed a great many in Middle French that have been lost to history.

Should any theater practitioner wish to follow up dramaturgically on my thoughts about viable musical analogues, the detailed list below is designed to help with the first steps toward obtaining permission for use. Again, do note that rights may be held by lyricists, composers, performers, corporations, and others besides. It may, therefore, be necessary to seek separate permission from more than one entity. In each and every instance when a song pops up in these dozen farces, I indicate the professional registry—there may be more than one—that administers the rights to that song. The vast majority of artists are affiliated with either ASCAP or BMI and, as of this writing, a joint search of both repertories is now possible through Songview (Halperin, "Music Rights"), which also indicates percentages of ownership rights held. You will likewise find any official identification numbers assigned to a given song by ASCAP (www.ascap.com), BMI (www.bmi.com), MPL Music Publishing (www.mplcommunications.com), Music Theatre International (www.mtishows.com), SESAC (www.sesac.com), and on the rare occasion, the licensing portal at www.raycharles.com. When a song title is not listed in any repertory but an artist number is, I try to supply the latter (IPI, e.g., for ASCAP). And, inasmuch as my goal is to translate *language* as opposed to oft irrecuperable melodies, I provide the names of composers and lyricists only, if known, rather than those of artists who might have popularized the song in question. For simplicity's sake, I do not follow the usual order of "music and lyrics by," nor do I list collaborators by priority of contribution, as is often done. Instead, the artists appear in alphabetical order, except when I cite songwriting teams, for example, that it would be jarring to hear as anything other than, say, "Rodgers and Hammerstein." I also prefer to cite music creators by their more recognizable names: Buddy Holly instead of Charles Hardin Holly, Freddie Mercury instead of Farrokh Bulsara, and so forth. At no time do I appropriate any artist's trademark interpretation of any song.

Finally, it bears reemphasizing in no uncertain terms that *before contemplating production, theater practitioners are required to investigate and resolve any and all issues of copyright, fair use, or royalty arrangements related to any of the following, to which I make scholarly references in this anthology.*

"Achy-Breaky Heart." By Kenneth Gregory Watters. SESAC Work Number: 55896468.

"All My Trials." By Joan Baez. ASCAP Work ID: 310153330.

"All She Wants to Do Is Dance." ASCAP Work ID: 310240843.

"Amazing Grace." By John Newton. (1779).

"Amazing Journey." By Peter Townshend. BMI Work #33852.

"Amen." By Jerry Goldsmith. BMI Work #34271.

"America the Beautiful." Katherine Lee Bates and Samuel Ward. BMI Work #34771.

"And When I Die." By Laura Nyro. BMI Work #40714.

"Anything You Can Do." By Irving Berlin. ASCAP Work ID: 310056043.

"A Tisket, a Tasket." Traditional.

"Baby Got Back." By Anthony L. Ray. BMI Work #72106.

"Baby, It's You." By Burt Bacharach, Mack David, and Barney Williams. ASCAP Work ID: 320111553.

"Baby, What a Big Surprise." By Pete Cetera. ASCAP Work ID: 320230915.

"Bad Company." By Simon Kirke and Paul Rodgers. ASCAP Work ID: 320187240.

"Bad Moon on the Rise." By John Cameron Fogerty. BMI Work #79979.

"Barbara Ann." By Fred Fassert. BMI Work #87434.

"Battle Hymn of the Republic." By Julia Ward Howe. (19th c.)

"Bibbidi Bobbidi." By David Mack, Al Hoffman, and Jerry Livingston. ASCAP Work ID: 320044162.

"The Big Muddy." By Pete Seeger. BMI Work #114413.

"Big Rock Candy Mountain." Traditional.

"Big Spender." By Cy Coleman and Dorothy Fields. ASCAP Work ID: 320137955.

"Black Magic Woman." By Peter Alan Green. BMI Work #121091.

"Bohemian Rhapsody." By Freddie Mercury. ASCAP Work ID: 320199817.

"Both Sides Now." By Joni Mitchell. ASCAP Work ID: 360095229.

"Bottle of Wine." By Tom Paxton. ASCAP Work ID: 320130096.

"Brother, Can You Spare a Dime?" By Yip Harburg and Jay Gorney. ASCAP Work ID: 320093878.

"Burning Love." By Dennis Linde. BMI Work #160887.

"A Bushel and a Peck." By Frank Loesser. ASCAP Work ID: 320102867.

"Bust a Move." By Matt Dike, Luther Rabb, and Marvin Young. ASCAP Work ID: 320348316.

"Bye-Bye, Birdie." By Lee Adams and Charles Strouse. ASCAP Work ID: 320119564.

"California, Here I Come." By B. G. De Sylva, Al Jolson, and Joseph Meyer. ASCAP Work ID: 330004507.

"Carry That Weight." By John Lennon and Paul McCartney. BMI Work #187794.

"Celebration." By Eumire Deodato Almeida et al. ASCAP Work ID: 330279293.

"C'est moi." By Alan Jay Lerner and Frederick Loewe. Music Theatre International. https://www.mtishows.com/camelot.

"C'est si bon." By Henri Betti and André Hornez. ASCAP Work ID: 887366085.

"Les Champs Elysées." By Pierre Delanoë, Michael Wilshaw, and Michael Deighan. BMI Work #849309.

"Chevaliers de la table ronde." Traditional.

"Concrete and Clay." By Thomas Moeller and Brian Parker. BMI Work #239352.

"Crazy Love." By Russell Young. ASCAP Work ID: 330259797.

"Cry Like a Baby." By Dewey Lindon Oldham Jr. and Daniel Pennington. BMI Work #261591.

"Dang Me." By Roger Miller. BMI Work #275944.

"De-Lovely." By Cole Porter. ASCAP Work ID: 340019152.

"Doctor, My Eyes." By Jackson Browne. ASCAP Work ID: 340138550.

"Do It [till You're Satisfied]." By Billy Nichols. BMI Work #309081.

"Dominique." By Soeur Sourire, aka Jeannine Deckers. ASCAP Work ID: 340100063.

"Don't Leave Me This Way." By Kenneth Gamble, Cary Grant Gilbert, and Leon Huff. BMI Work #323300.

"Do-Wacka-Do." By Roger Miller. BMI Work #1719799.

"Dry Bones." ["Dem Bones."] By Jay Weldon Johnson and J. Rosomond Johnson. (19th c.)

"Everything's Alright." By Andrew Lloyd-Webber and Timothy Rice. ASCAP Work ID: 250061588.

"Everything's Coming Up Roses." By Stephen Sondheim and Jule Styne. ASCAP Work ID: 350034303.

"Evil Woman." By Jeffrey Lynne. BMI Work #393757.

"Fat-Bottomed Girls." By Brian Harold May. BMI Work #406587.

"Field of Opportunity." By Neil Young. ASCAP Work ID: 360219907.

"Frère Jacques." Traditional.

"Gee, Officer Krupke." By Stephen Sondheim and Leonard Bernstein. Music Theatre International. https://www.mtishows.com/west-side-story.

"Get Happy." By Harold Arlen and Ted Koehler. ASCAP Work ID: 360219907.

"Get Ready." By William [Smokey] Robinson. ASCAP Work ID: 370083240.

"Gimme That Old Time Religion." Gospel song. (19th c.)

"Girl from Ipanema." By Vinicius de Moraes, Norman Gimbel, and Antonio Carlos Jobim. BMI Work #470303.

"Girls Just Want to Have Fun." By Victor Carstarphen, Robert Hazard, Cyndi Lauper, Gene McFadden, Richard David Morel, John Cavadus Whitehead. ASCAP Work ID: 372137750.

"God Bless America." By Irving Berlin. ASCAP Work ID: 370029559.

"God Rest Ye Merry Gentlemen." Traditional.

"Goin' Down." By Suketu Khandwala, Taylor Momsen, and Benjamin Phillips. BMI Work #11639290.

"Good Lovin'." By Rudy Clark and Arthur Resnick. BMI Work #494823.

"Good Old-Fashioned Lover Boy." By Freddie Mercury. BMI Work #495994.

"Gotta Dance." By Hugh Martin. ASCAP Work ID: 370048707.

"Go Your Own Way." By Lindsey Buckingham.[1]

"Greensleeves." ["What Child Is This?"] Traditional ballad.

"The Hallelujah Chorus." From George Frideric Handel's *Messiah* (1741).

"Hand in My Pocket." By Glen Ballard and Alanis Morissette. BMI Work #2028578.

"Heaven Sent." Jingle. By Buddy Weed.[2]

"Hello Dolly." By Jerry Herman. ASCAP Work ID: 380106250.

"Hey Diddle Diddle." Nursery rhyme.

"His Love Makes Me Beautiful." By Bob Merrill and Jule Styne. ASCAP Work ID: 380108632.

"Hit Me with Your Best Shot." By Edward Sydney Schwartz. ASCAP Work ID: 380218380.

"Hit the Road, Jack." By Percy Mayfield. BMI Work #571691.

"Hodie Christus Natus Est." From *Ceremony of Carols*. By Benjamin Britten (1942).

"Hokey Pokey." Traditional.

"Hosanna." By Andrew Lloyd-Webber and Timothy Rice. ASCAP Work ID: 381488533.

"Hot Blooded." By Louis A. (Andrew) Grammatico and Michael Leslie Jones. ASCAP Work ID: 380199428.

"How Long?" By J. D. Souther. ASCAP Work ID: 380147929.

"I Cain't Say No." By Richard Rodgers and Oscar Hammerstein II. ASCAP Work ID: 390003762.

"I Can't Get No Satisfaction." By Mick Jagger and Keith Richards. BMI Work #608621.

"If I Only Had a Brain." By Harold Arlen (ASCAP IPI #1307353) and E. Y. Harburg (ASCAP IPI #13397497).[3]

"I Got Plenty o' Nuttin'." By George Gershwin, Ira Gershwin, and DuBose Heyward. ASCAP Work ID: 390020583.

"Il est de nôtres." Traditional.

"I'll Be There for You." By David Crane, Marta Kauffman, Michael Jay Skloff, Philip Solem, Danny Wilde, and Allee Willis. BMI Work #2033645.

"I'll Get You." By John Lennon and Paul McCartney.[4]

"I'll Take You There." By Alvertis Isbell. BMI Work #643764.

"I'm a Woman." By Jerry Leiber and Mike Stoller. BMI Work #4175708.

"I'm Called Little Buttercup." By William Schwenk Gilbert, Nicholas Cameron Patrick, and Sir Arthur Seymour Sullivan. From *H.M.S. Pinafore* (1878). BMI Work #4257023.

"It's in His Kiss." By Rudy Clark. BMI Work #744118.

"It's Raining Men." By Paul Jabara and Paul Shaffer. BMI Work #1226921.

"I Whistle a Happy Tune." By Richard Rodgers and Oscar Hammerstein II. ASCAP Work ID: 390083480.

"Jacob's Ladder." Spiritual.

"Jailhouse Rock." By Jerry Leiber and Mike Stoller. BMI Work #757227.

"Johnny B Goode." By Chuck Berry. BMI Work #773553.

"Joshua Fit the Battle of Jericho." Spiritual.

"Jubilation T. Cornepone." By Gene de Paul and Johnny Mercer. ASCAP Work ID: 400022800.

"Just One Look." By Gregory Carroll and Doris Payne. BMI Work #788840.

"Knockin' on Heaven's Door." By Bob Dylan. SESAC Work Number: 514919.

"Let 'Em In." By Paul and Linda McCartney. ASCAP Work ID: 420198209.

"Let's Get It On." By Marvin Gaye and Edward Townsend. BMI Work #857218.

"Let's Hear It for the Boy." By Dean Pitchford and Thomas Snow. BMI Work #858383.

"Like a Virgin." By Thomas Kelly and William Steinberg. ASCAP Work ID: 420307199.

"Little Less Talk and a Lot More Action." By Keith W. Hinton and Jimmy Alan Stewart. BMI Work #880887.

"Little Tin Box." By Jerry Bock and Sheldon Harnick. BMI Work #883643.

"Longfellow Serenade." By Neil Diamond. SESAC Work Number 514272.

"The Lord Bless You and Keep You." Traditional hymn.

"Losing My Religion." By Robert Baskaran, William Berry, Peter Buck, Michael Mills, John Michael Stipe, and Brian Wakefield. BMI Work #20325189.

"Love Is a Battlefield." By Mike Chapman, Randall Hargove, and Holly Knight. ASCAP Work ID: 882360621.

"Love, Reign o'er Me." By Pete Townshend. BMI Work #924510.

"Lovesick Blues." By Cliff Friend and Irving Mills. ASCAP Work ID: 420097327.

"Magic to Do." By Stephen Lawrence Schwartz. ASCAP Work ID: 886449522.

"Maria." By Richard Rodgers and Oscar Hammerstein II. ASCAP Work ID: 430030594.

"La Marseillaise." By Claude Joseph Rouget de Lisle. (18th c.)

"The Mess-Around." By Ahmet Ertegun [Nugetre]. BMI Work #981371.

"Michael Finnegan." Traditional.

"More, More, More." By Gregg Diamond. ASCAP Work ID: 430240205.

"My Boyfriend's Back." By Bob Feldman, Gerald Goldstein, and Richard Gottehrer. BMI Work #1028431.

"My Way." By Paul Anka, Claude François, Jacques Rivaud, and Gilles Thibaut. BMI Work #1044656.

"Nothing Compares 2 U." By Prince. ASCAP Work ID: 440162807.

"Now I Lay Me Down to Sleep." ["All Night, All Day, Angels Watching Over Me."] By Otis Leon McCoy. (19th c.)

"O Come, All Ye Faithful." [*Adeste fidelis*]. Traditional (ca. 1600s or 1700s).

"Oh Happy Day." By Philip Doddridge. (18th c.)[5]

"Oh, Mary, Don't You Weep." Spiritual.

"Old Dope Peddler." By Tom Lehrer. ASCAP Work ID: 450017026.

"Once in a Lifetime." ["Letting the Days Go By."] By David Byrne, Brian Eno, Christopher Frantz, Jerry Harrison, and Martina Weymouth. BMI Work #1117241.

"One, Two, Three." Len Barry [Leonard Borisoff], Lamont Dozier, Brian Holland, Eddie Holland, John Medara, and David White. BMI Work #1126577.

"On the Wings of a Nightingale." By Paul McCartney. ASCAP Work ID: 450177005.

"Over the Rainbow." By Harold Arlen and E. Y. Harburg. ASCAP Work ID: 450062263.

"Pa-, Pa-, Pa-, Papageno." From *The Magic Flute*. By Wolfgang Amadeus Mozart (1791).

"Papa Don't Preach." By Brian Elliot. ASCAP Work ID: 460257114.

"Papa's Got a Brand New Bag." By James Brown. BMI Work #1149944.

"Petticoat Junction." By Paul Henning and Curtis Massey. BMI Work #1169258.

"Pickin' Up the Pieces." By Richie Furay. BMI IPI #57552074.[6]

"Plop, Plop, Fizz, Fizz." [Alka-Seltzer jingle.] By Thomas Dawes. ASCAP Artist IPI Number: 88568319.[7]

"Poor Jerusalem." By Andrew Lloyd-Webber and Timothy Rice. ASCAP Work ID: 460132212.

"Poor, Poor Pitiful Me." By Warren Zevon. BMI Work #1189347.

"Put on a Happy Face." By Lee Adams and Charles Strouse. ASCAP Work ID: 890113209.

"Rag Doll." By Bob Crewe and Bob Gaudio. BMI Work #1223896.

"Rag Doll." By Holly Knight, Joe Perry, Steven Tallarico, and James Vallance. ASCAP Work ID: 480200315.

"Respect." By Otis Redding. BMI Work #1244564.

"The Rhythm Is Gonna Get You." By Gloria Estefan and Enrique Garcia. BMI Work #1248618.

"Ride a Cock Horse to Banbury Cross." Traditional.

"Rock Around the Clock." By Max Freedman and James Myers. ASCAP Work ID: 480039358.

"Row, Row, Row Your Boat." Traditional.

"Run for the Roses." By Dan Fogelberg. ASCAP Work ID: 480149122.

"Seven Deadly Virtues." By Alan Jay Lerner and Frederick Loewe. Music Theatre International. https://www.mtishows.com/camelot.

"76 Trombones!" By Meredith Willson. ASCAP Work ID: 490040443.

"Shake a Tail Feather." By Otha Hayes, Verlie Rice, and Zephire Williams. BMI Work #1318017.

"Shambala." By Daniel Moore. BMI Work #1319243.

"Shiny Happy People." By Bill Berry, Peter Buck, Mike Mills, and Michael Stipe. SESAC Work Number: 689794367.

"Show Me the Way to Go Home." By James Campbell and Reginald Connelly [aka Irving King]. (1925).

"Signed, Sealed, Delivered, I'm Yours." By Lee Garrett, Lula Mae Hardaway, Stevie Wonder, and Syreeta Wright. ASCAP Work ID: 490293528.

"The Simple Joys of Maidenhood." By Alan Jay Lerner and Frederick Loewe. Music Theatre International. https://www.mtishows.com/camelot.

"Since You've Gone, [My Heart Is Broken Another Time]." By Gary Busey. ASCAP Work ID: 490359716.

"Sisters Are Doin' It for Themselves." By Ann Lennox and David Allan Stewart. ASCAP Work ID: 790710124.

"Sit Down, You're Rocking the Boat." By Frank Loesser. ASCAP Work ID: 490071624.

"Skip to My Lou." Traditional.

"So Long, Farewell." By Richard Rodgers and Oscar Hammerstein II. ASCAP Work ID: 490089142.

"Someone to Lay Down Beside Me." By Karla Bonoff. BMI Work #1376250.

"Spread a Little Sunshine." By Stephen Schwartz and Roger Hirson. Music Theatre International. https://www.mtishows.com/pippin.

"Spring Carol." From *Ceremony of Carols*. By Benjamin Britten (1942).

"Stairway to Heaven." By Robert Plant and Jimmy Page. ASCAP Work ID: 490294198.

"Stop in the Name of Love." By Lamont Dozier, Brian Holland, and Eddie Holland. BMI Work #1413855.

"Suspended from Class." By Tracyanne Campbell. ASCAP Work ID: 493817573.

"Sweet Gypsy Rose." By Irwin Levine and Russell Brown. BMI Work #1294630.

"Sweet Painted Lady." By Elton John and Bernie Taupin. BMI Work #1440132.

"Sympathy for the Devil." By Mick Jagger and Keith Richards. BMI Work #144456.

"Take Me to the Pilot." By Elton John and Bernie Taupin. BMI Work #1450840.

"That Old Black Magic." By Harold Arlen and Johnny Mercer. ASCAP Work ID: 500035232.
"That Smell." By Allen Collins and Ronnie Van Zant. BMI Work #1483429.
"That's the Way I Like It." By Harry Wayne Casey and Rick Finch. BMI Work #1481515.
"These Boots Are Made for Walkin'." By Lee Hazlewood. ASCAP Work ID: 500170925.
"They're Coming to Take Me Away, Ha-Ha." By Jerry Samuels. ASCAP Work ID: 500221503.
"This Old Man." Traditional.
"Three Is Company Too." By Donald Nicholl and Joe Raposo. ASCAP Work ID: 500265976.
"The Times They Are A-Changin'." By Bob Dylan. SESAC Work Number: 514866.
"Tits and Ass." By Marvin Hamlisch and Edward Kleban. ASCAP Work ID: 892861121.
"Treat Her Right." By Roy Head and Gene Kurtz. BMI Work #1542510.
"Trouble." By Lenka Kripac and Thomas Salter. ASCAP Work ID: 505224635.
"Twist." By Hank Ballard. BMI Work #1561070.
"Two Tickets to Paradise." By Eddie Money. BMI Work #1564326.
"Virgin." ["Not a Virgin Anymore."] By Annie Poe, Kenneth Burgomaster, and Matthew Wilder. BMI Work #5369139.
"Vogue." By Madonna [Ciccone] and Shep Pettibone. ASCAP Work ID: 520105119.
"Waited So Long." ["Daddy, I'm No Virgin."] By Carly Simon. ASCAP Work ID: 530179450.
"War Is a Science." By Stephen Schwartz and Roger Hirson. Music Theatre International. https://www.mtishows.com/pippin.
"We Hasten with Eager Footsteps." (*Wir eilen mit Schwachen.*) By J. S. Bach.
"We May Never Love Like This Again." By Joel Hirschhorn and Al Kasha. BMI Work #1617187.
"We May Never Pass This Way Again." By Darrell Crofts and Jimmy Seals. BMI Work #1617190.
"What a Girl Wants." By Shelly Peiken and Guy Roche. BMI Work #4993749.
"What'd I Say." By Ray Charles. BMI Work #1631628; also licensed through https://raycharles.com/music/singles-discography/.

"What's the Buzz?" By Andrew Lloyd-Webber and Timothy Rice. ASCAP Work ID: 530169050.

"When Johnny Comes Marching Home." By Patrick Gilmore [aka Louis Lambert]. (19th c.)

"When the Saints Come Marching In." Traditional.

"Who's Sorry Now?" By Burt Kalmar and Harry Ruby. ASCAP Work ID: 530081448.

"Wrigley's Spearmint Gum [jingle]." By Steve Karmen. ASCAP Work ID: 57001664.

"Ya Got Trouble." By Meredith Willson. ASCAP Work ID: 550000489.

"You Can Leave Your Hat On." By Randy Newman. ASCAP ID: 550069602.

"You Give Love a Bad Name." By Jon Bongiovi, Desmond Child, and Richard Sambora. ASCAP ID: 550147303.

"You Got Me Wrapped [Around Your Little Finger]." By Beth Rowley and Benjamin Castle. BMI Work #9833096.

"You Keep Me Hangin' On." By Lamont Dozier, Brian Holland, and Eddie Holland. BMI Work #1720690.

Notes

Introduction

1. For an excellent initiation to this vast historical and theological subject, see Ozment, *Age of Reform* and *Protestants*; and *Christian Spirituality*, ed. Raitt.

2. For more on the Basoche, see Harvey's signature *TB*; Bouhaïk-Gironès, *Les Clercs de la Basoche*; *ROMD*, chap. 3; *FF*, 4–13; and *PF*, chap. 1.

3. The procurator general of Paris, a rough equivalent of an attorney general, cited by Sainte-Beuve in *Tableau historique*, 193–95; and in *DBD*, 107–8, 221–22.

4. Cited by Lebègue, *Mystère des actes des apôtres*, 30–31.

5. François Vinchant, *Annales de la province et comté du Hainaut*, 5: 267, cited in *DBD*, 223.

6. Rousse devotes vol. 5 of *TFFMA* to these societies; also discussed at length by Reid in "Carnival in Rouen" and "Triumph of the Abbey," both analyzed by Guynn in *PF*, e.g., 30–31.

7. As this book was going to press, *Representations* published a dazzling special issue in 2021, titled "Practices of Devotion" edited by Eleanor Craig, Amy Hollywood, and Chris Trujillo (https://online.ucpress.edu/representations/issue/153/1; accessed 15 March 2021).

8. On this rich topic—*confession sans repentance* in the *Roman de la Rose* (v. 6924)—see, e.g., Tentler, *Sin and Confession*, 3–30; and, more generally, *PF*, 111–125.

9. See Pouchelle on "secret places" as both the female reproductive organs and the latrine (*Body and Surgery in the Middle Ages*, 134), the latter the site of the messy denouement of *The Shithouse* (*HD*, #2).

10. The *Constitutions* of 1322, cited in Baverstock, *Priest as Confessor*, 63. You can see a lovely image of an outdoor confession here: https://www.medievalists.net/wp-content/uploads/2014/11/Medieval-priest-giving-confession.jpg (accessed 13 April 2021).

11. For my revision of Goffman's "bracketing" in *Frame Analysis*, see *MBA*, 8–11. I coined the term "pseudoperformativity" in "History Trouble," by which I mean the *appearance* or *fantasy* of a performative that is not one.

12. See Hardison's seminal revisitation of E. K. Chambers and Karl Young in *CRCD*, Essay 1; *ROMD*, 54–68; and Dox, *Idea of the Theater*, 74–85.

13. I draw here on Cusa's "coincidence of opposites": a thing "either is or it is not. It is and it is not. It neither is nor is not." See, e.g., Hopkins, *Concise Introduction*, 8–9; and Colie, *Paradoxia Epidemica*.

14. *Rose*, vv. 5537–38; quoted in Horgan's translation, p. 85. From a massive bibliography, see, e.g., Kelly, *Internal Difference and Meanings*, 43–53; and Fleming, "Words and Things," chap. 3 of *Reason and the Lover*.

15. *Rose*, vv. 6981–82; and Horgan, p. 106. N.B.: Heldris de Cournälle's thirteenth-century *Roman de Silence*, the summa of language, gender, cross-dressing, and performance, features two characters named Eufémie and Eufème. Coincidence? I think not.

16. Montaiglon elides *coilles* or *vit* in #2, *Blue Confessions*, *ATF*, 1: 375; and in #11, *Slick Brother Willy*, *ATF*, 1: 321.

17. See also Hequembourg, "*Literally*: How to Speak like an Absolute Knave." I've also blogged about this in "To Laugh or Not to Laugh," https://pennpress.typepad.com/pennpresslog/2019/04/to-laugh-or-not-to-laugh.html (accessed 21 July 2019).

18. *Théâtre et propagande*, ed. Beck, vv. 220–21. Estelle Doudet is one of the few to have studied the politics of this fascinating play in "Les Clefs de l'Église."

19. *Chronicle of Adam Usk, 1377–1421*, ed. Given-Wilson, 120–21; below, #12, § "Plot."

20. For Sébillet, who also treats the *blason*, see *APF*, 161, 169–74; *AG*, 9–12; for the selected legislation, see *MES*, 329–38.

21. On Baudrillard, "Simulacra," 178; and Eco, "Interpreting Drama," 105, see *MBA*, e.g., 11, 43–46, 128–29.

22. See *HDTW*, 14–24; Gould, "The Unhappy Performative," esp. 28–31; and my discussion of the relevance of this terminology for medieval theater studies in *MBA*, 34–36, 109–20.

23. MacKinnon, *Feminism Unmodified* (201, 218, 144, 128), cited and discussed by Steiner, *Scandal of Pleasure*, 66, 69, 211.

24. See Penley on Ed Cray's *Erotic Muse* (40) in "Crackers and Whackers," 104.

About This Translation

1. The most complete records of medieval performance in France are *RTC* and Rousse's amplification thereof in *TFFMA*, vol. 4 (his magisterial unpublished, five-volume *thèse d'état*).

2. For more details, see *RF*, 1: 15–19; Faivre, *Répertoire*, 9–28; *RFlorence*, 7–16; and Droz, *RTLS*, xi–xiv.

3. On 23 March 2016, I accessed the *RLV* here: http://gallica.bnf.fr/ark:/12148/btv1b90631556/f1.image.r=24341%20Valli%C3%A8re.

4. Martin's editions are available only online at https://sottiesetfarces.wordpress.com/about/ (accessed 19 March 2019). The Table of Contents appears on the "Préface" page.

5. Cited in translation by Virginia Scott in her exceptional *Women on the Stage*, 59–72; see also Susannah Crowder's resurrection of the lives of four women in the theater of Metz in *Performing Women*.

6. See it here: https://www.youtube.com/watch?v=BwO4B_pxI7s (accessed 21 January 2017).

7. The present farces do not stage the Benedictine Monks (Black Monks), the Cistercians (White Monks), or the Carthusians (silent monks); so, I won't take them up here. Too bad about the Benedictines: I was dying to work in the Trappist monks and their famous beer. For an initiation into medieval monasticism, I highly recommend volumes 16 and 17 of *Christian Spirituality*, i.e., *Origins to the Twelfth Century*, ed. McGinn and *High Middle Ages to Reformation*, ed. Raitt; the engaging introductions by Geltner to *Making of Medieval Antifraternalism* (1–9) and Rayborn to *Against the Friars* (1–31); and the excellent entry on "Medieval Monasticism" in the *Catholic Encyclopedia*: http://www.newadvent.org/cathen/10472a.htm (accessed 17 February 2017).

8. See the still useful *New Schaff-Herzog*, 2: 418; or 1: 213 of the revised ed.

9. For further elaboration, see *FF*, 49–50, 374–75; *HD*, 29–30.

10. Between 1360 and 1641, the coins minted as 1 *livre tournois* were called *francs* and, per the Littré, were worth 20 *sous*; these were eventually replaced by the *écu* in 1577, the primary gold coin in circulation in France.

Actors' Prologue

1. "Losing My Religion." By Robert Baskaran, William Berry, Peter Buck, Michael Mills, John Michael Stipe, and Brian Wakefield. BMI Work #20325189.

Play 1. *The Con-Man's Confession*

1. For more on the *société joyeuse des conards*, see Reid, "Carnival in Rouen" and "Triumph of the Abbey."

2. Matilda's *vous* could be for the audience or for an initially unseen Connor. Protection from *vilenie* (v. 4) also connoted *venereal* evil; plus, the purgative language is that of catharsis: *purger il se convient / Par tres vraye confession* (vv. 8–9).

3. *Quaresme* (v. 25) looks as much like "Lent" (*caresme*) as it does a variant of the number four.

4. With *vous n'avés plus sens qu'une beste* (v. 48), I hear an echo of Psalm 73:22: "So foolish was I, and ignorant: I was as a beast before thee."

5. Alternatively, one could break the scene here and have Connor deliver the rest as a soliloquy.

6. In the original (fols. 3–4), this whole long speech (vv. 74–100) is attributed unambiguously to Roger; but v. 80 is missing at the crucial juncture: *Et s'on ne veult a moy entendre / . . . / Ainsi je me suis bien passé / Quatre ans sans estre confessé* (vv. 79–82). This is farce, I know, but what are the odds that *both* men would have gone *four years* without confession? If you buy the coincidence, you could add this line to Roger's previous speech: "And that's how I've managed to go four years without confession." Or Connor could interrupt with: "Right, but I haven't been for four years and I'd kinda like to keep it that way."

7. Another possible meta-allusion to the *Conards* with *Je ne fais pas* conart *ni lourt* (v. 85; my emphasis). Interestingly enough, Roger speaks of "mon *curé*" (v. 86), possibly implying that he confesses at a different church nearby. Note also the spelling of *absolution*, which looks suspiciously like *assault*: *Je dy ouy, lors il m'assault* (v. 91).

8. Given the Easter setting and the mention of a *larre* (v. 99), the term typically employed for the three thieves crucified with Jesus, I've added the Barabbas reference.

9. To account for a marked difference of language and tone, I've doubled Connor's lyrical apostrophe: *Mon povre cueur forment souspire / Quant je ne puis trouver sejour / Pour alleger ma grief douleur / Que jour et nuyt si ne me fine, / Je suis bien mis a discipline* (104–8).

10. *Vueillés abreger* (v. 127): *abreger* often appears in the theological distillations of the quodlibet; see, e.g., my "Theater of Scholastic Erudition," 345–56. And, yes, there are three terms of endearment within the space of five verses: *mon amy doulx*, *beau filz*, and *mon amy* (vv. 124–27).

11. *Sire, je suis [. . .] bien souvent, / Que j'ay ouvré huyt jours ou tant / Sur deux clochers merveilleurs hauts / Et n'ay eu pour jour que deux saulx* (vv. 139–42). *Deux saulx* almost certainly means money—two *sous*—but it also looks like a "jump" or even a "fall." Plus, when Connor says *s'a esté par ma follie* (v. 145), it sounds vaguely like how the French would begin confession: *C'est ma faute, c'est ma très grande faute.*

12. The official is a *prevost* (v. 158), a cross between a judge, a magistrate, an attorney general, and a chief of police (key players in my next volume). Martin thinks that the delict in question is working on a Sunday or a religious holiday (*SFQS*, note 86).

13. In this exchange, the joke is about sleeves and sackcloths: *Dont il te fault aller en lange* followed by Connor's *Tousjours je suis jusqu'a la manche* (vv. 199–200). A *lange* is normally some kind of penitential shirt made of rough wool.

14. These charming allusions to a near personified "shirt"—a forerunner to Bridget Jones's "skirt?"—are also reminiscent of *Jenin, Filz de Rien* (*RBM*, #20), scheduled for my next volume as *Who's Your Daddy?*

15. Among Connor's more theologically consonant statements: *Or suis je de tous mes pechez, / De quoy j'estoye moult chargez / Asoubz et ay remission / Par ce prestrë et vray pardon* (vv. 247–50). Meanwhile, a *joyeuse chançon / Pour l'amour de Marion* (vv. 253–54) sounds as Marianic as it does pastoral, as in Adam de la Halle's popular *Robin et Marion* (in *FCMF*, 77–104).

16. The specific denomination is a *poujoyse* (*RTLF*, 62n); see above, "ABT," § "Money, Money, Money."

17. The Middle French *envoi* reads: *Seigneurs, ne prenez en diffame / Nostre petit esbatement. / Nous prirons Dieu du firmament / Qu'il vueille vous et nous garder / Et mieulx que Rifflart confesser* (vv. 274–78). Or, if you don't mind switching to pentameter, you could try: "God bless us! God forgive us our transgressions! / He'll do without the con jobs at confession."

Play 2. *Blue Confessions*

1. For Liebman's comedy, see https://www.youtube.com/watch?v=60I_GK7E3FQ or https://www.youtube.com/watch?v=8hbH9j8Sz1Q (both accessed 28 February 2017).

2. On the musicality of processionals, see Collins, *Production of Medieval Church Music-Drama*, 143–49; Ogden's comprehensive *Staging of Drama in the Medieval Church*, 39–121; and, for farce's own sacrilegious spin on it, *HD*, 215–25.

3. See *MTOC*, 170–85; Goebel, *Felony and Misdemeanor*, 170–71; and Ashley on the obligation to participate in pardon parades, "Social Functions," 43–47.

4. This is Penley's reading of male characters in porn ("Crackers and Whackers," 104). On the theory and practice of sodomy, see Jordan, *Invention of Sodomy*; Burgwinkle, *Sodomy, Masculinity, and Law*; and Goldberg's groundbreaking *Sodometries*.

5. On "Estula," see Bloch, *Scandal of the Fabliaux*, 35–36; and #3, *Highway Robbery* (§ "Plot").

6. For music, and with thanks to S. C. Kaplan, "Goin' Down"© by The Pretty Reckless covers it, as would Britten's "Hodie,"© Lenka's "Trouble,"© etc.

7. For *empesché* (1: 373; *RF*, 6: 392, v. 5), with heretical connotations in *Con-Man's Confession* (*RTLF*, v. 166; #1, § "Characters and Character Development"), also meant "troubled," "tormented," "hot and bothered," "horny," or, for Martin, that the Priest didn't know what to do with his erection (*SFQS*, note 5).

8. In *RBM*-a, this is the first mention of Margot's husband (later than in *ATF*, 1: 373): *Ha! sire, de ce suis honnye, / Car le curé de nostre ville / Angrossie m'a d'une fille, / Que j'ay donnée à mon mary* (*RF*, 6: 396, vv. 25–28). Is Margot revealing her pregnancy to the bastard-child's baby-daddy? Is she lactating under an ample cape? Is she hiding yet another baby bump?

9. It's *Romme* in the *ATF*, the papal city of Rome (1: 373); but in *RBM*-a, it's *Rosne*, i.e., the Rhône (*RF*, 6: 398, v. 41), associated with the contested papal site and cardinals' debauchery at Avignon (*RF*, 6: 399n; *SFQS*, note 11).

10. In *RBM*-a, the legalistic agency is more "absolute": *Serez absolute pour certain* (*RF*, 6: 400, v. 53). And could *a plain* (*ATF*, 1: 374) be a pun on pregnancy? She's all filled up?

11. This is that moment about "lodging" vs. "having lodged" (*RF*, 6: 404, vv. 75–79; above, § "Language"). As Margot's account becomes increasingly graphic, this could be the moment to hint at fiddling about.

12. *Lequel tenoit entre ses doys, / A plain poing, une gente chose* (*ATF*, 1: 375). Compare this to when Slick Brother Willy takes his genitals in hand (see #11, note 22).

13. At *ATF*, 1: 375, he might deliver this line à la Dana Carvey's Church Lady from *SNL*. Here is where the original *couille* (*RBM*, iii) was suppressed (*ATF*, 1: 375).

14. With its *capuchon* (*ATF*, 1: 376)—a hood, cape, or cloak, usually for women—this sounds like a not-so-veiled pun on the Capuchin monks and their mini-Monks: members of the Order of Friars Minor Capuchin. Founded in 1529, this austere order drew inspiration from the teachings and missionary work of Francis of Assisi.

15. If the latticed opening functions here as a glory hole, is a sausage passed through?

16. Here is *fatrouillé* (*ATF*, 1: 377; above, § "Language").

17. This is the possible lapsus discussed above (§ "Language"), where the Priest may be implying a present "warming up" (*ATF*, 1: 377). A good moment to drop that Bible.

18. This graphic moment from *RBM*-a is much shorter than the corresponding description in *ATF* (1: 377) and almost too pornographic to conjure visually: *Encore vous recite / En ce vert boys d'ung hermite, / Qui tenoit en son poing ung membre / Très dur; l'a boute à mon ventre / Plus q'ung petit à faire saulce. / Il parut bien que je fus faulse / Quant son membre tyra l'hermite: / Il estoit plus mol q'une mitte. / Je m'en confesse et repens* (*RF*, 6: 406–8, vv. 80–88).

19. *As* penance or *instead of* penance? Two different readings from the two versions: "*pour* pénitence" (*ATF*, 1: 378) vs. "*en lieu* de penitance" (*RF*, 6: 414; v. 100). Meanwhile, there's something deeply obscene about the Priest's brothers of the belt and *seigner* (be it bleeding, signing, or belting): *Qu'à tous les freres de nostre ordre / Et à tous ceulx qui seignent la corde* (*RF*, 6: 414; vv. 102–04); see #6, *Brother Fillerup*, § "Plot."

20. Compare this passage from *RBM*-a (*RF*, 6: 416–18, vv. 112–17) to the final scene of *Blind Man's Buff*, when servant Thomasina—or the actress playing her—is offered up to the audience as a whore for sale (*FF*, 191–93).

21. This was as close as I could get to Martin's ingenious recovery of the double entendre—in oral homonymy only—of *in secula secolorum* (1: 379 [*sic*]). While it means "forever and ever," the Latin would have been pronounced "*ces culs-là, ces culs l'auront*," yielding something like: "[The assholes have it!] In those assholes [out] there! Those assholes will *win*!" or "Those assholes will get it *in the end*!" (*SFQS*, note 45).

22. Possible closing music: "Let's Hear It for the Boy";© "Papa Don't Preach";© or "Amen"© from *Lilies of the Field*.

Play 3. *Highway Robbery*

1. See *RFlorence*, 178n. At one point, the Highwayman speaks a phrase that stumped Cohen: *Sire Mors, mon amy* (vv. 179)—or *Morise* (*SFQS*, note 74)—but I suspect wordplay that I've teased out below (note 21). *Mors* sounds an awful lot like a cross between "Sir Death" and "Bite me, good sir!, goddammit!" (*mor bieu*).

2. Saint Julian, recognizable to any reader of the *Golden Legend*, the *Decameron*, or Gustave Flaubert's *Trois Contes*, was the patron saint of travelers along with such farce-leaning types as carnival workers, clowns, jugglers, and fiddlers. See, e.g., http://sourcebooks.fordham.edu/halsall/basis/julian.asp (accessed 10 June 2018); and the lovely image of Julian and his oar in *SFQS*.

3. Here is the Middle French of the *Brigant*'s musical opening (vv. 1–12):

> *Je suis desconfit de quinquaille,*
> *Tout mon argent est despendu.*
> *A malle hart soit-il pendu*

Qui soustient ne denier ne maille!
Or n'est-il rien qui ne me faille
Et grant planté d'escuz vieulx.
Ma robe a le ventre creux
Depuis que je n'ay eu nul gaige.
Tout me fauldra en mon mesnaige,
Du pain, du lart et du fourmaige.
Je ne le tiendray pas à saige
Qui passera ains que je couche.

4. When the Priest says *je ne crains rien* (v. 25), I hear a spin on Psalm 23:4, which, like most of his "theology," is garbled.

5. In the *RC*, *A mort! A mort!* (v. 37) is attributed to the *Brigant*; but it's the usual cry of the *victim*, not the perp. Koopmans suggests addressing the anomaly via staging (*RFlorence*, 174n); but I suspect that the line has simply been misattributed. I've split the difference.

6. *Je te mettray la dague au corps, / Par la chair Dieu, se tu dis mot* (vv. 51–52): with this sacrilegious, sexual, noneuphemistic evocation of the wounding of Christ's flesh, the Highwayman switches to the familiar *tu*.

7. While Koopmans stresses that *ma tasse* is a synonym for "purse" or "pocket" (vv. 55–56; *RFlorence*, 174n), the image of the collection plate or beggar's *cup* works well.

8. At vv. 80–83, this is the mangled *Sursum corda*, the antiphonal exhortation that congregants "lift up their hearts" at Mass. It includes "The Lord be with you.—And also with you" (*SFQS*, note 29; above, § "Language"). It seems to have crossed here with the *Benedicite Dominum* of Lauds, "Praise the Lord and magnify Him forever."

9. *Je me confesse à Dieu* (v. 85): we have seen this pun before on *à Dieu* ("to God") and *adieu* ("bye-bye") in *Confession Lessons* (*FF*, 133).

10. *Dictes voz besongnettes* (v. 91) sounds like an obligation to pray the rosary but the expression also refers to sex (*SFQS*, note 33).

11. And here come the *espinettes*: *Quant je vois par my les santiers, / Une ronce ou une espinette / Me happe par my ma jambette, / Incontinent je maulgroye Dieu, / Et la coupe par le mellieu, / Voire tout bas, sans mot sonner* (vv. 101–6).

12. *Si fois-je quant n'y puis actaindre* (v. 109): for Martin (*SFQS*, note 41) and Koopmans (*RFlorence*, 176n), this is when the thief gets the purse. I think he's still struggling to lay hands on it.

13. *Avez-vous point veu en la bource / A ces gallans et joué de force?* (vv. 111–12): this is a double entendre on those purse-snatching scissors (*RFlorence*, 176n; *SFQS*, note 43) to "get in by force" or "cut it off." Ouch either way.

14. Even for farce, the coincidence is far-fetched: earlier, the Highwayman mentioned that exact figure (v. 67) before even getting in (vv. 132–33); see also *RFlorence*, 176n.

15. A confession that is *parfaicte* (v. 135) is both "perfect" and legally "complete."

16. Recall that a *chappon* or capon—as in *coq au vin*—is a castrated cock; compare with *Chicken Pie and the Chocolate Cake.*

17. The incomprehensible original reads: *Dea, julfhange!* (v. 147), clearly, an error (*RC*, 81n; *RFlorence*, 177n). I might be way off, but it could be something auditory like *je le fange*: something like getting it all hellaciously "muddy," which fits the situation.

18. There is a triple entendre for *vous avez grant somme* (v. 153), which denotes a "heavy burden," a "large sum," and even "to be sleepy." I've read the line slightly differently from Koopmans, who suggests that the thief is "tired," so he sleeps late on Sundays instead of going to Mass (*RFlorence*, 177n).

19. Here is that fearsome double-edged knife of the *trippière* (above, § "Characters and Character Development"). It sounds almost like a song: *Je mengay l'autre jour des trippes / A une tripière qui passoit / Et luy abbatis son bacquet, / Tant que la gresse cheut à terre / Et laissé là mon couteau* (vv. 158–62; see also *SFQS*, note 62).

20. This is the alleged moment of absolution with the farcical, kitchen-Latin spin on the *Gloria Patri: E[r]go asuote / De la crouste d'ung pasté / Sicut erat sempiternum / Spiritus sancti amen* (vv. 176–79; above, § "Language"). The Latin *should* be: *Gloria patri et Filio et Spiritu Sancto: Sicut erat in principio et nunc et semper; et in saecula saeculorum, amen*, i.e.: "Glory to the Father, and to the Son, and to the Holy Spirit. As it was in the beginning, and now, and ever shall be, world without end. Amen." See also *SFQS*, notes 71 and 72.

21. Here is "Maurice": *Sire Mors, mon amy* (vv. 179; above, note 1).

22. *Vertu bieu, je eschape bien aucy, / Que je n'é pas laissé* l'endosse. */ Mor bieu, je le reviens par cy, / Je m'en vois à mon avanture / Confesser mes parroisiens / Prenés en gré l'esbatement, / Sire Dieu le vous pardonne. / Adieu vous dy pour maintenant* (vv. 181–88; my emphasis). *Se faire endosser* is slang for sodomy (*SFQS*, note 76).

23. Maybe consider something like "Carry That Weight."©

Play 4. *Confessions of a Medieval Drama Queen*

1. For musicological guidance on the complexities of rondeaux and motets, see Upton, "Unfolding the Rondeau"; Leach, "Genre(s) of Medieval Motets"; Boogaart, "A Prism of Its Time"; and Hartt, *Critical Companion*, "Introd."

2. There is, e.g., in the *RLV*, a *Morallité de Science et Anerie* (#39); see *TFR*, 332–39; and a whole anthology of them in *Martin en sa gloire*, ed. Bideaux. For more on the Conards, see *PF*, 30–31.

3. See D. W. Robertson's foundational, Augustine-inspired discussion of *sapientia* and *scientia* in *Preface to Chaucer*, 22–51. Johnny Slack-Jaw (#9) returns from Heaven with similar *science*.

4. Recall that Naples (v. 499) was ground zero for both the plague and syphilis. The Italians called the former "the French disease"; the French called the latter the Neapolitan one (*le mal de Naples*) (*RFlorence*, 658n).

5. You can see an edition of Ronsard's signature carpe diem sonnet here: https://www.bacdefrancais.net/quand-vous-serez-bien-vieille-ronsard.php (accessed 3 August 2019).

6. On all these locales, see *RC*, xxiv–xv; and *RFlorence*, 654n, 661. On *Sainct Marry* (v. 345) and the *Sainte Hostie*, a French analogue of the Croxton *Play of the Sacrament*, see *DBD*, 118–30; and my "Theater Makes History," 1010.

7. While "I'll Get You" has no BMI Work #, the vast majority of Beatles songs appear in that registry.

8. "If I Only Had a Brain" is not listed in the ASCAP repertory, but other such titles from the *Wizard of Oz* are.

9. You might be more familiar with the copyrighted gospel arrangement by Edwin Hawkins, ASCAP Work ID: 150028565.

10. Personally, I hear something like "Seven Deadly Virtues"© from *Camelot*. Or one might hit each woman with a power spot and have her dance to her own theme song. Try, e.g., "Vogue"© for Dolly, "Sweet Painted Lady"© for Jezebel, "Rag Doll"© (Crewe and Gaudio) for Tartuffie.

11. I've restored, per Koopmans, verse 4, omitted by Cohen (*RC*, p. 369): *D'amours les fais comme on peult ouÿr* (*RFlorence*, 647n). At v. 15, Dolly sounds suspiciously like Machaut's Lady Fortune in the *Remède de Fortune*, whence my intertext for *A l'ung je ris, et l'autre je regarde*. Here is some of the Middle French for Dolly's decasyllables which, again, I've scripted in pentameter: *Il est temps d'ung peu se resjouyr / Et deviser de ce qui est passé, / Dire motz tous plaisans à ouyr / D'amours les fais comme on peult ouÿr / Sans que jamais on se treuve lassé, / Les tours, les fais, le train entrelassé, / La façon, la ruse et le moyen / Parquoy la femme tout veu et compassé / Peult attraire de l'homme tout son bien. . . .* (*RC*, vv. 1–8 only; *RFlorence*, 647–48).

12. Although she speaks many seven-foot lines (heptameter), I've rendered Jezebel's whole speech—a single sentence, by the way—in the canonical octosyllables: *Je me polis, je me farde, / Je suis dehet, frisque en point, / Je tiens mon cul sur la ba[r]de / Je l'emboure tousjours à point, / Je congnois la note et le point / De larder celuy qui larde, / Je tiens la gorre sur mon point. . . .* (vv. 18–24; *RFlorence*, 648). Her use of *embourer*—attending to the bottom—recalls the principal activity of *RC*, #36, the *Farce des femmes qui font rembourer le bas*; see also *RFlorence*, 648n.

13. Here are Tartuffie's octosyllables, which I've scripted in alexandrines: *Doy-je estre mise arrière? / Je veuls triumpher honnestement, /Je sçay la façon et manière / De bien pomper secretement, / Je fais mon cas couvertement / Par ce point nully ne me note, / Je besongne ne occultement / En contrefaisant la bigotte* (vv. 30–37).

14. A "hilli-ho" from Charles Dickens's Mr. Fezziwig. For Koopmans, this speech evokes a proverb about leisure being the only treasure: *Il n'est trésor que de vivre à son aise* (*RFlorence*, 648n). For more on dance, see *MFST*, 93; 100; 156.

15. In addition to suggesting cleverness, trickery, subtlety, and malice, Dolly's *braguer en quignet ou en coing* (vv. 54–57) is about corners. Could there also be a connection with *le petit coin*—the *toilet* of toiletries—and "quinny," the archaic British term for the vagina?

16. *Pour dire "le dyable m'enport!"* (v. 107) sounds suspiciously like the curse that summoned the Devil in disguise in *Cooch E. Whippet* (*RC*, #41; *FF*, 355). The women's debate also recalls that of *Match/Point/Counterpoint* (*HD*, 178–82).

17. *J'ay humé maint oeuf mollet / Pour faire luyre mon visaige* (vv. 109–10): to peel a soft-boiled egg is "to play a trick on someone" (*RFlorence*, 649n).

18. In lyrical heptameter, this is the first of two references to Bagnolet: *J'ay esté à Baignollet / Ouyr le rossignollet, / Chanter son doulx chant ramage / En esté* (vv. 111–14; later at v. 334).

19. For *saint Cornille de Compiègne* (v. 118), see Koopmans, ed. *Pronostications*, 71–72n; and *DSI*, 1002. This is an allusion to Pope Cornelius, a protector of many horned—horny?—critters and cuckolds.

20. Here's Saint Julian again (as in #3, *Highway Robbery*, note 2).

21. With regard to her inductive, experiential, or "scientific" knowledge (*toutes sciences*), the agency of *apprendre* is difficult in *tous les jours du nouveau aprent* (v. 148). Is Theologina learning, teaching, or both?

22. A priceless meta-moment about translation: *Elle a veu les translatés / De latin en françoys vulgaire* (vv. 150–51).

23. Jezzie's rhyme of sweating and emotion—*j'en sue* and *esmeue* (vv. 183–85—might have something to do with the later flush of VD (below, note 42).

24. Here is Theologina's description of her perilous journey (above, § "Language"): *Par* le moyen de saincte Croix */ En ce pays l'ay aportée / Sus ung [mulet] empaquetée, / Mais, quant vint passer le plus fort, / L'asne au pied d'une vallée / Cheut toute bride avallée / Et de ce pas demoura mort* (vv. 197–203; my emphasis). Regarding the *moyen de saincte Croix*, I was tempted to go with an absurd Virgin Islands–style pun but, per Koopmans, it's a synonym for the coin of the realm, likely connoting the ongoing sale of indulgences (*RFlorence*, 651). Could she be hinting that she received the bull in exchange for sexual favors?

25. Theologina's crucial speech, reproduced below in its entirety, foreshadows a legal and theological denouement based on the strict interpretation of the bull.
Original Middle French (vv. 220–35; my emphasis):

LA THEOLOGIENNE
Je voys lire, faictes silence,
Vous la verrés bien solennelle,
Oncques n'en vistes une telle,
Elle est emple et generalle,
J'ay besongné par cautelle
Sur la clausulle principalle.
En lisant la bulle
A tous et toutes faisons sçavoir
De nostre auctorité moyenne
Nous donnons puissance, pouvoir

A madame la Théologienne
D'oÿr femmes de tous estatz
Interroguer d'ab oc et ab ac
Et les confesser de tous cas.
Ainsi signé: Teste de Fol.
Il n'y fault pas ung seul mot,
Elle est en planière forme.

Koopmans reads *interroguer d'ab oc et ab ac* (v. 231) as "willy-nilly" (*RFlorence*, 652n); but I deem that inconsistent with the play's ongoing focus on legalese and illiteracy (v. 155).

26. Connotations of purgative enemas as well as catharsis here with *Tresbien purgeray en effait / Vos consciences de tous cas* (vv. 243–44).

27. *Dire . . . ung seul motet* (vv. 247–48): Dolly won't leave out a single word nor leave off singing her motet.

28. Some charming double entendres with *les* sainctz corps *des moynes* (vv. 309–10). Also the *pellerinage de Saint Mors* (v. 308) refers to Saint-Maur-des-Fossés just east of Paris (*RFlorence*, 654n). And remember *Sire Mors* from *Highway Robbery* (above, #3, note 1)? "Saint Moritz" also offered protection from the plague (*DSI*, 740–45, 1090).

29. How could I resist? The Salvador *Dali* Museum is located in Montmartre.

30. Here's how I've handled *voulenté repute le fait* (v. 332); above, § "Language."

31. I've replaced the second reference to Bagnolet (v. 334) with a more familiar landmark: the nearby Père Lachaise cemetery.

32. In this exchange (vv. 359–67), pretending to pee (*faisant semblant de pysser*) and the herbed smell of sex (*margolaine*) could have sprung directly from the *RC*'s *Blind Man's Buff* (*FF*, 181–82). Koopmans concurs (*RFlorence*, 655n).

33. I couldn't resist a play on the word for scarlet: *migraine* (v. 369).

34. As in *For the Birds* (*HD*, 123–24), this likely song lyric puns on cuckoo and cuckold: *En ces boys, qui sont si vers, / Soubz arbre de fueilles ramu, / En ces boys, qui sont si vers, / Pour ouyr chanter le coqu* (vv. 374–77). I've conveyed some of the pastoral violence with an allusion to "Under the Linden Tree" from the *Carmina Burana* (e.g., Klinck, *Anthology*, 95–96).

35. At vv. 404–7, the overripe metaphor intimates less the "perfume of sex" and more the unsavory odor of menstruation: *ce tresmauvais vent / De la chemise* and the *paillard vent de la chemise* (v. 407; *RFlorence*, 656n). See also McCracken, *Curse of Eve*, 1–20.

36. For *demy pié* (v. 413), Koopmans came up with 16 centimeters (6.3 inches); but he is unsure as to whether it measures male or female body parts. I don't understand the confusion.

37. This legalistically liturgical language implies absolution to come: *S'autres pechés aves commis / Par oubliance ou obmis, / Que pour l'heure ne vous recorde, / A Dieu criez misericorde / Que du tout vous soyent remis!* (vv. 423–27).

38. Metacommentary with two uses of *contrefaire* (vv. 460–66): once for remaking the body (*mon corps tout contrefait*), once for pretending to be virgin (*en contrefaisant la pucelle*). Actual "revirginization" appears later as a miracle of Saint Muffie in the opening monologue of #10, *The Pardoners' Tales*.

39. Some amusing terminology for the game of sex: *nicque-nocque* (backgammon) and *planter la broque / Au fin plus près de mon cu!* (vv. 476–78), which sounds very much like the shit-kebabs of *RC*, #45, *Blind Man's Buff* (*FF*, 182).

40. For *Croque, / C'est bien joué* à la boy tu (vv. 478–79), Cohen wasn't sure (*RC*, 378n). Was it pronounced *boite* or *bete*? If the former, it could be part of the wordplay on illiteracy (*ne a ne boys* [v. 445]); or an intertext with the *boite* of the Dutch farce, *Blow in the Box* (Prins, *Medieval Dutch Drama*, 101–11). Per the Littré, I also find something like card playing or bowling.

41. *Velà ung mauvais relatif* (v. 484) is a fascinating term of art in logic, theology, or grammar, reinforced by Jezzie's subsequent reference (v. 486) to her own fine mind (*engin tressupelatif*).

42. The allusion to Syria—*en Surie* (v. 501)—seems odd but it's clearly wordplay on sweating (*suer*) as both a symptom (*RC*, 378n) and a cure for syphilis (*RFlorence*, 658n).

43. It's partridge in the original, the subject of much proverbial wisdom (*HD*, 66); but quail works better. In this passage, *la gorre* (v. 510) straddles a meaning between fashion and syphilis.

44. A particularly legalistic query: *Fistes-vous jamais nul fin tour / Prejudiciable au mestier?* (vv. 518–19).

45. At vv. 522–27, the man in question sounds like the gout-ridden Fouquet of our next play, #5, *Confession Follies*. More unsavory wordplay on taste (*qui qu'en gouste*), "gout" (*la goutte*), or "droplets" and "drip" of gonorrhea. And if "dead as a doornail" was good enough for *Piers Plowman*, it's good enough for me.

46. *Je dis que moy etant en fleur / Grunant par gorre florissante, / J'ay porté pour plus grant honneur / Mainte pierre reluysante / Enchassée et sans châsse* (vv. 541–45). For Koopmans, these "shiny stones" are pockmarked remains of buboes.

47. *Vous en avés mainte place / A vostre front, on le voit bien* (vv. 546–47): a particularly dense two lines in that *front* could be both that pockmarked forehead or a synonym for the vagina.

48. Tartuffie names a specific place—*aux Brières*—which is in the Essonne; *dessus* is a reference to the tenor's part of a musical score (*RFlorence*, 659n), befitting that motet; and her partner is a *gorrier* (v. 574), a male version of Jezzie's *Gorrière*.

49. This is the ambiguous moment invoked above (§ "Language"): "Si *voz faitz ne sont amendables, / Tout droit yrés à damnation*" (vv. 582–83), either "iffy" or "determinative." When Theologina speaks of *cas desraisonables*, she might be indicting "unreasonable" or "unnatural" behavior (v. 579). And *remplies d'obstination* (v. 581; later, v. 603)

implies a near heretical "ensconcement" in sin, all the more prosecutable. If one wishes to foreshadow the denouement, one could add this aside to the audience: "and I'm not saying one way or the other." Is Theologina implying that Dolly, Jezzie, and Tartuffie have a way out *if* they make reparations? Or is she stating quite forcefully that, *therefore*, their misdeeds are irreparable, so they're going straight to hell? You'll see, and so will they.

50. Here, I am inspired by two bits: *SNL*'s Fred Armisen and Vanessa Bayer as the "friends of" such tyrants as Qaddafi or Saddam Hussein: e.g., https://www.youtube.com/watch?v=XsZGZe4LSH0; and Brooke's confession to Elle Woods about liposuction in *Legally Blonde*: https://www.youtube.com/watch?v=APiRfhfH3KA (both accessed 19 January 2019). At vv. 584–90: *parfaire* is, again, a legal term; *contricion*, a theological one; and *par fiction*, another metacommentary. But the real kicker is: *J'ay fait à Dieu barbe de feurre*, which Koopmans deems a synonym for mockery or hypocrisy (*RFlorence*, 660n). The philology, however, links it to the notorious tithe owed to the Church.

51. With the singular pronoun for the three-person Trinity, Tartuffie's language is more or less theologically correct: *De tout le mal que oncques je fis / Duquel point ne me recorde. / Je prie le Père et le Filz / Et* luy *crye misericorde / A deulx genoulx devotement* (vv. 597–601; *RFlorence*, 660n). Unless she means the Son only.

52. Dolly's line is slightly ambiguous: *Absolutions nous sont baillées / En nous donnant benediction* (vv. 604–5). She could also mean: "Check it out girls: Nice blessing. I guess we're absolved!"

53. Here now, the most important speech of the play, foreshadowed all along by ambiguous legalese: *Soufit, puis qu'estes confessées, / Point n'aurés d'absolution, / Car je dis par conclusion / Que maintes femmes par compass / Sont oÿes de confession / Et après toutes audicions / Ne sont absoutes de leur cas, / Puis ma bulle ne s'estent pas / Donner absolution planière* (vv. 606–14). The document signed by Jack Asse makes no explicit mention of absolution (above, note 25). Key, therefore, to production will be determining whether or not Theologina has been planning to get off on a technicality all along.

54. In a rather indeterminate ending—compare it to Guynn's assessment of the *Pathelin* (*PF*, 69–108)—the audience is left hanging too when Theologina vows to seek another dispensation: *A Romme iray sans cesser, / Courant la poste à diligence, / Pour veoir si pourray passer / Touchant ce cas une dispance, / G'y voys faire assistance / En pourchassant de obtenir / Le point d'absouldre en substance / Adieu jusques au revenir!* (vv. 619–26). Absolution pervades the equivalent of the typical *envoi* asking the audience's forgiveness for any offenses.

55. *Se aucun se vient enquerir / Qui nous sommes, je ordonne / Qu'on nous trouvera sans faillir / Grans grammairiens de Narbone* (vv. 629–32). The Parisian Collège de Narbonne was on the rue de la Harpe (*RC*, 378n; *RFlorence*, 660n).

Play 5. *Confession Follies: Folie à Deux?*

1. I considered providing "underdetermined" stage directions, so as not to constrain your vision of the events; but *Confession Follies* needs a script that makes sense, even if you wind up altering it. Believe it or not, my earlier but much too repetitive draft of this translation was comprised of two free-standing *Follies*: one in which the Fool was Fouquet, the other in which he was the Valet.

2. Compare, e.g., with the tragic lives of chambermaids in #7, *Bro Job*, § "Characters and Character Development"; and in my "Theater Makes History," 993–1004.

3. A frequent prayer, the *Te Deum [laudamus]* was recited in thanksgiving ("praise the Lord"), as was the *Tu autem Domine miserere nobis*, in connection with death: "But Thou, O Lord, have mercy upon us."

4. The only anomaly in this scenario—Mandy addressing the bedridden valet as *vous*—is easily explained if Mandy, who recognizes the valet, is addressing "Fouquet," consistent with the ruse.

5. *Douce mémoire en plaisir consommée / En plaisir consommée* (1: 271; *MFST*, 83; 207), followed by eight more A-rhymes, is a song lyric. Given the unpalatability of staging Fouquet's abuse of Gwynnie as pleasure, I've gone with Bozo as the singer.

6. Technically, this nine-verse line (1: 272) belongs to Mandy; but it makes more sense in Gwynnie's mouth. Given a possible misattribution, I've doubled it.

7. For a different sensibility, try "Yessa, massa?" (1: 272).

8. Note that, as yet, Gwynnie has said not said exactly that. That wish comes later and often (1: 274, 278, 283).

9. *Verte veine* (1: 273) sounds sexual to me; but it might also refer to the proverb *Qui voit ses veines voit ses peines*, said of an elderly person whose veins are more visible through transparent skin.

10. This account could have come directly from the annals of domestic violence; see, e.g., Davis, *Fiction in the Archives*, 77–110; or Skoda, *Medieval Violence*, 193–231.

11. *Il n'a ne confort ne amys* (1: 274) recalls the Boethius-inspired *Comfort d'Amy* of the great fourteenth-century poet and musician Guillaume de Machaut.

12. Suddenly mindful of the need for an alibi, Gwynnie suggests a *bouteille de sainct pot* (1: 275), a small bottle of holy water (Di Stefano, "A Chaque Saint," 137–38; *DSI*, 1111–12).

13. With a thrice-spoken refrain, this *rondeau triolet* might play as a *comédie-ballet*: *Et puis, hay, où va Mannette? / Y a-il quelque anguille sus roche?* (1: 276). It also channels the proverbial wisdom associated with bottom-feeding eels (*DBD*, 79–90).

14. *Avoir mal à son amatrix* (1: 276) is precisely where Gwynnie will say it hurts in MASQUERADE #1. It's also a reference to the female pudendum. Compare with a similar expression in *Bro Job*, #7, sc. 1.

15. Since I hear a pregnancy pun in *toute plaine* (1: 277)—a meaning attested as early as the twelfth century—I've doubled the rapid-fire dialogue to bring it out.

16. And here are the most difficult lines of the play. They are mutilated, irregular, obscure, and potentially rife with omissions (albeit transcribed correctly from *RBM*, fol. 3). Since the rhyme scheme is off, I also recommend that the whole thing *sound* off: poorly syncopated, poorly "rapped," accompanied by bad dance steps, *emphásis* on the wrong *sylláble*, etc. Among other things, the Fool seems to channel the title character of *Cooch E. Whippet* (*Martin de Cambray*) when advising that Mandy invoke the Devil as part of her role-play (*FF*, 355). His reference to *Martin baton*, the title of another farce about getting women to shut up (Rouen, ca. 1600; *RTC*, 165–67; Faivre, *Répertoire*, 278–79), not only resonates with the infamous "rule of thumb" of wife-beating (*baton* = "stick"): *Martin* is Cooch's Middle French name. Among the difficulties: two puzzling uses of a slash as punctuation—could the curious diacritical be a musical call to repeat the line?: *Si elle* te triche, *voicy / Martin baton qui en fera / La raison. Tourne vers elle, / Et pleure et lui fait grand / Serment, donne-toy au dyable / Hardiment; il n'y a point / De dangier, non, ne jeu. / Tous mes sacrements / Et j[é] ma cautelle et / Malaise je feray du messire / Morice et luy dis que // Je t'ay fait veu et promesse, / Mais que j'aye confessé / Fouquet que je seray plus; // C'est que un* chouquet *vist // Où elle fait son domicille* (1: 278; my emphasis). And the rest depends on what the Fool means by *si elle te triche*. If correct as written, the clause means: "if she harms you, [Mandy]." If it's an erroneous transcription of *si elle* me *triche*, it could mean: "if she, [Gwynnie] is cheating on *me*." Meanwhile, Godefroy was stumped by the two last lines. A *chouquet*—rhymes with *Fouquet*—might be a chopping block.

17. In the salutations of the *rondeau triolet*, "Father Maurice" says: *Bonjour, ravice, bonjour ma soeur* (1: 279–80), with *ravice* stumping Godefroy again. I do find a Latin *ravice* denoting "virgin," with connotations of "rape" or "ravishment" (*ravir*). One wonders too about a connection with *rabice* for "rabies." Also, it's not clear whether the Fool is addressing one and the same woman as both *ravice* and *soeur*. Or is Mandy one and Gwynnie the other? If you prefer Fouquet as the Maurice-Impersonator, you could still have Bozo trailing him the whole time, imitating him.

18. The magic touch of *la main legiere* (1: 280) picks up on the earlier magician metaphors; but it also applies to horses, as in "giving free rein." If you believe that Gwynnie falls for the Maurice-impersonation, she could play the scene resentful of the ersatz Father's interest in Mandy, or she could try to guide his hands with "Easy does it. Just like last time."

19. This is the Fool's odd complaint that he's not in the woods with Mandy (above, § "Characters and Character Development"): *Pleust à Dieu que moy et la chambrière / Fussions emmy ses bois, / Et elle m'eust presté son harnoys / Affin que je luy esclarcice* (1: 280). *Harnoys* is militaristic, equine, and vaginal; and the past tense suggests multiple previous visits to the woods.

20. *Je fains quand je suis entour vous / Les membres me redissent tous, / Je suis plus hardy qu'un suisse* (1: 281). *Vous* signals that Gwynnie is the addressee; and the remark is ironic. The Swiss were as stereotypically cowardly as they will be in #9, *Johnny Slack-Jaw*.

21. At 1: 282, I've added the stage direction to tease out the homonymy of the next line's *Paix! Paix!*, a homonym for "fart."

22. The aphorism is *Commère, si vous estes mauvaise / Mesnagère, je vous feray bonne nourrisse* (1: 282, with a triple "r" in "*nourrrise*"). Granted: this is probably funnier if it's *Fouquet* learning about his wife's adultery (as in *Confession Lessons* and as Faivre thought). But it can still work for *Bozo*, who might be horrified that his own sexual advances on the mistress are now being revealed to *Mandy*.

23. *Faulse trahison, Dieu te mauldie / Quant par toy me fault mourir* (1: 284): this is the odd *tutoiement* discussed above, § "Plot."

24. While difficult to grasp, this could well be another song lyric in dialect: *Va debinelle, ouystaignelle à l'i grégois, / Va debinelle, etc.* (1: 284). *Grégois* would normally be related to Greeks; and *débiner* is badmouthing (*faire la mauvaise langue*).

25. *Vasselle* (1: 285), the ungrammatical "female vassal," also looks like "doing the dishes." It sounds almost like the later Classicist *je suis votre serviteur*: i.e., the sarcastic opposite of "at your service" (*FF*, 255), which is perfect for Mandy.

26. *C'est cest enfant, c'est cet enfant / Qui fut fait en ses gachères, / C'est cest enfant, c'est cet enfant / Qui fut fait emmy ces boys* (2: 285): this is clearly another song, conveniently about the birth of a child . . . conceived in the woods? Or you could go another way with "What child is this got laid to rest on mama's lap was creeping?"©

27. To maximize the allusion to Saint Veronica, who wiped Jesus's face (1: 287), I've added a stage direction akin to the dirty, nasty face-painting of *The Kettle-Maker* (*HD*, 101–4, 115).

28. What *can* the Fool mean by *Et à la femme à messire Maurice* (1: 287)? Father Maurice's *wife*? His *concubine*? Priests did have concubines, and one makes a tragic historical appearance as a rape victim in 1395 (see my "Spectacle of the Scaffolding").

29. If, like many others, this farce were played at Lent, the fasting makes sense (1: 288). Compare with similar language in *Confession Lessons* (*FF*, 120).

30. Even the aphoristic *envoi* is in poetic disorder: *Adieu, de par tous les diables; / Adieu, seigneurs; contemplez en effect / Qu'il n'est finesse que d'une femme; / Fin contre fin autre deçoy* (1: 288).

31. "And When I Die"© would both hint at Gwynnie's pregnancy and authorize the audience to "carry on."

Play 6. *Brother Fillerup*

1. My translation of *Jehan de Lagny* (*RLV*, #31) is projected for my next volume. For the two extant versions of the song, see *SFQS*, "Préf"; and Martin's edition of *Jehan de Lagny*, note 5: https://sottiesetfarces.wordpress.com/2019/07/25/jehan-de-lagny/ (accessed 14 January 2021); and *MFST*, 268. Oddly, he reads a stage direction about *Perrete, povre garce* (4: 7) as an indication that she is not, in fact, *Perrete Venés Tost*.

2. See https://www.youtube.com/watch?v=XRhi8Tk9nNE (accessed 17 December 2018).

3. The advice of "Treat Her Right"© is eerily similar to Brother Filbert's; and its "hey, hey, hey, hey" refrain would be in keeping with the standard medieval plea for silence. Or you could try "How Do You Solve a Problem like Perrette?"© Or give *Perrette* a theme song on the order of "Daddy, I'm No Virgin,"© "Not a Virgin Anymore,"© "What a Girl Wants,"© "A Girl Who Cain't Say No,"© etc.

4. What's in a whole list of names? Here, it's *Mais il n'est Trubert ne Herbert, / Guillebert, Robert, ne Lambert...* (4: 6). "Guillebert" is the star of #11, *Slick Brother Willy*.

5. The original stage direction reads: *Perrete tousse et sa metresse tient son front* (4: 9). Since *le front* could also denote the vagina or, for that matter, the virile member, could he really "grab her by the pussy" (or by something else)?

6. *Da, usque me he* (4: 10) sounds vaguely Latinate, almost an echo of Psalm 72:8 about dominion from sea to sea: *Et dominabitur a mari usque ad mare, et a flumine usque ad terminos terrae*. I've worked that into his next line.

7. *C'est de la teste, / Dont je ne puis prendre liqueur; / Puys il me vient descendre au coeur, / Et cela me respont à l'ayne* (4: 11). This is the first reference to *ayne* (above, § "Plot").

8. *Ouvrés n'en ainsy que de cyre* (4: 12): in addition to "to perfection" (*SFQS*, note 44), the practice of writing on wax is a classic memory image that we have seen before in *Monk-ey Business* (*FF*, 447n).

9. After *prent ses lunettes, puys escript une recepte*, here is a sample of Filbert's closing set-piece, where frequent use of the subjunctive renders agency ambiguous. For example, until the rest of the syntax makes things clear, the oft-repeated *prengne* or *prenne le galant* could mean "may she take the stud" or "may the stud take *her*." And "hokey-pokey" fits the garrison metaphors nicely. See also *SFQS*, notes 61–81.
Original Middle French (4: 12–14; my emphasis):

FRERE FILLEBERT
(En luysant.)
Recepte pour le cotillon
Que la povre garce a perdu.
Sy l'un d'eulx se trouve esperdu,
L'un sera pour l'autre enseigner;
Que bientost la connvyent [convient] saigner.
Puys apres fera gargarin
D'un bon clistere barbarin,
Et pour luy remplir bien ses vaines,
La fault seigner *entre deux aynes*
Tant qu'elle en puisse estre assouvye.

We've met the *barbarin* enema before in *Playing Doctor* (*FF*, 433n); and *gargarin* might well be evocative of swallowing—gargling?—a little something.

10. The women utter their refrain four times (4: 13–14). Twice, it's *Sainct Jehan! Dieu vous doinct bonne vye*, literally, "In the name of Saint John, God give you a good

life"; and twice, it's *Dieu vous doinct bonne vye et longue*, "May God give you a long and happy life." One is tempted to think that the wish applies to a *bon vit* too, "a good dick"; but the masculine adjective doesn't have enough poetic feet.

11. While *motet* often means "a few words" (*SFQSS*, note 85), one wonders, in such a musical play, whether Filbert might be calling for all or part of a motet—*un petit motet de chanson* (4: 14). Modern musical analogues might include: a reprise of "Treat Her Right"© or "Hand in My Pocket";© but, again, I'd go with a parody of *Petticoat Junction*.

Play 7. *Bro Job*

1. The original order in the *RBM* is Domine Johannes, Troussetaqueue, La Nourrice, and Saupicquet (1: 435).

2. King also translates several excerpts in this unpublished, unpaginated conference paper.

3. See *RTC*, 118; *SFQS*, note 7; and compare with *ATF*, 2: 435–38 and *RPF*, 5: 78–80.

4. It is unknown whether Montaiglon also consulted a Lyon edition apparently published by Barnabé Chaussard in 1549.

5. The publication history is complex and occasionally confusing. The Costé edition can be consulted at http://gallica.bnf.fr/ark:/12148/bpt6k83475b?rk=21459 (accessed 17 December 2018).

6. Montaiglon gives the date of 1831; but the title page of the Crapelet/Silvestre edition reads 1830. As for the coda, the Gothic lettering makes it difficult to distinguish *chauffer* ("heat up") from *chausser* ("slip on," as in shoes); but either works. See also *RTC*, 9–10.

7. *Perrette answers and says to her mistress* (*Respond Perrette et dict à sa maistresse* [*RPF*, 5: 77]); see below, note 12.

8. The protonotary is present at slightly different moments in the *Caquet* (*RPF*, 5: 80) vs. the *RBM* (2: 439). Pope Clement I appointed the first twelve protonotaries to write the lives of the martyrs, a lofty mission with such benefits as assigned seats in the papal chapel. See the entry in Diderot and D'Alembert's *Encyclopédie*: https://fr.wikisource.org/wiki/L'Encyclopédie/1re_édition/PROTONOTAIRE (accessed 8 February 2018).

9. I also considered "Hot-to-Trottie," "SmokinHot," "Juicy Lucy," "Salty," "Spicy," and "Sassy." In "Caught in the (One-)Act," King liked "Sassy" (and "Tuck-up-your-Tail" for Troussetaqueue); but I've reserved "Sassy" for Soeur Safrete of #12, *Immaculate Deception*.

10. From multiple songs registered to Fleetwood Mac, "Go Your Own Way"© is listed in neither the ASCAP nor the BMI repertories. The best place to start might well be https://globalmusicrights.com/artist/1412025.

11. I've condensed his greatest hits (*RPF*, 5: 74–77), but here is a sense of the original: *Chamberières, vueillez moy pardonner / Si je pretendz descouvrir voz finesses; / Je n'entendz point les bonnes blazonner; / Chamberières, vueillez moy pardonner. / Aux maulvaises je vueil le tort donner, / Que chascun sçait plus communes qu'asnesses; / Chamberières, vueillez moy pardonner / Si je pretendz descouvrir voz finesses* (*RPF*, 5: 71).

12. Here is a taste of the *Caquet's* reported speech: "*Madame vient, il se fault retirer; / Tost, mon amy, tost sortez par derrière; / Ma maistresse se pourroit fort irer; / Pour tant, amy, retirez-vous arrière; /—Dieu vous gard, dame!"—"Et puis, ma chamberière, / Avez-vous bien nostre logis gardez?" / O! qu'elle est saoulle! O! que la première / Est encore pleine, et vous n'y regardez!* (*RPF*, 5: 77). Some clarity on the maid's (in)delicate condition emerges in the Costé edition, where the text reads not *premiere* but *pannetière* (p. 6). Instead of glasses of spirits, we seem to be talking about buns in the oven.

13. Who exactly is in the mood? In the *RBM*, it's a question of the *Master's* desires: *Il sembloit donc, à ses dictz, / Qu'*il fut tendre *du petit ventre* (*ATF*, 436; *RBM*, xii–xiii). In the *Caquet*, it's the *wife's* desire to garrison: *Et sembloit, à oyr ses dictz, / Qu'*elle eust mal *en son petit ventre* (*RFP*, 5: 79).

14. Martin thinks that a *femme de pied* "has her feet on the ground" (*SFQS*, note 10); but, given all the militarism of the Mistress's *logis*—a synonym for "vagina" (*SFQS*, note 12)—I also see "boots on the ground." She's a real "foot soldier" or "infantryman" (2: 436). The line is even explicit in the *Caquet*: *Elle se mect à l'advant-garde / Pour repcevoir les premiés coups* (*RFP*, 5: 80).

15. As in the *Caquet* (*RPF*, 5: 80), this account is peppered with reported speech (2: 436–47).

16. Martin understands the opposite: i.e., that Pricker-Upper would have been "proud to have refused him" (2: 437; *SFQS*, note 14).

17. Exceptionally, I amplify the narrative with this account from the *DNC* (*ATF*, 2: 426), which demonstrates what is needed to please her and her thingy (*complaire*).

18. *Elle sent trop souvent le masle; / Je croy qu'elle encharge d'un filz* (2: 438): some marvelously ambiguous wordplay here in that a wet nurse would surely have a kid "hanging on her breast," but a promiscuous one might be pregnant with a kid of her own.

19. Some wonderful metacommentary on *tresteaulx*, the legal or theatrical "stage" (2: 438). Martin sees an allusion to a medieval dining table, typically a board atop two-by-fours (*SFQS*, note 23).

20. More on the sheets with *Tu n'es point orde à tes drappeaulx, / Car tu es souvent remuée* (2: 438). Martin understands it to mean that there is too much action for the sheets to collect dust (*SFQS*, note 24). If you don't mind the anachronism, you could add: "She's a one-woman spin-cycle!"

21. *Elle veult faire bonne buée; / Elle manie souvent le pissot*: the *pissot* is both a washtub spigot and the male member that plugs holes (*rescourre*) (2: 438–39; *SFQS*, notes 26, 28). The washtub also makes for an intertext with the beloved *Washtub* (*La Farce du Cuvier*) of my next volume.

22. A contradiction: Florence has just said that she feels sick if she *doesn't* drink something in the morning (2: 438–39).

23. I've made my best guess at what sounds like a proverb straddling ankles, plugs, and sex acts: *Tu semble aux sainctz de la paroisse, / Tousjours as la cheville au trou* (2: 439).

24. With uncharacteristic *pudeur,* Martin reads *baiser* (2: 439) as "kissing" (*SFQS,* note 34).

25. *Ce n'est pas jeu. / J'entends que les bastons à feu / Y ont cest an sonné si ferme, / Qu'ils ont estonné tout le germe / De toutes mes dames de* Carmes, / *Qui n'a peu proffiter ne* croistre / *En sorte que ayent peu engrossir* (2: 441–42 and *RBM,* iii; my emphasis). In this curious speech with two orphaned rhymes for *Carmes* and *cloistre,* it seems that the nuns are pregnant . . . but, then, they're not. Perhaps Saint Muffie has worked the revirginizing magic invoked in #10, *The Pardoners' Tales* (sc. 1); or perhaps, as in #12, *Immaculate Deception,* the nuns know how to manipulate the firestick (the portable hand-cannon known as a *baton à feu*) in such a way as to avoid pregnancy. I've added some extra dialogue—Matthew 3:12 seemed appropriate—consistent with possible rhymes with the orphans: *armes/Carmes* and *croistre/cloistre* ("cloister"). For Martin, at stake here is the spear-tipped *arquebuse,* which he reads as a penis headed to the anus; and the firearms are so noisy that they cause spontaneous abortions in pregnant nuns (*SFQS,* note 51).

26. *En lieu de verjus, / J'ay entendu qu'on mist du jus / D'un clistère au moine (se) dit-on / Pour l'eaue béniste d'un chappon* (2: 442). In the *RBM,* this is still part of Florence's speech (fol. 3, col. 2); but it's likely meant for Pricker-Upper. And notice the capon, as castrated a critter as the gelding (*hongre*) of Brother Fillerup's prescription (#6, *RFMSJ,* 4: 14).

27. This is not quite the traditional envoi, which I've doubled here: *Veoir se l'endouille est rostie. / Je m'en vais d'une autre partie. / Prou vous face la compaignie* (2: 447). Martin deems it a later addition (*SFQS,* notes 79 and 80).

28. "Don't Leave Me This Way"© easily does double duty here and might be preferable to "Sisters, Go Your Own Way!"©

Play 8. *The Resurrection of Johnny Palmer*

1. See, e.g., Young, *Drama of the Medieval Church,* 1: 149–77.

2. See Knight, "Medieval Theater of the Absurd"; *AG,* 78–91; and Arden, *Fools' Plays,* 160–68. The sotie is relatively neglected, but not by Dull in *Folie et Rhétorique dans la sottie.*

3. On the importance of the *monde à l'envers* and its association with popular culture, see Bakhtin, *Rabelais and His World*; Gurevich on "the medieval grotesque" (*Medieval Popular Culture,* 176–210); and, for an iconographic approach, Robert-Nicoud, *World Upside Down,* esp. 52–101.

4. For a pictorial account, see Boureau, *Myth of Pope Joan,* 50. Pope Joan is also the subject of Dietrich Schernberg's *Play of Lady Jutta* of 1565 (*Medieval German Drama,* ed. Wright, 159–219).

5. On the Pinecone sculpture, see Gruber, "Thirteen Things"; and, for a picture, see https://commons.wikimedia.org/wiki/File:Cortile_della_Pigna_(Vatican_Museums)_September_2015-2.jpg (accessed 19 December 2018).

6. The Alka-Seltzer jingle is listed in the ASCAP registry along with many other Dawes titles; but there is a request to contact them for more information (accessed 3 July 2019).

7. Chimney sweeping (*ramonner*) is a favorite metaphor for the sex act, as in the *Farce nouvelle du Ramonneur de cheminees* (*RC*, #30 and *RBM*, #36).

8. *Las onc depuis mon cueur n'eut joye* (v. 26) is clearly the verse of a song that also appears in *RC*, #6, the *Queues troussées* (*SFQS*, note 9), and in the sotie of *Deulx Gallans et Sancté* (*RLV*, #12).

9. It is challenging to translate the slang of *Si n'es-tu point sur le suc / Comme estoit mon frère Jenyn* (vv. 32–33). *Suc* is related to "blood," "head," or "neck," but for Koopmans, this might well be another instance of *verlan*: *suc = cu[l]s* (*RFlorence*, 710n). For Martin, it could also be the head of a tonsured fool like Brother Johnny (*SFQS*, note 18).

10. The *beau père* of v. 38 might technically be her father-in-law; but he could also be a good-looking Father Confessor to confess 'er.

11. There is something otherworldly about *ababou, tanfarara, tanfarara* (v. 91; above, § "Language"): a devilish tone reminiscent of conjuring the Devil in the *Miracle of Theophile* (*MFP*, 174–75). See also *MFST*, 190.

12. Martin has identified *Jamais mon cueur joye n'aura* as another song lyric, #326 in the *Jardin de Plaisance* (*SFQS*, note 44); see also *MFST*, 93; 232.

13. Deleted from the *RC*, this line—*Au plus parfond?*—was restored by Koopmans (*RFlorence*, 713). That's why I had him "beyond the moon" and "under the rainbow" above; plus, there are more "moons" to come, as in the music of *happe la lune* (vv. 203–4; *MFST*, 222).

14. The boat-related imagery above was for the music of *Ils sont en gallée gallée* (vv. 153–54; *MFST*, 230). With *mais est-il venu mon cousin* (v. 157), the same confusion about identity ensues for Caillette as for Toni's brother (*Répertoire*, 382). Here, a comma determines whether Toni is referring to Johnny as "my cousin" or calling Birdie "Cousin." Inbred *cousinage* might help to explain the characters' overall stupidity.

15. At vv. 188–92, the *larons* could also be evocative of the two thieves crucified with Jesus; so you could substitute "Bar-bar-bar, bar-bar-a-bas!"© As for the pirates, could they be connected to Chaucer's *Pardoner's Tale* or *Shipman's Tale* or, better yet, to pirated *editions* of our play?

16. Toni says only one word: *maire* (v. 194), which sounds like "uterus," "Mayor," or "shit"—until, *Ubu-Roy*-like, you hit the "d" (above, § "Language"). Koopmans thinks it means "calm down" (*RFlorence*, 715n).

17. If you're unfamiliar with the Southern California spectacle of The Pageant of the Masters, check it out here: https://www.foapom.com/pageant-of-the-masters/ (accessed 21 December 2018). It goes well with Joanie's later advice about their house: *Il fault qu(e) au vif elle soit pourtraicte* (v. 277).

18. This set-piece is in pentameter: *Nous sommes de l'ordre de saint Baboyn.* / Ilz chantent tous: / *L'ordre ne dit mye de lever matin, / Dormir jusqu'à prime et boire bon vin / Et chanter matines sur ung pot de vin* (vv. 231–34). See also *MFST*, 263–64.

19. Perhaps this moment led to the misperception that Birdie and Toni are brothers (above, § "Characters and Character Development"): Mon frère, *or allez, / Vous nous avez bien ravallez / Au ressuscitement de Jenin!* (vv. 255–57).

20. *Sans faire longue station, / J(e) y feray bientost besongner* (vv. 281–82): *besogner* might mean many things, including business on the toilet; plus, these *stations* reminded me of pageant wagons and the stations they might depict.

21. *Mais la chaire est-elle persée? / J(e) y vueil faire mon aisement* (vv. 297–98). With the *aisement* of relieving oneself (*SFQS*, note 130), this seat is sounding more and more like Pope Joan's Seat of Shit.

22. *Faire chière lye au nys* (v. 324) clearly denotes feasting and festivities (*RFlorence*, 719n); but I also hear that *Ubu-Roy*-like wordplay mentioned above (§ "Language") with *faire chier*, as in "to make someone shit" or, even now, "to bug someone."

23. *Vive les enfans Beauvais! / Si concluons par motz exprès* / La Resurrection Jenyn / A Paulme, *nostre amy très, / Adieu vous dy jusqu'à demain!* (vv. 326–30).

24. Appropriate choices might be: "One Child,"© a reprise of "My Cousin's Back,"© or such drinking songs as "Bottle o' wine, fruit o' the vine"© or "Show me the way to go home."©

Play 9. *The Resurrection of Johnny Slack-Jaw*

1. On *sapientia* vs. *scientia*, see Robertson, *Preface to Chaucer*, 22–51; cited in #4, *Drama Queens*, note 3. For Renaissance Platonism, see esp. Colie, *Paradoxia epidemica* and Kristeller, *Renaissance Thought*. Maistre Pierre Doribus also boasts about the invisibility trick in a *Sottie nouvelle* of *RT*, #9, v. 36.

2. In *Trois Galants et un Badin* (*RLV*, #40), e.g., a certain Naudin dreams that, as God, he is married to the Virgin Mary. See *RF*, 11: 26n; *RTC*, #108, 141–42; Faivre, *Répertoire*, #66, 181–83.

3. See *RTC*, 228; *CM*, 148–51; and Tissier's extensive gloss of Johnny's entire account (*RF*, 11: 40n–48n). *Saint Jacques en Galisce* (2: 24) is the *Sainct Jacques* of Compostela, as in the Camino de Santiago, the famous pilgrimage (*RF*, 11: 41n) and also mentioned in #2, *Blue Confessions*.

4. *Et sainct Paul atout son espée, / Qui avoit la teste coupée / A sainct Denys, se* luy *sembloit, / Et* sainct Françoys *les combatoit, / Frappant sur eulx, patic, patac* (2: 24; my emphasis). Like Tissier, I suspect that this should read *les Françoys*, "the French," by analogy to the other nationalistic fighters (*RF*, 11: 40n). The typography of *ATF* even looks like King Francis I (*Francois Ies combatoit*). And the perspective is confusing too: Did it "seem to" *Saint Dennis* or to *Johnny* that "he" had beheaded Saint Paul? I suspect that *se* luy *sembloit* should have been *se* me *sembloit*.

5. This joke appears in multiple versions online but try this one: http://www.jamesfuqua.com/lawyers/jokes/afterlife.shtml (accessed 14 May 2018).

6. On the Harrowing of Hell, see, e.g., Young, *Drama of the Medieval Church*, 1: 149–77; cited in note 1 of #8, *Johnny Palmer*.

7. We've seen *verlan* in #8, *Johnny Palmer* (§ "Sets and Staging") and in *Monk-ey Business* (*FF*, #9), where the lead character is nicknamed "Verjus," *jus-vert* in *verlan* (*FF*, 432n). And Furetière gives that example of *verjus* in the *Dictionnaire Universel* (1690), even without terming it *verlan*: "On dit aussi, C'est verjus ou jus verd, pour dire, C'est la même chose"; cited in Lefkowitz, *Talking Backwards*, 51.

8. *Nenin par le jez et mandore par le lenton* doesn't quite match phonetically but it does come close: *nennin* is an emphatic Middle French "no"; a *jai* is a jaybird; a *mandeur* is a bailiff; a *mont d'or* is a cheese, which sounds suspiciously like a golden mount or a vagina; and *lenton* sounds a bit like *longtemps* ("for a long time")—plus *landon* is a synonym for "muzzle," the most pronounced part of Johnny's anatomy. For more on the meaning of *landore*, see *RF*, 11: 30–31. My thanks to Chadi Ben Youssef for suggesting that this could be a metalinguistic pun on the shape of the articulatory apparatus when the drunken character speaks. Other possibilities for his name: Johnny Johnson, Johnny Jawbone, Johnny Lazy-Bones, Johnny Wino, Johan Johan (as in John Heywood's *Johan Johan* of 1533), Johnny Jabber-Wocky (because he's fearsome, jabbers, and *wocks* funny), and so on.

9. Other farces dependent on an overarching joke include *The Student Who Failed His Priest Exam* (*FF*, 144–45) and *Cooch E. Whippet* (*FF*, 334–35).

10. In "'Je viens . . . / d'estrange contrée,'" King favors an absurdity-enhancing, red-and-white-checkered tablecloth for Johnny's shroud (351n). For the master trope of the tavern, see Cowell, *At Play in the Tavern*.

11. You can see and hear the Heaven Sent perfume jingle, produced in the 1960s for Helena Rubinstein, here: https://www.youtube.com/watch?v=Gym7LD47k98 (accessed 3 July 2019). As of this writing, it was not listed in any copyright registry that I could locate.

12. Try "Magic to Do,"© or the Heaven Sent jingle about a scent that was "a little naughty but heavenly"© or, for a completely different sensibility: "How Long?"© or "Oh Mary, Don't You Weep."©

13. I hear a song in *Or est-il mort, helas! helas! / Jenin Landore, mon mary, / Mon espoir, mon bien, mon soulas. / Or est-il mort, helas! helas! / Quand m'en souvient, je pers esbas, / Et ay le cueur triste et marry. / Or est-il mort, helas! helas! / Jenin Landore, mon mary* (2: 21). After the Priest adds *Quand il estoit ensepvely*, rhyming couplets return.

14. *Il estoit assez bon folastre / Et se marchoit de bon biés* (2: 22) is a mouthful. While Godefroy had a big question mark for *biez*, perhaps it's a precursor to today's *bonne descente*: the spirits "go down easy."

15. *Benedicite, / Nostre-Dame de Reconfort!* (2: 22): Tissier reminds us that that church was in close proximity to one of the most famous publishers of farce: Barnabé Chaussard of Lyon (*RF*, 11: 38n).

16. *Atout sa chappe bien doublée* (2: 24): while this could be a hat or a cape, I also hear echoes of an instrument of torture (*chape de plomb*): a different "full metal jacket" for a different "Iron Man." I doubt it's the *chappe* as "oyster opener" but, in this fishy context, you never know.

17. I couldn't resist the parallel to the famous "Anne Elk" bit from *Monty Python's Previous Record.*

18. *Clerice, tu es tout gentil. / Maquereau c'est poisson d'apvril; / Ainsi es-tu, je te le jure; / La fin de ta bonne adventure, / C'est que tu aymes ton repos* (2: 31): I've interpolated quite a bit to tease out the complex meaning of one of the best moments of the play. With more thanks to Noah Guynn: in Eloy D'Amerval's fifteenth-century *Livre de la Deablerie*, we also find Lucifer insulting Satan as a *macquereau infame* and a *poisson d'apvril* (vv. 321–23).

19. There was a terrific ghost costume in *At Cross Purposes* (*FF*, 224–25; *RF*, 11: 25, 56n–58n); so, I couldn't resist channeling Eddie Izzard's Holy Ghost bit from *Dress to Kill.*

20. *Sans faulte* (2: 34) is an interesting turn of phrase that means "certainly" but also "without sin."

21. I've doubled the particularly short envoi: *Adieu vous dis, je prens congé* (2: 34), which rhymes with the preceding *Si j'estoys un peu reposé.*

22. You might try "Papa's Got a Brand New Bag"© or "Losing My Religion."©

Play 10. *The Pardoners' Tales*

1. For more on *pardonneurs* vs. *triacleurs*, see *RF*, 5: 232–26; *DLU*, 48; and esp. chap. 8 of Katritzky, *Women, Medicine*, e.g., 126–27. Farcically enough, the term *theriaque* was gendered both masculine *and* feminine.

2. If you don't know the *SNL* bit, try: https://www.nbc.com/saturday-night-live/video/theodoric-of-york/n8661 (accessed 26 May 2019).

3. Soon to pop up in #11, *Slick Brother Willy*, Saint Woody also appears in *Pots and Scams* (*HD*, 115). See *DSI*, 52–55, 135–37, 192–94, 198–99, 214, 316–17; and Di Stefano, "À Chaque Saint," 130–31.

4. For Claude Duneton, the expression "seems to date from the seventeenth century" (*La Puce*, 174). See Patrick Brault's fascinating blog on untranslatable expressions: https://blog.ted.com/40-idioms-that-cant-be-translated-literally/comment-page-10/.

5. Try any of these: a medieval lyric *tenson*, a gender-bent "I'm Called Little Buttercup,"© "Respect,"© "The Old Dope Peddler,"© Mary Magdalene's "Everything's Alright"© from *Jesus Christ Superstar*, or a zany update of Steve Martin's King Tut bit, https://www.youtube.com/watch?v=FYbavuReVF4 (accessed 20 January 2021).

6. Here is a taste of the lyrical opening, the first five verses of which I've doubled: *Sainctes parolles pacificques / Soient entre vous residens / Par vertu de sainctes relicques / Qui reposent icy dedans. / Messieurs, il y a long-temps / Que ne visitay ce pays; / Mais, s'il plaist à Dieu, je pretens / De vous faire tous esjouys. / J'aporte icy de[s] ouyes / De sainct Couillebault confesseur / Et de saincte Velue, sa soeur, / Dont il appert de grans miracles. / Je vous vueil compter les obstacles / Et les miracles qu'ilz ont fait* (2: 50).

7. Here are the somewhat inscrutable miracles of Saints Woody and Muffie: *Cestuy monsieur sainct Couillebault, / Delivra, je le vous afferme, / Une juifve estant à l'assault / D'enfant et n'estoit à terme* (2: 51).

8. Those were my rough translations of both the meter and the absurdity of the Middle French onomastics: *Maintenant fault que labeure / A nommer les confrères anciens / Qui furent de leur confrarie. / Jehan Pigault, Bietrix Barbarie, / Colin Mulet et Jehan Bigace, / Jenin Gringecte, Jehan La Gace* [sounds like "John, the slut"], / *Tassin Pigard, Perrin Bicorne, / Jehan Sousseron, Jehanne La Sorne, / Martin Marteaulx, Regnault Frasie, / Pierre Sourys et sa maignie* (2: 51). Later names to follow are: *Jehan Beaufort, Tassin Lebrun, / Jehan Fort-en-guelle* (2: 52) and *Jehan Huart, Colin forte here, / Pierre boit bien, Guillot tout neant* (2: 53). Do add some local dignitaries too, especially given Tissier's speculation that the second list, in metric disarray, was originally longer (*RF*, 5: 250n).

9. For *raisiner*, Tissier gives a legalistic reading of "to yield" (*se résigner*) (*RF*, 5: 248n); but I incline more toward Rabelais's hint about writing *Gargantua* while drunk (*CFRW*, 5). *Raisiner* also denotes "drinking wine" (Clark, *Vulgar Rabelais*, 98).

10. A *lanternier* (2: 54) is someone fixated on foolish, useless things (*RF*, 5: 253n) and a possible shout-out to the *Farce des femmes qui font accroire à leurs maris de vecies que ce sont lanternes* (*RC*, #25).

11. The fascinating use of *de commune juré* is consistent with the historical emergence of bourgeois towns (2: 54; later 2: 55–56).

12. The Pardoner's above referenced piggy-wiggy foretells yet more animal imagery: recall that Saint Anthony was often depicted in the company of a porker, as here: https://commons.wikimedia.org/wiki/File:Tentation_de_Saint_Antoine.jpg (accessed 12 September 2021). While most challenging to translate, the Snake-Oil Salesman's curious line about bird eggs appears to reference the same reset of pregnancy that was earlier attributed to Saint Muffie: *Messeigneurs, vecy l'oeuf d'un moyne / Qui fut ponnu en Barbarie, / Qui est plain quand la lune est plaine / Et tary quand elle est tarye* (2: 54). I agree with Tissier that *l'oeuf d'un moyne* is a sparrow's egg (*RF*, 5: 254–55n); but it's also the word for "monk." To my ear, the whole thing is evocative of the fabliau of the thief on the rooftop who tries to kiss the moon: "Le Larron qui embrassa un rayon de lune" (*Fabliaux et contes*, 45–47).

13. It was before Caiaphas, not Pilate, that Peter denied Jesus three times; see also *MFST*, 202. The reference to Noah's ark (*la grand arche de Noë*) is likely related to the upcoming allusion to Mount Ararat in Turkey (2: 55; *RF*, 5: 255n–256n). I also like Matt

Sergi's idea that this is a sight gag: try having the Pardoner produce a large plank along the lines of the proverbial ramrod up somebody's ass.

14. An error in *RBM*, fol. 2v, col. 2 attributes three speeches in a row to the *Triacleur* (*RF*, 5: 258n).

15. More wordplay on *de commune juré* with *esse juré cela*? (2: 56; above, note 11). For Tissier, *Pâques* could have been *Parques*, i.e., the three Fates, who were seated near Hades, the aforementioned Cerberus, and the upcoming Persephone (*RF*, 5: 258n)—also the name of the harridan of *Wife Swap* (*HD*, #9).

16. The specific plant is *la barbe de Proserpine* or "Persephone's Beard" (2: 57; *RF*, 5: 259n; *FFMA*, 2: 169). But its hellacious origins require a different pun in English.

17. At 2: 58, the basket (*une hotte*) recalls Virgil hanging in his *corbillon* in #4, *Drama Queens* (Figure 2) and *Basket Case* (of my next volume): *La Farce de la Femme qui fut desrobée à son mari en sa hotte et mise une pierre en son lieu* (*RC*, #23).

18. At 2: 58: Machiavelli's famous *Mandragola* is contemporaneous with our farce (*RF*, 5: 263n). Also, recall that there was only *one* phoenix in the entire world (*RF*, 5: 263n); that Mount Athos was a sacred site of orthodox Christianity where no women were allowed; and that the pelican nourishing its young with its own blood was a preferred New Testament symbol, as in Thibaut de Champagne's thirteenth-century *Deus est ensi com li pelicans* (for the Folger Consort's rendition, see https://www.youtube.com/watch?v=8b6r02ZmTU4 [accessed 25 December 2018]).

19. Another nod to the Melusine legend with Geoffrey Big-Tooth (2: 58–59), probably Geoffrey II of Lusignan (ca. 1198–1248), who owed that moniker to a protruding canine tooth (*RF*, 5: 264n–65n).

20. Some complex wordplay here on *baulx* and *bau* (2: 59), the latter, another rafter-like *chevron* mentioned above (2: 59), whence my *truss/trust* pun above.

21. *Deux coquins ne vallent rien / a un huys* (2: 60) seems as concrete a reference as any to the *Chicken Pie and the Chocolate Cake* (*FCMF*, 151–58; above, § "Plot"), the moral of which is likewise that you can't knock twice at the same door for both dinner and dessert.

22. To my ear, this is a delightful setup. You'll see why later: *je me tiens seur, / Se mon mary estoit icy, / Certes, il seroit bien marry / Se très bien ne vous festoioit / Car aussi certes il souloit / Se mesler du mesme mestier* (2: 61).

23. *Vous ne demourrez pas derrière / Par ma foy jusques à un escu* (2: 61): my reading diverges from Tissier's (*RF*, 5: 270n); but, to make room for both, you could add this *sotto voce* to the audience: "I'll be into these boys for a least a hundred bucks a head!"

24. Actually, it was the Snake-Oil Salesman who handed her the *coffret* (2: 60–61); but the Pardoner would be happy to invent anything about what's in it.

25. On *adieu, pou fille*, Tissier puzzled out a synonym for *povre garce* (like Perrette of #6, *Brother Fillerup* [*RF*, 5: 271–72n]). But there is a character called *Puoc fille* or *Peu-File*

in the *Farce des Trois Commères*, projected for a future volume of mine. For a summary, see *RTC*, 213–14; and *Répertoire*, 106–7.

26. For the big payoff, I draw on this fantastic cold open from "The Boys in the Bar" (*Cheers*, 1983): https://www.youtube.com/watch?v=Km8n48oAJmo (accessed 1 June 2018).

27. What a pair! Stained or unstained "britches" or *brayes* (2: 63) will reappear in #11, *Slick Brother Willy*, and #12, *Immaculate Deception* (*haut de chausse*). Compare with a report by Philippe de Vigneulles in his *Chronique* (4: 99) that, in 1511, an unscrupulous German salesgirl had filled her pots of butter with "old breeches full of shit" (*dez vielle braye toutte brenoize*); see my "Theater Makes History," 1006.

28. And, to me, this is the final payoff (2: 63): despite the Alewife's earlier proto-Clintonesque language, her husband isn't dead at all!

29. This is one of the shorter *envois*: *Je m'y en vois; adieu, vous dy, / Et prenez en gré, je vous prie / Adieu, toute la compagnie* (2: 63).

Play 11. *Slick Brother Willy*

1. Excellent initiations to the *ars praedicandi* include Wenzel, *Art of Preaching*; and Murphy, *Three Medieval Rhetorical Arts*.

2. The fabliau of "The Franciscan's Breeches" ("Les Braies au Cordelier") relates similar events. On the tale's legacy from ancient Greek comedy to Poggio Bracciolini (1380–1459), see Tissier's extensive comparison (*RF*, 6: 191–201). To get a sense of what *braies* looked like, see this fourteenth-century pair from the Catalonia Love Breviary: https://commons.wikimedia.org/wiki/File:Braies_14th_century.jpg; or this whole collection here: http://postej-stew.dk/2016/11/medieval-mens-underwear/ (both accessed 12 September 2021).

3. We've met, e.g., William-the-Geek (Guillaume) in *At Cross Purposes* (*FF*, #7); Willy-the-Valet (Guillot) in *The Shithouse* (*HD*, #2); Will (Guillemin) in *Pots and Scams* (*HD*, #3); and the Wilhelminas of the *Farce of the Fart* (*FF*, #1), *Cooch E. Whippet* (*FF*, #11), and, of course, the *Pathelin*.

4. Here is some of the sermon (1: 305–7; my emphasis), which I've translated into both prose and verse. The added length is in keeping with Willy's lopsided dominance of the play; but feel free to delete one or the other.

> *Original Middle French*
> *Foullando in calibistris,*
> *Intravit per boucham ventris*
> *Bidauldus, purgando renés.*
> *Noble assistence, retenez*
> *Ces mots pleins de devotion;*
> *C'est touchant l'incarnation*
> *De l'ymage de la brayette,*
> *Qui entre, corps, aureille et teste,*
> *Au precieulx ventre des dames.*

Si demandez entre vos, femmes:
"Or ça, beau père, quo modo?"
Le texte dict que, foullando,
En foullant, et faisant zic zac,
Le gallant se trouve au bissac.
Entendez-vous bien, mes fillettes?
S'on s'encroue sur vos mamelettes,
Et qu'on vous chatouille le bas,
N'en sonnez mot, ce sont esbas,
Et n'en dictes rien à vos mères.
De quoy serviroient vos aumoyres,
Se ne vouliez bouter dedans?
Se vous couchez tousjours à dens,
Jamais n'aurez les culz meurtris,
Foullando in calibistris. . . .
Mes dames, je vous recommande
Le pauvre frère Guillebert.
Se l'une de vous me demande
De fourbir un poy son haubert,
Approchez, car g'y suis expert.
Plusieurs harnois ay estrenés,
Bidauldus purgando renes.

5. Here is Willy's next set-piece (1: 309): *Ma dame, ayez de moy mercy, / Ou mourir me fault avant aage, / Mon las cueur vous baille en ostage; / Plaise vous le mettre à son aise. / Je vous dis en foy de langaige / Ce qui me tient en grant mesaise.* See also *SFQS*, note 57.

6. *S'une foys je suis sur mes oeufz, / Je bausmeray sur le tetin* (1: 310): "walking on eggshells" takes on new meaning in that "protecting one's eggs" is "protecting one's balls"; plus the precious balm released on the tits is sperm (*SFQS*, notes 7, 60–62). I guess that's one way of following the advice about avoiding pregnancy. Philipot preferred the militaristic *haumer* (*RF*, 6: 223–24n), which is by no means incompatible, e.g., with the later *combatu* (1: 312): "banging the cunt"? (*SFQS*, notes 76 and 77).

7. Here's that rhyme of *purgatoire* and *suppositoire* (1: 311; above, § "Language"). Also present: the infamous enema, the *clystère barbarin*, from *Playing Doctor* (*FF*, 443n), so called because it's "barbaric" and "made with rhu*barb*" (*RF*, 6: 226n).

8. The spelling of "starvation" or "keeping someone waiting" (from *affamer*) is clearly gendered for the eye as *affemmement* (1: 311); see also *RF*, 6: 227n; and *SFQS*, note 72.

9. *Mourir de soif emprès le puis* (1: 312) channels one of Villon's most celebrated verses. See, e.g., Galway Kinnell's translation of the "Ballade du Concours de Blois," http://www.tau.ac.il/~tsurxx/Blois/Blois.html (accessed 14 November 2014).

10. Or Willy could sing himself to sleep instead. For Martin, this soliloquy takes place in the street; but, either way, it's a skillful way of marking the chronological transition from one day to the next (*SFQS*, note 86).

11. *Hé, gentil tétin,* [or *matin*] / *Que tant tu me tiens en l'oreille. / Pour une qui* s'appareille, / *Ung vray chef-d'oeuvre de nature, / Mon corps veulx mettre à l'aventure; / A les sangler pour la pareille / Mon corps et membres* j'appareille, / *N'escondire pas créature. / Pour une, et ce.* [*qui s'appareille,*] / *Si son mary dort ou veille, / Mais que accès j'aye à la figure, / Je veulx que l'on me defigure / Se point un grain je m'esmerveille / Pour une.* [*qui s'appareille*] (1: 313; my emphasis). At fourteen lines, this could almost be a sonnet but, in *RBM*, it's a *rondeau* (fol. 2; 1: 313). My reading diverges from those of Martin and Tissier. The former thinks that Willy is hinting at continued flirtations with other women (*SFQS*, notes 86–94); the latter, that Willy is fixing *himself* up for *Blanche* (*RF*, 6: 231n–32n). I find the primping more reciprocal. One might also add, as a transition: "Get ready 'cause here I come!"©

12. Tissier thinks that Marvin slept in his clothes (*FFMA*, 2: 246).

13. This is where Tissier stunningly suggests that Willy is caressing his willy (1: 316; *FFMA*, 2: 249; above, § "Sets and Staging"). Physically, Willy is *à bazac* or *basac*—"laid out" or "destroyed"; so, it makes sense to call on Saint Fermin, the first archbishop of Amiens (*RF*, 6: 239n). He was also known as *Saint Frémin l'accroupi*, "the squatter," i.e., Willy's current position. And a Frenchman scrunched up like a frog? *Quelle coincidence*!

14. Technically, it's Saint Valéry, to whom the Church of Meullers is consecrated. Is that a wink at the play's signature (*SFQS*, note 126)? I've gone with a more recognizable saint associated with coupling.

15. A tip of the hat, of course, to Villon's "Ballade des Pendus"; see, e.g., Kinnell's translation (*Poems*, 25–156) and Craig Bertelot's at http://medieval.ucdavis.edu/20C/Villon2.html (accessed 16 December 2018).

16. Some excerpts now from Willy's Villonesque Will (*ATF*, 1: 318–19; my emphasis):

Original Middle French
Je suis mort si je me remue.
J'ay desjà le cul descouvert.
Et pour ce, frère Guillebert,
Mourras-tu si piteusement?
Deux motz feray de testament.

Devant que laisser m'accueillir
Et qu'on m'ait couppé le couiller,
A Cupido, dieu d'amourettes,
Je laisse mon ame à pourveoir,
Pour la mettre avec des fillettes;
(Car) j'ay esté bien aise à les veoir.

La dame aura mon coeur, pour veoir,
Pour qui me fault icy perir:
Frère Guillebert, te fault-il mourir?

. . . Je prye à tous les bons yvrongnes,
Se frère Guillebert est trespassé,
Qu'ilz disent en lavant leurs trongnes,
J'ay bien gardé le temps passé
Mon gentil gosier de sotir:
Frère Guillebert, te fault-il mourir?

17. *Fourbir les custodi nos* (1: 318): this rub-a-dub-dub of lady parts against precious relics—a fertility ritual for women struggling to conceive (*SFQS*, note 149)—foreshadows the play's closing gestures.

18. Here's part of Brother Willy's parody of last rites—kitchen Latin and all—which would doubtless have been instantly recognizable (see also *SFQS*, note 159; *RF*, 5: 245–46n). *In manus tuas, Domine, / Nisi quia domine ne / Tedet spiritus et pelli / Confiteor deo celi / Ut queant quod chorus vatum . . . / Hé, te perday-je, beau baston? / . . . Hé, Dieu, comme tu me gravonnes; / Adieu, gentilz tesniers pelus* (1: 319–20).

19. At 1: 320, the Latinate *c'est ille* ("here it is") and, a bit later, *ce sont ille* ("here they are") are consistent with a pair of two, which goes for the *bissac*, the britches, the drawers, the underwear, etc.

20. In light of Marvin's inadequacy, *baiser* is likely "to kiss" (1: 320).

21. *Par Dieu, (si) ne m'y rairez-vous plus, / Ronge cul ravoir sainct Françoys* (1: 321): we are invited sacrilegiously to envision cold, naked butt cheeks and a nasty castration that bloodies Willy's behind (see *SFQS*, note 178). Ouch. For Tissier, Willy means "you're really not gonna let me get back to the monastery" (*RF*, 6: 248n–49n).

22. For *Je croy qu'il ne m'y trouvera point* (1: 321), Martin understands Willy to be muttering that nearsighted Marvin won't recognize him (*SFQS*, notes 181 and 182). This is where Tissier makes his decorous suggestion that Willy should *hide* his member with his hands (*FFMA*, 2: 252).

23. Believe it or not, the Middle French terms for "cuckold" and "hoo-hoo" (*huihot* or *wihot*) are homonyms: *Vous faictes fourbir le huihot / Et on m'appellera huihot* (1: 323); see also *SFQS*, notes 201 and 202; *RF*, 6: 255n. And, yes: Marvin really does invoke the Devil four times but, in contradistinction to *Cooch E. Whippet* (*FF*, #11), the Evil One does not show up.

24. The *RBM* calls for Blanche to deliver this line (fol. 5), which is probably an error. But it would work if you had her watch and eavesdrop from a distance.

25. *Encor, s'on ne nous eust congneues, / Jamais nous ne les eussions eues* (1: 325; *SFQS*, note 215). There is some ambiguity in that the final "e" of *congneues* would not have been heard when spoken. I'm not sure that Agnes would say that to Marvin, but it could be an aside.

26. Agnes is talking about the britches—*les chausses*—but the text reads *les choses* (1: 326), a different thingy!

27. *Sans plus de plaict* has a juridical ring (1: 326–27). Martin further believes that, while kissing the drawers would affect one's breath (*l'aleine*), the text should read *la laine*, i.e., "pubic hair" (*SFQS*, notes 230 and 231).

28. At 1: 327, Martin understands that, à la *Bro Job* (#7), Blanche is asking for a nice big shot (*SFQS*, note 232), a metonymic confusion, to be sure.

29. *Que chascun voyse à son degré. / Adieu, Messieurs, prenez en gré* (1: 327): for Martin, the *envoi* calls for both a procession and an acceptance of a wife's adultery (*SFQS*, notes 233 and 234). I hear an invitation that spectators kiss the relic and that they literally watch their "steps" (*degrés*) upon exiting; see also *Getting Off on the Wrong Foot* (*FF*, 453–54n).

30. For oh-so obvious reasons, one could go with "Let's Hear It for the Boy[s]"© or "The Mess-Around."©

Play 12. *Immaculate Deception*

1. Sister Goody, *Soeur de bon Coeur*, is "The Second Nun"; but in the original cast list (*RLV*, 204v) her name appears before that of "The First Nun," Sister Crybaby (*Soeur Esplouree*). I've put the cast in the proper order.

2. There is an error in the digitized *RFMSJ*, vol. 2 at https://books.google.com/books?id=g1hXAAAAcAAJ&printsec=frontcover&source=gbs_book_other_versions_r&cad=3#v=onepage&q&f=false (accessed 26 January 2021). It breaks up our play on p. 17, with pp. 18–30 appearing at the end of the volume.

3. For Streisand's rendition of "His Love Makes Me Beautiful,"© see https://www.youtube.com/watch?v=rIaHWp5DlFY (accessed 27 January 2021).

4. On the *miserere* and the seal of the confessional, see, e.g., the *Catholic Encyclopedia*: http://www.newadvent.org/cathen/10352c.htm and http://www.newadvent.org/cathen/13649b.htm (accessed 27 January 2021).

5. On *chanter* vs. *dire* and *cantare* vs. *dicere*, see Treitler's groundbreaking "Oral, Written, and Literate Process"; and Jonsson and Treitler, "Medieval Music and Language."

6. See also *FFMA*, 4: 315n; *SFQS*, note 46; Brown, *MFST*, 281; and, on the song's antisemitic and anti-Protestant connotations, Draughon and Knapp, "Gustav Mahler." In *SFQS*, Martin gives us a peek at the Godard score of "Dormez-vous, fillettes?" here: https://sottiesetfarces.files.wordpress.com/2017/08/robert-godard.png (accessed 13 April 2021).

7. For more on these convent sites, see *RF*, 11: 266n–67n, 279n; *SFQS*, notes 21 and 68; plus this helpful resource: http://www.monasticwales.org/glossary.php (accessed 27 January 2021).

8. I refer to "Maria"© or "Concrete and Clay":© https://www.youtube.com/watch?v=VGhSGpocyZo (accessed 27 January 2021).

9. See, e.g., *SFQS*, note 45; *RF*, 11: 249–50, 268–69n; and Rey-Flaud, *La Farce*, 134.

10. See, e.g., this Polish nun's coif (1939), courtesy of Wikipedia: https://en.wikipedia.org/wiki/Cornette (accessed 13 April 2021).

11. While "Pickin' Up the Pieces"© is not listed in the BMI repertory, multiple other titles by Furay are.

12. In addition to "Concrete and Clay"© and "Maria,"© one could try, for either the opening or closing numbers, "Gimme That Old Time Religion,"© "Papa, Don't Preach,"© "Girls Just Want to Have Fun,"© "That's the Way I Like It," or "Fat-Bottomed Girls"!©

13. At 2: 8, the scholastic *a quia*, "to be reduced to silence," is nothing if not tongue in cheek given Bunny's upcoming take on the sisterly vow of silence.

14. Martin thinks that by *par envye* (2: 13), Sister Crybaby means "jealousy," "envy," or "spite" (*SFQS*, note 26); but, to my eye, it could also read *par enuye* (*RLV*, 207r), as in the *ennui* ("distress" or "anger") befitting her emotional state.

15. *Nostre bon pere confesseur / En aura le miserere* (2: 14): instead of the *miserere*, I've offered biblical language consistent with prayer (*RF*, 11: 268n) and the "misericord," the chamber where discipline is administered (above, § "Sets and Staging"). Martin understands the line to mean that Brother Hard-On will have heard their prayer (*SFQS*, note 27).

16. Alternatively, Sisters Goody and Frisky could accompany her but remain on their knees, eyes averted, and in silence throughout Scene 2.

17. Tissier posits that *devers nous* (2: 14) is the royal "we," as befits Mother Superior's station (*RF*, 11: 269n). For Martin, it's a Freudian slip in that she is not alone (*SFQS*, note 30).

18. For Tissier, *faire la resserée* (2: 16) denotes Sister Bunny's refusal to engage in sex (*RF*, 11: 271n); but Martin sees an allusion to a special astringent for deflowered women. Its tightening effects re-create the impression of virginity on the wedding night (*SFQS*, note 35). The pharmaceutical miracle of Saint Muffie (above, #10, *The Pardoners' Tales*, note 7)?

19. As in #4, *Drama Queens* (note 50), I imagine the inaudibility routines of *SNL* or *Legally Blonde*.

20. Her response is limited to one word—*ficatores* (2: 16)—which requires much teasing out in English. For Martin, it's the rub-a-dub-dub *fricatores* of lesbian sex (*SFQS*, note 36); whereas Tissier sees Latinate "fashioning" and an almost *foie-gras*-like goose-stuffing (*RF*, 11: 271n). "Goosing," though, doesn't seem to be Bunny's anti-anal specialty.

21. *Voz huys sont ils tous fermés? / Filletes, vous dormés, / Quant pour vous sont consommés, / [Ouvrez-les moi si m'aimez] / Dormés vous filletes? / Filletes, vous dormés. / [Dormez-vous seulettes?]* Mes sens d'amours enflamméz *[Mais, sans amour enflamés], / Dormés-vous, filletes? / Filletes vous dormés / [Dormez-vous seulettes?]* (2: 18; my emphasis). I've included additional lyrics from Godard's contemporaneous score (above, § "Language"); and adapted Tissier's take that the gentlemen callers are on fire for the sleeping nuns (*RF*, 11: 274n).

22. *Venite et aprochantes, Madamus, agenouillare / Quia voz fecit mouillare / Le boudin? il est bon à voir* (2: 18). Tissier prefers *bedaine* to *boudin*—the "belly" to the "sausage" (*RF*, 11: 275n)—but the one doesn't rule out the other: all the more so in that

Martin recalls that *Saint Boudin* is often paired with *Sainte Fente* or Saint Muffie (*SFQS*, note 51).

23. The number five hundred—*cinq cens* (2: 20)—is a homonym for the five senses, *les cinq sens*, also the subject of *Les Cinq sens de l'homme* (*RBM*, #61; *ATF*, 3: 300–324).

24. In the *Tiers Livre*, the tale turns toward violent rape and incest: "it had not been by her consent: it had been by violence and by the strength of Friar Stickitinstiff" (*CWFR*, 312–13; *RF*, 11: 239–47).

25. Per Tissier, this is a parody (2: 26) of the *ne respicas* prayer preceding communion (*RF*, 11: 284n); and, per Martin, it's an invocation of Paul to Romans 2: 3 (*SFQS*, note 83).

26. Mother Superior switches to *tu* and also calls Sister Bunny *rusée* (2: 26), which recalls one of the title characters of Coquillart's mock trial, the *Plaidoyé d'entre La Simple et la Rusée* (see, e.g., *ROMD*, 233–43).

27. *Ne jugés poinct! / Les jugemens sont odieulx / Au seigneur, qui est Dieu des Dyeulx. / Vous le sçavés de poinct en poinct. / Paul, glorieulx apostre sainct, / Dict que celuy n'aura refuge / D'excuse qui sera tasché / Et que luy mesme il se juge / S'il est subject à tel pesché* (2: 26–27). This speech—Martin's suspected interpolation (*SFQS*, note 88)—reprises Matthew 7:1 and Romans 2:1; see also *RF*, 11: 285n.

28. This macaronic statement is almost incomprehensible: *Tu fessisti sicut et nos, / Par quoy absolvo te gratis, / In pecata nunc dimitis / In corbennem, comme au passé; / Plus oultre, vade in passé* (2: 29–30). *Fessisti* seems to be a conjugation of *faire*; but it's clearly a pun on *Fessue* too. As a literal translation, Tissier proposes (and Martin largely agrees): "You have done as we all have done. I absolve you without [requiring you to perform] penance for your sins. And now, fill your baskets! Continue to enjoy [sex or orgasms] (*joir*) as in the past. Now go in peace. Thank you" (*RF*, 11: 288–89n; *SFQS*, notes 97–101). At issue: the meaning of *gratis*, seemingly "dispensed from penance," and *incorbennem*, which seems to invoke both a "basket" and a "good heart." For Martin, the latter would mean *dans un cœur bon*, from *in cor bonum et devotum*.

29. Most of the *envoi* is in pentameter: *Conclusion: Je trouve erreur caché, / Que cestuy la veult un pesché reprendre / Du quel il est taché & empesché, / Et par lequel enfin on le peult prendre, / Vous le pouvez en ce lieu cy comprendre. / La faulte en est à voz deulx apperceue, / Tesmoing l'abeesse aveques seur Fesue. / En prenant congé de ce lieu, / Une chanson pour dire adieu* (2: 30). I know, I know: the drafting of *Romeo and Juliet* might not have begun until 1591.

30. And what could be more fitting than a parodic finale à la *Full Monty*? "You can leave your hat on!"© Unless you prefer "Sisters Are Doin' It for Themselves."©

Appendix

1. From multiple songs registered to Fleetwood Mac, "Go Your Own Way" is listed in neither the ASCAP nor the BMI repertories. The best place to start might well be https://globalmusicrights.com/artist/1412025.

2. You can see and hear the Heaven Sent perfume jingle, produced in the 1960s for Helena Rubinstein, here: https://www.youtube.com/watch?v=Gym7LD47k98 (accessed 3 July 2019). As of this writing, it was not listed in any copyright registry that I could locate.

3. While "If I Only Had a Brain" is not listed in the ASCAP repertory, multiple other titles are (such as "Over the Rainbow").

4. While "I'll Get You" has no BMI Work #, the vast majority of Beatles songs appear in the BMI registry.

5. You might be more familiar with the copyrighted gospel arrangement by Edwin Hawkins, ASCAP Work ID: 150028565.

6. While "Pickin' Up the Pieces" is not listed in the BMI repertory, multiple other titles by Furay are.

7. The Alka-Seltzer jingle is listed in the ASCAP registry along with many other Dawes titles, in this instance, with a request to contact them for more information (accessed 3 July 2019).

Bibliography

Editions of French Farces

Le Caquet des bonnes chambrières. Pièce #6, *Poésies des XVe et XVIe siècles*. N.p. [Ed. Francisque Michel.] Paris: Crapelet, 1830.

Le Caquet des bonnes chambrières, déclairant aulcunes finesses . . . In *Recueil de poésies françoises*, vol. 5, ed. Montaiglon, 71–83.

Caron, Pierre Siméon. *Collection de différents ouvrages anciens, poésies et facéties*. 11 vols. Paris, 1798–1806.

Cohen, Gustave, ed. *Recueil de farces françaises inédites du XVe siècle*. Cambridge, Mass.: Mediaeval Academy of America, 1949. [*RC*]

Droz, Eugénie, ed. *Le Recueil Trepperel: Les Sotties*. Geneva: Droz, 1935. [*RTLS*]

Droz, Eugénie, and Halina Lewicka. *Le Recueil Trepperel: Les Farces*. Travaux d'Humanisme et Renaissance, 45. Geneva: Droz, 1961. [*RTLF*]

Faivre, Bernard, ed. and trans. *Les Farces: Moyen Âge et Renaissance*. 2 vols. Vol. 1: *La Guerre des sexes*; vol. 2: *Dupés et trompeurs*. Paris: Imprimerie Nationale, 1997–99.

La Farce de Pathelin. See *Pathelin*.

La Farce des Trois commères. Ed. Paul Meyer, "La Farce des Trois Commères." *Romania* 10 (1881): 433–42.

Farce d'un Pardonneur, d'un Triacleur et d'une Tavernière (*Farce Nouvelle tresbonne et fort joyeuse à trois personnages d'un Pardonneur, d'un Triacleur et d'une Tavernière*). Ed. and trans. Ernest Fièvre and Paul Fièvre. http://www.theatre-classique.fr/pages/programmes/edition.php?t=../documents/ANONYME_PARDONNEUR.xml (accessed 10 February 2018).

Fournier, Édouard, ed. *Le Théâtre français avant la Renaissance*. 1872; rpt. New York: Burt Franklin, 1965. [*TFR*]

———. *Variétés historiques et littéraires, recueil de pièces volantes, rares et curieuses*. 10 vols. Paris: P. Jannet, 1855.

Jacob, [Paul Lecroix]. *Recueil de farces, soties et moralités du quinzième siècle*. Paris: Delahays, 1859.

Koopmans, Jelle, ed. *Le Recueil de Florence: 53 farces imprimées à Paris vers 1515*. Orléans: Paradigme, 2011. [*RFlorence*]

———, ed. *Recueil de sermons joyeux: édition critique avec introduction, notes et glossaire.* Geneva: Droz, 1988. [*RSJ*]

Le Roux de Lincy, Antoine, and Francisque Michel, eds. *Recueil de farces, moralités et sermons joyeux, publiés d'après le manuscrit de la Bibliothèque royale.* 4 vols. Paris: Téchener, 1837; rpt. Geneva: Slatkine, 1977. [*RFMSJ*]

Mabille, Émile, ed. *Choix de farces, soties et moralités des XV*[e] *et XVI*[e] *siècles, recueillies sur les manuscrits originaux.* 2 vols. Nice: J. Gay & Fils, 1873–93; rpt. Geneva: Slatkine, 1970. [*CFSM*]

Manuscrit La Vallière (recueil de farces, moralités et sermons joyeux): Fac-similé intégral du manuscrit 24314 [i.e.: 24341] de la Bibliothèque nationale de Paris. Geneva: Slatkine, 1972. [*RLV*]

[Martin, Thierry, ed.] *Sotties et Farces du XV*[e] *et du XVI*[e] *siècle.* Online edition published under the pseudonym of "Maître Antitus." https://sottiesetfarces.wordpress.com/ (accessed 14 February 2017). [*SFQS*]

Montaiglon, Anatole de, ed. *Recueil de poésies françoises des XV*[e] *et XVI*[e] *siècles: Morales, facétieuses, historiques.* Vol. 5 of 13. Paris: Jannet, 1856. [*RPF*]

Montaiglon, Anatole de, and Gaston Raynaud. *Recueil général et complet des fabliaux des XIII*[e] *et XIV*[e] *siècles.* 6 vols. 1872–90; rpt. Geneva: Slatkine, 1973; and New York: Burt Franklin, n.d. [*RGCF*]

[*Pathelin*]. *La Farce de Pathelin.* In *"La Farce de Pathelin" et autres pièces homosexuelles: Edition critique bilingue,* ed. Thierry Martin, 59–202. Montpellier: GayKitschCamp, 2011.

———. *Maistre Pierre Pathelin, farce du XV*[e] *siècle.* Ed. Richard T. Holbrook. Paris: Champion, 1937.

Picot, Emile, ed. *Recueil Général des Sotties.* 3 vols. Paris: Firmin Didot, 1902–12. [*RGS*]

Poésies des XVe *et XVI*[e] *siècles, publiées d'après les éditions gothiques et des manuscrits.* Paris: Silvestre, 1830–32.

Recueil du British Museum: Fac-similé des 64 pièces de l'original. Introd. Halina Lewicka. Geneva: Slatkine, 1970. [*RBM*]

Le Recueil Trepperel. See also Droz, Eugénie.

Rousse, Michel, ed. *Le Théâtre des farces en France au Moyen Âge.* 5 vols. Unpublished dissertation/*thèse d'état.* University of Rennes 2 1983. [*TFFMA*]

Tissier, André, trans. *Farces françaises de la fin du Moyen Âge.* 4 vols. Geneva: Droz, 1999. [*FFMA*]

———, ed. *Recueil de farces (1450–1550).* 13 vols. Geneva: Droz, 1986–2000. [*RF*]

Viollet-le-Duc, M., ed. *Ancien Théâtre françois.* 10 vols. Paris: P. Jannet, 1854–57. [*ATF*]

Medieval Farces in English Translation

Axton, Richard, and John Stevens, trans. *Medieval French Plays.* Oxford: Basil Blackwell, 1971. [*MFP*]

Blow in the Box. In *Medieval Dutch Drama*, trans. Prins, 101–11.

Boucquey, Thierry, trans. *Six Medieval French Farces*. Lewiston, N.Y.: Edwin Mellen, 1999. [*SMFF*]

The Chicken Pie and the Chocolate Cake [*Le Pâté et la Tarte*]. In Mandel, *FCMF*, 151–58.

Enders, Jody, ed. and trans. *"The Farce of the Fart" and Other Ribaldries: Twelve Medieval French Plays in Modern English*. The Middle Ages Series. Philadelphia: University of Pennsylvania Press, 2011. [*FF*]

———. *Holy Deadlock and Further Ribaldries: Another Dozen Medieval French Plays in Modern English*. The Middle Ages Series. Philadelphia: University of Pennsylvania Press, 2017. [*HD*]

Halle, Adam de la. *The Play of Robin and Marion*. In Mandel, *FCMF*, 77–104.

Mandel, Oscar, trans. *Five Comedies of Medieval France*. 1970; rpt. Boston: University Press of America, 1982. [*FCMF*]

[*Pathelin*]. *The Farce of Master Pierre Pathelin*. Trans. Alan E. Knight. In Donald Maddox, *Semiotics of Deceit: The Pathelin Era*, 173–99. Lewisburg, Pa.: Bucknell University Press, 1984.

———. *Peter Quill's Shenanigans*. Trans. Mandel, *FCMF*, 105–38.

Prins, Johanna, ed. and trans. *Medieval Dutch Drama: Four Secular Plays and Four Farces from the Van Hulthem Manuscript*. Asheville, N.C.: Pegasus, 1999.

The Second Shepherd's Play. In *"Everyman" and Other Miracle and Morality Plays*, ed. Candace Ward, 12–35. New York: Dover Thrift Editions, 1995.

The Washtub [*La Farce du Cuvier*]. In Mandel, *FCMF*, 143–50.

Other Primary Sources

Aristotle. *De poetica liber Graece et Latine*. Ed. T. C. Harles. Leipzig: Siegfried Lebrecht Crusius, 1780.

———. *Poetics*. Ed. and trans. W. Hamilton Fyfe. In *Aristotle, "The Poetics"; Longinus, "On the Sublime"; Demetrius, "On Style,"* 1–118. Loeb Classical Library. 1927; rpt. Cambridge, Mass.: Harvard University Press, 1946.

Augustine of Hippo. *Confessions*. Ed. and trans. William Watts. 2 vols. Loeb Classical Library. 1912; rpt. Cambridge, Mass.: Harvard University Press, 1950–51.

———. *The Rule of Saint Augustine*. Ed. Tarsicius J. Van Bavel. Trans. Raymond Canning. New York: Image Books, 1986.

Beck, Jonathan, ed. *Théâtre et propagande aux débuts de la Réforme: Six pièces polémiques du Recueil La Vallière*. Geneva: Slatkine, 1986.

Bevington, David, ed. *Medieval Drama*. Boston: Houghton Mifflin, 1975. [*MD*]

Bideaux, Michel, ed. *Martin en sa gloire: Un livre d'ânes*. Paris: Garnier, 2010.

Bidler, Rose M. *Dictionnaire érotique: Ancien français, Moyen français, Renaissance*. Erotica Vetera: À la recherche d'un langage perdu. Montreal: CERES, 2002.

Boccaccio, Giovanni. *The Decameron*. Trans. Wayne A. Rebhorn. New York: W. W. Norton, 2013.

Chrétien de Troyes. *The Knight of the Cart*. In *The Complete Romances of Chrétien de Troyes*, trans. David Staines, 170–256. Bloomington: Indiana University Press, 1990.

La Chronique de Metz de Jacomin Husson, 1200–1525. Publié d'après le manuscrit autographe de Copenhague et celui de Paris. Ed. H. Michelant. Metz: Rousseau-Pallez, 1870.

Cornuälle, Heldris de. *Le Roman de Silence*. Trans. Regina Psaki. New York: Garland, 1991.

———. *Silence, a Thirteenth-Century Romance*. Trans. Sarah Roche-Mahdi. East Lansing, Mich.: Colleagues Press, 1992.

Diderot, Denis, and Jean le Rond D'Alembert. *Encyclopédie ou Dictionnaire raisonné des sciences, des arts et des métiers*. Vol. 5. Paris, 1767. Partially published in English as *The Encyclopedia of Diderot & d'Alembert: Collaborative Translation Project*. Ann Arbor: Michigan Publishing, University of Michigan Library, 2002–. http://quod.lib.umich.edu/d/did/ (accessed 21 June 2014).

The Distaff Gospels: A First Modern English Edition of "Les Évangiles des quenouilles." Ed. Madeleine Jeay and Kathleen Garay. Peterborough, Ont.: Broadview Press, 2006.

Dubin, Nathaniel E., ed. and trans. *The Fabliaux: A New Verse Translation*. New York: Liveright [W. W. Norton], 2013.

Duneton, Claude. *La Puce à l'oreille: Anthologie des expressions populaires avec leur origine*. Paris: Stock, 1978.

Eloy D'Amerval. *Le Livre de la Deablerie*. Ed. Robert Deschaux and Bernard Charrier. Geneva: Droz, 1991.

Les Évangiles des quenouilles. [Attributed to Fouquart de Cambray, Antoine du Val, and Jean d'Arras.] 1480; rpt. Paris: Jannet, 1855.

———. Ed. Madeleine Jeay. Paris: J. Vrin and Montreal: University of Montreal Press, 1985.

Everyman. In *"Everyman" and Other Miracle and Morality Plays*, ed. Candace Ward, 36–59. New York: Dover Thrift Editions, 1995.

Fabliaux et contes du Moyen Age. Ed. and introd. G. Chappon and Nelly Caullot. Paris: Hatier, 1967.

The Fifteen Joys of Marriage [*Les .XV. Joies de mariage*]. Trans. Brent A. Pitts. New York: Peter Lang, 1985.

Godefroy, Frédéric. *Dictionnaire de l'ancienne langue française et de tous ses dialectes du IXe au XVe siècle*. 10 vols. 1881–1902; rpt. Vaduz, Liechtenstein: Kraus Reprints, 1965. The 1880–95 version (8 vols.) is online at http://micmap.org/dicfro/search/dictionnaire-godefroy/ (accessed 18 October 2011).

Hassell, James W. *Middle French Proverbs, Sentences, and Proverbial Phrases*. Toronto: PIMS, 1982.

Hindley, Alan, Frederick W. Langley, and Brian J. Levy. *Old French–English Dictionary.* Cambridge: Cambridge University Press, 2000.

Hrotsvitha of Gandersheim. [*Paphnutius.*] *The Conversion of the Harlot Thais.* In *The Plays of Hrotsvit of Gandersheim,* ed. and trans. Katharina Wilson, 93–122. Garland Library of Medieval Literatures, 62, Series B. New York: Garland, 1989.

Isidore of Seville. *The "Etymologies" of Isidore of Seville.* Trans. Stephen A. Barney, W. J. Lewis, J. A. Beach, and Oliver Berghof. Cambridge: Cambridge University Press, 2006.

———. *Isidore of Seville's Etymologies: The Complete English Translation of Isidori Hispalensis Episcopi, "Etymologiarum sive Originum," Libri XX.* Trans. Priscilla Throop. 2 vols. Charlotte, Vt.: MedievalMS, 2005.

———. *Isidori Hispalensis Episcopi, "Etymologiarum sive Originum," Libri XX.* Ed. W. M. Lindsay. 2 vols. 1911; rpt. London: Oxford, 1962.

Izzard, Eddie. *Dress to Kill.* DVD. Ella Communications Ltd., 1999.

Jean d'Arras. *Melusine, or, The Noble History of Lusignan.* Ed. Donald Maddox and Sara Sturm-Maddox. University Park: Pennsylvania State University Press, 2012.

Jean de Meun [and Guillaume de Lorris]. *Le Roman de la Rose.* Ed. Daniel Poirion. Paris: Garnier-Flammarion, 1974.

———. *The Romance of the Rose: A New Translation.* By Guillaume de Lorris and Jean de Meun. Trans. Frances Horgan. Oxford: Oxford University Press, 1994.

Klinck, Anne L., ed. *Anthology of Ancient and Medieval Woman's Song.* New York: Palgrave Macmillan, 2004.

La Fontaine, Jean de. *The Complete Fables of Jean de La Fontaine.* Trans. Norman R. Shapiro. Urbana: University of Illinois Press, 2007.

Landes, Louis de. [Auguste Scheler?] *Glossaire érotique de la langue française depuis ses origines jusqu'à nos jours.* Brussels, 1861.

Littré, Emile. *Dictionnaire de la langue française.* 1863–77. http://littre.reverso.net/dictionnaire-francais/ (accessed 15 December 2015).

Marie de France. *The Lais of Marie de France.* Trans. Robert Hanning and Joan Ferrante. 1978; rpt. Durham, N.C.: Labyrinth Press, 1982.

Merceron, Jacques E. *Dictionnaire thématique et géographique des saints imaginaires, facétieux et substitués en France et en Belgique francophone du moyen-âge à nos jours: Traditions & dévotions.* Paris: Seuil, 2002. [*DSI*]

Molière, Jean-Baptiste Poquelin de. *Tartuffe.* Trans. Richard Wilbur. New York: Harcourt, 1963.

Molinet, Jean. *Les Pronostications joyeuses.* Ed. Rachel Koopmans. Geneva: Droz, 1998.

Moralité à sys personnages. [*Hérésie, frère Simonie, Force, Scandale, Procès, et l'Eglise.*] Ed. Jonathan Beck. In *Théâtre et propagande aux débuts de la Réforme: Six pièces polémiques du Recueil La Vallière,* 179–203. Geneva: Slatkine, 1986.

Murphy, James J., ed. *Three Medieval Rhetorical Arts.* Berkeley: University of California Press, 1971.

Navarre, Marguerite de Navarre. *The Heptameron of Margaret, Queen of Navarre*. Trans. Walter K. Kelly. [London: Bohn, 1864.] http://digital.library.upenn.edu/women/navarre/heptameron/heptameron.html (accessed 17 March 2016).

The New Schaff-Herzog Encyclopedia of Religious Knowledge. Vol. 2. Ed. George W. Gilmore, Charles Colebrook Sherman, Samuel Macauley Jackson, Albert Hauck, Philip Schaff, and J. J. Herzog. New York: Funk and Wagnalls, 1908. Revised edition by Lefferts Augustine Loetscher and Samuel Macauley Jackson as *Twentieth Century Encyclopedia of Religious Knowledge: An Extension of The New Schaff-Herzog Encyclopedia of Religious Knowledge*. Grand Rapids, Mich.: Baker, 1955.

Noah's Flood. In *"Everyman" and Other Miracle and Morality Plays*, ed. Candace Ward, 1–11. New York: Dover Thrift Editions, 1995.

Noomen, Willem, and Nico van den Boogaard, eds. *Nouveau recueil complet des fabliaux*. Vols. 1–2 of 5. Assen: Van Gorcum, 1983–84.

Paetow, Louis John, ed. and trans. *Two Medieval Satires on the University of Paris: "La Bataille des vii ars" d'Henri d'Andeli and the "Morale Scolarium" of John of Garland*. Berkeley: University of California Press, 1927.

Parfaict, François, and Claude Parfaict. *Histoire du théâtre françois depuis son origine jusqu'à présent, avec la vie des plus célébres poëtes dramatiques, un catalogue exact de leurs piéces, & des notes historiques et critiques*. 15 vols. Paris, 1745–49; rpt. New York: Burt Franklin, 1968. [*HTF*]

Pulci, Antonia. *Florentine Drama for Convent and Festival: Seven Sacred Plays*. Trans. James Wyatt Cook. The Other Voice. Chicago: University of Chicago Press, 1996.

Les Quinze [.XV.] Joies de mariage. See *The Fifteen Joys of Marriage*.

Rabelais, François. *The Complete Works of François Rabelais*. Trans. Donald Frame. Berkeley: University of California Press, 1991. [*CWFR*]

———. *Oeuvres complètes*. Ed. Guy Demerson. Paris: Seuil, 1973.

Redford, John. *The Play of Wit and Science*. Ed. Ben Byram-Wigfield. http://www.hoasm.org/IVM/PlayofWit.pdf (accessed 18 May 2019).

Rutebeuf. *Le Miracle de Théophile*. In *Jeux et sapience du Moyen Âge*, ed. Albert Pauphilet, 135–58. Pléaide. Paris: Gallimard, 1951. Published in translation in Axton and Stevens, *MFP*, 165–92.

Sébillet, Thomas. *Art Poétique françoys (1548)*. Ed. Félix Gaiffe. Paris: Edouard Cornély, 1910. [*APF*]

Songs of the Women Trouvères. Ed. and trans. Eglal Doss-Quinby, Joan Tasker Grimbert, Wendy Pfeffer, and Elizabeth Aubrey. New Haven, Conn.: Yale University Press, 2001.

Di Stefano, Giuseppe, ed. *Dictionnaire des Locutions en moyen français*. Bibliothèque du Moyen Français. Montreal: CERES, 1991.

Di Stefano [di Stephano], Giuseppe, and Rose M. Bidler, eds. *Toutes les herbes de la Saint Jean: Les Locutions en moyen français*. Montreal: CERES, 1992.

Tydeman, William, ed. *The Medieval European Stage, 500–1550*. Theatre in Europe: A Documentary History. Cambridge: Cambridge University Press, 2001.

[Usk, Adam.] *The Chronicle of Adam Usk, 1377–1421*. Ed. Chris Given-Wilson. Oxford: Oxford University Press, 1997.

de Vigneulles, Philippe. *La Chronique de Philippe de Vigneulles*. Ed. Charles Bruneau. 4 vols. Metz: Société d'histoire d'archéologie de la Lorraine, 1927–33.

Villon, François. "Ballade des Pendus." Ed. Louis Thuasne; trans. Craig Bertelot. http://medieval.ucdavis.edu/20C/Villon2.html (accessed 16 December 2018).

———. "Ballade du Concours de Blois." With a translation by Galway Kinnell. http://www.tau.ac.il/~tsurxx/Blois/Blois.html (accessed 14 November 2014).

———. *The Poems of François Villon*. Trans. Galway Kinnell. 1965; new edition Hanover, N.H.: University Press of New England, 1982.

Wenzel, Siegfried, ed. *The Art of Preaching: Five Medieval Texts and Translations*. Washington, D.C.: Catholic University of America Press, 2013.

Wright, Stephen K., ed. and trans. *Medieval German Drama: Four Plays in Translation*. Fairview, NC: Pegasus, 2002.

Secondary Sources

Agamben, Giorgio. *Profanations*. Trans. Jeff Fort. New York: Zone, 2007.

Andrews, Frances. *The Other Friars: The Carmelite, Augustinian, Sack and Pied Friars in the Middle Ages*. Monastic Orders. Woodbridge: Boydell, 2006.

Arden, Heather. *Fools' Plays: A Study of Satire in the Sottie*. Cambridge: Cambridge University Press, 1980.

D'Arcens, Louise. *Comic Medievalism: Laughing at the Middle Ages.* Cambridge: D. S. Brewer, 2014.

———. "Medievalist Laughter." In *Comic Medievalisms,* special issue of *postmedieval: a journal of medieval cultural studies* 5.2 (2014): 116–25.

Ashley, Kathleen. "Social Functions." In *A Cultural History of Theatre*, ed. Enders, 39–58.

Ashton, Gail, and Daniel T. Kline, eds. *Medieval Afterlives in Popular Culture*. The New Middle Ages. New York: Palgrave Macmillan, 2012.

Austin, J. L. *How to Do Things with Words*. Ed. J. O. Urmson and Marina Sbisà. 2nd ed. Cambridge, Mass.: Harvard University Press, 1978. [*HDTW*]

———. *Philosophical Papers*. Ed. J. O. Urmson and G. J. Warnock. 2nd ed. Oxford: Clarendon, 1970. [*PP*]

Bakhtin, Mikhail. *Rabelais and His World*. Trans. Hélène Iswolsky. 1965; rpt. Bloomington: Indiana University Press, 1984.

Bartsch, Shadi. "Don't Yield Ancient Literature and History to the Alt-Right." https://www.washingtonpost.com/opinions/dont-yield-ancient-history-and-literature-to-the-alt-right/2021/02/03/3632ad7a-6635-11eb-886d-5264d4ceb46d_story.html (accessed 14 April 2021).

Baudrillard, Jean. "Simulacra and Simulations." In *Selected Writings*, ed. and trans. Mark Poster, 166–84. Stanford, Calif.: Stanford University Press, 1988.

Baverstock, A. H. *The Priest as Confessor*. London: Cope and Fenwick, 1911.

Bayless, Martha. *Parody in the Middle Ages: The Latin Tradition*. Ann Arbor: University of Michigan Press, 1996.

Beam, Sara. *Laughing Matters: Farce and the Making of Absolutism in France*. Ithaca, N.Y.: Cornell University Press, 2007.

Beckwith, Sarah. *Christ's Body*. London: Routledge, 1993.

———. *Signifying God: Social Relation and Symbolic Act in the York Corpus Christi Plays*. Chicago: University of Chicago Press, 2001.

Bell, David. "Eroticizing the Rural." In *De-centring Sexualities*, ed. Phillips, Watt, and Shuttleton, 83–101.

Benston, Kimberly W. "Being There: Performance as Mise-en-Scène, Abscene, Obscene, and Other Scene." *PMLA* 107.3 (1992): 434–49.

Bergson, Henri. "Laughter." In *Comedy: "An Essay on Comedy" by George Meredith; "Laughter" by Henri Bergson*, ed. Wylie Sypher, 59–190. Garden City, N.Y.: Doubleday, 1956.

Bermel, Albert. *Farce: The Comprehensive and Definitive Account of One of the World's Funniest Art Forms*. New York: Simon and Schuster, 1982. Reprinted as *Farce: A History from Aristophanes to Woody Allen*. Carbondale: Southern Illinois University Press, 1990.

Bevis, Matthew. *Comedy*. Very Short Introductions. Oxford: Oxford University Press, 2013.

Bloch, R. Howard. *The Scandal of the Fabliaux*. Chicago: University of Chicago Press, 1986.

Boogaart, Jacques. "A Prism of Its Time: Social Functions of the Medieval Motet in Fourteenth-Century France." In *A Critical Companion to Medieval Motets*, ed. Hartt, 135–74.

Bouhaïk-Gironès, Marie. *Les Clercs de la Basoche et le théâtre comique (Paris, 1420–1550)*. Paris: Champion, 2007.

Boureau, Alain. *The Myth of Pope Joan*. Trans. Lydia G. Cochrane. Chicago: University of Chicago Press, 2001.

Boutarel, Maurice. *La Médecine dans notre théâtre comique depuis ses origines jusqu'au XVI*[e] *siècle: Mires, Fisiciens, Naurés*. [Caen: Le Boyteux,] 1918.

Bowen, Barbara C. *Les Caractéristiques essentielles de la farce française et leur survivance dans les années 1550–1620*. Illinois Studies in Language and Literature, 53. Urbana: University of Illinois Press, 1964.

———. "Le théâtre du cliché." *Cahiers de l'Association internationale des études francaises* 26 (1974): 33–47.

———. [Barbara Cannings]. "Towards a Definition of Farce as Literary 'Genre.'" *Modern Language Review* 56.4 (1961): 558–60.

Boyer-Xambeu, Marie-Thérèse, Ghislaine Deleplace, and Lucien Gillard. *Private Money and Public Currencies: The 16th Century Challenge*. Trans. Azizeh Adodi. Armonk, N.Y.: M. E. Sharpe, 1994.

Brown, Howard Mayer. *Music in the French Secular Theater, 1400–1550*. Cambridge, Mass.: Harvard University Press, 1963.

Brundage, James A. *Law, Sex, and Christian Society in Medieval Europe*. Chicago: University of Chicago Press, 1987.

Burgwinkle, William E. *Sodomy, Masculinity, and Law in Medieval Literature: France and England, 1050–1230*. Cambridge: Cambridge University Press, 2004.

Burgwinkle, William E., and Cary Howie. *Sanctity and Pornography: On the Verge*. Manchester: Manchester University Press, 2010.

Burke, Kenneth. *The Philosophy of Literary Form: Studies in Symbolic Action*. 3rd ed. Berkeley: University of California Press, 1973.

———. *The Rhetoric of Religion: Studies in Logology*. Berkeley: University of California Press, 1961.

Burns, E. Jane. *Courtly Love Undressed: Reading Through Clothes in Medieval French Culture*. Philadelphia: University of Pennsylvania Press, 2002.

Burrows, Daron Lee. *The Stereotype of the Priest in the Old French Fabliaux: Anticlerical Satire and Lay Identity*. Oxford: P. Lang, 2005.

Butterworth, Emily. *The Unbridled Tongue: Babble and Gossip in Renaissance France*. Oxford: Oxford University Press, 2016.

Bychowski, M. "The Isle of Hermaphrodites: Disorienting the Place of Intersex in the Middle Ages." *postmedieval* 9.2 (2018): 161–78.

Chailley, Jacques. Review of *Recueil de farces françaises inédites du XVe siècle*, ed. Gustave Cohen. *Revue de Musicologie* 32 (1950): 65–68.

Chambers, E. K. *The Mediaeval Stage*. 2 vols. Oxford: Oxford University Press, 1903.

Chambure, Geneviève de. "La Musique dans les farces." *Cahiers de l'Association Internationale des Etudes Françaises* 26 (1974): 49–59.

Christian Spirituality: High Middle Ages to Reformation. Ed. Jill Raitt. Vol. 17 of *World Spirituality: An Encyclopedic History of the Religious Quest*. New York: Crossroad, 1988.

Christian Spirituality: Origins to the Twelfth Century. Ed. Bernard McGinn. Vol. 16 of *World Spirituality: An Encyclopedic History of the Religious Quest*. New York: Crossroad, 1987.

Clark, Carol. *The Vulgar Rabelais*. Glasgow: Pressgang, 1983.

Classen, Albrecht, ed. *Death in the Middle Ages and Early Modern Times: The Material and the Spiritual Conditions of the Culture of Death*. Berlin: De Gruyter, 2016.

Cleese, John. "How to Write the Perfect Farce." *Guardian*. 17 February 2017. https://www.theguardian.com/stage/2017/feb/17/john-cleese-farce-bang-bang-fawlty-towers-rat-manuel-feydeau (accessed 28 May 2019).

Clopper, Lawrence M. *Drama, Play, and Game: English Festive Culture in the Medieval and Early Modern Period.* Chicago: University of Chicago Press, 2001.

Coldewey, John C., ed. *Medieval Drama.* 4 vols. New York: Routledge, 2007.

Colie, Rosalie. *Paradoxia Epidemica: The Renaissance Tradition of Paradox.* Princeton: Princeton University Press, 1966.

Collins, Fletcher, Jr. *The Production of Medieval Church Music-Drama.* Charlottesville: University of Virginia Press, 1972.

Cowell, Andrew. *At Play in the Tavern: Signs, Coins, and Bodies in the Middle Ages.* Stylus: Studies in Medieval Culture. Ann Arbor: University of Michigan Press, 1999.

Crane, Susan. *The Performance of Self: Ritual, Clothing, and Identity During the Hundred Years War.* Philadelphia: University of Pennsylvania Press, 2002.

Cray, Ed. *The Erotic Muse: American Bawdy Songs.* 2nd ed. Urbana: University of Illinois Press, 1992.

Crocker, Holly A., ed. *Comic Provocations: Exposing the Corpus of Old French Fabliaux.* Studies in Arthurian and Courtly Cultures. New York: Palgrave Macmillan, 2006.

Crowder, Susannah. *Performing Women: Gender, Self, and Representation in Late-Medieval Metz.* Manchester Medieval Literature and Culture. Manchester: Manchester University Press, 2019.

Dal Molin, Aria. "A Transalpine Theatrical Conversation: French Medieval Farce and Italian Renaissance Comedy." Ph.D., diss., University of California, Santa Barbara, 2015.

DaSilva, Zenia Sacks, and Gregory M. Pell, eds. *At Whom Are We Laughing?: Humor in Romance Language Literatures.* Newcastle upon Tyne: Cambridge Scholars Publishing, 2013.

Davidson, Clifford, ed. *Gesture in Medieval Drama and Art.* Early Drama, Art, and Music, 28. Kalamazoo, Mich.: Medieval Institute Publications, 2001.

Davis, Jessica Milner. *Farce.* London: Methuen, 1978; rpt. New Brunswick, N.J.: Transaction, 2003.

Davis, Natalie Zemon. *Fiction in the Archives: Pardon Tales and Their Tellers in Sixteenth-Century France.* Stanford, Calif.: Stanford University Press, 1987.

———. "Women on Top." In *Society and Culture in Early Modern France: Eight Essays by Natalie Zemon Davis*, 124–51. Stanford, Calif.: Stanford University Press, 1975.

Delepierre, Octave Joseph. *Description et analyse d'un livre unique qui se trouve au Musée britannique.* [London]: Au Meschacébé, 1849. [*DLU*]

Derwich, Marek. "Clothing." In *Encyclopedia of Monasticism*, ed. Johnston, 309–10.

Desmond, Marilynn. *Reading Dido: Gender, Textuality, and the Medieval "Aeneid."* Medieval Cultures. Minneapolis: University of Minnesota Press, 1994.

Diefendorf, Barbara B. *The Saint Bartholomew's Day Massacre: A Brief History with Documents.* Bedford Series in History and Culture. Boston: Bedford, 2009.

Diehl, Huston. *Staging Reform, Reforming the Stage: Protestantism and Popular Theater in Early Modern England*. Ithaca, N.Y.: Cornell University Press, 1997.

Doudet, Estelle. "Les Clefs de l'Église: Mise en scène et herméneutique d'une métaphore/accessoire dans le théâtre polémique Rouennais du XVIe siècle." In *Les Clefs des textes médiévaux: Pouvoir, Savoir et Interprétation*, 83–95. Ed. Fabienne Pomel. Rennes: Presses Universitaires de Rennes, 2016. Open Edition: https://books.openedition.org/pur/28879?lang=en (accessed 29 July 2018).

Dox, Donnalee. *The Idea of the Theater in Latin Christian Thought: Augustine to the Fourteenth Century*. Ann Arbor: University of Michigan Press, 2007.

Draughon, Francesca, and Raymond Knapp. "Gustav Mahler and the Crisis of Jewish Identity." *Echo: A Music Centered Journal* 3.2 (2001): n.p.

Dubin, Nathaniel E. "Creative Choices: Notes on Translating the Old French Fabliaux." In *Comic Provocations*, ed. Crocker, 175–92.

Dubruck, Edelgard, and Barbara Gusick. *Death and Dying in the Middle Ages*. New York: Peter Lang, 1999.

Dufour, Pierre [Paul Lacroix.] *Histoire de la Prostitution chez tous les peuples du monde*. Vol. 6 of 8. Brussels: Librairie Universelle de J. Rozez, 1861.

Dull, Olga Anna. *Folie et Rhétorique dans la sottie*. Geneva: Droz, 1994.

Eco, Umberto. "Interpreting Drama." In *The Limits of Interpretation*, 101–10. Reedition of "Semiotics of Theatrical Performance" (1977). Bloomington: Indiana University Press, 1990.

Egan, Keith J. "The Spirituality of the Carmelites." In *Christian Spirituality: High Middle Ages to Reformation*, ed. Raitt, 50–62.

Ehrstine, Glenn. *Theater, Culture, and Community in Reformation Bern, 1523–1555*. Leiden: Brill, 2002.

Enders, Jody. "Allegory Plays." *SEL: Studies in English Literature, 1500–1900* 55.2 (2015): 447–64.

———. "Comically Incorrect." *ROMARD* [*Research Opportunities in Medieval and Renaissance Drama*] 51 (2012): 75–82.

———, ed. *A Cultural History of Theatre*. Vol. 2: *The Middle Ages*. The Cultural Histories Series. London: Bloomsbury Academic, 2018.

———. *Death by Drama and Other Medieval Urban Legends*. Chicago: University of Chicago Press, 2002. [*DBD*]

———. "Delivering Delivery: Theatricality and the Emasculation of Eloquence." *Rhetorica* 15.3 (1997): 253–78.

———. "The Farce and Folly of Female Authority in a Sixteenth-Century View of the *Roman de Silence*." *Romance Notes* 33 (1993): 33–37.

———. "Foul Play: Rape, Murder, and the Medieval Theater of Everyday Life." Special issue on "Loi et littérature." *Cahiers de recherches médiévales* 25 (2013): 145–64.

———. "History Trouble: Reenactment and Pseudoperformativity at the Witch Festival of Nieuwpoort." *Theatre Journal* 65 (2013): 235–51.

———. "Introduction: Miscarriages of Justice." *A Cultural History of Tragedy*, ed. Enders, Coletti, Sebastian, and Symes, 1–14.

———. *The Medieval Theater of Cruelty: Rhetoric, Memory, Violence*. Ithaca, N.Y.: Cornell University Press, 1998. [*MTOC*]

———. *Murder by Accident: Medieval Theater, Modern Media, Critical Intentions*. Chicago: University of Chicago Press, 2009. [*MBA*]

———. "Of Protestantism, Performativity, and the Threat of Theater." Special issue, "Figuring Protest and Lament in the Sixteenth Century," ed. Dora Polachek. *Mediaevalia* 22 (1999): 55–74.

———. "Performing Miracles: The Mysterious Mimesis of Valenciennes (1547)." In *Theatricality*, ed. Tracy C. Davis and Thomas Postlewait, 40–64. Cambridge: Cambridge University Press, 2003.

———. "Rhetoric and Comedy." In *The Oxford Handbook of Rhetorical Studies*, ed. Michael MacDonald, 364–75. Oxford: Oxford University Press, 2017.

———. *Rhetoric and the Origins of Medieval Drama*. Rhetoric and Society, 1. Ithaca, N.Y.: Cornell University Press, 1992. [*ROMD*]

———. "The Spectacle of the Scaffolding: Rape and the Violent Foundations of Medieval Theatre Studies." *Theatre Journal* 56.2 (2004): 163–81.

———. "Theater Makes History: Ritual Murder by Proxy in the *Mistere de la Sainte Hostie*." *Speculum* 79 (2004): 991–1016.

———. "The Theater of Scholastic Erudition." *Comparative Drama* 27.3 (1993): 341–63.

———. "Violence, Silence, and the Memory of Witches." In *Violence Against Women in Medieval Texts*, ed. Anna Roberts, 210–32. Gainesville: University of Florida Press, 1998.

Enders, Jody, Theresa Coletti, John Sebastian, and Carol Symes, eds. *A Cultural History of Tragedy*. Vol. 2, *The Middle Ages*. The Cultural Histories Series. London: Bloomsbury Academic, 2020.

Everist, Mark. *French Motets in the Thirteenth Century: Music, Poetry, and Genre*. New York: Cambridge University Press, 1994.

Fabre, Adolphe. *Les Clercs du Palais*. 1856. 2nd ed. Lyon: N. Scheuring, 1875.

———. *Les Clercs du Palais: La Farce du Cry de la Bazoche*. Vienne: Savigné, 1882.

Fabre-Vassas, Claudine. *The Singular Beast: Jews, Christians, and the Pig*. Trans. Carol Volk. New York: Columbia University Press, 1997.

Faivre, Bernard, ed. "La Farce: Un genre médiéval pour aujourd'hui?" Special issue, *Études théâtrales* 14 (1998).

———. *Répertoire des farces françaises: Des origines à Tabarin*. Paris: Imprimerie Nationale, 1993. [*Répertoire*]

Fleming, John V. *Reason and the Lover*. Princeton, N.J.: Princeton University Press, 1984.

Fletcher, Alan, and Wim Hüsken, eds. *Between Folk and Liturgy*. Amsterdam: Rodopi, 1997.

Foucault, Michel. *Discipline and Punish: The Birth of the Prison*. Trans. Alan Sheridan. New York: Pantheon, 1977.

———. *Les Mots et les choses: Une archéologie des sciences humaines*. Paris: Gallimard, 1966. Published in translation as *The Order of Things: An Archaeology of the Human Sciences*. New York: Vintage Books, 1973.

Gatton, John Spalding. "'There must be blood': Mutilation and Martyrdom on the Medieval Stage." In *Violence in Drama*, ed. James Redmond, 79–92. Themes in Drama, 13. Cambridge: Cambridge University Press, 1991.

Geltner, Guy. "Brethren Behaving Badly: A Deviant Approach to Medieval Antifraternalism." *Speculum* 85.1 (2010): 47–64.

———. *The Making of Medieval Antifraternalism: Polemic, Violence, Deviance, and Remembrance*. Oxford: Oxford University Press, 2012.

———. *The Medieval Prison: A Social History*. Princeton, N.J.: Princeton University Press, 2008.

———. "Medieval Prisons: Between Myth and Reality, Hell and Purgatory." *History Compass* 4 (2006): 1–14.

Genty, Lucien. *La Basoche notariale: Origines et histoire du XIVe siècle à nos jours de la cléricature notariale*. Paris: Delamotte, 1888.

Gertsman, Elina. *Worlds Within: Opening the Medieval Shrine Madonna*. University Park: Pennsylvania State University Press, 2015.

Giles, Ryan D. *The Laughter of the Saints: Parodies of Holiness in Late Medieval and Renaissance Spain*. Toronto: University of Toronto Press, 2009.

Goebel, Julius, Jr. *Felony and Misdemeanor: A Study in the History of Criminal Law*. Philadelphia: University of Pennsylvania Press, 1976.

Goffman, Erving. *Frame Analysis: An Essay on the Organization of Experience*. Cambridge: Harvard University Press, 1974.

Goldberg, Jonathan. *Sodometries: Renaissance Texts, Modern Sexualities*. Stanford, Calif.: Stanford University Press, 1992.

Gould, Timothy. "The Unhappy Performative." In *Performativity and Performance*, ed. Andrew Parker and Eve Kosofsky Sedgwick, 19–44. New York: Routledge, 1995.

Gruber, Xaque. "Thirteen Things You Never Knew About Pinecones." *Huffington Post*. 16 August 2016; updated 6 December 2017. https://www.huffingtonpost.com/xaque-gruber/thirteen-things-you-never_b_11763858.html (accessed 18 May 2018).

Gurevich, Aron. *Medieval Popular Culture: Problems of Belief and Perception*. Trans. Ja'nos M. Bak and Paul A. Hollingsworth. Cambridge Studies in Oral and Literate Culture, 14. New York: Cambridge University Press, 1988.

Guynn, Noah D. *Pure Filth: Ethics, Politics, and Religion in Early French Farce*. The Middle Ages. Philadelphia: University of Pennsylvania Press, 2020.

———. "Translating Catharsis: Aristotle and Averroës, the Scholastics and the Basochiens." In *Rethinking Medieval Translation: Ethics, Politics, Theory*, ed. Emma Campbell and Robert Mills, 84–106. Woodbridge: Boydell & Brewer, 2012.

Haliczer, Stephen. *Sexuality in the Confessional: A Sacrament Profaned*. Studies in the History of Sexuality. New York: Oxford University Press, 1996.

Halperin, Shirley. "Music Rights Organizations ASCAP and BMI Join Forces for Much-Needed Publishing Data Platform." *Variety*. 21 December 2020. https://variety.com/2020/music/news/ascap-bmi-data-platform-songview-1234867925/.

Hanawalt, Barbara A. "Whose Story Was This? Rape Narratives in Medieval English Courts." In *Of Good and Ill Repute: Gender and Social Control in Medieval England*, 124–41. New York: Oxford University Press, 1998.

Happé, Peter. "The Protestant Adaptation of the Saint Play." In *The Saint Play in Medieval Europe*, ed. Clifford Davidson, 205–40. Kalamazoo, MI: Medieval Institute, 1986.

Happé, Peter, and Elsa Streitman, eds. *Urban Theatre in the Low Countries, 1400–1625*. Turnhout: Brepols, 2006.

Hardison, O. B., Jr. *Christian Rite and Christian Drama in the Middle Ages: Essays in the Origin and Early History of Modern Drama*. Baltimore: Johns Hopkins University Press, 1965. [*CRCD*]

Harris, Max. *Carnival and Other Christian Festivals: Folk Theology and Folk Performance*. Austin: University of Texas Press, 2003.

———. *Sacred Folly: A New History of the Feast of Fools*. Ithaca, N.Y.: Cornell University Press, 2014.

Hartt, Jared C., ed. *A Critical Companion to Medieval Motets*. Woodbridge: Boydell, 2018.

———. "Introduction: Approaching Medieval Motets." In *A Critical Companion to Medieval Motets*, ed. Hartt, 1–13.

Harvey, Howard Graham. *The Theatre of the Basoche*. Cambridge, Mass.: Harvard University Press, 1941. [*TB*]

Hayes, Bruce E. *Rabelais's Radical Farce: Late Medieval Comic Theater and Its Function in Rabelais*. Farnham: Ashgate, 2010.

Hellmann, J. A. Wayne. "The Spirituality of the Franciscans." In *Christian Spirituality: High Middle Ages to Reformation*, ed. Raitt, 31–50.

Henke, Rob. *Performance and Literature in the Commedia dell'arte*. Cambridge: Cambridge University Press, 2002.

Hequembourg, Stephen. "*Literally*: How to Speak like an Absolute Knave." *PMLA* 133.1 (2018): 56–70.

Hillman, David, and Carla Mazzio, eds. *The Body in Parts: Fantasies of Corporeality in Early Modern Europe*. New York: Routledge, 1997.

Holsinger, Bruce Wood. "Analytical Survey 6: Medieval Literatures and Cultures of Performance." *New Medieval Literatures* 6 (2003): 271–311.

———. *Music, Body, and Desire in Medieval Culture: Hildegard of Bingen to Chaucer.* Stanford, Calif.: Stanford University Press, 2001.

Hopkins, Jasper. *A Concise Introduction to the Philosophy of Nicholas of Cusa.* Minneapolis: University of Minnesota Press, 1978.

Huizinga, Johan. *Homo Ludens: A Study of the Play Element in Culture.* [Trans. R. F. C. Hull.] Boston: Beacon, 1955.

Hunter, David G. "Married Clergy in Eastern and Western Christianity." In *Companion to Priesthood and Holy Orders*, ed. Peters and Anderson, 96–139.

Jacobelli, Maria Katarina. *Il Risus paschalis e il fondamento teologico del piacere sessuale.* Brescia: Queriniana, 1991.

Janin, Hunt. *The University in Medieval Life, 1179–1499.* Jefferson, N.C.: McFarland, 2008.

Janko, Richard. *Aristotle on Comedy: Towards a Reconstruction of "Poetics II."* Berkeley: University of California Press, 1984.

Jeay, Madeleine. *Le Commerce des mots: L'Usage des listes dans la littérature médiévale (XIIe–XVe siècles).* Geneva: Droz, 2006.

Johnston, Ruth. *All Things Medieval: An Encyclopedia of the Medieval World.* 2 vols. Santa Barbara, Calif.: Greenwood, 2011.

Johnston, William M. *Encyclopedia of Monasticism.* Chicago: Fitzroy Dearborn, 2000.

Jonsson, Ritva, and Leo Treitler. "Medieval Music and Language: A Reconsideration of the Relationship." In *Music and Language*, 1–23. Studies in the History of Music, 1. New York: Broude Bros., 1983.

Jordan, Mark D. *The Invention of Sodomy in Christian Theology.* Chicago: University of Chicago Press, 1997.

Katritzky, M. A. *Women, Medicine and Theatre, 1550–1750: Literary Mountebanks and Performing Quacks.* Aldershot: Ashgate, 2007.

Kay, Andrew. "The Joke's Over: Academics Are Too Scared to Laugh." *Chronicle of Higher Education.* 14 March 2018. https://www.chronicle.com/article/Academics-Are-Too-Scared-to/242817 (accessed 26 July 2018).

Kelly, Douglas. *Internal Difference and Meanings in the "Roman de la Rose."* Madison: University of Wisconsin Press, 1995.

Kennedy, George A. *Classical Rhetoric and Its Christian and Secular Tradition from Ancient to Modern Times.* Chapel Hill: University of North Carolina Press, 1980.

Kent, Carol Anne. "Le Signe trompeur: Une étude du langage ambigu et mensonger dans quelques farces médiévales." Ph.D. diss., University of Toronto, 1997.

Kerr, Walter. *Tragedy and Comedy.* New York: Simon and Schuster, 1967.

Kibler, William W. *An Introduction to Old French.* New York: MLA, 1984.

Kieckhefer, Richard. "Major Currents in Late Medieval Devotion." In *Christian Spirituality: High Middle Ages to Reformation*, ed. Raitt, 75–108.

King, Sharon D[iane]. "Caught in the (One-)Act: Staging Sex in Late Medieval French Farce." Paper presented at the 14th Triennial Colloquium of SITM, Poznan, Poland. 25 July 2013. http://www.staff.amu.edu.pl/~pber/Sharon%20King.pdf.

———. "'Je viens . . . / d'estrange contrée': Medieval French Comedy Envisions the Afterlife." In *Death in the Middle Ages*, ed. Classen, 339–55.

Kipnis, Laura. "How to Look at Pornography." In *Pornography, Film, and Culture*, ed. Lehman, 118–29.

Kirby, Michael. *A Formalist Theatre*. Philadelphia: University of Pennsylvania Press, 1992.

Knapp, Steven, and Walter Benn Michaels. "Against Theory." In *Against Theory: Literary Studies and the New Pragmatism*, ed. W. J. T. Mitchell, 11–30. Chicago: University of Chicago Press, 1985. Reprinted from *Critical Inquiry* 8.4 (Summer 1982): 723–42.

Knight, Alan E. *Aspects of Genre in Late Medieval French Drama*. Manchester: Manchester University Press, 1983. [*AG*]

Kobialka, Michal. *This is My Body: Representational Practices in the Early Middle Ages*. Ann Arbor: University of Michigan Press, 1999.

———. "The Medieval Theater of the Absurd." *PMLA* 86.2 (1971): 183–89.

Kooper, Erik, ed. *Medieval Dutch Literature in Its European Context*. Cambridge: Cambridge University Press, 1994.

Koopmans, Jelle. *Le Théâtre des exclus au Moyen Âge: Hérétiques, sorcières et marginaux*. Paris: Imago, 1997.

Koopmans, Jelle, and Paul Verhuyck. "Les Mots et la Chose, ou la métaphore comme spectacle: Nouvelle étude sur la représentation scénique de l'acte sexuel dans la farce." https://www.researchgate.net/publication/280936285_Les_mots_et_la_chose_ou_la_metaphore_comme_spectacle_Nouvelle_etude_sur_la_representation_scenique_de_l'acte_sexuel_dans_les_farces (accessed 9 June 2019).

Kristeller, Paul Oskar. *Renaissance Thought: The Classic, Scholastic, and Humanist Strains*. 1955; rpt. New York: Harper and Row, 1961.

Lambdin, Laura Cooner, and Robert Thomas Lambdin, eds. *Companion to Old and Middle English Literature*. Westport, Conn.: Greenwood, 2002. ProQuest Ebook Central (accessed 6 February 2021).

Lea, Henry Charles. *A History of Auricular Confession and Indulgences in the Latin Church*. New York: Greenwood Press, 1968.

Leach, Elizabeth Eva. "The Genre(s) of Medieval Motets." In *A Critical Companion to Medieval Motets*, ed. Hartt, 15–41.

Lebègue, Raymond. *Le Mystère des actes des apôtres: Contribution à l'étude de l'humanisme et du protestantisme français au XVIe siècle*. Paris: Champion, 1929.

———. *La Tragédie religieuse en France: Les débuts (1514–1573)*. Paris: Champion, 1929.

Lefkowitz, Natalie J. *Talking Backwards, Looking Forwards: The French Language Game Verlan*. Tübingen: Gunter Narr Verlag, 1991.

———. "Verlan: Talking Backwards in French." *French Review* 63.2 (1989): 312–22.

Lefranc, Abel. "Les Dates du séjour de Rabelais à Metz (1546–1547)." *Revue des Etudes rabelaisiennes* 3 (1905): 1–11.

Le Goff, Jacques. *The Birth of Purgatory*. Trans. Arthur Goldhammer. Chicago: University of Chicago Press, 1984.

———. *La Civilisation de l'Occident médiéval*. Paris: Arthaud, 1964. Published in English as *Medieval Civilization, 400–1500*, trans. Julia Barrow. Oxford: Blackwell, 1988.

Lehman, Peter, ed. *Pornography, Film, and Culture*. New Brunswick, N.J.: Rutgers University Press, 2006.

Le Marchand, Bérénice. "Specular Dissection in French Renaissance Literary Blasons." *Dalhousie French Studies* 92 (2010): 21–31.

Lochrie, Karma. *Covert Operations: The Medieval Uses of Secrecy*. Philadelphia: University of Pennsylvania Press, 1999.

MacKinnon, Catharine A. *Feminism Unmodified: Discourses on Life and Law*. Cambridge, Mass.: Harvard University Press, 1987.

———. *Toward a Feminist Theory of the State*. Cambridge, Mass.: Harvard University Press, 1989.

Maddox, Donald, and Sara Sturm-Maddox. *Melusine of Lusignan: Founding Fiction in Late Medieval France*. Athens: University of Georgia Press, 1996.

Marshall, Mary Hatch. "Boethius' Definition of Persona and Mediaeval Understanding of the Roman Theater." *Speculum* 25 (1950): 471–82.

Maxwell, Ian. *French Farce & John Heywood*. Melbourne and Oxford: Melbourne University Press and Oxford University Press, 1946.

McCracken, Peggy. *The Curse of Eve, The Wound of the Hero: Blood, Gender, and Medieval Literature*. Philadelphia: University of Pennsylvania Press, 2003.

McLuhan, Marshall, and Quentin Fiore. *The Medium Is the Message*. New York: Random House, 1967.

Mohr, Melissa. *Holy Sh*t: A Brief History of Swearing*. Oxford: Oxford University Press, 2013.

Moi, Toril. *Sexual/Textual Politics: Feminist Literary Theory*. London: Methuen, 1985.

Monson, Craig. *Nuns Behaving Badly: Tales of Music, Magic, Art, and Arson in the Convents of Italy*. Chicago: University of Chicago Press, 2010.

Morrison, Susan Signe. *Excrement in the Late Middle Ages: Sacred Filth and Chaucer's Fecopoetics*. New York: Palgrave Macmillan, 2008.

Murphy, James J. *Rhetoric in the Middle Ages: A History of Rhetorical Theory from Saint Augustine to the Renaissance*. 1974; rpt. Berkeley: University of California Press, 1981.

———. *A Synoptic History of Classical Rhetoric*. New York: Random House, 1972.

Nayar, Sheila J. "*Coprus [sic] Christi*: The Scatological Tales of the Fabliaux." In *Comic Provocations*, ed. Crocker, 163–81.

Nederman, C. J., and J. True. "The Third Sex: The Idea of the Hermaphrodite in Twelfth-Century Europe." *Journal of the History of Sexuality* 6.4 (1996): 497–517.

Ogden, Dunbar H. *The Staging of Drama in the Medieval Church*. Newark: University of Delaware Press, 2002.

Olson, Glending. *Literature as Recreation in the Later Middle Ages*. Ithaca, N.Y.: Cornell University Press, 1982.

———. "The Medieval Fortunes of 'Theatrica.'" *Traditio* 4 (1986): 265–86.

Ong, Walter J. *Rhetoric, Romance, and Technology: Studies in the Interaction of Expression and Culture*. Ithaca, N.Y.: Cornell University Press, 1971.

Ozment, Stephen. *The Age of Reform, 1250–1550: An Intellectual and Religious History of Late Medieval and Reformation Europe*. New Haven, Conn.: Yale University Press, 1980.

———. *Protestants: The Birth of a Revolution*. New York: Doubleday, 1992.

———, ed. *The Reformation in Medieval Perspective*. Chicago: Quadrangle Books, 1971.

Paetow, Louis John. *The Arts Course at Medieval Universities with Special Reference to Grammar and Rhetoric*. Champaign: University of Illinois Press, 1910.

Parish, Helen. *Clerical Celibacy in the West, c. 1100–1700*. Burlington, Vt.: Ashgate, 2010.

Parker, John. *The Aesthetics of Antichrist: From Christian Drama to Christopher Marlowe*. Ithaca, N.Y.: Cornell University Press, 2007.

Parker, Patricia. "On the Tongue: Cross-Gendering, Effeminacy, and the Art of Words." *Style* 23.3 (1989): 445–65.

Parsons, Ben. "'A Riotous Spray of Words': Rethinking the Medieval Theory of Satire." *Exemplaria* 21.2 (2009): 105–28.

Penley, Constance. "Crackers and Whackers: The White-Trashing of Porn." In *Pornography, Film, and Culture*, ed. Lehman, 99–117.

Perfetti, Lisa. "Laughing at Learned Women in Medieval French Farce." In *At Whom Are We Laughing?*, ed. DaSilva and Pell, 107–20.

———. *Women and Laughter in Medieval Comic Literature*. Ann Arbor: University of Michigan Press, 2003.

Peters, Greg, and C. Colt Anderson. *A Companion to Priesthood and Holy Orders in the Middle Ages*. Brill's Companions to the Christian Tradition, vol. 62. Leiden: Brill, 2016.

Petit de Julleville, L. *La Comédie et les moeurs en France au Moyen Age*. 4th ed. Histoire du théâtre en France, 3. Paris: Léopold Cerf, 1886. [*CM*]

———. *Les Comédiens en France au Moyen Âge*. Histoire du théâtre en France, 2. Paris: Léopold Cerf, 1885.

———. *Les Mystères*. 2 vols. Histoire du théâtre en France, 1. Paris: Léopold Cerf, 1880; rpt. Geneva: Slatkine, 1968. [*LM*]

———. *Répertoire du théâtre comique en France au moyen-âge*. Histoire du théâtre en France, 4. Paris: Léopold Cerf, 1886. [*RTC*]

Philipot, Emmanuel. "Notice sur la farce de *Frere Guillebert*." In *Mélanges de linguistique et de littérature romanes offertes à Mario Roques par ses amis, ses collègues, et ses anciens élèves de France et de l'étranger*, 2: 237–41. Bade: Editions Arts et sciences, 1950–53.

Phillips, Richard, Diane Watt, and David Shuttleton, eds. *De-centring Sexualities: Politics and Representations Beyond the Metropolis*. London: Routledge, 2000.

Picot, Emile. *Le Monologue dramatique en France*. Rpt. *Romania* 15 (1866): 358–422; Paris: 1866–68.

———. *La Sottie en France: Fragment d'un répertoire historique et bibliographique de l'ancien théâtre français*. Nogent-le-Rotrou: Daupeley-Gouverneur, 1878. [*SEF*]

Pouchelle, Marie-Christine. *The Body and Surgery in the Middle Ages*. Trans. Rosemary Morris. New Brunswick, N.J.: Rutgers University Press, 1990.

Rayborn, Tim. *Against the Friars: Antifraternalism in Medieval France and England*. Jefferson, N.C.: McFarland, 2014. [*AF*]

Reeves, Andrew. "Teaching Confession in Thirteenth-Century England: Priests and Laity." In *Companion to Priesthood and Holy Orders*, ed. Peters and Anderson, 252–80.

Reid, Charles J., Jr. "The Priesthood and the Sacrament of Marriage." In *Companion to Priesthood and Holy Orders*, ed. Peters and Anderson, 217–51.

Reid, Dylan. "Carnival in Rouen: A History of the Abbaye des Conards." *Sixteenth Century Journal* 32.4 (2001): 1027–55.

———. "The Triumph of the Abbey of the Conards: Spectacle and Sophistication in a Rouen Carnival." In *Medieval and Early Modern Ritual: Formalized Behavior in Europe, China, and Japan*, ed. Joëlle Rollo-Koster, 147–73. Leiden: Brill, 2002.

Rey-Flaud, Bernadette. *La Farce, ou la machine à rire: Théorie d'un genre dramatique*. Geneva: Droz, 1984.

Robert-Nicoud, Vincent. *The World Upside Down in 16th-Century French Literature and Visual Culture*. Leiden: Brill, 2018.

Robertson, D. W. *A Preface to Chaucer: Studies in Medieval Perspectives*. Princeton, N.J.: Princeton University Press, 1962.

Robson, Michael. *The Franciscans in the Middle Ages*. Monastic Orders. Woodbridge: Boydell, 2006.

Romano, John F. "Priests and the Eucharist in the Middle Ages." In *Companion to Priesthood and Holy Orders*, ed. Peters and Anderson, 188–216.

Runnalls, Graham. Medieval Actors' Roles. Fribourg. http://toisondor.byu.edu/fmddp/roles/fribourg.html (accessed 19 June 2016).

Sainte-Beuve, Charles Augustin. *Tableau historique et critique de la poésie française et du théâtre français au seizième siècle*. Revised ed. Paris, 1869.

Saulnier, V. L. "Facéties." http://www.persee.fr/docAsPDF/bude_1247-6862_1977_num_36_4_3558.pdf (accessed 20 June 2016).

———. "Histoire d'un conte rabelaisien et le devoir du silence." *Bibliothèque d'Humanisme et Renaissance* 24 (1962): 545–58.

Scarry, Elaine. *The Body in Pain: The Making and Unmaking of the World*. New York: Oxford University Press, 1985.

Scott, Virginia. *Women on the Stage in Early Modern France: 1540–1750*. Cambridge: Cambridge University Press, 2010.

Sidhu, Nicole Nolan. *Indecent Exposure: Gender, Politics, and Obscene Comedy in Middle English Literature*. The Middle Ages Series. Philadelphia: University of Pennsylvania Press, 2016.

Skoda, Hannah. *Medieval Violence: Physical Brutality in Northern France (1270–1330)*. Oxford: Oxford University Press, 2015.

Sofer, Andrew. *The Stage Life of Props*. Ann Arbor: University of Michigan Press, 2003.

Solberg, Emma Maggie. *Virgin Whore*. Ithaca, N.Y.: Cornell University Press, 2018.

Spufford, Peter. *Handbook of Medieval Exchange*. London: Royal Historical Society, 1986.

———. *Money and Its Use in Medieval Europe*. Cambridge: Cambridge University Press, 1988.

Stanislavski, Constantin. *An Actor Prepares*. Trans. Elizabeth Reynolds Hapgood. New York: Theatre Arts, 1936.

States, Bert O. *Great Reckonings in Little Rooms: On the Phenomenology of Theatre*. Berkeley: University of California Press, 1985.

———. *The Pleasure of the Play*. Ithaca, N.Y.: Cornell University Press, 1994.

Di Stefano, Giuseppe. "À Chaque Saint sa chandelle: Pour un calendrier ludique." *Florilegium* 24 (2007): 125–42.

Steiner, Wendy. *The Scandal of Pleasure: Art in an Age of Fundamentalism*. Chicago: University of Chicago Press, 1995.

Stevens, John E. *Words and Music in the Middle Ages: Song, Narrative, Dance, and Drama, 1050–1350*. Cambridge: Cambridge University Press, 1986.

Sverdlik, Steven. "Crime and Moral Luck." In *Moral Luck*, ed. Daniel Statman, 181–94. Albany: State University of New York Press, 1993.

Symes, Carol. *A Common Stage: Theater and Public Life in Medieval Arras*. Ithaca, N.Y.: Cornell University Press, 2007.

———. "Knowledge Transmission: Media and Memory." In *Cultural History of Theatre*, ed. Enders, 199–211.

Taylor, Chloë. *The Culture of Confession from Augustine to Foucault: A Genealogy of the "Confessing Animal."* New York: Routledge, 2009.

Tentler, Thomas N. *Sin and Confession on the Eve of the Reformation*. Princeton, N.J.: Princeton University Press, 1977.

Toldo, Pierre [Pietro]. "Etudes sur le Théâtre comique français du moyen âge et sur le rôle de la nouvelle dans la farce et dans la comédie." In *Studi/Studj di filologia romanza*, ed. Ernesto Monaci, vol. 9, 181–369. Rome: Ermanno Loescher and Company, 1903. ["ETCF"]

———. "Rabelais et Balzac." *Revue des Etudes rabelaisiennes* 3 (1905): 117–37.

Tracy, Larissa. "The Uses of Torture and Violence in the Fabliaux: When Comedy Crosses the Line." *Florilegium* 23.2 (2006): 143–68.

Treitler, Leo. "Oral, Written, and Literate Process in the Transmission of Medieval Music." *Speculum* 56 (1981): 471–91.

Tugwell, Simon. "The Spirituality of the Dominicans." In *Christian Spirituality: High Middle Ages to Reformation*, ed. Raitt, 15–31.

Upton, Elizabeth Randall. "Unfolding the Rondeau: Form and Meaning in Early 15th-Century Chansons." http://www.sjsu.edu/people/gordon.haramaki/courses/practice/s1/Upton-Unfolding-Rondeau.pdf (accessed 14 January 2019).

Vickers, Nancy. "Members Only." In *The Body in Parts*, ed. Hillman and Mazzio, 3–22.

Walker, Jonathan. "Rhetorics of the *Obscaene*." *Theatre Survey* 48.1 (2007): 77–97.

Warren, Nancy Bradley. *The Embodied Word: Female Spiritualities, Contested Orthodoxies, and English Religious Cultures, 1350–1700*. Notre Dame, Ind.: Notre Dame University Press, 2010.

Wenzel, Siegfried. *Macaronic Sermons: Bilingualism and Preaching in Late Medieval England*. Ann Arbor: University of Michigan Press, 1994.

Williams, Bernard. *Moral Luck: Philosophical Papers, 1973–1980*. Cambridge: Cambridge University Press, 1981.

Witkowski, Gustave Joseph. *Les Médecins au théâtre de l'antiquité au dix-septième siècle*. Paris: A. Maloine, 1905. [*MTA*]

Wright, Stephen (Steve), webmaster. "Medieval European Drama in Translation." http://english.cua.edu/faculty/drama/index.cfm (accessed 26 September 2010).

Young, Karl. *The Drama of the Medieval Church*. 2 vols. Oxford: Clarendon, 1933.

Zumkeller, Adolar. "The Spirituality of the Augustinians." In *Christian Spirituality: High Middle Ages to Reformation*, ed. Raitt, 63–74.

Zumthor, Paul. *Essai de poétique médiévale*. Paris: Seuil, 1972.

Acknowledgments

My gratitude to many friends, colleagues, and collaborators is no laughing matter. They inspired me to think more broadly about what is to be made of farce on the worldwide stage. My favorite shop-talk sessions were with three long-time friends and colleagues: Leo Cabranes-Grant; Dan Jaffe; and a reviewer of this book for Penn, Noah Guynn, whose brilliance and generosity leave me almost speechless. Almost. They were later joined by wonderful new interlocutors: Sara McDougall and the inimitable Thierry Martin (aka Maistre Antitus), as well as a large group of actors and commentators who participated in read-throughs and performances (actual and, once the pandemic hit, virtual across three time zones via Zoom). I owe an enormous debt to Gordon Abra, Ellen Anderson, Leo Cabranes-Grant, Rita Copeland, Dorota Dutsch, Jane Faulkner, Noel Greer, Noah Guynn, Dan Jaffe, Erith Jaffe-Berg, Eric Jorgensen, S. C. Kaplan, Lizzie MacArthur, Rosemary Malague, Mariah Min, Jason Narvy, Cary Nelson, Samantha Pious, Courtney Rydel, Annika Speer, Heather Terbell, Andrew Warner, Bill Warner, Sarah Watson, and Simon Williams. Meanwhile, I remain *bouche bée* by what the Radford players were able to accomplish with *Cooch E. Whippet* (2017) and *Husband Swap* (2019) at the Mostly Medieval Theater Festival at the International Congress for Medieval Studies (artistic director, Lofton Durham). Frank Napolitano, Amanda Kellogg, and director David Beach met head-on the challenges of staging medieval comedy in the #MeToo era, provoking as much laughter as they did difficult but necessary conversations. And, then, enlivened via Zoom and which helped me to no end, there was the magnificent cold read by the participants in Matthew Sergi's Medieval World Drama Group at the University of Toronto by Alexandra F. Johnston, Élise LaFleur, Morgan Moore, Aras Pabedinskas, Linda Phillips, Tricia Postle, Colin Rowley, Marlow Stainfield, and Sergi himself.

In some thirty years at UCSB, there have been standout undergraduates too, like Matilda Criel, who quickly put her finger on Sister Bunny's central problem, and Laura Pastre, who wittily characterized the Priest of *Blue Confessions* as *sérieusement excité*. But then came Spring 2018, when a once-in-a-career class was the source of immeasurable delight. The hardy group had dared to enroll in a course devoted entirely to the twenty-four plays of my *Farce of the Fart* and *Holy Deadlock*; and I do believe that they taught me as much as I taught them, most notably: Helen Foley, Celie Mitchard, and Sandra Linares (for their stunning regendered update of *The Newlywed Game* [*HD*, #1]), along with Josselyn Beutler, Brittyn Davis, Hannah Drennan, Drea Godsey, Madeleine Higgs, Nick Pfister, Amanda Salas, and Dustin Stroeve. But that wasn't all: endless student creativity dominated a subsequent course on medicine and comedy, where rip-roaring adaptations were conceived and executed by Leah Akomolafe, Tatiana Alonso, Kirsten Annell, and Alison Kelton.

Once again, I thank the Interlibrary Loan Office at Davidson Library of my home institution, whose staff assiduously assisted me in securing even the most obscure documents, and our marvelous area librarian, Jane Faulkner.

In recent years, another conversation has gone live, as it were, as one of the most exhilarating of my life. It has been a pleasure and a privilege to come to know the incomparable Natalie Zemon Davis, whose erudition and flair for storytelling have not only brought early modern history to life: they have served as a model of intellectual generosity to emulate.

Last but never least, what would life be without someone with whom to share the laughter? That person has always been my one-of-a-kind husband, Eric D'Hoker. And that's no farce.